Round and About

Spain

A. F. Tschiffely

He began to make castellis
in Spaygne as louers doo

(Garden Roson 1475)

The Long Riders' Guild Press

www.classictravelbooks.com
www.horsetravelbooks.com
www.lrgaf.org

ISBN: 1-59048-268-9

First published by Hodder & Stoughton in 1952.

The sketch maps and decorations throughout the book have been specially drawn by the author.

Cover image of the author on his motorcycle, with thanks to Benno Affolter.

About the Author

Aimé Tschiffely

Though he was to become the most famous Long Rider in history, Aimé Tschiffely started life quietly enough in the small village of Zofinguen, Switzerland. The call of adventure and travel soon lured the young Swiss man to move to England in the early 1910s.

Aimé was a devout student and ardent reader. Having been offered a chance to teach at St. George's College, a boy's school in Argentina, Aimé moved to Buenos Aires in 1917.

Once again, it was the lure of travel which drove the fighter turned maths teacher to make an historic decision. In 1925 Aimé set out to ride 10,000 miles alone from Buenos Aires to New York city. For the next three years Aimé and his two Criollo geldings, Mancha and Gato, survived a litany of hardships unequalled in equestrian travel. The trio trekked through mud-holes, over quicksand bogs and across rivers, over the mountains of Bolivia and into the steep jungle valleys of Peru and across the Matacaballo ("Horse-killer") Desert.

Then, after being hailed as a hero by the President of the United States, the quiet Swiss traveller returned home with his horses to Argentina, and spent some time there. Then he went to the USA and in 1932 he returned to England and took up writing full time. His ensuing first book, *Tschiffely's Ride* sold more copies than any other Long Rider book in the twentieth century.

He later wrote *The Tale of Two Horses,* the story of this remarkable journey, as told by the horses themselves and written for children

Aimé died unexpectedly in January, 1954 due to complications related to minor surgery. Ever the traveller, Aimé had one more journey to make: his ashes were sent to his beloved Argentina, where they rest near the memorial for his horses on the El Cardal ranch.

In 1999 the Argentine Congress passed a law celebrating 20th September of each year the "Día Nacional del Caballo" (National Day of the Horse) – because that is the day Aimé arrived in New York in 1928.

Aimé Tschiffely wrote several books, all of which will be republished by the end of 2008. They are:

Tschiffely's Ride, which was translated into French, German, Finnish and Polish. This is the story of the greatest equestrian epic of the twentieth century, a journey that came about because a man and his horses refused to quit – ever! During the course of their travels Tschiffely, Mancha and Gato crossed deadly deserts, passed through jungles, traversed sky-high mountain passes – and rode on. They were assailed by vampire bats, mistaken for gods and navigated the Panama Canal – but rode on. Nothing stopped them. No one since has rivalled their accomplishments. The trio were hailed as heroes by the President of the United States.

A Tale of Two Horses, which was translated into Spanish, German and Swedish. It tells the story of the journey from Buenos Aires to Washington DC from the point of view of the horses! With a preface by the famous horseman R. B. Cunningham Graham, "The Tale of Two Horses" is amply illustrated with drawings by the author. No equestrian travel collection could be considered complete without this wonderful book!

Bohemia Junction, which one reviewer described as "Forty years of adventurous living condensed into one book." It is all that and more! Exotic people, faraway places and equestrian adventure make up the background to the explorer's autobiography. "Bohemia Junction" is packed with the amazing assortment of humanity that Tschiffely met during his lifetime of travel, including cowboys, prize-fighters, writers, Indians, and the eccentric riff-raff of three continents. From Cape Horn to New York, Tschiffely journeyed wherever his vagabond fancy took him. And each region explored had its quota of "bohemians" in the old sense of the word – men and women for whom love of adventure was a reality.

Bridle Paths: Through the ancient New Forest, over the lonely mountains of Wales, and across the rugged landscape of Scotland, the renowned author investigated the nooks and crannies of this island kingdom. Mounted on his gentle Cob mare, Violet, Tschiffely details the last roving adventure of its kind. "Bridle Paths" is a final poetic look at a now-vanished Britain, as it was before the advent of suburbia changed it forever.

This Way Southward: With the Second World War raging across Europe, the most famous equestrian explorer of the twentieth century decides to make a perilous journey across the U-boat infested Atlantic. His mission? To return to his old haunts in South America and under-take a harrowing 7,000 mile journey by car through Argentina, across the inhospitable regions of Tierra del Fuego and over the majestic Andes mountains.

Coricancha: A fascinating and balanced account of the conquest of the Inca Empire.

Ming and Ping: An adventure book for older children. The title characters go exploring South America together. They meet many tribes of Indians and learn about their way of life. Exhilarating and effortlessly instructive.

Don Roberto: A biography of Tschiffely's friend and mentor, Robert Cunninghame Graham. Upon completing his epic equestrian journey, Aimé arrived in London armed with little more than his unpublished manuscript. After weeks of disappointing rejections, the discouraged Long Rider was about to head back to Argentina. That's when "fate" intruded. Before catching the boat to South America, Aimé stopped by the Argentine embassy to say "adios" to his friends stationed there. One of these well-connected diplomats urged Aimé to make one last attempt at publication. He could, the diplomat said, arrange a meeting with that distinguished man of letters, Don Roberto. Young, unknown, poor and unpublished, Aimé hesitated to ask for help from this literary giant whom he had admired for years. Yet with the boat ticket in his pocket, and nothing left to lose, the hesitant equestrian explorer agreed to meet Don Roberto for lunch the following day.

Don Roberto, far from being aloof, was deeply interested in the younger man's unpublished manuscript. Aimé's battered manuscript was passed across the table, then duly delivered to Don Roberto's London publisher. Thus *Tschiffely's Ride* the book that lit the bonfire of modern equestrian exploration, came into being because of a chance meeting.

It is what transpired over the next few years that now concerns us. For what no one could have foreseen was the deep and lasting friendship which would develop between the older and childless Don Roberto and his hard-riding protégé. So when the need arose for a biography of Don Roberto, who better to write it than his close friend and protégé?

Little Princess Turtle Dove: An enchanting fairy story set in South America. Little Princess Turtle Dove is a delightful child who is the daughter of the Inca, or king, who brought peace and prosperity to the Indians. A mysterious woman grants her the power to talk to, and understand, animals.

Unfortunately Turtle Dove's eldest brother, the Inca's heir, turned into a nasty old man who bullied his subjects and his sisters. He locks her and her sisters up in prison, from which Turtle Dove is rescued by her pet llama, Keeyla, who has been given wings for the occasion.

Turtle Dove and Keeyla go to Faunaland, which is populated by all the animals of the world who go there after they die. Turtle Dove makes friends with the animals and birds, and learns about horses and ponies.

Sprinkled with easy to absorb geography and history, this delightful book belongs in every child's library.

For more information about this remarkable man, please visit
www.aimetschiffely.org.

The Spanish Civil War – Publisher's Note

The author makes frequent reference to the Civil War in Spain, which had ended only about a dozen years before the journey described in this book. Here is a very brief summary of that war.

The Spanish Civil War was a major conflict in Spain that started after an attempted *coup d'état* committed by parts of the army against the government of the Second Spanish Republic. The Civil War devastated Spain from 17 July 1936 to 1 April 1939, ending with the victory of the rebels and the founding of a dictatorship led by the Fascist General Francisco Franco and the defeat of the supporters of the Republic. Republicans (*republicanos*), gained the support of the Soviet Union and Mexico, while the followers of the rebellion, *nacionales* (Nationalists), received the support of Italy, Germany, as well as neighbouring Portugal.

The war increased tensions in the lead-up to World War II and was largely seen as a possible war by proxy between the Communist Soviet Union and the Fascist Axis of Italy and Germany. In particular, tanks and bombing of cities from the air were features of the later war in Europe. The advent of the mass media allowed an unprecedented level of attention (Ernest Hemingway and George Orwell were among those who covered it) and so the war became notable for the passion and political division it inspired, and for atrocities committed on both sides of the conflict.

Like other civil wars, the Spanish Civil War often pitted family members and trusted neighbours and friends against each other. Apart from the combatants, many civilians were killed for their political or religious views by both sides, and after the war ended in 1939, Republicans were at times persecuted by the victorious Nationalists.

INTRODUCTION

"Quien dice España dice todo": He who says Spain says all

For many years I had been wondering how much truth there is in this old Spanish saying, and I longed to become properly acquainted with this fascinating land of which I only knew the fringes. Having lived in South America, I knew something of the Spanish nature; but then it must be remembered that members of all nationalities change somewhat when they live abroad, and especially so in the New World. In the Argentine particularly, and also in Uruguay, I learnt something about the chief characteristics of Spaniards from different regions. Thus, for instance, I got to know that Basques are physically tough, and hard workers, that Catalunians are industrious and exceedingly thrifty, Aragonese stubborn and hard-headed, Galicians either brilliant, or slow-witted, and that Andalusians are so volatile, light-hearted and imaginative that when they are "wound up" and really let themselves go, a person who believes half of what they say is very credulous.

But how was I to travel through Spain? At the time when I conceived the idea of going there, tourists were allowed to take only £50 out of Britain, and the rate of exchange stood at 70 *pesetas* to the pound. Certainly not much wherewith to "step out", let alone to cover several thousand miles, as was my intention. Of course, I could have applied to the Bank of England to grant me – as an author – special concessions; but this would have involved the writing of long letters and the filling of forms – horrors against which my very stomach revolts.

As it happened, when I was about to give up the idea of going abroad, a Spanish professor came to London on a visit, and when the two of us met, during the course of our conversation he turned to me and said, "Come on, friend; courage. Pack up a few things and take the jump. Never mind money. You can always give a few lectures, and thus earn *pesetas.* I shall arrange them for you." That decided it, though there were several knotty problems to be solved before I was ready to depart to the land of my dreams.

As, previously, I had done most of my long-distance travelling on horseback, all my friends expected me to ride through Spain. But how could I buy a good horse with so little money at my disposal, let alone feed him for weeks? Quite out of the question. Even if a suitable animal were put at my disposal, it would take many weeks, or even months, to ride through so vast a country as Spain. Then, what about using a motor-car, or travelling in trains? No. Both too expensive, besides being uninteresting modes of travel. The idea of walking had certain attractions, but the factor of time had to be considered. So what?

I was thinking over the matter of transportation when a friend of mine came to my rescue with a brilliant idea. "Use a motorcycle," said the one who, years ago, had been a famous motor-cycle racer, and who continues to ride one of those machines for amusement. Enthusiastically he continued, "I have a friend who is a director of a famous firm of motor-cycle manufacturers. I shall write to him at once, and I'm sure he will be delighted to supply you with a really reliable machine."

And so it came about that a few days later I found myself in a huge factory in the Midlands, where one of the directors showed me their latest model of a powerful machine. One look at it was sufficient for me. "Heavens," I exclaimed, "I don't want to travel jet-propelled! Please remember that I haven't ridden a motorcycle for some thirty years." Catching sight of a much smaller – and therefore less speedy-looking – machine and pointing at it I said, "That's the type of mount I fancy."

After a few trial spins on the cycle, and instructions on how to keep it in good running order, when I thought my passport and a mass of other documents were in order, I bumped into new difficulties. My old driving licence had lapsed, so a new one had to be obtained. Time was getting short, and with it my temper as I became more and more entangled in red tape. When, sick and tired of it all, I was about to leave without my machine, the Royal Automobile Club – of which I was not a member – came to my assistance; I got a driving licence; insurance was attended to, and by the time the Club's efficient and speedy-working staff had finished with other formalities, and documents, etc., were handed over to me, my portfolio was a most imposing packet.

When I went to the French Consulate, in order to get a transit visa, they fairly staggered me by asking 8,000 francs for the privilege of travelling through la Belle France in a train. I could not help wondering if by any chance they wanted me to make up for deficits in the national budget. As I am writing this, I also wonder what the Inspector of Taxes will have to say when I reveal to him what I had to spend on preparations for my trip. If by any remote chance this book should turn out to be a good seller, the same gentleman would be there in the King's name to claim the lion's share of the profits. Such is the job of an Inspector of Taxes, and such is the lot of authors.

Thanks to my knowledge of Spanish, wherever I went I soon felt at home, and in the course of the innumerable conversations I held during the four months I spent travelling some five thousand miles through the Iberian peninsula, I learnt much. Politics being out of the sphere of my main interests in life, I will touch on this debatable subject only lightly, but, I hope, fairly, without taking sides. My main interests in any country are the people, the scenery, animals, the varieties of food and diverse drinks. Though in Spain are many marvels of olden times, and remarkable monuments can be seen almost everywhere, I shall refer only briefly to history, archaeology and architecture – subjects which have been masterfully treated by specialists, and, for that matter, quite adequately in popular guide-books.

My aim in writing this account of my wanderings is to attempt to take the reader with me, stage by stage, to introduce him or her to some of the many people I met, and to act, as it were, as interpreter and guide. A wise old Scottish friend of mine, whose voice never again shall I hear, once said to me: "If Spain didn't exist, someone would have to invent it." And how right he was, for he knew the land and its colourful people, as the saying goes, inside-out.

With this, friends who wish to follow me, let us set out and see what my latest travels had in store for me.

A. F. TSCHIFFELY

Chelsea, London, 1951

CHAPTER 1

VOYAGE FROM LONDON TO THE EASTERN PYRENEES OF FRANCE

The month of March was nearing its end when on a fine but chilly morning I was at Victoria Station half an hour before the 9 a.m. Continental Express was due to leave for Dover. As trains from the suburbs of London arrived at different platforms, and masses of passengers alighted, they brought to my mind worker ants hurrying along their narrow tracks. I was glad to think that after months of being confined to my desk, struggling with manuscripts and obstinate sentences, which refused to be set down clearly and simply on paper, at last I was a more or less free man. I could not help wondering what some of the business men, typists, secretaries and Government officials who hurried towards their respective offices would reply if they were asked what they thought of writing as a profession. Most likely the majority would have said that it is easy, "soft ", lucrative and delight-ful. Perhaps some of the young typists and stenographers would have gone as far as to say that it must be wonderful to recline on a couch, and whilst smoking cigarettes in a long holder to dictate stories to a gorgeous young lady secretary. Most of us have a sneaking fancy for the other man's job.

As I stood and watched what was going on near me, the porter I had engaged came to inform me that my presence was requested by the Customs House officials whose "pitch" was near the entrance end of the platform. Accordingly I threaded my way through groups of passengers who conversed in various languages, and presently found the man who wanted to see the documents concerning my motor-cycle. A brief-case and some of my pockets were bulging with papers and forms of every size, colour and description, and as I had not had time to sort them out, they were in dire disarray. However, after much searching and fumbling, I succeeded in finding what the official required, and shortly after, when the train began to move, and friends and relatives who had come to bid some of the passengers *bon voyage* confined their demonstrations of affection to blowing kisses and waving handkerchiefs, I sat down in the corner of a carriage, mopped my brow and heaved a deep sigh. At last I was on my way to Spain. Presently, as the train gained speed and rumbled over Grosvenor Bridge I looked in the direction where, in my nearby home, I had left much unfinished work. The Thames, which has been called "Liquid History", looked at its best. The rays of the sun illuminated a fine curtain of mist through which, towards the west, could be seen the Chelsea Embankment, and further along, towards the majestic bend of the river, Cadogan Pier, and in the distance the Albert and Battersea Bridges and the outlines of the towering chimneys of the Lotts Road gas works. Whilst looking in that direction I could not help wondering how my friends, the swans, were faring in their favourite haunt, just where the river begins to bend, at the far end of Cheyne Walk.

During the journey towards Dover I made the acquaintance of three fellow-travellers, one of them an elderly English lady who was on her way to the south of France. She told me that this was the first holiday she had had since the outbreak of the Second World War, throughout which she had worked as a volunteer in a canteen. The other two were an Englishman and his French wife, who were on their way to the north of France where a relative was dangerously ill. Chatting about this and that, we passed the time quickly, and then we arrived at Dover, where some of the passengers acted as if they feared that the cross-channel steamer was about to sail without them. Being in no mood to scramble and push, I waited until the first rush was over, and then looked for my porter, who seemed to have disappeared. When at last I found him, and he placed my luggage before a young Customs House official who wore the uniform of a budding stage admiral, and who acted as if he were some knowing big chief of the Criminal Investigation Department, the fun started . . . for him. Two panniers, made to be fitted on to the motorcycle, contained spare parts, such as chains, clutch wheel, inner tubes, spark plugs, screws, nuts and other accessories, which were essential for so long a journey as the one I was about to make. Evidently suspecting that I was trying to take these spare parts abroad in order to sell them, the official argued that they, not being part of the motor-cycle, could not leave England. Naturally, I disagreed; so in order to settle the matter, haughty Mr. Busypants, the young Customs official, trotted me to his Chief. Having been told what brought the two of us before him, he did not even bother to look at the contents of the panniers, but said that, of course, I could take the things with me. Visibly annoyed by this decision, Mr. Busypants then led the way back to the counter where my other belongings had been left. I did not mind in the least having to open my suitcases, but when, instead of searching through them, the young official picked up a large leather-bound address book which happened to be on the top of clothes in one, and proceeded to turn over the leaves and read names and addresses, my blood began to simmer.

Before entering into the Customs House, another official – a very polite and civil person – had already asked me how much money I had on me, and when I informed him that I had exactly what travellers are allowed to take with them, he took my word and let me pass without further questioning. Young Mr. Busypants, however, was a different type of human species, with other ideas of dealing with travellers. When he had finished with my address book, and asked me to hand over to him my wallet, and when he began to turn it inside out, my blood began to boil, but I held my peace. For some mysterious reason, only known to officials of a certain type, Mr. Busypants did not search through my suitcases. After having handed me back my wallet, he marked my luggage with chalk: whereafter, indignant and humiliated, I was allowed to board the ship. So much for a thoroughly nasty Customs House official.

On board the channel steamer, travellers who sat in groups gave one the impression of being refugees. Although the ship rolled only very slightly, a few were seasick, whilst others sat apprehensively. Everywhere in the corridors were suitcases, bags and other luggage, and whilst wandering about I noticed that several passengers were busy counting their money. After an uninteresting meal of cold meat and salad – for which I had to pay a ridiculously high price – I went to the upper deck to watch the French coast approach. From the distance, the sun-bathed beaches near Calais looked inviting, but as we drew nearer and the ravages of war became visible, the region lost much of its attraction. The ship having been docked with speed and high efficiency, there followed another stampede by those of the passengers who appeared to fear that the Paris-bound train would leave without them. Unlike the more or less silent and stolid English railway porters, the French *porteurs* did a lot of shouting and scurrying about, and there were several heated arguments among them. However, eventually the veritable storming of the train came to an end, *porteurs* walked away counting their tips, and when the train left the dockyard, I was all alone in a second-class compartment. After about half an hour two very polite French officials came to ask me for my passport and enquire if I had anything to declare. Without fuss or bother, and without even making me open my suitcases, they stamped my documents, whereafter I was left alone until, some hours later, the train steamed into the Gare du Nord in Paris. Fortunately Cook's Travel Agency in London had advised their representatives in Paris that a traveller from London had a motor-cycle on the train, and that the machine would have to be transported through Paris, to Austerlitz Station, in time to catch the evening train bound for Barcelona. When I found Cook's man, he proceeded to lead the way towards the deposit where the two of us arrived just in time to meet a porter who was proudly pushing along the motor-cycle. Soon a number of his colleagues formed a circle round him, and when I came on the scene, and they guessed that I was the owner of the brand-new machine – parts of which were still wrapped up in paper – asked me if it was a "deertrahc." It took me quite a while to guess that the mysterious word was meant to be "dirt track." Having handed in my bill of lading, I was at liberty to take away the cycle, and, as the porter took it towards a car Cook's man had brought with him, a little crowd of loafers followed the little procession. As bad luck would have it, the car was too small to hold my machine, so after much fuss, shouting and gesticulation on the part of several porters and other onlookers, all of whom tried to be of assistance with words and deeds, eventually the greatly admired "deertrahc" was loaded on a huge single-decker bus, in which it – as well as Cook's man, myself and the rest of my luggage – were transported to Austerlitz Station. The machine having been weighed and consigned to Barcelona, and my belongings having been put into a compartment, I thought my troubles had come to an end, and that the rest would be plain sailing. But alas for the frailty of human hopes! As will be seen later, when least expected I ran into really serious trouble, and into an adventure which more than satisfied my appetite for such.

When I left London, my total capital consisted of £50. Of these forty were in travellers' cheques, three in tens and five in twos. Besides these I had £5 in one pound notes and the remaining five pounds in French currency.

The brand-new carriage in which I had installed myself at Austerlitz Station was very comfortable and spotlessly clean. The train, being driven by electricity, ran along very smoothly on the well levelled and ballasted track. This time I was not as lucky as I had been during the journey from Calais to Paris, when I had a compartment all to myself. Still, my five travelling companions – two middle-aged married couples and a young Basque, all typically French, and therefore very talkative – were quite pleasant. One of the women, who was rather stout, soon became so friendly that she took great pains to tell me all her family history, and occasionally, when she recounted some of the trials and tribulations endured in these difficult and hard times, her husband chimed in with additional information or corrections of statements made by his wife. In the circumstances, my spoken contribution to the conversation had to be limited to nodding or shaking my head, with an occasional, "*Oui, oui, naturellement,*" "*Evidemment,,*" "*Certainement,*" and similar interjections to show that I was in full agreement with everything told to me. So, who says that diplomacy is dead? The Basque, who was a young, good-looking and athletic man; told me a great deal about rugby football and the game of *pelota;* so time passed quickly until an attendant walked along the corridor, ringing a sonorous hand-bell, announcing that dinner was ready. What with tips I had given in Paris, the cost of freight of motor-cycle from there to Barcelona, and other incidentals, my capital in French money had dwindled alarmingly. Whilst I was talking to the Basque, the two French couples opened wickerwork baskets from which they produced all sorts of tempting foods, as well as fruit and wine. With napkins tucked into collars or tied round their necks, and others spread over laps to prevent their clothes from being soiled, the epicures started their meal, thereat the Basque rose and at the same time asked me if I was going to the dining-car to eat. Although I did not know exactly how my funds stood, I decided to risk it, so soon after the two of us were seated opposite each other at a table for four. The occupants of the other two seats were tremendously broad-shouldered and corpulent men, both of whom sported, tied to the lapels of their jackets, thin red ribbons of the Legion of Honour. Whilst watching them tuck away the food placed before them, I could not help wondering if the *Légion d'honneur* dishes out special orders for gourmands. When my companion – the Basque – asked me if I would "split" a bottle of red wine with him, and explained it would work out "*plus économique*" than if we bought a half-bottle each, I immediately agreed. The meal we were served was excellent and so was the wine, and when it came to paying the bill I found it to be quite reasonable. I was about to give the *garçon* a tip, when the Basque caught hold of my outstretched hand, and informed me that tipping was out of place, twelve per cent having already been added to the bill. With this statement on high finance the two *légionnaires* fully agreed. My by this time very meagre reserves of French currency having been put back into my pocket, we four table companions began a lively conversation. When – as is inevitable in France – it veered to politics, and I was asked what I thought of the situation, I explained that in such matters I was utterly ignorant, and that politics and politicians were of no interest to me. "*Mais c'est impossible*" the two *légionnaires* exclaimed in unison, and then went on telling me all about soaring prices, strikes and rumours of strikes, graft, profiteering, black market and so on. Over and over again they repeated, "*Ici il faut du vrai patriotism, ici il nous faut une forte discipline!*" Whenever they said "*forte,*" and at the same time struck the table with their heavy powerful and hairy hands, making glasses and cutlery jump and jingle, I fully understood and appreciated what they meant.

Being one of the unfortunate travellers who cannot sleep in trains, I had not wasted money on a berth, so when our conversation came to an end, we returned to our respective compartments. Upon arriving at mine, I found that all the blinds had been lowered and that only a bluish purple electric bulb gave a very faint light. The two French couples were already fast asleep, and very soon my companion, the young Basque, joined in the concert of deep breathing, wheezing and snoring, whilst I sat in my corner, longing to switch on the light in order to read a book I had brought with me. When the atmosphere became so hot and stuffy that it produced a choking feeling in my throat, I went out into the corridor. After an hour or so, tired of standing up, I returned to my compartment, but after a while the heat was such that perspiration dripped off me like water when a dog emerges from a stream. Once more I rose in order to seek relief in the corridor, and whilst carefully stepping over outstretched legs, I noticed that the sleepers' faces were also wet with perspiration. I had not been outside very long when, one by one, out of different compartments came passengers, like so many rabbits when a ferret drives them out of their warren. All mopped themselves and complained that the heat inside the compartments was *simplement plus supportable.* Apparently something had gone wrong with the regulator, and when the guard came on the scene, and unlocked a steel cupboard in which was a kind of automatic switch-board, he said that something had gone wrong, and that there was absolutely nothing he could do to switch off the electric heaters. This announcement caused much vociferation and waving of arms among the onlookers, who frequently used the word *scandale,* but eventually the guard retired; shrugging his shoulders, at the same time half raising his arms and showing the palms of his hands. There was only one thing the passengers could do: return to their respective compartments and let in cold but healthy fresh air. The heat had given us all such a thirst that when, after what seemed an eternity, the train stopped in a town, there ensued a veritable stampede to a buffet on wheels which, despite the time of night, was still doing business. And so the train sped on towards the south. On the platform of one important station at which we stopped I saw what at first I thought must be members of some expedition bound for some unexplored regions of the world. Then, as I gazed at heavy rubber boots, sou'-wester-like headgear, peculiar leather and oil-cloth jackets and topcoats, thick leather belts and mysterious cases, tins and baskets, I began to wonder if the little army assembled on that platform was about to fight off an invasion of Martians. Turning to a fellow passenger who happened to be standing near me in the corridor, I asked him if by any chance he knew something about those amazing apparitions, and the equipment they carried. *"Mais oui, monsieur,"* he replied, *"ce sont des pêcheurs et des chasseurs."* I laughed inwardly at my ignorance and my heart went out to those brave fishermen and hunters who defied the cold and darkness of the night, in order at the first crack of dawn to practise their respective sports.

Early in the morning we were in the *Midi,* nearing the foothills of the Pyrenees, and shortly after sunrise the dark-blue waters of the Mediterranean came in sight. The little towns and villages through which we passed were quaint and picturesque, and after a breakfast of excellent *café au lait* and delicious crackly rolls and butter, I began to take a new interest in life.

In one of the compartments adjacent to mine, travelled a pleasant-looking young Spaniard with three children and a nurse. The oldest, a boy about six, was a live-wire who could not sit still for a minute, and the other two were equally mercurial and equally troublesome. In and out of the door they dashed, down the corridor, father and nurse chasing after them to prevent accidents. Every now and again a child would get slapped, and when it howled, a bout of kissing followed, and so the game went on until long-suffering papa began to look tired and weary. The good-looking little imps were up to all manner of tricks, and whenever the oldest kept still for a few moments, it was to ask papa question after question. On one occasion, as the two stood in the corridor, just outside my compartment, and looked out of the window, the boy began to lick the thick brass hand-rail which protected the glass. When papa saw what the boy was doing, he pulled him away, saying, "Stop licking the rail, it is dirty." "Dirty?" the boy replied. "It isn't dirty, look how it shines." "I tell you it *is* dirty," senior came back in a tone of authority mixed with exasperation. "How can it be dirty when it shines?" the boy piped, looking up at his father with big black eyes. "Well then, if it isn't dirty, it is dangerous. Do you hear, dangerous, I tell you!" "Why dangerous?" the boy insisted. "Because it is full of microbes." "What are microbes?" "Oh, tiny little animals, so tiny you can't see them, but if they get into your mouth they make you ill," father explained. And so questions were fired by the youngster, and answers given by papa until he sighed and raised his eyes towards heaven. At long last, when the would-be teacher thought he had explained the transmission of microbes from one person to another to his pupil's satisfaction, the little one asked, "If there really are microbes on that rail, who put them there, and whose are they?"

"Oh," papa shouted, fairly snorting with temper, "they are the microbes of a general!" And with this he staggered back into his compartment, holding his head in both hands.

If that inquisitive little boy remembers that final reply, and takes the warning, in years to come the ranks of anti-militarists will be swelled with one new member, but in the meantime, I am sure, his father continues to suffer the joys of parenthood.

Brilliant sunshine and old picturesque villages at which I gazed through the window were of such interest to me that time passed quickly. The two French couples and the young Basque with whom I had shared the compartment having said "*Adieu*" to me at one of the stations, I was left alone until at another stopping-point three peasant women came to disturb my peace. In wicker baskets they carried vegetables, loaves of bread and other foodstuffs, and after a while the honking of a goose solved the mystery of one basket which was covered with a stitched-on piece of sack-cloth. Until we reached the next station the trio chattered and gossiped incessantly, and when they alighted I gave them a hand with their belongings. At Cerbère – which is the French border town – officials came to ask for passports and *douane* papers, which they stamped without questioning. Some time later, when at last the train steamed on and slowly clattered into a tunnel, I knew that upon emerging from it I would find myself in Spanish territory. Being a bit of a romantic, and somewhat childish, I was quite excited, and I wondered what the near future might have in store for me. After a while, the smoke of the engine assumed lighter tints, until, upon coming out of the tunnel it suddenly became a swirling bright cloud of light-grey, and when this lifted, I got my first glimpse of Spain; on my left the dark-blue Mediterranean, and on my right steep rocky mountains and hills. Presently the train came to a halt at Port Bou station, where all passengers were requested to alight, and to pass into a large shed where the Immigration and Customs House officials were ready to do their work. Judging by the wild rush most of the passengers made to be first, one might have thought they were trying to escape from an earthquake, and although a Civil guard with his three-cornered hat shouted that there was no hurry, and that the train would not leave until the last passenger was on board, the pushing and elbowing continued. At several pigeon-holes in a wooden partition, passports had to be handed in, later to be withdrawn at one at the far end of the row. As nobody made even as much as an attempt to form a queue, there ensued more pushing and elbowing, and therefore, when a struggler managed to get to the pigeon-hole, and had been attended to, it was only with great difficulty that he or she could squeeze a passage out of the crowd. Most of the members of this scrummage being Spaniards, the language of Cervantes predominated, but there was a fair sprinkling of Frenchmen, Italians, Britons, Swiss and several others whose languages I did not understand. Fortunately, all were good-humoured, and therefore there were no complaints, though all heaved sighs of relief upon extricating themselves from the various groups of thrusters. My passport having been handed back to me, I went into the Customs House department alongside, and after a little searching found my luggage, which the official passed without making me open anything. Next, I went in search of the motor-cycle, but, although I looked everywhere, and asked various porters and officials if they had seen a *motocicleta,* all shook their heads. I knew that the machine had been on the train at Cerbère, the French border-town, so I wondered what could have happened to it between there and Port Bou, only a short run, mostly through the tunnel?   Rushing along the platform I went to look into the luggage van, which, to my dismay, proved to be empty; and so the mystery deepened until, after many more frantic enquiries on my part, an official calmly informed me that the machine had been unloaded at Cerbère, it being against rules and regulations to bring it into Spain by train. Although I argued that the *moto* had been freighted through directly, from Paris to Barcelona, and that in France no objection had been raised to this procedure, the Spanish official merely shook his head, and said that he could not help it, and that he was merely acting according to regulations. Other officials who listened to this debate were most sympathetic with me, and when one suggested that I go and see the *autoridad militar,* I hastened to an adjacent office where, at a table which did duty as desk, sat a man, dressed in civilian clothes.   As it turned out, he was the *autoridad militar,* and when I put my case before him, he listened impassively. Having heard my story, he shrugged his shoulders languidly, raised his eyebrows, and said that the machine could not be brought into Spain on a train, and that, I being a tourist, it was necessary for me to ride it into the country overland.

What a situation! Here was I, at last in Spanish territory, and my motor-cycle still in France, on the other side of a tunnel which passes through a high mountain. As I stood, pockets fairly bulging with documents of all kinds, I was at my wits' end when a young man – who turned out to be a Catalan – came on the scene.

"Come with me," he said, "don't waste your time here. I will tell you what to do." And so, downcast and bewildered, I followed the newcomer who led the way to a corner of the Customs House shed where the two of us discussed the situation. Meanwhile, the last travellers, having finished with border formalities, betook themselves to the waiting train which presently steamed out of the station. As I watched its tail-end pass the door of the Customs House shed in which I stood, both Barcelona and France seemed to be far away, and I was overcome by a sickly feeling in my empty stomach.

CHAPTER 2

ADVENTURE AT THE SPANISH BORDER
ARRIVAL IN BARCELONA

From the moment of setting foot on Spanish soil I had been in such a hurry and flurry that only when the obliging and sympathetic Chief of the Customs House department, Cook's Travel Agency man, the young Catalan and I stood talking things over, that I heard the real reason why my motor-cycle had been left in France. Apparently, if the machine had been transported into Spain on the international train, it would have become automatically "imported", and therefore I would have had to pay enormously high duties. Furthermore, possessing no import permit, I would, in any event, have had to store the cycle in bond until I could obtain the necessary document for its release; and in Spain such matters take time.

During a short council of war it was decided that the only way out for me was to hire car and chauffeur, drive back to Cerbère over a high mountain pass, and then ride the motor-cycle back into Spain. Whilst telephone calls were being made to the Spanish and French border posts, informing the guards about my predicament, and requesting them not to delay me longer than necessary, the Catalan hurried off to fetch his car. When he returned and told me to jump into the antediluvian contraption, I wondered if it would be capable of taking us to our destination and back. Leaving my luggage in the Customs House, I squeezed myself into the vehicle which, even as its motor ticked over, shook and shivered like an old dog in a sleety storm. The driver, having jumped in, put the engine into gear with much noise and grating, and presently the two of us drove through the small town, soon to come to a road which led up a long and very steep incline. After much climbing and rounding of sharp curves we reached a small stone-built house in front of which a wooden barrier and a chain made further progress impossible. This was the Spanish border post; so we halted, and the guards stationed there requested me to step inside in order to obtain an exit permit. Forms having been filled in and stamped, and my already imposing-looking passport having undergone a similar treatment, I was allowed to depart; the barrier and chain were raised, and on we drove over a stretch of no-man's-land until, upon rounding another curve, we reached another chain which indicated that on the other side of it began French territory. Again I had to go through tedious formalities; more signatures, rubber stamps and forms, and then I was allowed to re-enter France; the chain was lowered to the ground, and off we rattled in our antiquated vehicle, the radiator of which spouted steam like a miniature geyser. Soon the steep downgrade began, and with it my apprehension. The twisting road had no protections to avoid driving over its sides, where gaped deep ravines and precipices, but despite this my chauffeur drove on merrily, now at alarming high speed. Even in a modern car with efficient brakes the experience of rounding hairpin bends at such speed would have been enough to test the nerves of seasoned racing drivers, so when I suggested to my companion to proceed with a little more caution, he merely laughed, and speaking to me over his shoulder said that his *coche* knew the way and all its tricks almost as well as he did himself, having made the crossing "millions of times." Though, un-doubtedly, this was a gross exaggeration, due to bad simple arithmetic or imagination, the general state and appearance of our rattle-trap suggested that it could not make many more, if this one was not to be its last. As we rounded bends, sometimes I looked down into the deep-blue waters of the Mediterranean sea, and then again into a ravine which appeared, disappeared and re-appeared with horrible frequency, whilst I sat in the back of the car, holding my breath and clutching a thin hand-rail in front of me. Fearing that if I again spoke to the driver, he might easily turn round to give his reply, I refrained from making any further suggestions. We were about half-way down the mountain when the town of Cerbère came into view below. With its nice beach and chalets on the little horse-shoe-shaped sea front, it looked most attractive, and I longed for the moment when we should arrive down there. After having whisked round several more sharp curves, just as I was looking forward to being able to heave a deep breath of relief, we passed a neat well-populated cemetery which gave me much food for thought, but soon after, to my great relief, we were down at sea-level, and on our way to the nearby railway station, where I alighted with shaking knees. It being about 1 p.m., the narrow streets of the little town were practically deserted, and when we reached the station it looked like a peculiar kind of palace of the Sleeping Beauty. Not a soul was to be seen anywhere, only deserted platforms, a few forlorn porters' hand-trucks and shiny rails on their black oil-stained sleepers. The various *guichets* and doors at which we knocked were either shuttered or locked, but finally, peeping into the goods' deposit, there we found two porters, sitting half asleep with cigarettes dangling down from their mouths. Having apologized for disturbing their peace at so unheard-of a time, the Catalan explained the object of our visit. With a sigh and a groan, one of the men rose, went to a greasy board that was fixed to a wall, and from a nail took a key. Then, slouching in front of us, he led the way towards a deposit where, to my joy, I saw the motor-cycle, looking as if it were enjoying a *siesta,* too. Having handed my bill-of-lading to the porter, I was about to push the machine out of the deposit, when the man, pointing at the document, told me that on it was clearly written "*Parree à Barcelone,*" and that, therefore, 1 could not claim or withdraw *la moto* in Cerbère. This led to a heated argument in which the Catalan took a prominent part, siding with me. There was so much shouting and gesticulation that, after a while, even the other porter came to see what was amiss, and when my protector, the Catalan, suggested we fetch the station master, the porters' jaws dropped and arms fell limply by their sides. Upon recovering their faculty of speech they informed us that he was at home, and that he would not thank us for molesting him at such an hour. And so arms were raised once more and the argument was resumed. Between bursts of verbal machine-gun fire I produced document after document to prove my identity and show that I was the owner of the machine, but all my efforts were in vain; the porters stubbornly stuck to the annoying reply that on my bill-of-lading was clearly written "PAR-REE À BAR-CE-LONE." Changing my tactics, I handed out cigarettes and substantial tips, which were accepted in a casual manner, as if they were merely a matter of course.

Whilst the four of us smoked, I explained, suggested, pleaded, vouched, testified and appealed, until, suddenly, the Catalan stepped forward, caught hold of the handle-bars of the cycle, and with an oath and some rude remarks concerning the status and pedigree of the porters, began to push the machine towards the door. The two victims of this tirade were so surprised by this storm of abuse that for a while they stood, listening and watching, and then, running after my would-be saviour, in their turn they pleaded and appealed. Eventually it was agreed that I sign a written statement to the effect that the machine had been withdrawn against the porters' advice and at my own risk and responsibility. This done, I handed over the bill-of-lading and another good tip, and then the Catalan and I took the cycle out of the station, leaving the two porters to argue between themselves. Our museum-piece of a car being too small to hold the motor-cycle, and having no ropes wherewith to tie it on the roof or to the back or sides, the Catalan suggested that I follow whilst he drove to the house of a friend of his where he had some business to do. According to regulations, petrol tanks of motor vehicles must be empty when such are transported on trains, and therefore, having no "juice", and there being none available anywhere without coupons, whilst my guide slowly drove through the little town, I followed behind him, pushing the motor-cycle, parts of which were still wrapped up in packing paper. Our little mechanized fighting column came to a halt outside a baker's shop where the Catalan filled two sacks with appetizing-looking loaves of white bread, with which he intended to do business on the other side of the border where, owing to the shortage of wheat, the baking of white bread is illegal. The two sacks, as well as cakes and a few mysterious parcels, having been loaded, the Catalan asked the baker to lend him a strong rope, but as he could not supply us with what we needed, a house-to-house search was made until, at last, a man appeared, carrying, partly round his neck and partly dragging behind him, what from the distance appeared to be a gigantic boa-constrictor. The illusion was made more realistic by a terrific *mistral* which had begun to blow in all its fury, making the man reel about as if he were about to be strangled and crushed. The "monster" turned out to be a rope, stout enough to withstand the strain of towing a battleship.

By that time a few boys and young men had assembled to look at my motor-cycle, with its mysterious letters and number – JAB 376 and

GB – on plates fixed to the front and rear mudguards. Whilst making preparations for the trip back to Spain, I had to answer numerous questions which were fired at me, but eventually the Catalan and I were ready; the thick rope was fastened to the bumper of the car and to the middle of the handle-bars of my motor-cycle, I bestrode my mount, fixed to which, behind me, was a nasty-looking luggage carrier – which wedged me completely in between it and the handle-bars – waved farewell to the onlookers, adjusted my hat, heaved a deep breath, and then, with a lump in my throat, shouted to the Catalan, "*Vamos,*" "Let's go." Slowly the rope took the strain, and after a few wobbles on my part, we were off, once more towards the high, break-neck pass. How I wished I were riding a horse, instead of being towed on a motor-cycle! As we approached the foot of the winding road, the top of the pass seemed to be very far away, and I felt like a shipwrecked mariner clinging to a raft in a hurricane. To say that I felt uncomfortable would be putting it mildly, for thirty-five years had passed since I had ridden a shaft-driven motor-cycle, and now, to make things even worse for me, the *mistral* grew in fury as I was being towed to higher regions. What with trying to keep my balance whilst rounding curves, and leaning to one side or the other to prevent being blown over, I hadn't time – let alone inclination – to cast a glance at the cemetery I had seen on my way down to Cerbère. Rounding curves and hairpin bends we climbed higher and higher, and as we proceeded the *mistral* hit me with ever increasing force. Although the trilby hat I wore was pulled down to my ears, it threatened to leave its anchorage, but I was so busy steering the motor-cycle that I could do nothing about it, so I left my hat to its fate, which, I felt sure, was to end its days at the bottom of a ravine. By degrees the Catalan drove faster and faster, until I tooted the horn frantically, a signal he luckily understood, and which made him pro-ceed with more caution. What seemed to me an interminable nightmare came to an end when we reached the French border post, where more forms had to be filled in, and rubber stamps affixed to my passport before I was allowed to leave France. Whilst the Catalan and I were inside the little stone house, there was an alarm, and upon going to investigate its cause, we found that the motor-cycle – which had been freed from the rope – had been blown over by the *mistral,* and that the force of its blasts was such that the machine was being dragged along as if it were made of light cardboard. Having recovered it, the border

guards stamped my documents and accepted a tip for the promptitude
with which they had attended to me, and then the Catalan and I made
ready to depart. The chain which hung across the road was lowered,
and I started to freewheel downhill, towards the Spanish border post.
There, once more, I had to obtain permission to enter into the Land of
the Hidalgos. Forms having been filled in, declarations regarding currency matters and the motor-cycle having been signed, and more
stamps having been affixed to my over-worked passport, a Spanish
officer shook me warmly by the hand, and at the same time expressed
his heartfelt hope that luck would accompany me, and that I would
enjoy my tour through his beloved *patria.* When I offered him and his
companions a tip wherewith to buy themselves a few bottles of wine,
they refused to accept it, so I placed the bank note on a desk, and went
to mount the cycle. Before I had time to get away, the officer came
chasing after me, and after a short friendly scuffle pushed the intended
tip into a side pocket of my jacket. The chain having been lowered, and
the wooden barrier lifted, I waved *adios,* and freewheeled downhill into
Spain. The law was being complied with; I *rode* the cause of all this
trouble, fuss and inconvenience across the border, though my latest ride
was that of a modern, Don Quixote. My Sancho Panza, the Catalan,
followed behind in his old liver-shaker, filled with white bread and
other things about which no questions were asked by French and
Spanish border officials, who evidently wink an eye when they deal
with an old friend. Thanks to the fact that I was no longer being towed
along, the steep winding road now lost much of its former terror, but, as
the *mistral* still blew in all its fury, I proceeded with utmost care.
Before our two-vehicled convoy reached the bottom of the incline, the
mistral died down, and by the time we arrived at the station, only light
gusts of wind reminded me of my recent experiences in the high
regions.

A thoughtful official had asked the station restaurant *chef* to remain
on duty until I should return, so soon after my arrival the Catalan and I
enjoyed a belated lunch and a bottle of excellent wine. Whilst we were
eating, a friend – who had been expecting me to arrive in Barcelona on
the morning train – telephoned to ask what was amiss, and when I
explained the cause of my delay and informed him that I would be on
the evening train, he laughed heartily and promised to be at the station
to meet me.

Although, besides my passport and masses of other documents, I had no written recommendation of any kind, in Port Bou the officials and porters who took me in hand were so friendly and obliging and helpful that very soon I felt quite at home. Towards evening, when I boarded the train and sat down in a compartment, upon thinking over my recent adventures, I laughed inwardly, but upon sorting out papers, documents, bank-notes and odds and ends which made my pockets and brief-case bulge, I suffered a rude shock. During the course of the day I had changed fifteen pounds in travellers' cheques into Spanish currency, and now, as I counted what was left of my ready funds, I found that during the day I had spent some fourteen pounds. This meant that I was left with roughly thirty-six pounds; certainly not much wherewith to make a tour of several thousand miles. But there it was, nothing could be done about it; I had mistaken Spanish bank-notes for French ones, and therefore most of the tips I had given were absurdly generous. No wonder the two porters in Cerbère had allowed me to take away the motorcycle, and no wonder all the other tips I had given in the course of my hectic whirlwind day had so pleased their recipients.

Though slow, the train journey from Port Bou to Barcelona was pleasant and most interesting, and the scenery I gazed at through the window enchanting At first the train wound through deep rocky valleys, and here and there I had a fine view of the mighty Pyrenees which – it being early spring – were still clad in a mantle of glittering white. Some of the clouds which slowly drifted over them assumed fantastic shapes and threw shadows which gave life to the landscape. Every patch of land and terrace on mountainsides where vines or vegetables could be grown was cultivated and kept free from weeds. The almond trees were in full bloom, their pink blossom and first delicate green shoots of leaves contrasting marvellously with the wild surroundings. Here and there, on rocky eminences, stood ruined forts and castles which gave the impression of having been there ever since the very mountains and hills came into being. Some of the villages and two or three towns through which we passed, or where the train halted, looked almost prehistoric, and they and the people who lived in them differed entirely from any I had seen during my extensive travels through various parts of the world. At one station, three men joined me in my compartment, and soon the four of us conversed as if we had known one another for years. At first, until the newcomers realized that

I spoke Spanish, they carried on their conversation in Catalan, but, Spaniards being a polite people, after that they refrained from making use of their native tongue, of which I understand not a word. We were busy chatting when a young man in civilian clothes came along the corridor of the train and opened the door of our compartment.

After having turned back the lapel of his jacket, thus showing a badge which was concealed under it, he asked us to produce passes and passports. Although, in a joking manner, my companions were distinctly rude to the official in plain clothes, he merely smiled, and when he was satisfied with the documents produced by us, retired under a veritable bombardment of jibes and wisecracks concerning his mission and manner of earning a living. Especially near the border, such officials appear when least expected, it being their task to catch people who do not comply with existing regulations connected with security measures.

Darkness fell before our belated train steamed into Barcelona, where two old friends (a professor whom I shall merely call by his Christian name, Julio, and his charming wife, Rosemary, a Scottish-Patagonian) awaited my arrival. Number of licence plate, number of motor, frame, tyres and so on having been noted by a policeman, I was allowed to take the motor-cycle out of the station, where Julio half filled its tank with petrol he had purposely brought in his car. This done, his wife drove me towards their home, whilst her husband followed behind us on the cycle, pleased as a sand-boy. Upon reaching the outskirts of the town, we began to climb, and finally stopped at the foot of a high hill where my friends live in a *torre* (tower), as chalets are called in their region. The hospitality with which my good hosts overwhelmed me was almost embarrassing, and when in the early hours of morning one of the party suggested that we retire to sleep, I, for one, did not object. As I lay in bed, thinking over recent happenings, I found it difficult to believe that two nights previously I had slept in London, and that now, at last, I was in Spain, and about to find out for myself what the country and its people are like.

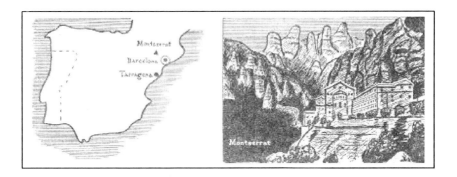

CHAPTER 3

BARCELONA – TARRAGONA – MONTSERRAT

Bright sunshine pouring in through the window of my bedroom greeted me on awakening next morning. Prosaic things like unpacking, making arrangements to give lectures, obtaining petrol coupons and so on having to be made, my host and I had a long programme before us. From his *torre* (chalet) I had a good view of nearby gardens, all blazing with flowers. On a ridge above us, a row of Castilian pines, looking for all the world like peculiar tall umbrellas, was silhouetted against the cloudless sky, and agave plants and oleanders gave a sub-tropical touch to the landscape. From the kitchen came sounds of the cook singing Flamenco songs, the tricky appoggiaturas of which have something distinctly North African about them. As if taking up the challenge, a caged budgerigar screeched and chattered away merrily, pigeons cooed and sparrows chirped as if in heated debate. After breakfast my host drove me into the city, where much had to be done.

Before going off on some errand, Julio, my host, asked me later to meet him at a certain *café,* situated at the top end of the *rambla.* As in the Argentine a *rambla* is a pleasure pier, I was puzzled as to why I should be asked to go all the way down to the beach, but when it was explained to me that in the case of Barcelona the *rambla* is a wide kind of boulevard with traffic lines on either side, I began to understand. Apparently the word is of Arabic origin, meaning a dry river bed. In due time I strolled along the animated promenade with its permanent bird and flower markets along the centre, and at the appointed hour went to the *café*, there to wait for my friend, who, incidentally, unlike the vast majority of his countrymen, is very punctual and systematic in everything he does. Accordingly, when he turned up, on the dot of time, the two of us sat down to have an *aperitivo*, and at the same time to talk over our plans for the immediate future. Whilst thus occupied, a stocky and rather corpulent boot-black came to ask me if I would allow him to shine my shoes. About forty years of age, he was such a jovial-looking fellow that I asked him to get busy, and whilst he sat in front of me on his little wooden stool, and brushed and rubbed for all he was worth, I conversed with Julio. How it was done is still a mystery to me, but after a while when a gentle tapping at the sole of my shoe made me look down in order to see what the man was doing to it, I discovered that he was busy nailing on a rubber sole, and that the job was nearly finished. Naturally, I protested, whereupon the boot-black pushed back his beret to scratch his head with one hand. Looking up at me, he smiled sheepishly, and proceeded to explain that my soles badly needed protection. My brogues being practically new, it dawned on me that the man was trying to trick me into buying a set of rubber soles from him, so in a mild fit of temper I called him an *atorrante*. As it happens, this is a typically Argentine slang word, meaning a low-down ruffian or bounder. "Oh, *señor*, what a pleasure to meet and to be of service to one who comes from the Argentine!" the boot-black exclaimed with assumed enthusiasm and joy. "What a delightful and expressive word . . . *'atorrante, a-tor-ran-te!'*" Whilst repeating the word slowly, his black, roguish eyes were raised towards heaven, feigning a state of ecstasy. Clasping together his grubby hands as if in prayer, he pressed them to his heart, and continued, "*Madre mia*, what wonderful memories this brings back to me . . . Argentina, the land of plenty, Argentina, the blessed land where I spent the best years of my life! Oh, *señor*, what a pleasure to meet one who comes from there, what a joy to hear that beautiful word, *atorrante!*"

At that moment a nice-looking little girl, aged about seven, came running towards him on tiptoe, and from behind covered both his eyes with her hands, at the same time asking, "Who is it?" "Carmencita," he exclaimed, and then hugged and kissed the child whom he introduced to us as his daughter. A few moments later, as swiftly as the child had come, she ran away, soon to be lost from view in the crowd which circulated near us in the sunshine.

After this little interlude, my heart softened, so I told the bootblack to go ahead with the tacking-on of the rubber soles. Whilst tapping away, he began to tell me all about his experiences in the Argentine where he had spent several years, sometimes in places I know well. Being a native of Bilbao, the important sea-port in the Basque country, he had spent most of his youth working in ships and later became a sailor. During a trip to Buenos Aires, when times were hard in his homeland, he decided to "hop" his ship, and so it came about that upon landing in the Argentine he deserted. Being a sailor, and therefore resourceful and able to set his hands to many different kinds of work, he became a baker's assistant, and as such earned more money than ever before he had received for services rendered. After having spent some two years in Buenos Aires, he shifted his camp to the provinces, and later became the chief baker in a well-known hotel in a summer resort at the foothills of the Andes. When the season came to an end, he decided to go and have another look at Buenos Aires and to enjoy some of the money he had saved. In the city, being a good and healthy Basque, he got drunk, and whilst he took a much needed rest, sleeping on a bench in a park, a policeman arrived on the scene to offer the carouser the hospitality of a cell. When it came to checking up on the new official guest's identity, and it was discovered that he had no documents of any kind, and that, in fact, he had entered the country illegally, the unfortunate ex-sailor and master baker was escorted to the first Spanish ship to set sail for its home port. And thus it came about that after an absence of several years, the Basque was taken ashore in Bilbao, where, for having deserted his ship, he was jailed for nine months. Shortly after his release he worked his way across the country to Barcelona where, eventually, he became a boot-black, and got himself a wife who, according to him, is the best washerwoman in the town.

When my rubber soles were tacked on to my thick-soled shoes, they were so heavy that I walked along like a deep-sea diver on dry land, and although my purse was lighter by twenty-five *pesetas,* I did not begrudge the jovial Basque his money. For several days after, whenever I saw him hovering about his favourite hunting ground, looking for other victims, I greeted him with an "*Adios, atorrante!*" which pleased him immensely. As will be seen, four months later I was to see that *simpático* rogue in a very different role.

I greatly enjoyed my walks through Barcelona, with its fine Plaza de Catalonia and magnificent thoroughfares. In the Gothic quarter, with its grand Levantine Gothic cathedral and many romantic buildings, I loved to peep into antique shops and into *talleres* where craftsmen carry on their ancient trades and arts. In crude but picturesque *tascas* (taverns) I drank wine and conversed with patrons, all of whom were most friendly. This city, with its million and a quarter inhabitants, is built on a gently undulating plain which slopes up to hills. Being sheltered from the *mistral,* in winter the climate is mild, but in summer, especially when a north-east wind blows, it can get hot and rather "clammy". At one time Barcelona rivalled Genoa and Venice as trading city of the Mediterranean, and about twelve centuries ago when the Moors captured this veritable Babel, they gave it the name of Bardjaluna.

When two elderly English ladies of my hosts' acquaintance arrived in Barcelona, they expressed their wish to be taken to a bull-fight. Strangely, although the two had been intimate friends for many years, in some respects their inclinations and tastes varied greatly. Thus, for instance, the frail and gentle-looking one – of all things – was a most enthusiastic all-in wrestling and boxing "fan," whilst the other had an abhorrence for these or any other violent kind of sport. And yet, whilst the three of us sat, watching six bulls being fought, whenever something dangerous happened, the admirer of real "he-men's" sports covered her eyes, and asked her friend to give her a running commentary of what was going on in the sandy arena below us, and whilst this was being done, listened intently, with a bottle of smelling-salts held to her nose.

One of the *matadores* was so cautious in approaching his bull that the onlookers began to whistle, cat-call, boo and howl, and whilst this commotion raged, suddenly from the spectators' enclosure a young man leapt into the ring, and was about to play the bull with his jacket, when he was grabbed and ejected. In Spain such exasperated hot-headed interveners in bullfights are called *"espontáneos."* Policemen and attendants are always on the look-out for such dare-devils, who out of sheer bravado expose themselves to the great danger of facing the onrush of a formidable fighting bull.

As, later on, I shall dedicate a whole chapter to bullfights and to the technicalities and general atmosphere connected with them, I will say but little about the one I saw on this occasion. Before dismissing the subject temporarily, I must add that bullfighting is not a competitive sport in the true sense, but a spectacle, an exhibition of daring, skill and grace, a primitive feast of joy mixed with terror. To many people the name "Spain" is synonymous with "bull-fighting," but yet I have met many Spaniards who have never seen – or wish to see – one of those bloody spectacles. To-day Association Football is Spain's favourite sport. Wherever I went, to towns, villages and even hamlets, I saw men and even small boys kicking about balls, from real footballs down to tin cans and rags tied together. If football could be played in bullrings, even the largest among them would be much too small to accommodate the enormous crowds which flock to see any important match. The masses in Spain are wildly, almost madly, football-minded, but in spite of this, the ancient and traditional art of bullfighting remains, as do stag and fox hunting in Britain.

As it happened, during the bullfight in Barcelona, two gorgeous, very effeminate and over-dressed young Englishmen sat near us, evidently getting a great thrill out of watching the *matadores* with their tight-fitting trousers. Strangely, I was to see the same pair at different times and in different places during my travels, and as will be seen later, these veritable flowers were to be given the nicknames of "Milo" and "Mila."

Owing to the lack of foreign currency and gold reserves – which were taken out of the country by the "Reds" during the civil war – only very few motor cars are being imported into Spain. Necessity being the mother of invention, ingenuity and resource, it is amazing to see what Spanish mechanics are capable of doing with old cars and motors. Some of these veritable mechanical wizards can recondition almost any rusty Methuselah of a motor or car, and I know of two brothers who carry on a very successful business doctoring and "dolling up" ancient motor-cycles, which leave their workshop running perfectly and look-ing as good as new.

Petrol being scarce and expensive, in Barcelona many of the taxis are driven by gas which is generated in veritable field-kitchens fixed on the backs of the vehicles. Charcoal and almond shells being burnt to provide locomotive power, smoke and sometimes flames are emitted from these affixed contraptions. The fact that many of the taxis have curtains over their windows, and that several I saw had the back win-dow completely covered over with a layer of thick paint, puzzled me until a friend explained that this was being done for a very good reason, and that taxis without this safeguard were "taboo" with certain members of Barcelona's community, and therefore lost quite a number of "fares." Near the outskirts of the city my reliable informant pointed out to me a building which I took to be a small hotel, but which, he explained, was an expensive *moblada,* or a house of assignation where rooms are let to couples. The entrance to this particular one is so cleverly and thoughtfully designed that when prospective guests arrive in a car, it is impossible for anyone to see them alight from it, excepting the *chef de reception,* who awaits clients inside the entrance door which is reached by walking along a kind of porchway made of awning with flaps which fit tightly against incoming vehicles. As guests leave the establishment by another door with identical contraptions provided for the sake of privacy, apparently the *moblada* is doing a constant and roaring business, and no wonder taxi-drivers who are accessories in many of Barcelona's amorous escapades, equip their vehicles with curtains which protect "fares" from the gaze of the inquisitive. And no wonder, also, that many a young *señorita* has left her parental home under the pretext of going to Mass or Confession, when in reality she merely went for a ride in one of those convenient taxis with curtained-off windows.

Far be it from me to suggest, or even remotely to insinuate that riding in the type of taxi here described is a kind of sport or favourite pastime in Barcelona. I merely mention the foregoing details for the benefit of tourists who, after hours of strenuous sightseeing in that attractive town, may wish to rest for an hour or so.

Newly-made friends took me to several quaint and interesting taverns and restaurants where we spent pleasant and amusing hours, eating savoury foods, drinking excellent wine and listening to strange though captivating music and singing. One such place was situated in a side street, in the quarter of the town where merrymakers assemble at night, and it was the first of its type I visited in Spain. A short entrance corridor led into a spacious kitchen, with a huge cooking range in the middle, and along its walls and in a large alcove at the end of this original dining-room were tables and chairs for guests who wished to eat on the ground floor. A narrow winding stair led up to a wooden gallery, whence, whilst dining, we had an excellent view of what was going on below. The proprietor of the restaurant – an enormously fat

man who acted as chief chef – was a jolly soul, and amazingly quick
and active for a man of his size and proportions. Having finished our
meal, we went to a nearby tavern run by gipsies who, upon realizing
that my companions – whom they knew well – were *de juerga* (on the
spree), rushed to bring wine and brandy. Two guitars appeared as if by
magic, and after a prolonged spell of tuning them in and playing short
"twiddly bits," the two musicians caught each others eyes, nodded
slightly, and began to strum away. The boss of the tavern, a powerfully-
built and fairly corpulent gipsy, and several of his friends, seated
themselves in a semi-circle near the guitarists, and, in turn, broke into
weird fascinating song. During short intervals they helped themselves
freely to wine, cigars and cigarettes, and when those which had been
placed on the table were finished, they calmly asked for more to be
produced. The cunning rascals never finished a glass of wine, so the
boss saw to it that clean ones were brought at short intervals, and filled.
Thus, after about an hour, on the table and on the floor near our
entertainers were platoons and battalions of full and half-full glasses,
and the place was littered with cigar and cigarette ends. By degrees, as
music and alcohol began to show their equally intoxicating effects on
the gipsies, they became more and more enthusiastic and vehement.
Joined by the waiters – one of them a mere boy – the other gipsies who
came in from the street, they beat complicated rhythms with hand-claps
which varied in tone and volume, until, unable to resist any longer, one
rose and slowly walked into the circle of singers and onlookers. For a
little while he stood motionless, as if gazing at his feet, apparently
oblivious of the audience round him, but as, by degrees, the strumming
of the guitars and the hand-clapping grew louder, he slowly raised his
eyes until he seemed to be looking for something on the ceiling.
Presently, he stretched himself up to his full height and a sort of shiver
seemed to run over him. Then, suddenly he stamped the floor with his
feet, twisting his narrow hips and writhed like a snake, and as his
amazing rapid stamping grew faster and faster and his weird
contortions and twists and turns more frenzied, the hand-clappers urged
him on with frequent exclamations of "*Olé!*" When, after a crescendo
stamping of feet, the dance came to an abrupt end, applause broke
forth, mixed with many loud "*Olés!*" Before they died down, the
exhausted performer – who until then had appeared to be in a trance –
suddenly became himself again. Laughing and making gestures

conveying apologies for an imperfect performance, the prima donna accepted a cigarette and a glass of wine, which, after having taken a sip out of it, he placed alongside the others which were lined up on the floor near his chair.

So many gipsies and outsiders joined our party, that when one of my friends suggested we go to his house and there continue the spree, the boss of the establishment and several of his gipsy friends immediately agreed that this was a splendid idea. Accordingly, in a surprisingly short time the cafe was emptied of its mostly non-consuming *habitués,* who had merely come in for a free entertainment, lights were turned out, the door locked, and, packed into three cars like sardines, we were on our way to the outskirts of the town, there, in a luxurious house with a spacious hall, to make merry. Upon entering it, the gipsies fairly gaped at objects of art and furniture, and when their boss, gathering courage, sampled a large leather-covered armchair, into which he sank with an exclamation of admiration and ecstasy, his dusky clansmen laughed boisterously. "If I had one of these," the stout man said, groaning and sighing, "I'd never get out of it. I'd sleep in it, eat in it, and die in it." However, when bottles of wine, cigars and cigarettes were brought by a smiling servant – who evidently, despite the late hour, looked forward to a night's fun – the stout one fairly catapulted himself out of the springy armchair, and rushed to the table on which the objects of his anticipation were being deposited, and set to, helping himself and his companions. Having tuned in their instruments, the two guitarists began to strum away, and the rest of us joined in, clapping our hands. Every now and again a gipsy sang one of those strange wailing songs, or if the music and the hand-clapping had the desired effect on some member of the party, he rose from his seat to do a solo dance. As night wore on the dancing became more and more furious until, when daylight began to appear, for a *gran finale* several of the dusky merrymakers improvised a most realistic dance representing a bullfight.

Instead of going to bed, as they could have done, the servants watched and listened from the top of the staircase, and when, dog-tired, I went to bed, they started on their day's work, singing cheerfully.

My hosts and newly-made friends were so keen to entertain me that it looked as if I would never get away, but besides one or two trial runs, during which the machine behaved splendidly, I also made several excursions from Barcelona, among them one to Tarragona and another to Montserrat. In Villafranca del Panades, a quaint little town in that region, was born the great 'cellist Casals. Even whilst at the peak of his fame, every year he conducted the local orchestra and played in the main square, the money thus collected going to local charities. The trip to Tarragona provided me with the first taste of Spain, as I wanted to see it. Before reaching the town, on a hill situated some three miles from it, the road led past a wonderfully preserved Roman triumphal arch, which dates back to the beginning of the second century. Over two thousand years ago, during the Second Punic War, the town was captured by the Romans who made it their headquarters, and constructed a good harbour and strong fortifications. According to a local belief, Pontius Pilate is said to have been born in the massive Tower of Pilate, which to-day is used as a prison. Besides Roman and Moorish constructions, Tarragona has a cyclopean wall which is said to date back to pre-historic times.

As I walked through the cobbled streets of the town, admiring ancient buildings and monuments, children watched me as if I were a strange being from another world. A bearded beggar, wearing rags, happened to pass me, and when he seated himself in the shade under a tall tree, I went to give him a few coins. Having thanked me for the small gift, in perfect French he asked me if I hailed from France, and went on to express his hope that I enjoyed my visit to his country. This led to a long conversation between the two of us, the filthy beggar doing most of the talking. He told me that at the age of twenty he had gone to wander through France where he spent several years, going from one region to another, just to see a bit of the world, sometimes doing an odd job, but mostly as a tramp. To my surprise the man seemed to be interested in people, their customs and habits, and even in traditions and history, and he had wandered about observing things with keen eyes. What had brought him to the pitiful state in which I saw him, he did not reveal to me, but I was left in no doubt that he was perfectly contented with his lot.

On my way back to Barcelona I followed a winding road which led along the rugged coast which is of great beauty. In these parts is Sitges, a fashionable seaside resort, with its fine beach and many crazily built houses, some of which are owned by rich people from all over the world who spend the summer season in these pleasant parts. My next excursion took me to Montserrat, the grotesque "serrated mountain" with its famous Benedictine monastery.

It was a perfect early spring morning when, accompanied by several friends, I started out from Barcelona. Following an excellent road, we were soon out of the city, and found ourselves in rolling country, planted with olives and vines, with here and there almond trees in full bloom. Every now and again we passed through picturesque villages and hamlets, and after having been on our way some two hours, ahead of us, out of a plain the outline of what appeared to be a colossal fantastic castle came in sight. We were on the plateau of Catalonia out of which rises Montserrat, the "Montsagrat" or Sacred Mountain of the old Catalans. My guides pointed out to me several particularly weird rock formations, all of which have local names, such as the *calavera* (skull), the *dedos* (fingers), the *flautas* (flutes), "giants", "sentinels", and "procession of monks", etc. Upon reaching the foot of this strange mountain, I discovered that most of it is a kind of reddish clay slate and "pudding stone" (conglomerate), or consolidated gravels which once upon a time must have been beach or sea deposits which were thrown up during a tremendous upheaval of nature, millions of years ago. A good winding road took us through pine-woods, and past crevices, fissures and gorges in which grow box and other evergreen shrubs. Upon rounding the numerous curves, new fantastic rock formations came in sight, until I thought that what I was seeing was part of a weird dream. After having visited the Benedictine monastery which is believed to have been founded before the Moorish conquest of Spain (A.D. 717) we continued our uphill journey until we reached the bottom of a funicular which takes cool-headed passengers up an enormous rocky precipice to the Turó de San Jerónimo, Montserrat's highest peak, 4,070 feet above sea-level. Having entered a kind of square tram-like box which holds about twenty passengers, we waited for a while, and presently we began to move very slowly. Up and up we went in our car, which is suspended from strong steel cables, and presently, high up above us the other car came in sight, on its downward journey towards us. Several of the passengers who were afraid of giddiness took good care not to look out of the windows, but after about a quarter of an hour, when we reached the little station at the top of the gaping rocky wall, and they stepped out of the car, the nervous ones heaved sighs of relief, and laughed off their recent experience.

To my surprise I found that the top of the mountain was covered with box and shrubs, some of which scented the chilly air. Unfortunately the sky became overcast, and whilst we followed a winding footpath which leads to the highest point, the temperature dropped rapidly, shifting fogs came rolling towards us, and rain began to fall, making us shiver. The information that on clear days from where I found myself, marvellous views can be obtained of the Catalonian plains, as far as to the Pyrenees, and sometimes of the Mediterranean Sea, and even of the Balearic Islands, did not help to cheer me up, and when it began to rain in torrents, and lightning flashed in the clouds around and below us, we decided that it was high time to beat a retreat. As we slithered along the footpath towards the top station of the funicular, I could not help wondering what would happen if lightning struck the steel cable from which we would soon be dangling in the box car. However, the return journey was accomplished without incident, and all of us were glad to have a warming drink in the restaurant near the monastery. As explained already, it is believed that a Benedictine settlement existed on Montserrat before the Moorish conquest, but according to a legend, the settlement is even older, and a small wooden image of the Virgin is said to have been made by Saint Luke, and to have been brought to Spain by Saint Peter. According to the popular story, during the Moorish invasion the image was hidden and subsequently forgotten until, nearly two centuries later, shepherds accidentally found it in a cave. When the happy discoverers attempted to take the image to the nearest town (Manresa), despite its diminutive size, it made itself so heavy that it could not be moved, and so it came about that a monastery was built wherein to house the miraculous image.

Having seen a great deal of Barcelona and its surrounding regions, assisted by Julio, my excellent host, I gave the motor-cycle a thorough overhaul, prepared my equipment, and after another short trial run was ready to set out on my tour.

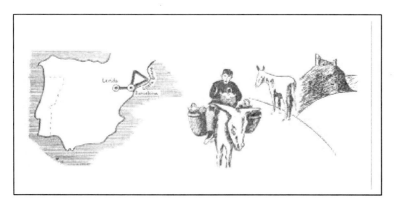

CHAPTER 4

BARCELONA – COSTA BRAVA – LÉRIDA

As from the French border I had travelled to Barcelona by train in order not to miss anything that might be interesting, I decided to make a big loop towards the Pyrenees, in a northerly direction, or, in other words, to go back to where I had come from, but this time on the cycle.

Being a cautious driver, I felt greatly relieved when the city with its heavy traffic lay behind me, and I rode merrily along a good coastal road where I was practically alone. Being in no hurry, I travelled at speeds ranging between fifteen and twenty miles per hour, and therefore was able to see and observe things. Every hour or so, upon coming to spots whence fine views could be obtained, I stopped to have a short rest, or to take photographs. The road wound along the "Rugged Coast" (Costa Brava), up hill and down dale, through strongly smelling pine and cypress woods, past carefully cultivated fields and through villages with narrow streets. Here and there, on the steep slopes of hills, black goats grazed, making perfect pictures with the deep-blue sea and sky. Early in the afternoon I halted in a little village where, in a small wayside tavern I had a meal consisting of smoked ham, bread and red wine. Towards evening, after a ride of some seventy miles, I reached San Feliu, a picturesque seaside resort and fishing port. The little hotel at which I stopped was empty, as were all the others, but I was told that in mid-summer accommodation is at a premium.

Having deposited my few belongings in the bedroom, I went down to the empty dining-room, there to chat with the owner of the establishment who was seated at a table, watching his wife and another woman who were busy mending linen sheets. I noticed that before him were placed a small inkpot, a pen and a large sheet of greenish-buff paper, evidently some kind of form. With an apology for having to bother me, he explained that what I looked at was the *triptico,* an official questionnaire all foreigners have to fill in. As in Barcelona my host had attended to this formality, this was the first time I had to suffer with the tiresome – and in my opinion quite unnecessary – red tape. Seating myself at a nearby table, with a nib, the points of which were crossed like a lounge lizard's legs, I began to make the necessary entries, of which seventeen were required: date of arrival, whence, number of passport, origin of passport, object of voyage, father's name, mother's name, and so on. The paper, on which I tried to write clearly, was of such poor quality that the nib frequently stuck into it. Divided into four sections under the imposing headings of *Matriz, Salida de Extranjeros, Parte* and *Entrada,* four times I made the seventeen entries, and when, suffering from writer's cramp, I handed the sheet back to my host, he thanked me most profusely for having saved him a lot of bother. Apparently visitors are expected to fill in only one section, and it is up to the owners of establishments to attend to the other three. Together with my passport the *triptico* was sent to the police station, whence, after some time, it was returned with a blank form, to be filled in at my next halting place. Being as yet a stranger to Spanish ways, at the time I did not realize that in that happy-go-lucky land even officialdom does not take *papeleo* (paper business) seriously; but as I had saved my host a great deal of hard and tedious work, he became very friendly. In the evening, after having strolled through the little town and its picturesque surroundings, and I sat alone in the dining-room, eating, he joined me for a chat, in which, after a while, the solitary waiter also took part. As usual in similar circumstances, the topic of our conversation changed from one subject to another, but when the Civil War was brought up, they had a great deal to say about it. According to my interlocutors, although their little home town, San Feliu, was of no importance, it was subjected to many air raids, during which a number of people were killed. So many were the stories I heard about the Civil War that it was getting late when we rose to go for a short stroll before turning in for the night. A full moon shone on the sea, transforming it into an animated sheet of silver, and small waves washing up the beach sang their dreamy song of ages. Here and there, among the wooded hills, twinkled lights of chalets, and although from two taverns near the port came sounds of talking and singing, shortly after having placed my head on the pillow, I fell into a deep sleep.

Early next morning I was on my motor-cycle, heading towards a nearby hill whence a marvellous view of the Costa Brava can be obtained. Contrary to its appearance on the previous day, the sea now was of cobalt and green-jade colour, and so transparent that submerged rocks and reefs were visible. After a short halt I proceeded, soon to find myself among fields in their spring gala attire of every shade of light-green, with here and there, where linseed was being cultivated, a square patch of yellow. In the distance, towards the north-west, towered the snow-covered Pyrenees whence blew a cold penetrating wind which, together with the rays of the sun, made the skin of my face tingle. Everywhere, in fields and vineyards, peasants – men, women and children – were busy weeding, and as I passed they looked up and waved greetings.

On the brow of a low hill, a particularly picturesque old house attracted my attention, and upon going closer to have a good look at it, I discovered that it was a pottery works. A man who was busy carrying round lumps of clay to boards on which to dry them in the sun, greeted me with a friendly *"Buen dia, señor"*, and whilst the two of us stood, making banal remarks about the weather and the beauty of our surroundings, an elderly woman came out of the house to offer me a glass of wine. "It is grown in our vineyard," she said, "just a wine of the region; please tell me what you think of it." Having tasted a little, in all sincerity I complimented her on the quality of the liquid, whereupon she smiled with visible pride.

"What a picturesque old house, yours is," I remarked between sips, to which the woman replied that, indeed, it was very old, having been owned by the family for many generations. "You see, *señor,* here we carry on the oldest craft in the world. We are potters. Come and have a look at our primitive installations."

The tour of inspection over, I had to accept another glass of wine, and whilst we sat on stools, talking about pots and jars, the woman asked me where I had learnt Spanish. When I told. her that I had lived in the Argentine for many years, she became very interested, and enquired if by any chance I knew a Señor So-and-So in Buenos Aires. I explained that Buenos Aires has over three million inhabitants, and that in consequence I regretted having to say that I did not know the person to whom she referred.

"He happens to be my son," the woman went on. "He is very well known in Buenos Aires. He is the manager of an important American bank there. Ever since travel by air has become so rapid and easy, every year he comes here to spend two or three weeks with us."

Now I remembered; I had met the man, though I do not know him well. Both the woman and her husband were so delighted that they wanted me to stay for a meal, but as I had a long way to drive before evening, I thanked them for the kind offer, and shortly after departed.

From the parts in which I found myself (Catalonia), countless people had emigrated to different parts of the Americas, and the same has been the case with Galicia and the Basque country. However, on the whole, Spaniards are stay-at-homes, and in many regions emigration is a rarity. Over-population and its inevitable consequences, as well as, to a certain extent, high taxation, have driven the most enterprising and courageous to seek a living across the seas.

In a Catalonian mountain village where I stopped to buy some oranges at a tiny shop, the elderly woman who ran it told me that in all her life she had never gone more than a few hundred yards from her birthplace. She, also, had relatives in South America, and although they had repeatedly invited her to join them, she much preferred to stay at home, and to live in a state bordering on abject poverty.

Travelling northwards, towards the nearby Pyrenees, I made a big loop, on the way passing through the historic old towns of Gerona and Vich (pronounced "Vick"). In many parts, and for long stretches, the minor roads I followed were bad, and the country mountainous, rugged and wooded. Most of the villages were primitive but picturesque, and the people very friendly. Steep, winding roads, on which there was practically no motor traffic, gave me ample opportunities of improving my handling of the motorcycle, and as I became more and more confident, I wished for no better means of transportation. In a car, one is apt to become sleepy, and one is unable really to "take in" the scenery. Furthermore – and very important in my case – a traveller who arrives in a village or small town in a car, looks too prosperous, and consequently it is more difficult to make contact with the people. A motor-cycle is, as it were, the tourist's donkey. Though most of the powerful machines are apt to make a great deal of noise, they are, to use the modern and chewed-out word, "democratic." Fortunately, my cycle, even when driven at top speed, was remarkably silent, and, better still, it consumed but very little petrol (roughly 120 miles to the gallon).

In a little town near the Pyrenees, upon seeing a petrol pump, I decided to fill my tank. The pump being unlocked, and as near it stood an empty chair, I tooted to attract the invisible attendant's attention. Nothing happened, so over and over again I tooted, until, at last, a boy came to see what was the matter. "Oh, you want the *duwño!*" (owner) he said, as if surprised, "he is down the road in the *café. Un momento,* I will call him."

With this the youngster ran away, soon to reappear seated on a bicycle which he pedalled towards the tavern. At least ten minutes must have passed before several men came slouching out of the door, where they formed a group, evidently to finish their conversation. Eventually, after the boy with the bicycle had pointed in my direction several times, one of the talkers detached himself from the others and slowly came towards me. Without apology for having kept me waiting so long, he filled my tank, and then proceeded to tell me all about an argument he and his friends had had in the *café,* over the selection of the football team which was to represent Spain in the world tournament in Rio de Janeiro. No wonder I was kept waiting for so long, for as I was to find out later, this event was to overshadow and put into the background all other happenings in the world as far as the masses in Spain were concerned. The "GB" plate on my motor-cycle having given the man the clue where I came from, he proceeded to ask me many questions about football, as it is played in England, and upon realizing that I knew a little about the game, he became so enthusiastic that he invited me to return to the *café* with him. His friends were still talking and arguing outside, and when I arrived with my machine, conversation ceased, all eyes were fixed on the cycle, about which comments were made in whispers. "*Muy maja*" (very spruce), one ventured to tell me, at last.   The ice having been broken, I was asked so many to me technical questions about the machine that I became almost giddy. Was it a two- or four-stroke engine she had? What was her horse-power and top speed? What was this gadget and that? What was the consumption of petrol? and so on. When the petrol-pump man introduced me to the assembly as. an expert *futbolista,* and suggested we go into the *café* for a little refreshment, everybody agreed, and soon after, whilst we sat at table, I was subjected to a bombardment of questions regarding football in England, in the Argentine, Uruguay and in other countries. When, at last, I made ready to depart, one of the company asked me if I had had my midday meal, and when I replied that I would eat a snack anywhere along the road, a shout went up, several voices ordering the waiter to bring me *butifarra* (a kind of sausage) and *munchetas* (beans). Despite my protests, I was made to eat, and when, before leaving my pleasant company, I offered to pay for what I had consumed, there was almost a riot, and when I insisted the waiter was pushed behind the counter, and I was escorted outside to where my motor-cycle stood. Such is Spanish hospitality.

The wooded mountains over which the twisting and winding road led reminded me of parts of Switzerland. Rosemary was in blossom, and its fragrant smell mixed with that of pine, so I inhaled deeply, almost greedily. Near the old town of Vich I struck an excellent highway which leads back to Barcelona. At a cross-road, I was about to overtake a lorry which had slowed down, when I saw two motor-cycle policemen who made a signal to stop. As the lorry came to a standstill, I halted beside it, whereupon one of the policemen politely told me that there was no need for me to stop, and that they were merely about to search the lorry for contraband. "A little rest will do me good," I said, pushing my machine to the side of the road, and when the lorry had been searched and allowed to proceed, the two policemen came to have a look at my cycle with expert eyes. One of them insisted on giving me a cigar, and whilst we chatted, and I told them about my proposed tour through their country, both became most enthusiastic. At it happened, the two men hailed from Galicia, so they told me much about the beauty and charm of their home regions, and even gave me the addresses of their respective families, whom they had not seen for a long time. Having conversed for well over an hour, during which, incidentally, I was given several useful tips about riding a motor-cycle through difficult country, I departed, and towards evening arrived at the house of my friend, Julio, in the outskirts of Barcelona. When his charming, typical Spanish-looking daughter saw me, she fairly shrieked with laughter, and upon recovering sufficient breath to utter a few words she said, pointing at my face, "What have you done to it? Oh, how funny you look!"

Ever since midday I had felt a sharp tingling under my left eye, and presently, upon having a look at myself in a mirror, I noticed that one cheek was badly swollen and sunburnt. Strong sunshine and a continuous cold wind blowing from one direction had affected my skin, and although the young lady smeared over the affected parts with some ointment, making me look like a gargoyle, the swelling increased, and by next morning my left eye was completely closed. Naturally, I became the target of many jokes and "wisecracks," but in order to avoid a similar happening in future, Julio presented me with a mica shield which was to prove invaluable, and much more practical than goggles; for never again, throughout my tour, did sun or wind affect my face.

During two or three days which preceded Palm Sunday *(Domingo de Ramos)*, there was a great deal of movement and activity in Barcelona. All along the wide *rambla* were stalls where the branches of palms were sold. Having been kept in pits filled with lime and sulphur for several weeks, the leaves and stems were of a bright light-yellow, and many of the branches were worked into intricate patterns and shapes of various sizes. As purchasers – men, women and children – walked along, they looked like a disorganized army of lancers. On Palm Sunday processions are held, people going to different churches to have the palms blessed. Later they are fixed to balconies or to walls inside the house where they remain for a whole year, when they are replaced by new ones. Date-palms require careful cultivation. There are two kinds: the male and the female. The pollen is sprinkled over the female by husbandmen. The leaves of male palms and of barren female are cut for Palm Sunday.

Another method for bleaching the leaves is by doing this on the trees, binding them up tightly. This can be done only once in four years, lest the trees suffer too much. A tree yields about ten leaves. The binding up of them is tricky. The *hortelano* (husbandman) climbs up the high trunk by means of a rope passed round his waist, thus half walking up the tree.

Throughout Spain, but especially in Seville, Good Friday and Holy Week are great occasions. Every region has its own particular traditions, ceremonies and forms of interpreting this religious festival. The procession I watched in Barcelona, though it is not as spectacular as in other cities, was most impressive. The hooded penitents reminded me of the Ku Klux Klan, then there were the be-helmeted Romans and images surrounded by hundreds of burning candles on litters carried by many men.

Whilst watching the slow-moving procession I felt a very slight tugging at the strap of my camera case, and upon looking down to see what was the cause of this, I discovered that a pick-pocket was trying to extricate the camera from it. Turning round quickly, I grabbed the would-be thief by the lapels of his ragged coat. I was about to punch the rascal's jaw, but upon seeing that he was a miserable weak-looking man of about fifty, I merely gave him a good shaking, whereafter he made off as fast as he could. The whole thing happened so quickly and silently that only one man who stood near me saw it. "Why didn't you give the old *pillo* (rogue) a sound kicking?" he said, and with this turned round to go on watching the procession.

Catalans being hard-working thrifty people – who, according to an old saying, can produce bread from stones – Barcelona, the capital of their province, is a prospering town. Among its chief industries are the manufacture of textiles, machinery, paper and iron ware. Owing to lack of housing accommodation, in one part of the city there is a large colony of crudely-built hutments. For a long time, Catalans have striven for home rule, for they resent the high taxation to which they are subjected, and even more so the fact that most of the money they contribute to the National Treasury is spent in Madrid and on projects from which they derive no benefit. In this respect Catalans are very much like the Scots who strive for home rule.

My trial run along the Costa Brava and up towards the north having been made without mechanical or other troubles arising, I felt much more confident than before, so after having made minor adjustments to the machine – my friend Julio doing most of the work – I was ready to have the real "go" at Spain, Madrid being my first important objective.

The sun was shining brightly when, not too early one morning, I fixed the two panniers and the suitcase to the cycle. By means of leather straps, my practically new raincoat was secured to the top of my luggage, I cranked up, bade farewell to my hosts who had come to the gate to see me depart, and then rode away merrily. As it was *Sábado de Gloria* (Holy Saturday) here and there groups of children were assembled. When the clocks struck and chimed 10 a.m., the youngsters began to make a great noise with rattles *(carracas)* and by beating tins and wooden boxes.

Striking out in a south-westerly direction, soon the last houses of Barcelona's suburbs were behind me, and after about an hour, upon stopping to have a short rest, and to see if the luggage behind me was in order, I had a rude shock. My precious raincoat had disappeared, the straps which were supposed to secure it having been badly adjusted, with the result that bumps and vibrations had caused it to fall off. Thinking over matters, I came to the conclusion that it would be useless to go back in search of what I had lost, for surely by this time a passer-by had picked up my coat, and the chances of retrieving it were vastly against me. Eighteen guineas had gone, and as I was in no position to replace what I had lost, there was no alternative but to go ahead and trust to luck. Should it come on to rain, well, I should have to seek shelter or simply get soaked to the skin. Whilst I sat by the wayside, thinking over my misfortune, two motor-cycle policemen came riding towards me, so I rose and signalled to them to stop. Upon hearing about my loss, they asked me to give them an address in Madrid, to which in case they found the raincoat they could send it. No sooner had I handed them what they required than they cranked up and disappeared as if they were chasing some bandits. However, the coat never reached me, so I can only hope that some poor and deserving person became its new owner.

The country through which I rode at a leisurely pace is rocky and hilly. Here and there, perched on strategic heights, were ruins of old castles. On stretches and patches of arable land grew symmetrical rows of almond and olive trees, and in the spaces between them wheat was cultivated. It being Easter Day, people in villages were making merry, bands playing music, and joyous young people rode on carts decorated with flowers, greenery and coloured paper. Whilst riding along, they sang songs of the region, and as I passed them, they waved and shouted greetings. Between villages and small towns I had the road practically to myself, and when, at long intervals, I met a mule or donkey-drawn cart, the driver was almost invariably asleep, lying down whilst the animal plodded along. It was surprising to observe the animals' "road sense," for all of them kept to the right side, which the majority of Spanish motorists do only during spells of absent-mindedness. But more about donkey and mule sense later, and about driving in the delightful Land of the Hidalgos.

During the late afternoon, now feeling like a seasoned motorcyclist, I rode over a bridge which spans the river Segre. I had arrived in Lérida, the ancient town of Celtiberian origin. There it stood before me, with its old houses built up the slopes of a steep hill, at the top of which is the fort and the old cathedral built in the late Romanesque Transition style. Like most Spanish towns, Lérida has a fascinating history. Owing to its strategic importance, in 49 B.C. Caesar captured it, and later the Visigoths, Moors and the French (1642). The foundations of a bridge which was blown up during the Civil War are Roman.

Having admired the view before me for a while, I went to ask a policeman if he could recommend some *económico* hotel. Delighted to be of assistance, he pointed to a nearby house, where, soon after, the proprietor and a waiter did their utmost to make me feel comfortable and at home.

The lower part of the town is modern, but a steep climb up narrow streets, cobbled with flat circular stones laid edge upwards, takes one to the old section. Although I wore thick-soled brogues, walking over those stones was most uncomfortable, and I had to proceed with care lest I should slip and fall. From a painter's or photographer's point of view, the old part of Lérida, with its narrow streets and ancient hovels, is most picturesque. Everywhere children played, women gossiped from balconies, some of which are so close together that from them hands could be shaken across the street. Here and there, squatting on stools, other women played cards, old packing-cases doing duty as tables. Upon nearing the top of the hill I came to the walls of the ancient fort from which the town's name is derived, in Celtic *il* or *hil* meaning "castle" and *erd* "height". Below me, the irregular shapes of the houses with their tiled roofs and the surrounding country made a romantic sight. Threading my way along a rough footpath, I came to a place where a woman, wearing a dirty black dress, squatted outside the entrance of a small tunnel. She was busy cooking something in a pot, placed over a small fire on the ground. For a moment I was puzzled, but then it dawned on me that the woman, and most likely her husband and children, lived in the excavation under the wall of the old fort. Continuing my ramble, I came to two or three similar caves, all of which were inhabited by poor people. Later I heard that these tunnels were dug during the Civil War, when attackers attempted to blow up the strongly defended fort. To-day the old cathedral and the fort are used as barracks.

Retracing my steps, I went downhill to the modern part of the town, where, in the Calle Mayor (Main Street), crowds of well-dressed men and women were parading about, their gay voices reverberating through the narrow street. Groups of raw recruits in ill-fitting uniforms mingled with the crowd, or stood at corners, self-consciously eyeing particularly good-looking *señoritas* as they passed in threes and fours, laughing, chatting and revelling in the veritable sun-bath of admiring looks thrown in their direction by men.

Having seen enough, I went back to my hotel, to seat myself at one of the tables outside its entrance door. The waiter being nowhere to be found, the porter brought me a glass of sherry, and whilst I sipped the golden fluid, he stood at my side, chatting away as if we were old acquaintances. About sixty years of age, he was a typical Catalonian, lively and full of talk and information. The last red after-glow of a beautiful sunset was reflected on the nearby river, and bats flitted about erratically in the balmy evening air. Talking incessantly, the old porter at my side interspersed his weighty statements with adages and proverbs, of which there are countless in Spanish. The international football match between Spain and Portugal had been played that evening in Lisbon, so even after it had ended in Spain's favour, crowds of enthusiasts were assembled before loudspeakers in the street, eagerly listening to "post mortem" comments and greetings broadcast by some of their heroes, the victorious *futbolistas.* The porter took but a very casual interest in the great *victoria,* and when, in order to change his flow of conversation, I asked him if he was an *aficionado* ("fan") of bullfighting, he fairly snorted, "Much too expensive! Bulls and bullfighters no good nowadays! As far as I am concerned they can all go to the devil!" When I asked him about the Civil War, though he had a great deal to say about it, he did not reveal on which side his sympathy had been. Pointing at a bridge which had been blown up during the "Reds'" retreat towards the north, he said, "That was done with barrels of *dinamitra* (dynamite). Evidently he liked the Spanish word, *dinamita,* with an "r" thrown in, for every time he used it the "r" was rolled as if in imitation of an explosion. Whilst my informant was holding forth, a car drew up near us. A plate with a black "F" indicated that it came from France, and that its two occupants were tourists. Presently a rather attractive woman stepped out of the car, and in very broken Spanish began to ask the porter some questions. To begin with she wanted to see the hotel's menu, and when this was produced she asked many questions regarding quality, quantity, prices, etc. Having obtained the required information, she went to consult her male companion, who remained seated at the wheel. After a while she returned and asked to see the *patrón,* and when he came on the scene, and the prospective client started to haggle about prices, suggesting reductions here and there, eventually, having shown great patience, he politely told her that, if the prices were not to her liking, he would much prefer it if she went to some other *restaurán,* of which there were several in the town. As, prior to departing, the female tightwad made her way towards the car, the porter scratched his stubby grey hair and murmured, *"Vaya, que franchuta!"* (Gosh, what a Frenchie).

Shortly after I left Lérida, the scenery changed completely. The road led over high passes and across semi-arid plains, where the soil is so rocky and dry that according to a fanciful description there it is easier for builders to mix their mortar with wine than with water. A terrific *Castellano* – as the wind blowing from the heights of the Castilian plateau is called – often made me swerve and wobble from one side of the road to the other. In summer this wind can be very hot, but as I passed through these parts early in April, it was bitterly cold and penetrating. The raincoat I had lost would have come in very useful, but as it was, the best thing I could do to protect myself was to stuff newspapers into the sweater I wore under my jacket. Besides this improvised but excellent protection, the mica shield was a god-send and gauntlet gloves kept my hands and wrists warm. Here and there, jagged rocky hills reminded me of certain high parts of Bolivia. If an Aymara Indian had suddenly appeared, the illusion would have been perfect. At intervals I saw shepherds looking after scraggy sheep. One who happened to be seated on a rock alongside the road was about to have his simple midday meal when I halted to have a short rest. He was an intelligent looking blue-eyed man, about twenty-five years of age. To protect himself against the cold wind, over his tattered clothes he wore a goat-skin with long black and white hair. Over his shoulder was slung a *mochila* (knapsack), from which he took a piece of dark-brown bread and a small bottle containing milk. Having replied to my *buenos dias* (good morning), with a flashing smile he said, *"Si le gusta, señor"* (If you like, sir), and at the same time held out his food to me.

"*Gracias, que aproveche*" (thanks, may it do you good), I replied, this being the customary negative answer to invitations to share a meal. "I trust that I'm not disturbing you," I went on, at the same time petting the shepherd's dog who had come up to sniff me. The young man said that his life was a lonely one, and that, therefore, it gave him pleasure to have my company, and that he was glad and felt honoured because I had stopped to speak to one as poor and humble as he. For about half an hour the two of us sat in friendly conversation, but what interested me most was to learn something about my interlocutor's life and family. Without complaining, he told me that as no rain to speak of had fallen for nearly two years in the region, things were very bad. Indeed, on my way I had noticed that where wheat had been sown, the crop was very thin, and most of the ears I had tested were empty. "Even if it came on to rain now, it is too late. Bread will be very scarce; so what we are going to eat, only God knows. Unless Argentina sends us wheat, we peasants face a very bleak future. However, *paciencia,* hope is a great thing."

Having taken my leave I made ready to resume my journey, and as I rode away I heard the shepherd sing a weird plaintive song of the region.

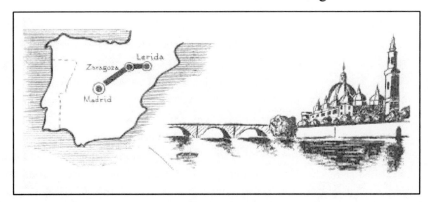

CHAPTER 5

LÉRIDA – ZARAGOZA – MADRID

In the high, semi-barren but yet strangely picturesque regions between Lérida and Zaragoza the sun shone brightly, but cold penetrating
winds blew incessantly. In Spain the tops of high passes –a number of
which I had to negotiate in this region – are called *puertos* (a word
which also means "seaport" or "haven"). From some of these heights,
fine views of the surrounding regions can be obtained. The villages
through which I passed, or where I stopped to eat brown bread, cheese
or a few slices of *chorizo* (a strongly flavoured kind of pork-sausage),
and to drink a glass of wine, were very ancient and, despite their
primitiveness, romantic, and in some cases weird. No trees shade the
adobe houses with their brown-tiled roofs and whitewashed walls,
which are of very simple design, but the people who live in them have
the stamp of nobility. They are the purest Iberians. Parched by the sun
and furrowed with wrinkles, the lean aquiline faces of many of these
peasants are fine studies of character. Though proud and dignified and
opposed to all innovations, the typical Castilian is a friendly and kind
soul. The struggle for existence, and centuries of hardship and fighting
have left their outward and inward marks. Owing to the prolonged
drought, the outlook for the future was dismal, but yet only a few old
women to whom I spoke complained. The men carried on their work,
attending to their semi-barren fields and looking after flocks of scraggy
sheep.

As I neared Zaragoza, the hills became lower, and eventually I reached the city which is situated in the midst of what might almost be described as a desert. Upon arriving at the banks of the river Ebro, I beheld the fine sight of the cathedral of the Virgin of Pilar, with its coloured domes reflected in the waters. The city is surrounded by masses of *huertas* (vegetable gardens and orchards), watered by means of small canals. The old part of Zaragoza, with its ancient fortress-like *solares* (houses in which the nobility used to live) is particularly interesting.

In startling contrast with the villages and small country towns through which I had passed, where food was scarce and of the simplest, even the modest hotel in which I stayed in Zaragoza had a menu which would have satisfied exacting gourmets. By that time I was becoming accustomed to the lateness of the hours during which meals are taken in Spanish cities and towns. Breakfast is served between 9 and 11 a.m., lunch from 2 until as late as 4 p.m., and dinner never before 9 p.m. Even if a guest arrives after 11 p.m., it is quite in order, and servants make no complaints. In many places I have seen people sit down to dinner after midnight.

After having walked about Zaragoza, whenever I returned to my hotel, looking forward to sitting down and reading, to my dismay and annoyance a trio of young bloods *(curci,* as such are called in Spain) were in the hall, showing off with a portable English radio set. In order to impress the other guests, they turned it on full blast, thus doing their best to drown the horrid noise made by the hotel's infernal box of agony which was tuned in to a different transmitting station. Not satisfied with this, when the time came to sit down to meals, they proudly carried their pet into the dining-room, and placed it on the table at which they sat, talking and arguing, at the same time gesticulating elegantly. Irritated by the noise, I looked over my newspaper several times and wriggled in my chair. At a table near mine happened to sit a tall middle-aged man who, judging by his general appearance, must have been a country gentleman on a visit to the town. Unable to stand the blaring of the wireless any longer, I asked the waiter to go and suggest to the young smarties to reduce the volume of sound. Accordingly, he went, and when his polite request was dismissed with a waving of hands and a slight shrugging of shoulders, as if to say, "Go away, we don't care," the tall gentleman near me rose, crossed the dining-room to where the offending trio sat, and, without saying a word, picked up their radio set. Having switched it off under their noses, he handed it over to the waiter with the curt instruction to take it to the "kennel" *(perrera)*. This done, he slowly returned to his table, and, before resuming his seat, turned to me and with a slight bow said, "*Disculpe, señor*" ("Pardon, sir").

This sudden and unexpected intervention had such an effect on everybody in the place that for the rest of the meal all that could be heard were the noises made by knives, forks and spoons, and occasionally a few whispers and giggles by young ladies. As far as the radio fiends were concerned, they finished their dinner, blushing and in silence. So much for a Castilian lesson in manners, and for three pupils who knew how to take it.

Spain's topography is so varied and often bewildering that it has been called the "Land of the Unexpected." When one bears in mind that the average height above sea-level is 2,000 feet, and that the climate changes greatly in different regions – from cold to warm and even hot, and from wet to dry – it is advisable to be prepared for the contrasts one meets whilst travelling. With startling suddenness everything changes in this "Land of Contrasts," as I prefer to call it; the scenery, vegetation, colour of the rocks and soil, the people, the languages and dialects they speak, the food they eat and the wines they drink, their music, songs and traditional costumes, and also their character; in short, differences and contrasts are as great as, say, between the north of Scotland and the South of Italy. Whilst travelling, I began to understand the real meaning of the old adage, "*Quien dice España dice todo*" (He who says Spain says all).

Between Zaragoza and Madrid I had to cross several more high passes, and for long stretches the road wound through tortuous deep and rocky valleys. Owing to the topography, the construction of highways and railroads, and their upkeep, involves great expense and much labour. In Primo de Rivera's time, many fine highways were constructed, but since the Civil War, owing to lack of funds and modern machinery, both the highways and railroads have greatly deteriorated. However, much is being done to remedy matters, and consequently, as already pointed out, on the whole the main highways are fairly good, though here and there stretches are bad. Distances between towns being great, and most of the country mountainous or rough, the problem of highways and railroads is gigantic.

In some parts of Castile the red or brownish-grey clay-built houses match the colour of the rocks and the soil, and the same is the case with ruined castles and forts which proudly stand on heights dominating valleys and other strategic points. Some of the small towns and villages with their low-built houses look like stony growths from the arid soil. As I proceeded, there were narrow gorges and gullies between towering walls of jagged rock, stretches of windswept arid plain, here and there a green valley, shepherds with flocks of sheep, herds of goats which thrive on apparently nothing, the road winding up and up, colder and colder, wind blowing furiously, then seemingly interminable series of curves, below warmer and more sheltered parts, families working in fields, praying for rain, almond trees in blossom giving a welcome touch of colour, peasants waving greetings, then another ruined castle, all but shouting defiance from its rocky height, a dry river bed, some miles further along another, and yet another, then an ancient village with rough cobbled streets, women and girls at a fountain filling pitchers, donkeys standing by patiently, waiting to carry them home, then again out into open, bleak, barren country, uphill, down dale, curves, steep zigzagging, every now and again a heavy two-wheeled cart drawn by fine mules, one in front of the other, very occasionally a lorry or car, sun shining brightly, but in high places or on plains cold wind, gusts often so strong and sudden that I wobbled from one side of the road to the other. And so on towards Madrid.

On the way, the little town of Calatayud, situated in the green valley of the river Jalon, offered a pleasant change. Thanks to irrigation canals and abundance of water, all the fields were green, birds sang every-where, and swallows recently arrived from Africa, wheeled and circled about, voicing shrilly as if out of sheer joy. In the steep hill which overlooks the town live many cave-dwellers, and on the top of it stands the ruin of the Moors' castle of Ayub from which the town has derived its name *(al-Kalah-Ayub,* the Castle of Ayub).

Unlike some of the other cave-dwellers I saw in different parts of Spain, those of Calatayud are very poor. Despite the fact that water has to be brought up from the valley, and that sanitary arrangements are non-existent, the ancient dwelling places are kept remarkably clean. In some places, the climb up to the caves is so steep that donkeys cannot reach them, and therefore men, women and children make the tiring trips up and down, carrying as much as their strength permits. Almost all the people I saw there were dressed in rags, and all the children went about bare-footed. What the inhabitants of these caves exist on is a mystery to me. However, they appear to be quite happy, and the majority of the children looked healthy and were as clean as youngsters can be when left to play in the open.

In different parts of Spain such colonies of cave-dwellers have existed for many centuries, and many of these comfortable abodes have been occupied by countless generations of the families who now live in them. To most of us the word "troglodyte" conveys something prehistoric, but in Spain millenniums have spanned the gaps to modern times.

About twenty miles from Calatayud, after having passed through a deep gorge with bleak rocky mountains on either side of me, I came to another picturesque town, Alhama de Aragon. Its thermal springs were already known to the Romans who made use of the warm waters to cure rheumatism. Later the Moors changed the name of *Aquae Bilbilitanae* to *al-Hammah* (meaning the hot well).

A high jagged hill which overlooks the town is also perforated with many cave dwellings, inhabited by poor families. The hill is so steep that the climbing of it is a feat fit for a chamois, but, despite this, the cave-dwellers think nothing of making several journeys up and down, to work in the fields below and to bring home what food they are able to buy, water, firewood and other necessities.

Thanks to its thermal springs, Alhama de Aragon is a prospering place. I happened to be having lunch in a nice *fonda* when several men arrived in a car. Having taken a table alongside the one at which I sat, they ordered food and wine, and then began to talk away as if trying to squeeze a whole day's conversation into one hour. As the chatterers were seated so near me, I could not help hearing most of what they said, though sometimes so many spoke at the same time that the combined conversations sounded like a waterfall heard at close quarters. Eventually, one of the men who had evidently just returned from a voyage to the Argentine, got the upper hand in this veritable battle royal of vocal self-expression, and after a while all his table companions listened to him in silence. Some of the stories he told about what he had seen and experienced in South America were so fantastic that I held my breath. Lions, tigers, boa-constrictors, man-eating wild horses – he had seen them all. And when it came to the size of Buenos

Aires and the height of its buildings, according to the lecturer's descriptions, New York must be merely a village with adobe huts. When
the waiter placed some cutlets before the speaker, these reminded him
of other startling things he had seen. "The pampas," he said, at the
same time making a sweeping gesture with both arms, "are at least a
hundred times the size of Spain, and they are as flat as a billiard table.
The cattle, sheep and horses you see there – millions and millions of
them – move about like the spreading waters of a flood. Just think," he
went on, now gravely and with emphasis, "in one of the several
slaughter-houses in Buenos Aires alone, they kill ten thousand bulls
every day, and the figures for sheep are simply astronomical."

The man was still holding forth when I rose to depart, and whilst I
settled my bill with the waiter, he put his face close to mine. Nodding
his head in the direction of the speaker, he whispered, "*Que fenómeno!*"
(What a phenomenon), and, winking an eye, added, "I have worked in
the Argentine ten years."

Sometimes, when least expected, we see little scenes which make
lasting impressions on our memories. This happened to me as I was
riding along the slope of a high hill situated in mountainous country. A
group of peasants were tilling a small field above me, and in their
setting looked so picturesque that I halted to watch them for a while.
Whilst enjoying this peaceful scene, I heard the faint sounds of singing
which gradually became louder and louder. Presently, on a winding
footpath above me, appeared a boy, seated facing backwards on the
hindquarters of a mule. The animal was laden with *botijos;* earthenware
pots which contain water or wine. Evidently the sagacious mule knew
whither it was expected to go, for despite the fact that the boy was not
in a position to guide it, it carefully picked its way over the narrow
stony track, until it reached the group of peasants. The *botijos* having
been unloaded, the animal – with its rider still sitting facing backwards
– turned round to begin the homeward journey. Brilliant sunshine illu-
minated the hillside on which, here and there, stood almond trees in full
bloom, and as the boy jogged along, singing merrily, his strange
Flamenco song with its weird intricate cadenzas, sung in a throaty
falsetto voice, sounded very African, and suited the setting to perfection.

In Spain, jars and pots for holding water or wine vary a great deal in
different regions. The word *jarra* (jar) is derived from the Arabic *harra*

or *dharra.* Besides the ordinary earthenware jars and bottles, there are a great many of different shapes and sizes. *Botijos* have a handle and two beaks, one for filling and the other for pouring out, *cántaros* are plain, and *porrones* – which usually are made of glass – have one long pointed beak through which the wine is poured into the mouth, without touching the lips. The correct handling and manipulation of a *porron* requires much practice, and considerable marksmanship. Experts in the art of using them are able to hold the container at arm's length from their mouths, and to pour a fine stream of the liquid between their slightly parted lips, without wasting a single drop, let alone staining their clothes. Similar skill is required in using the *bota,* the classical Basque wine-skin, which has the great advantage of not being fragile. Peasants, especially shepherds, carry their *botas* fastened to a strap which is slung over their shoulders. If they wish to keep the liquid cool whilst working, the wine-skin is deposited in some shady spot.

About eighty miles from Madrid I spent a day in a little village named Alcolea del Pinar, so named on account of the many pine trees which grow in the region. The extraction of rosin is a source of revenue in this otherwise poor district where, besides scraggy sheep and a few pigs, animals do not thrive. The sheep are of such poor type that the average weight of a fleece is only about four pounds. When I told a shepherd that in southern Chile I had seen a *plantel* (nursery) of forty thousand sheep which gave an average of twenty-eight pounds per fleece, he looked at me with incredulity written on his face. If I had told him that I have seen several Merino rams whose fleeces weighed as much as thirty-six and even thirty-eight pounds, I am sure he would have thought I was trying to insult his intelligence.

I do not think that selective breeding, or the introduction of other types of sheep, would produce good results in some of the regions I visited in Spain. There is little about the breeding and handling of sheep that could be taught those hardy and knowing Spanish shepherds. They know – and for countless generations have known – which type of animal manages to exist in some of the arid regions, and I am convinced that if other breeds were introduced, the expensive experiment would prove to be a failure. In every country in the world, the art of sheep and cattle farming varies greatly, and it is futile to make comparisons as to efficiency. Climatic and other conditions have the last say.

In the village of Alcolea del Pinar I stayed in a neat little hostelry run by a family. The women were busy in the kitchen, and two little girls and a young man did the waiting in the dining-room. The few guests who came in for meals were mostly lorry drivers, on their way to or from Madrid. Throughout Spain, it is customary for restaurants and inns to display a picture of General Franco. Accordingly, in a prominent place hung a mass-produced print of him, but as someone in the house was evidently a bullfight enthusiast, the walls of the dining-room were covered with photographs of *matadores* in every conceivable position. Upon seeing me have a close look at the photographs – a few of which were signed – the young man who acted as waiter came to tell me all about them. Proudly he pointed out to me one that was signed by the famous "Manolete" who had eaten a meal in the establishment.

In the evening I went for a walk through the ancient village and its immediate surroundings. Most of the low houses are stone-built and have heavily-tiled roofs. In some of the old abodes – which once upon a time must have been inhabited by peasants – sheep or pigs are kept, and I observed that stone floors and bedding are kept remarkably clean. At sunset-time, when shepherds returned home with their flocks of sheep and goats, I watched them from a rocky eminence near an old stone-built church, round the tower of which swallows circled, screaming joyfully.

When the time came to have my evening meal, the young man who had done duty as waiter during the afternoon was invisible, and his place was taken by a pretty girl of about eleven. Though fair-skinned, she had large sparkling black eyes, and her dark hair was carefully plaited. When I asked her who she was, without a trace of shyness she replied that she was one of the daughters of the house, and that her brother, the waiter, had gone to attend to the animals. After that she chatted away merrily, telling me much about various people in her village. When my meal was ready, the dainty way in which she served it would have been a lesson to many an experienced waitress.

Later in the evening, whilst I sat in the dining-room, reading some of the old magazines which were piled up on a table, several middle-aged and elderly peasants came in to talk over glasses of wine. As they entered, all greeted me in a friendly manner, and when they were seated round a table, and wine was served, they offered me a glass, and at the same time invited me to join their circle. Thinking that this was only a matter of form, I thanked them for the offer and resumed my reading.

"You'll be getting sore eyes, *señor,*" one of the party shouted to me after a while. "Anyway, more lies and rubbish are printed than spoken, so why not come and sit down with us? We can see you are a stranger and that you come from afar, and we don't like to see you sit there all alone."

I rose, went over to the group of friendly souls, and having introduced myself to them, joined the circle. Naturally, my new friends must have been curious to know where I came from, but as they were much too polite to ask personal questions, I started by telling them what had brought me to their village. Then, for a while, we talked about any banality, and eventually the conversation veered to the Civil War. I was told that the very inn in which we sat had been the headquarters of the Italian General Staff. According to my informants, the "big shots", as well as the "voluntary legionnaires" under their command, had a grand time until the first shot was rumoured to have been fired by a "Red", whereafter the *Italianos* bolted so fast that it would have taken a racing car to keep up with them.

How my new friends laughed as they recounted – true or not – episodes connected with the Italian intervention in the Civil War! One of the stories that has stuck in my mind is about a general who is supposed to have made a grandiose after-dinner speech; all about Italian valour, the glories of Mussolini, and so on. For an hour the orator held forth, quoting great poets, passages out of operas, and using language that became more and more floral as he went on. Another general, who was listening to this marvellous display of verbal fireworks, leaned over towards another general who sat beside him, and whispered into his ear, "*Che bello che parla!*" (How beautifully he speaks).

Similar stories and yarns about the Italians' participation in the Spanish Civil War kept our little assembly in fits of laughter, until an elderly peasant, with an intelligent face that might have been carved out of walnut, took up the word. "Indeed," he said, "the *Italianos* who were sent over here were anything but fighters. After all, most of them did not want to come, and didn't even know what our war was about. I often wonder what their brothers are like over there in Italy, but if they run away from danger as Mussolini's boys did over here, it goes to prove that they are civilized. We Spaniards, the English, Germans and others, fight like demons; we walk into machine-gun fire to be killed like flies, for honour and glory, of course. Surely, a really civilized man doesn't fight. He works, he builds, he is interested in life, he is an artist, he does not kill to order, he wants to live, and therefore runs away from threatening death. So long as things were quiet, and the campaign merely a pleasant outing, the *Italianos* thoroughly enjoyed themselves, but when the alarm – as it happens a false one – was given that the Reds were swooping down on them, they bolted, leaving their rifles and equipment behind. Now, in my opinion, the very fact that they preferred flight to fight, goes to prove they are civilized, and that we who take pride in fighting are barbarians."

This statement started a heated though friendly argument which lasted until it was time to go to bed. Even after the little party broke up into two sections, whilst walking slowly away in opposite directions, every now and again they stopped to discuss a particularly knotty or interesting point, all the while gesticulating, and sometimes shouting in order to add weight to statements.

On the following morning I was on the road early, riding through hilly and in parts rocky country. At about 10 a.m. I stopped at a little inn, run by a solitary woman who had two children. Her crude but cosy establishment was situated in a narrow gulley, the entrance to which is overlooked by a ruined castle perched on a hill. A number of trees and green patches gave cheer to the otherwise dismal place, and I was glad to be sheltered from the cold wind which had blown ever since I started out. The woman gave me a cordial reception, and whilst she cooked me a dish of fried eggs and ham, I passed away the time, looking at cheap highly coloured prints which adorned the walls of her small dining-room. One of the pictures, entitled "*Jesus y los Pescadores*" (Jesus and the Fishermen), particularly attracted my attention, for it was a gem of its kind. Standing on the shore of a very blue lake, it depicted the Saviour, wearing a white and red Roman toga. He is seen pointing at a grill on which a fat fish is being fried, and near it kneels an apostle, offering his Master a basket filled with newly-caught fish. Immediately behind this group is the lake, and close to the shore a Canadian canoe, in which six centurions are busy pulling out a net filled with fish. The background of this masterpiece is even more remarkable; pink, red and purple Tyrolese mountains are reflected in the water, pine trees grow alongside palms, and to crown it all, on a nearby hill stands a Moorish castle. I was admiring another detail – a kind of blood-red starfish at the Master's feet – when the woman entered with the food. Seeing me standing there, gaping at the picture, she came alongside me and said, "*Bonito, muy bonito*" (Pretty, very pretty), and then, pointing at the starfish, remarked, "*Besugo, muy bueno*" (Bream, very good). I did not bother to tell her that there is quite a difference between starfish and bream, but before proceeding on my way I complimented her on an excellently cooked meal and on the quality of the wine she had given me. Just as I was about to ride away she reminded me that I had forgotten to mention something. "Thanks for the compliment," she shouted, "I'm glad you like my picture of Jesus and the Fishermen".

Guadalajara impressed me as a dismal place. The very origin of its name, *Wad-al-Hadjara,* meaning "Valley of Stones," suggests nothing cheerful. The sprawling palace of the Duke del Infantado, built some five hundred years ago, I found to be by far the most interesting sight in the town. Strangely, its namesake in Mexico is much sung about, but I doubt if any Spanish poet or writer of songs has bothered about the original Guadalajara.

Upon reaching Alcalá de Henares (a little over twenty miles from Madrid), I made a pilgrimage to the other commonplace church of Santa Maria, in which Cervantes was baptized, on the 9th of October, 1547. His family came originally from Galicia, and his father settled in Alcalá de Henares some thirty years before the great genius was born. Though poor, the family sent young Miguel (Cervantes) to Madrid where he spent several years studying under Lopez de Hoyos, a philosopher and theologian. As far as I know it has not been definitely established whether or not Cervantes was born in Alcalá de Henares, and therefore three or four towns and villages situated on the Castilian plateau claim this honour.

As an aside, it may be of interest to some readers to know that the average educated English person for self-expression and general communication uses roughly 3,000 words. Milton's vocabulary was 12,000, Shakespeare's 25,000 and that of Cervantes 36,000.

After Alcalá de Henares, a short ride brought me down to an undulating diluvial plain, situated roughly 2,000 feet above sea-level. Here and there the uninviting expanse is furrowed by depressions, most of which are strewn with sand and gravel, which suggest that in far remote times – probably in the glacial age – these depressions must have been beds of rivulets and streams.

It was about noon when, ahead of me, Madrid came into sight, with the snow-capped Guadarrama mountains in the distance in the north, the dark-blue outline of the Sierra de Gredos ahead in the west, and the mountains of Toledo at the horizon in the south-west. As I was about to make my first visit to the capital, I stopped the engine, and seated myself by the wayside, where for some time I studied a plan of the city and its thoroughfares. I was happy and satisfied, for, so far, all had gone well with me and the machine, and I had enjoyed every minute of my solitary travels.

CHAPTER 6

MADRID – CORDOVA – SEVILLE

The approaches to Madrid are so uninteresting, that they can be described as being dismal. Of course, the same can be said of most capitals and large cities, so in this sense the pride of Spain is not an exception.

As I was riding along slowly, I wondered what the place must have looked like a thousand years ago, when it was merely a fortified Moorish outpost which the dusky conquerors called *Madjrit,* from which the modern city derives its name. Before I realized exactly where I was, I found myself in lively traffic and in one of the main streets leading towards the centre of the city. Being a total stranger to it, I had decided upon arrival to call on an old friend who is in an important official position, for surely he was the person most likely to be able to tell me where I could stay without having to spend too much of my limited funds. As I proceeded, traffic became heavier, policemen blew whistles, bells at pedestrian crossings clanged at regular intervals, red, amber and green lights flashed, there were signs of one-way streets and "No Entry"; so, in order to be on the safe side, I got off the machine and pushed it. When a policeman saw me, he came to ask if I had a breakdown, and if he could be of assistance, and when I explained that I was a stranger and that I was merely pushing the machine in order not to *meter la pata* (put my foot in it), he laughed heartily. Having told me which way to go, he added, "*Señor,* now just get on your *moto.* I'm sure you are a much better motorist than hundreds of those who drive

through this city, so don't worry. *Que le vaya buén* (farewell). I am
delighted to have been of service to you."

A few minutes later I overshot a turning I should have taken, when
another policeman came to my assistance. He explained that I could not
turn round in that particular street, and informed me that I would have
to proceed some five hundred yards farther, there to turn round a
monument in the centre of a *plaza,* and then come back. When I
jokingly pleaded that it was a very long way, even on a motor-cycle,
the policeman replied with a twinkle in his eye, "*Bueno, señor,* then
turn round here. I'm not looking."

Upon reaching my destination, it being lunch-time, the offices of
my friend were deserted, with only a porter there on duty. When I
telephoned to his home, he immediately invited me to go and have
lunch with him, but being covered with dust, I preferred not to meet
company. When I asked a passing postman if he knew of some modest
eating place in the immediate neighbourhood, he directed me to one
situated in a nearby side-street. Upon getting to the place, I found that it
was exactly what I wanted. A little kind of *café* was attached to a store,
and in it were a number of workmen, eating, drinking and playing
cards. Having purchased some slices of sausage and some bread, I
placed my lunch on the marble top of a small table, the wrapping paper
doing duty as a plate. This simple meal and a glass of wine was all I
wanted, so after having finished eating, I passed away the time
watching and listening. Near me sat two men and a boy who were street
cleaners, then there were two postmen, a group of plasterers and house
painters, some wearing caps made of newspaper. All were bespattered
with whitewash and paint, and made the best of their time off from
work. Everybody in the place laughed, joked and talked loudly, and the
men behind the counter were so quick and jolly in attending to their
clients that it was a joy to watch them. Every now and again little boys
and girls came in to buy bottles of wine, evidently to take home to their
parents. I was astonished when a grubby bare-footed little urchin trotted
in and asked for a bottle of champagne. After a while, two tram
conductors came to seat themselves at my table, and soon after the
three of us chatted as if we had known one another for years. When
they told me that they earned only fifteen *pesetas* (roughly three

shillings[1]) per day, and I asked them how they could live on so little,
they explained that their wives and daughters earned a little, washing,
cleaning and doing needlework, and that they themselves did odd jobs
in their spare time. This was my first insight into the lives of Spaniards
of their status, but later on I was to learn much more about the
conditions under which people of their social class live. Most labourers
and low-grade employees earn only twelve *pesetas* or even less per
day. Considering the price of food and clothes, it is a mystery to me
how the masses in Spain contrive to exist. But more about this later.
Despite their poverty, my table companions appeared to enjoy life, and
whilst we sat together, every now and again they exchanged jokes and
good-natured personal gibes with some of their friends and
acquaintances who sat near us.

Later I returned to my friend's offices, and soon after he arrived,
thanks to his assistance, I was installed in an excellent inexpensive
boarding-house in the very centre of the city.

Being keen on getting to Seville for the great annual Fair – which
lasts a week – I spent only two days in Madrid, of which I was to see
much later. During the first night in the city I had an amusing experience. After having dined with some newly-made acquaintances, I
strolled back to my *pensión*. Upon reaching the door, and finding that it
was locked, I looked for the bell, and, finding no button which to press,
or handle which to pull, I knocked several times. As no one came to let
me in, I did this several times, knocking harder and harder, but, as
before, in vain. I was beginning to wonder if by any chance I had come
to the wrong door when a man, wearing a peaked cap and a heavy
khaki-coloured overcoat, and carrying a formidable stick appeared
beside me. Taking him to be a policeman or some kind of special constable, and thinking that he must be taking me for a potential burglar, I
feared the worst. On the principle that offensive is the best defensive,
before the apparition had time to speak to me, I asked, "Who are you?"

Having looked me up and down, the man in uniform replied, "I am
Pepe, the *sereno* (night-watchman). You are a stranger. Do you live in
the *pensión*?"

When I explained that, indeed, I was a stranger, that I lived in the

---

[1] *Editor's note:* Before 1971 Britain's currency consisted of twelve pennies to
the shillings and twenty shillings to the pound.

pensión, and that I found myself locked out, the man produced an enormous key with which he proceeded to unlock the massive. wooden door.   Before letting me in, he explained that every evening it was locked, and that, as night-watchman of the immediate neighbourhood, it was his duty to keep an eye on houses, and to open doors for people. "Remember," he went on, "next time you find yourself locked out, clap your hands vigorously. I'm always somewhere near. I shall hear you, and you won't have to wait long, before I come to let you in."

Later I discovered that in many parts of Spain night-watchmen have remained an institution since the olden days. At intervals, throughout the night, one hears the noise of hand-clapping, which indicates that belated birds seek admission to their houses or lodging-places. Night-watchmen are registered and officially recognized by the authorities, and all carry heavy sticks, in some cases "loaded" with lead. These guardians are paid a small salary by householders and shopkeepers, but they rely mainly on tips. Thus, certain "pitches" can be quite lucrative, and therefore, when a night-watchman thinks of retiring or of changing over to another district, he hands over his domain to the man who makes the best offer for it. In this way the job of being a night-watchman has developed into a mild sort of "racket," but it must be admitted that it has its uses, and, above all, that it adds romance to night-life. After this first meeting with Pepe, I had several long and interesting conversations with him, and whenever I found myself locked out and gave the classical signal, within a few moments he came rushing along to let me in, and, of course, to receive his tip for service rendered.   One night, when a young reveller, who had imbibed too freely, insisted on fighting our middle-aged Cerberus, he tapped the offender on the head with his trusty staff of office, thus re-establishing peace and quiet in his domain. As at this stage I left by car for Seville, and returned to Madrid a few days later, more about the capital after this side-trip.

When my friends, Julio and his Scottish-Patagonian wife (who had been my hosts in Barcelona), passed through Madrid on their way to Seville, they picked me up in their car, and so the three of us set out, looking forward to a grand time at the great annual fair. Julio – who is a Galician – insisted on singing songs of his home regions, but his wife preferred Flamenco songs, for which she has a passion. My contribution to this enthusiastic – though not very artistic – recital of songs consisted of a few from the Argentine, Mexico, America and England, including several parodies which were much appreciated by my two listeners who, fortunately, were not critical as far as the quality of my voice is concerned. After all, we were on our way to Seville, and the fair comes but once a year; perhaps, as far as we were concerned, but once in our lifetime.

When the outskirts of Madrid were behind us, we found ourselves on the semi-barren rolling plateau of Castile. In the distance, towards the west could be seen the mountain range of Toledo, jagged and dark-blue, extending along the horizon.   A cold wind blew incessantly, driving a mass of rolling clouds across the cobalt sky. We were over two thousand feet above sea-level, and heading almost dead straight towards the south. About twenty miles out of the city, upon reaching a low hill on the steep slopes of which stands a dismal-looking ancient village, we stopped to have a look at some of the cave dwellings in which poor families live. These dwelling places are situated near the highway which we followed, and as the entrances to them are square, and in most cases white-washed, I decided to take a photograph of them. No sooner had I got out of the car than several children – all bare-footed and dressed in rags – came running down the hill to beg. The youngsters were so nice, and looked so poor, that I gave them a few coins, whereafter I turned to look round for a suitable subject to photograph. Before I had time to get my camera ready, out of caves and miserable adobe houses came flocks of children and women carrying babies, all stampeding and almost tumbling down the steep hillside in my direction. Within a few moments I was surrounded by a mob of beggars who fairly screamed for *una limosnita por amor de Dios* (a small alms, for the love of God). All held out their hands and pleaded, and when I tried to get away, some of the more daring ones caught hold of my jacket and tugged at my sleeves. During this wild mêlée I caught a glimpse of my friend, Julio, who, camera in one hand, was pushing, almost fighting off assailants with the other. Both of us had to struggle hard to get back to the car, and when we tried to close the door, women and children held on to it, whilst others climbed on the running-boards and clung on to the car's mudguards and bumpers. With great presence of mind Julio blew the claxon horn, started the motor, and began to drive away slowly. This made hangers-on let go of their holds, and as he gradually increased the speed, the last had to let go their grip on the still open door of the car. Upon reaching the top of the hill, we halted, and upon seeing that the coast was clear, we ventured out to take some photographs of the village La Guardia, which I shall never forget. Later a Spanish historian told me that there the Spanish inquisition claimed its first victim.

Though the plateau over which we drove is practically devoid of trees, here and there we came to a green oasis. It is said that several centuries ago, trees and even large forests flourished there, but that they were gradually cut down by many generations of charcoal-burners, and also to be used as timber, and partially because the old Castilian peasants believed that trees gave shelter to birds which did great damage to their crops. In old writings about these regions is mentioned the existence of woods and forests in which kings and grandees hunted stags, boars, wolves and even bears. To-day the Government is doing much towards the reforestation of many regions, and even along some of the highways many miles have been planted with rows of trees, some of which have already grown considerably. Thus it can be foreseen that within a few years motorists will drive through fine shady avenues, and that the general aspect of these regions will undergo great changes.

We were on the central plateau of Castile, and now in its dismal arid sector, La Mancha, made famous throughout the world by Cervantes. In the distance, in the north-west, was the dark-blue outline of the Sierra de Gredos, much nearer, in the west, the mountains of Toledo, and ahead of us in the south, the Sierra Morena which figures prominently in *Don Quixote.* As I looked at our surroundings, and recalled some of the passages of this tremendous book, I realized more than ever before its amazing satire. What a setting for a hero with lofty and chivalrous but false and unrealizable ideals! I could not help remembering my entry into Spain, when I was towed on my motor-cycle over that high pass at the border, and I wondered if that was not an adventure worthy of a Don Quixote. Incidentally, but very few people realize the humour of the name "Don Quixote" or "Quijote," as it is spelt nowadays. (The "x" as well as the "j" are pronounced gutturally.) *Quixote* is an old Spanish word, meaning "greaves" or "cuisse", these being the names for the armour which in olden times protected the front part of knights' thighs. Therefore translated into plain modern English, *Don Quixote* means "Sir Thighguard."

I was delighted when we came to some windmills which made me almost expect to be seeing Cervantes' gloomy knight appear from behind them on his famous skinny steed. However, these windmills were big and fairly high, whereas Don Quixote's "giants" were of the old Castilian type, only about nine or ten feet high. I am told some of these are still in use in certain districts of La Mancha, but I did not see any of them. Apparently they are not gyratory, but, being small, they can be turned by hand, so as to make the blades catch the wind. The mills I saw were not of the gyratory type, but faced in the direction whence blow the prevalent winds.

Upon approaching the Sierra Morena we passed through the vale of Pefias, famed for its wine. Men with mules were weeding and plough-ing between the rows of vines which were beginning to grow their first tender-green leaves. All the animals I saw were in excellent condition, and their harness clean and in a good state of repair. Here and there, where fields are irrigated artificially, some of the *malacates* (hoisting machines) are very primitive. To a large crudely made wooden wheel – which is placed vertically – are attached a number of earthenware jars or calabashes, and as a mule or ox slowly trudges round and round, pulling a pole, at the end of which a wooden gear works on the water wheel, these jars or calabashes revolve, dipping into the water below, and emptying themselves as they rotate downwards from the top. In order to prevent the animals from getting giddy from continuously going round in a small circle, they are blindfolded, though this is not necessary in all cases.

Shortly after having passed through the picturesque little town of Valdepeñas we started a long and steep climb. The winding road, with its many sharp curves, led through woods and wild ravines and gullies, and upon reaching the top of a high pass an amazing panorama spread before us. The wild country we had left behind us changed to a scene of southern luxuriance, and we found ourselves gazing at the magical charm of the Andalusian sky and sub-tropical vegetation. To the east and to the west of us spread rows of jagged peaks which looked purple in a slight haze and strong light, and at our feet before us spread a vast expanse of undulating country, green everywhere, and the gentle hills and slopes with countless rows of symmetrically planted olive trees, the silvery-green leaves of which, viewed from the distance, vibrated like an animated carpet. The sky, which on the Castilian plateau had been cobalt, changed its colour to ultramarine, and the neat whitewashed farm houses with geranium and other bright flowers blazing in window-boxes hit the eye as the blare of a trumpet hits the ear.

Having gazed in silence at this inspiring panorama, we proceeded towards the old town of Cordova, where we arrived early in the evening. There being much to be seen in this ancient capital of the Moors – which once upon a time was the Mecca of the West and the nursery of science and art – I lost no time in setting out to make a preliminary exploration. The first thing that struck me were the masses of swallows which shrieked shrilly as they played their joyous evening game, darting, banking and wheeling about near the towers of old churches. Wherever I went in Spain these noisy boisterous games of the swallows attracted my attention, and often I looked on, fascinated by the birds' speed and elegance of flight, and by the acrobatic twists and turns they performed with astonishing ease.

Whilst wandering through the narrow roughly-cobbled streets in the old sector of the town, I made mental pictures of life as it must have been there in the time of the Romans, Visigoths and Moorish caliphs who, in turn, invaded and ransacked the town. Unfortunately, particularly after the defeat of the Moors, the victorious and fanatical Christian Spaniards marred and destroyed many works of art. For this we must not blame them too much; for who in those days took an interest in archaeology? More than seven centuries ago, after St. Ferdinand had captured Cordova, the marvellous Moorish mosque was consecrated as a Christian church. It was then that the mosque, as well as other buildings, was partially mutilated during the work of transformation. Have we improved since those days? People who cast stones at the Spaniards of those remote times for having committed what they indignantly call "vandalism" would do well to remember the ruthless bombings and bombardments (on both sides) during the Second World War. On that occasion so-called Christians fought among themselves, and in the name of civilization, freedom, right and what-not, with the help of modern science blew to smithereens thousands of irreplaceable works of art, not to mention tens of thousands of non-combatant fellow Christians, including women and children.

To-day the marvellous old Mussulman temple of Cordova, with its nineteen aisles and labyrinth of nearly a thousand pillars, must be one of the most remarkable and curious Christian churches. Unfortunately, during the various stages of transformation to make the mosque suitable for Christian services, certain harmonious proportions of the original building were destroyed, but, nevertheless, it has remained a unique gem of its kind.

Until late that night I wandered about the old town of Cordova. The main street of its new sector was thronged with people who were out for a stroll and a little fresh air, and the *cafés* were filled with men. Entering into one, I pushed my way between the crowded tables to a vacant seat in a corner, whence I could observe things. Nearly every social class of Cordova was represented in the place. At a round table near the entrance, sat a group of peasants, rough and tanned by the sun. They chaffed each other, argued and occasionally laughed boisterously. Next to them, grave, as if the responsibility of his position weighed heavily on his shoulders, sat one who appeared to be a kind of local "big chief", surrounded by minor officials and a few hangers-on. At another table a group played cards, and a little farther along lolled a bevy of young bloods who must have thought themselves to be the exquisites of the town. Whereas all the other clients in the establish-ment laughed and talked and argued, and sometimes struck the table with their fists to add emphasis to a particularly weighty statement, time seemed to be hanging heavy on the young sheiks' hands. Despite the late hour, several families, including small children, were sitting at different tables, the youngsters eating cakes and licking ice-creams.

Having sipped a glass of aromatic *manzanilla* (a light sherry wine), I resumed my wanderings. Upon reaching a spacious square, in the middle of which is a large equestrian statue, a peculiarity about it made me stop to peer at it. The night being dark, and the town badly illu-minated – owing to shortage of fuel – all I could see was the outline of the horse and rider who appeared to be headless. Wondering if, perhaps, it had been shot off during the Civil War, I walked towards the monument to have a close look at it. I had hardly left the sidewalk when I heard the shrill noise of a police whistle being blown several times in rapid succession, so loud and frantically that I thought a crime must have been committed in the serene old town of Cordova. As I continued my walk towards the monument, the whistling grew more and more frantic, and presently an excited policeman, who wore a white helmet, appeared at my side. "Haven't you heard my *pito*?" he shouted at me. When I replied that, indeed, I had, and that I had been wondering what all this whistling signified, the custodian of law and order informed me that I had no right to cross the road until he gave me the signal to do so. Seeing that I was a stranger, he immediately changed his tone of voice to a more friendly one, and explained that in blowing the whistle he had merely acted "in favour of my safety," it being dangerous and against regulations to cross the road until the signal to do so was given by him. As he spoke, a solitary donkey, laden with earthenware jars, trotted past us, followed by its owner. When I explained to the policeman that I wanted to have a close look at the monument, he saluted me gravely, and at the same time said, "*Muy bien, siga, señor*" (Very well, go on, sir). As I walked away, he blew his whistle, thus giving me the official right-of-way.

A close look at the monument revealed that it represents the "Gran Capitan" (Gonsalvo, 1453-1515), who contested Granada and who drove the French out of Italy. The monument being cast in bronze, and the rider's head being – what I took it to be – painted white, no wonder I could not distinguish it against the walls of buildings on the opposite side of the square. When I walked away, satisfied that I had not been seeing the statue of a headless rider, the policeman dutifully blew his whistle to hold up the non-existent traffic, whilst I crossed the street to rejoin the crowd of strollers who thronged the main street. As I passed him, he once more gave the "all clear" signal, and when I said "*Muchas gracias*" he smiled and saluted me once more, at the same time saying, "*De nada, señor*" (For nothing, sir).

Early on the following morning I resumed my wanderings through the old part of the town. The narrow streets with their rough cobble-stones were humming and buzzing with life and activity, as such do in old Spanish towns. Donkeys and mules carried heavy loads of vege-tables, pots and pans, fruit, etc., whilst their owners, the vendors, advertised their wares in loud throaty voices. Among the peddlers was a rag-and-bottle man, followed slowly and dreamily by his donkey which pulled a small cart. The collector of rubbish blew a horn to call out servants and housewives, and two ubiquitous Galician knife-and-scissor sharpeners played their shrill tunes on a small pan-pipe whilst pushing along their wooden, one-wheeled contraptions which became sharpening machines when turned upside down.

Throughout Spain, all knife-sharpeners hail from two villages near Lugo, in Galicia. When a boy has reached the age to fend for himself, his father presents him with one of those wheel-barrow-like machines, and so the youngster sets out to face the world. In South America, Mexico, and formerly in the U.S.A. and in different parts of Europe, many knife-sharpeners hailed from the same two villages, and before the First World War broke out some reached even Japan and China. During their wanderings through the world, many of these thrifty adventurers made "good," and several of the more enterprising and lucky ones among them amassed great fortunes.

Apart from the little pan-pipes which they play to announce their presence, these craftsmen have other traditional tricks to attract attention. Some carry with them a pair of outsize scissors which they open and shut, thus making a loud clicking noise. Others make the large wooden wheel revolve by means of a pedal, and when this sets a rough grind-stone revolving, they hold to it an old handsaw, or a sheet of metal, thus producing a loud, ugly and piercing noise.

From the outside the cathedral (formerly the Moorish mosque already referred to) presents a rather dismal appearance. The high walls and some of the huge gates which still preserve their Arabic character suggest a fort rather than a temple, but upon passing through one of the two gloomy gates at its north end, one enters into a veritable fairyland; the "Court of Orange Trees" *(Patio de los Naranjos),* which in Moorish times was the court of ablutions. Rows of orange trees, which happened to be in full bloom, threw off an intoxicating scent, and the fountain in the middle gave a feeling of perfect peace and suggested Oriental repose.

I could have spent days in this labyrinth of beauty, but time was short, so I moved on slowly. Outside once more, as I passed near one of the side-gates, three attractive *señoritas,* who wore becoming *mantillas,* were busy gossiping and laughing. Here was an enchanting picture; so on the sly I prepared my camera, turning away from the group, lest they become self-conscious, or turn their backs on me. Just as I was about to press the trigger, one of the young ladies caught sight of me, whereupon she quickly told her companions of my intention. With a merry, teasing laugh the three fled through the gate, but although I called after them, *"Señoritas, no sean malas, un segundo, por favor!"* (Young ladies, don't be naughty, one second, please), only one of them reappeared at the gate for an instant, teasingly to wave a hand in my direction, whereafter she vanished. Whilst writing this, I can still see that little group of beauties in a perfect setting, and I sigh at the thought of having missed by a second or two the "shooting" of a fine romantic picture.

Continuing my wanderings, I came to the Alcazar Nuevo, which to-day is used as a prison. As I passed its massive gate, outside which stood an armed guard smoking a cigarette, from the inside – evidently from a courtyard – came the noise of many people chattering, men, women and – I thought – children. There was something distinctly mediaeval about most prisons I saw in Spain; in fact, one or two of the fortifications and castles used as such, date back to the days of the Romans.

I was looking for the garden of the Alcazar, but being unable to find it, I asked the prison-guard how to get there. As it happened, it was quite near, and well worth visiting. Most of the old city walls have disappeared, and so have the *solares* (mansions) of the once-upon-a-time rich and mighty. The few *solares* which remain have undergone great changes, though the outside shells of them remain as of old. The garden of the old Alcazar, though not large, was one blaze of colour, and the towers, turrets and balconies along sun-baked walls made a fine background for lemon, orange and tall palm trees. In a corner of a large vacant lot of land – which long ago must have been a garden – stood an old dilapidated house which fascinated me. Standing on the very edge of a wall which overlooks the river Guadalquivir (the Moors' "Great River"), though in a state of disrepair, its architecture and situation, in fact everything about it, was most attractive and quaint. As I gazed at it, and listened to the croaking of frogs in pools of the practically dried-up river, I wished I were a rich man; for if I had sufficient money, I would buy that house, restore it, re-plant what must have been its garden, and live there happily ever after. For some time I sat on a little circular Roman rampart, wondering what my immediate surroundings must have looked like centuries ago. Then, as in mind I travelled through many parts of the world I know well, and I remembered the countless palaces, villas, mansions, and luxurious houses in which some of my fellow-men live, for the thousandth time in my life I came to the con-clusion that I must be a failure. After all, what do I possess? Health? Yes. Common sense? Perhaps. Ambition and vigour? . . . I thought again. Vigour when it comes to doing certain things. Ambition, for what? To be what? To end as what? Ambition to LIVE, to learn and to see as much of the world and its people. Amass wealth at the expense of sacrificing LIFE, and perhaps honour, self-respect and even friends? No!

Remembering that Julio and Rosemary must be waiting for me, I rose to go to our appointed meeting place near the old Moorish bridge which spans the river. Upon arriving there, finding that they had not yet arrived in their car, I had a good look at the fine stone bridge with its several massive stone arches, the foundations of which date back to Roman times. From the middle of this, the Moors' *Bib al-Kantara,* I had a fine view of the town, and of a Doric triumphal arch which once upon a time must have been one of its main gates. Men and women driving cattle, laden mules and donkeys, passed over the bridge, whilst groups of idlers sat on the stone embankment, chatting in the warm sunshine. After several exceptionally dry years, the river was merely a trickle of green slimy water among a mass of rocks and stones which suggested that the waters can be formidable when in flood. In the river-bed, where grass and even small shrubs grow, a few cattle and donkeys grazed, and every now and again one of the latter brayed, finishing the horrid asinine song with diminuendo gurgly-wheezy sighs as if in agony.

Returning to the town end of the bridge, I passed away time watching people buy *churros* at a nearby stall. *Churros* are flour fritters, and great favourites in many parts of Spain. To make them, a slightly sweetened paste is squeezed into boiling olive oil through a metal container with a pointed spout, and when the stream of paste – which is about as thick as an average-sized finger – is cooked brown, the *churro* is ready for eating. In cities, many labourers would not begin a day's work without having eaten such fritters, which are sold at many street corners. To many Spaniards hot *churros* are the equivalent of the Italian's spaghetti.

Whilst waiting for the car to arrive I got into conversation with two elderly men who, upon discovering that I was a tourist, told me not to miss seeing the house in which Manolete, the famous bullfighter, had lived with his widowed mother. Although I had heard and read much about this popular hero, I listened to the two old men's tales about him; about the vast sums of money he had given to hospitals and charities, and how, finally, a week before retiring from the bullring, he met his tragic death. Whether it was due to superstition – of which bullfighters have many – or to over-confidence in himself, I do not know; but the fact remains that the man who had been so generous to others, had no private doctor, ambulance or plasma with him when he gave his last performance in a small town, with the result that several hours after a bull of the redoubtable Miura breed horned him high up in the thigh, loss of blood caused his death, which was deeply lamented throughout Spain, even among the masses who are not interested in bullfighting. Undoubtedly, simple blood transfusions would have saved his life, but, "It was written," as the Arabs say.

When Julio and Rosemary appeared, I bade farewell to my two chance acquaintances, and soon after old Cordova was behind us. After the bleak, cold and windswept plateau of Castile, it was a delight to be in the undulating districts of Andalusia with their exuberant semi-tropical vegetation, balmy air – and deep-blue sky – which is "fire" in the summer. Teams of oxen, placed in single file, slowly pulled ploughs up and down gentle slopes, men urging on the beasts with a variety of weird-sounding cries. Wild flowers grew everywhere, small fields were of every shade of green, some of which, carpeted with poppies or wild mustard, were vermilion or golden yellow; in fact the countryside fairly vibrated with every colour of a painter's palette. With such a climate and a riot of colour and gaiety, no wonder Andalusians are volatile and imaginative, for their character is merely a reflection of nature. How could a Castilian have the character of an Andalusian, or vice-versa?

All the houses and farms in this region are painted a dazzling white, and several cottages and tiny hamlets which are situated on little plains seemed to be floating on bright blue, almost purple lagoons, masses of wild iris being responsible for this optical illusion. The ancient Roman and Moorish town of Carmona, which occupies the summit of a rocky forbidding-looking ridge rising high over the fertile country below, offered a startling change. Viewed from below, the yellowish-brown ramparts and towers which command a view of the whole plain of Andalusia look most impressive, arrogant and defying.

After Carmona, once again we drove through undulating plains, with here and there a quaint old village, or we passed rich people's villas; snow-white and Moorish-looking with square-built *miradores* (belvederes) and *azoteas* (flat roofs). Most of them had magnificent wrought-iron gates – invariably painted a shiny black – and grates before windows, and the gardens were a blaze of colour, with here and there orange, lemon and palm trees, to give shade. Most of the flowers in window-boxes were geraniums and red carnations, and on some of the towers and roofs storks stood on their nests, made of sticks and twigs piled up high. At last a sky-line of towers, turrets and belfries came into sight, and soon after we drove over a bridge which spans the tawny river Guadalquivir. We had arrived in Seville.

CHAPTER 7

SEVILLE

"*Quien no ha visto a Sevilla no ha visto una maravilla*" (He who has not seen Seville has not seen a marvel), an old saying goes. When we arrived, the town was dressed in its gala attire, and it fairly hummed with life and joyous activities. Hotels and private houses were packed with visitors from many parts of the world, and therefore one had the feeling of being in Babylon itself.

My two companions had been invited to stay with a friend, but as there was no more room in his overcrowded flat, he made arrangements for me to put up in a small *pensión* in the old sector of the town. There some of the winding streets are so narrow that whilst driving through them slowly we almost scraped the walls of the houses on either side of us. Just before reaching a tiny square, the streets became so narrow that driving through them was impossible so we walked, following a twisting alley. Despite its narrowness, I was surprised that it is called a *calle* (street). The small and very modest *pensión* in which, by a miracle, my friend had found accommodation for me, was run by a pleasant middle-aged woman, whose clients were impecunious clerks, two or three elderly men and several visitors from country districts. Whereas in the luxury hotels guests spent several hundred pesetas per day on apartments and food – for it must be remembered that the Fair comes but once a year – all I paid in my *pensión* was 45 pesetas, or, say, roughly eight shillings, but, for some peculiar reason, breakfast was not served in the establishment. The small room to which I was taken was at the top of the ancient house. Being under the roof, it had a slanting ceiling; its walls were immaculately whitewashed, and it had a tiny square window which overlooked a courtyard and the pictures-quely tiled roofs of neighbouring houses at the back. There being no running water in the vast majority of the houses in the old sector of the town, a wooden stand with a small enamel basin stood in a corner for purposes of external cleanliness, and near it was a pitcher containing water. I was informed that if at any time I wanted more, a servant would fetch it from a nearby fountain. Then there was a small table, rather weak in the legs, an affliction from which suffered also a solitary chair and a night-table, made of an old packing-case artistically painted over. The bed, though spotlessly clean, was so narrow that I wondered what would happen if I tried to turn over in it. However, as I was to discover in due time, the feat could be accomplished, but the mattress, with a kind of miniature mountain range hidden from ocular detection in its interior, presented a problem of comfort that even a contortionist would have found difficult to solve. After having made several experiments, eventually I discovered that by twisting my body into an open kind of "L" shape, and lying on one side so as to make the mountain range pass between my hip-bone and the last rib, I could sleep like the proverbial log.

The few meals I had in the *pensión,* though simple, were quite good, helpings generous and the food well cooked. Whenever something was being fried in the kitchen, the oil in which this was being done filled the whole establishment with a most unpleasant smell. This happens all over Spain, and is due to the fact that all the good olive oil is exported, and that the rationed substitute for it is a mixture of various inferior vegetable oils. Apart from certain minerals, fruit, wine and olive oil, the country has no exports worth mentioning wherewith to earn foreign currency, and therefore, ever since, during the Civil War, the "Reds" walked off with the entire gold reserve, "For export only" has been the battle-cry, especially so in the case of olive oil. Laws and regulations being made to be broken, and Spaniards being what they are, many of them are enriching themselves in the black market which is being carried on quite openly, and, as far as I could see, without interference on the part of the higher authorities. However, as far as the masses – who can barely live on the money they earn – are concerned, they must try to forget what pure olive oil tastes like, and put up with the rationed substitute, the smell and taste of which, especially when hot, is penetrating and nauseating.

During the busy week I spent in Seville, the *pensión* and my bed saw very little of me, but it was most convenient to have a *pied-à-terre,* a kind of retreat to which to be able to go when utterly exhausted.

If I were to write all about the beauteous things and wonders I saw in this semi-mediaeval city which the Andalusians call "the Fair" and "the Proud," my account would fill a volume. On approaching Seville, the traveller is apt to be disappointed, for all he sees from the fertile *vega* (plain) is a confused mass of turrets, belfries and belvederes above which towers the most conspicuous landmark; the rectangular belfry of the Giralda, capped by a small dome, on which stands a bronze female figure representing Faith. It is well over ten feet in height, of considerable weight, and the figure, holding the banner of Constantine, is the revolving vane (in Spanish, *giralda* or *giraldillo)* which gave the name to the lofty tower.

When I began my explorations in the old sector of the city, my first disappointment upon entering it gave way to ecstasy and rapture. Winding narrow streets and alleys suddenly and unexpectedly lead to little squares with shady trees which look most picturesque against the surrounding white walls. Everywhere is a quaint mingling of Moorish and Eastern architecture which brings to mind stage directions and music, such as Mozart's *Don Juan* and *Figaro,* Bizet's *Carmen* and Rossini's *Barber of Seville.* Viewed from the outside, the houses with their high, whitewashed walls and little balconies, give no clue as to what they look like inside, but if one peeps through artistic wrought-iron gates, one sees marble-paved courts full of flowers, leafy plants and shrubs, and in some of these *patios* are ornamental wells or murmuring fountains. Most of the windows of these romantic houses face the courts, with their surrounding Moorish pillars and arches. The narrow streets have the advantage that in summer, during the hot hours, the sun's fierce rays strike the ground and walls for only a short time.

Every nook and corner of Seville abounds in poetry, legend and history. More than two thousand years ago, the Phoenicians traded and settled in Sephela (meaning "Plain"), from which, it is believed, Seville derived its name. Then came the long rivalry between Rome and Carthage, until, in 45 B.C., Caesar captured the town. Some four and a half centuries later it became the capital of the Goths, and in A.D. 712, after a siege, it fell to the Moors, who gave it the name of Ishbiliya. The new conquerors held sway until, in 1248, Ferdinand III ("The Saint") conquered it, subsequently expelling 300,000 Moors who migrated to Granada and North Africa.

The atmosphere of many of these great events still clings to Seville. In 1493, when Columbus returned from his first voyage of discovery, the city obtained the monopoly of all the trade with the New World, and thus became the most important port in Spain. Besides Columbus, many other men and women whose names were destined to become immortal, wandered through Seville's narrow streets. Among them are the gentle Isabella, Pizarro, Cortes, Velasquez, Murillo, de Soto and other giants of the Church, adventure, art, music and literature. It was in those times of daring and adventure that Alonzo de Ojeda – whose character and achievements find no parallel but in the pages of Cervantes – rushed up to the highest point of the Giralda – over three hundred feet above the ground – and, running out along a pole which was being projected for some repairs to the dome, turned a pirouette in mid-air. Having accomplished this acrobatic dare-devil feat, he saluted the ladies with a wave of his hat, and ran back to safety. According to a chronicler, "all this was done for giving pleasure to Her Majesty." Trying to cap this crazy feat of daring, at about the same period another daredevil rode up to the tower on horseback; an extravagance which, no doubt, satisfied the vanity of the rider, but which must have left his willing steed in a sorry state.

Unfortunately I arrived in Seville too late to see her world-famous *pasos* (processions) of Holy Week. As pointed out in a previous chapter, these manifestations of sentiment and fervour vary a great deal in different parts of the country. Much has been written about Seville's spectacular processions, her *saetas* (spontaneous songs of praise or lament, sung by individuals, mostly gipsies), her different *confradias* (brotherhoods whose members wear high-pointed hoods of different colours) and the bejewelled images which are carried through the streets on litters, surrounded by hundreds of burning candles. But, as already related, I arrived too late to see these scenes in which Faith is so marvellously allied to art, beauty and emotion, scenes which are unequalled in the whole Catholic world, including Rome herself. However, sights and experiences of a very different nature offered me ample compensation for what I had missed.

The ground on which the Fair is held is situated within a stone's throw of the new part of the city. For gaiety, beauty, colour and animation I have seen nothing to equal those unforgettable scenes which delight and amuse even the most exacting lovers of pleasure. Arranged in a huge square, with wide avenues running through it, a whole town of *casetas* is erected for the occasion. Long lines of these square awning tents are fitted with wooden platforms facing the "streets," and in addition, in some cases, with reception rooms behind. All the *casetas* are decorated with flowers and coloured electric bulbs, and round the platforms chairs for the families and friends are arranged in the shape of a horse-shoe, the open end facing the "street" whence crowds watch the dancing. At night, countless electric lights illuminate the fairground which is overhung with garlands, flags and bunting. At about noon the fun begins. Masses of riders, men and women, canter along or parade in groups, all dressed in becoming regional costumes. The men, wearing the typical garb of *ganaderos* (stock-men), leather chaps *(zahones)*, short jackets and wide-brimmed *Cordoves* hats *(sombreros paveros)* with their flat tops and sitting on high-cantled *jerezano* saddles with ornate iron or silver stirrups, make a fine sight as they pass on their fiery high-stepping Andalusian steeds, bedecked with fine trappings. In many cases the cavaliers are accompanied by a young lady who, wearing the colourful flounced skirt typical of Seville, sits sideways on the croup, holding on to her companion with one hand, and on to the horse's tail crupper with the other. Incidentally, I saw several *señoritas,* who, thus seated on horses, made such desperate use of this "handle" that by the time they dismounted, the underneath part of the animals' tails must have been very sore. Besides such caval-cades, there are luxurious carriages, filled with beauty and grace, drawn by teams of magnificent horses and mules, all of the same colour and conformation. What amazing mules I saw during that Fair! Decorated with a mass of coloured tassles and *cascabeles* (little round bells), these spirited, elegant, high-stepping animals are worthy of drawing the carriage of any king or potentate. The vast majority of the women and even small girls who go to the Fair, wear the regional dress: many-tiered skirts – generally either red or blue in colour, with white spots – and, almost invariably, with becoming red carnations stuck into the hair. Only a few wore combs and mantillas which are an interference when dancing. It was a grand sight to see bevies of *señoritas* sally forth from houses, setting out in the direction towards the Fair. Excited, and with the gleam of hunting tigresses in their eyes, they walked along elegantly, chattering, laughing and their skirts rustling. All carried castanets, and every now and again clicked a rhythm with them, like drummers of old nervously and softly rehearsing the roll for the charge into battle.

During the six days the Fair lasts, Sevillans get but little sleep, for the dancing and fun goes on until the early hours of morning. Visits are made from *caseta* to *caseta* where food and wine – chiefly *manzanilla* (white sherry) – is served to all callers. Everywhere music and the clicking of castanets is heard, and late into the night masses of people watch the dancing and the equestrian parade which continues uninterruptedly. Vendors of balloons, trumpets and toys mingle with the crowd and add colour to the animated scene. Out to make hay whilst the sun shines, the gipsies from Triana across the river, take every advantage they can whilst the Fair lasts. Those among them who are good dancers or singers, perform in those of the *casetas* where the best money for such extra entertainment is paid.

Many anecdotes are told about the Andalusians' ready wit and repartee. A favourite among them is about a Sevillan who, acting as guide to an American tourist, showed him some of the ancient buildings. Every time, after having looked at one of them, the American asked how long it had taken to build it. If the guide replied that this one had taken fifty years, and that one a hundred, the American sniffed with contempt, and said, "Wal, I guess in the States our boys would do the same thing in a year." And so the sight-seeing tour continued, and as the American became more and more boastful about the speed of building in his homeland, saying that the Alcazar with its exquisite arches, gardens and courts, could easily be built in six months in the U.S.A., the Andalusian merely listened and made no reply. When the pair came to the cathedral and its adjoining Giralda standing on foundations which once upon a time were those of the Roman temple of the goddess Diana, and later a Moorish mosque, which five and a half centuries ago was re-built as a Christian church – the total area of which comes second to that of St. Peter's in Rome, and surpasses that of St. Paul's Cathedral (in London) by 40,000 square feet – again the American asked how long it had taken to do the job. "I really couldn't tell you," the Andalusian replied, scratching his head, "it wasn't here yesterday."

On Easter Sunday and during the week of the Fair, Seville's celebrated *corridas* (bullfights) are held. The *Plaza de Toros* was built to hold some 15,000 spectators who are reputed to be the most critical in Spain. Every day the place is packed to full capacity, for the bull-fighters who perform there are the very best in the land, and the animals are chosen from the most renowned herds.

In some of the taverns I visited could be seen groups of men who looked different and whose dress varied from the ordinary *habitués*. Most of them were clean-shaven, tanned brown by the sun, lean and quiet-spoken. They wore wide-brimmed, flat-topped *pavero* hats previously described, short jackets, and invariably carried a thin staff, not quite as long as an alpenstock. These somewhat reticent men – who evidently hailed from country districts – so excited my curiosity that I asked a waiter who they might be. "*Señor*," he replied, casting a respectful glance in their direction, "they are *ganaderos;* they are in the employ of the big breeders of fighting bulls." Seeing that I was interested, the waiter – who revealed himself as a great bullfighting enthusiast – proceeded to tell me all about these men's work; how they look after the dangerous beasts, how they are selected and finally brought to the bullring. "You must go to the *apartado de toros*," he went on, "it is very interesting." When I asked him what he meant by this, my willing informant told me that not far outside the city were some corrals where all the bulls to be used during the week were selected and parted out into groups of six, to await their turn in the bullring. "Don't miss seeing the *apartado*," he concluded, "it means a long walk, but I assure you it's worth it."

Fortunately, shortly after this conversation with the waiter, I met my friends, Julio and Rosemary, who drove me to the corrals in their car. My informant was quite right, for even if I had had to go afoot to the *apartado de toras*, the long walk would have been well worth-while.

A great crowd was assembled near a number of square corrals with adobe walls in which, here and there, were peep-holes through which people looked at the formidable bulls. Occasionally, when it seemed as if two of the beasts were about to start a fight, one of the *ganaderos* who kept a vigilant eye on them, picked up a stone or a lump of earth, and with a gruff cry of warning threw it at the aggressor. Invariably this brought the quarrel to an end, and it was surprising to see how afraid the fierce beasts were, even of a small pebble. Some of the *ganaderos* ventured – though cautiously – into the corrals, and it was obvious that the bulls knew them. On one side of these enclosures was a long grand-stand and terraces on which people sat at tables, taking refreshments. Enormous quantities of large prawns, lobsters and several other varieties of shellfish were being consumed during this social event, and, of course, Seville's inevitable *manzanilla,* though the latter only in moderation. Here and there, surrounded by a small group of connois-seurs and friends, stood a bullfighter, with eagle eyes observing the beasts, their conformation, general condition and the shape of their horns, and trying to detect any peculiarity of movement on which his life might depend.

As my friends and I seated ourselves at a table on one of the crowded terraces, to watch the strange scene below, whilst having some refreshment, vendors of cigars and cigarettes – the latter mostly contraband American brands, such as "Camel", "Lucky Strike" and "Chesterfield" – slowly walked among the crowd, shouting, "Cahmel, Looky, Chesterr!" and others, with baskets filled with large sweet-smelling carnations called out *"Claveles, claveles, señor, compre unos para la señorita!"* ("Carnations, carnations, sir, buy some for the young lady"). And all the time, elegantly dressed women, beautiful young ladies and their male consorts (or escorts) ate more shellfish, sipped *manzanilla,* laughed and conversed, whilst down below the bulls, now getting accustomed to their strange surroundings and noise, became serene and some of them lay down to rest. On the horizon beyond the corrals the last afterglow of the sun threw a dark-red curtain across the sky, and every now and again the soft breeze blew into my nostrils the warm rich smell peculiar to the bovine family, contrasting strongly with that of carnations, *manzanilla* and smoke of tobacco. On the morrow, a group of six animals out of one of those corrals would be transferred to the bullring in the nearby city, and as, one by one, they would be released into the round sandy arena, to tear into it like the proverbial bats out of hell, the bullfighters would be there to begin their dangerous display. In the meantime, in the corrals on the outskirts of the city, as the bulls settled down to their last sleep, in the grand-stand and terraces people continued to eat, drink and be merry, and when darkness fell on Seville, we made ready to return to the Fair with its thousands of bright lights, music and dancing.

It must have been about 2 a.m. when, tired out, I bade my friends goodnight, and started on my way to the *pensión* where I hoped to sleep for several hours. Upon reaching the old part of the city with its labyrinth of narrow, winding streets, I found that the district was in total darkness, all the electric current being used to illuminate the fairground. Being fairly good at finding my way – even in places I do not know well – I walked along confidently, but after a while the unpleasant thought assailed me that I was lost. Fortunately I had a cigarette lighter with me, and with the help of its flickering light found the narrow alley in which was my lodging place. Upon reaching the door, and finding that it was locked, I clapped my hands several times, calling the night-watchman. It was pitch-dark, and, although the noise I made echoed through the miniature canyon in which I stood without seeing anything, my calls met with no response. Accordingly, over and over again I clapped my hands, until, finally, about fifty yards from where I stood, a door opened, with the result that a bright beam of light was thrown against the wall of a house opposite. Presently a shadow appeared coming out of the door; it was the night-watchman. Whilst inwardly rejoicing, I heard noises which made me think that the house out of which my saviour came must be a tavern, and as I was longing for a cool drink before going to bed, when he reached me I told him to come with me and have whatever he fancied.

The little tavern into which the two of us entered, was very old-fashioned and cosy, and filled with smoke. On crude benches placed alongside wooden tables sat several men, drinking wine and playing cards. Leaning unsteadily against the counter stood two tipplers, who made loud noises which were supposed to be song. Having got me into focus, both greeted me almost affectionately, and proceeded to offer me anything in the line of drink I might fancy, "*champán*" – as they pronounced "champagne" – if I wished. Feeling thirsty, and not wishing to give the "cold shoulder," I accepted a bottle of beer, and whilst I drank, the two "soaks" began to tell me their life story. Both hailed from Aragon, but worked in Seville, where, according to their assurances – repeated over and over again with many hiccups – they were happy, their *patrón* being a nice and generous kind of person. In a state bordering on tearfulness, and swearing on the memory of their departed mothers, they told me that they imbibed only once a year, just to do honour to the Fair. When I replied that I did not doubt their statement, and added that a man must have a little fun and relaxation, even if only once in a year, my words so pleased them that one of them insisted on singing for me a song of his beloved home region. Whilst his companion listened, now with tears streaming from his eyes, it was only with great difficulty that I managed to suppress a fit of laughter. Although what was supposed to be a musical treat sounded like the weird howling of a dog, the card players went on with their game, whilst the boss of the establishment, both elbows on the counter, his chin cupped in his hairy hands, listened intently, every now and again exclaiming, "*Olé!*"

After having drunk two or three cups of *ersatz* coffee, the songsters sobered up sufficiently to talk more or less sensibly, but upon remembering that this was their "one" day in the year, they ordered the next round of coffee to be served with brandy. The night-watchman, who was sitting on a stool near us, was not overlooked, and when I offered him some sausage and bread, he set to work, eating with such gusto that it was a pleasure to listen to him. As my two companions gulped down their coffee and brandy, I expected to see them become more fuddle-headed, but to my surprise the strong drink had the contrary effect on them. During the ensuing conversation, among other things we talked about horses and mules, and when my two interlocutors asked me what I thought of the Fair, and if I had seen the *feria de los gitanos* (the Fair of the gipsies), when I replied in the negative they assured me that it was very interesting and strongly recommended that I should not miss it. "Seeing that you are interested in horses," they said, "you must meet El Guajiro." When I asked for information concerning this, to me, unknown person, they informed me that he was a gipsy who enjoyed considerable fame as a trainer of horses, and with the help of a pencil and a piece of paper proceeded to give me directions how to reach Triana, situated on the other side of the river Guadalquiver, where he lives. To my surprise, I discovered that my two new friends knew a great deal about horses, mules and cattle, and we yarned away so merrily that I forgot all about being tired and going to bed. When at last we parted, the first signs of approaching dawn appeared, and by the time the sun had risen I reached a large field where the gipsies' *feria de ganado* (cattle fair) was already in full swing. Everywhere stood groups of horses, mules and donkeys and here and there bovines, sheep and goats. Many of the gipsies camped under carts or waggons, whilst others did the same under awnings, beneath which dirty mattresses, straw or heaped-up grass did duty for beds. Here and there were stands where food and wine were being sold, and despite the early hour, at such places men were assembled, most of them bartering, haggling and arguing over prices and quality of animals. Though the majority of the horses I saw were not of the type I would like to own, here and there I spotted a fine specimen. I was looking at such a one, when a dusky gipsy, about thirty years of age, came sidling up to me, and whispered, "*Señor,* I have a much better horse over there. Come with me, I will show him to you. The price I ask for him amounts to a gift."

"Sorry," I said, "I'm not here to buy, but merely to look, but I shall be pleased to accompany you to see what your animals look like." And so the two of us went to a group of some eight or ten horses which stood among that veritable sea of animals. The would-be seller had certainly spoken the truth, for the horse he especially recommended was a fine-looking specimen, in excellent condition and well-groomed for the occasion. When the gipsy asked me to make an offer for the animal, I repeated that I had not come to buy, and added that I was merely a tourist, and an impecunious one at that. With a cunning twinkle in his eyes, and a faint sarcastic smile coming over his face, he replied that he could tell the difference between a sight-seer and a buyer, and that, having observed the manner in which I had looked at several groups of horses, he knew very well that I had come to buy. Jokingly the two of us argued for a while, and although I did my best to make the man believe me that I spoke the truth in saying that I had not come to acquire horses, he just laughed, and said, "*Vaya, señor, no me venga con cuentos!*" (Go, sir, don't come to me with yarns.) Eventually, trying the age-old trick of horse-copers, he playfully slapped me on the shoulder and said, "Well, if you don't want to buy, then surely you won't refuse to come and have a glass of wine with me!"

"Tell me, does a duck swim?" I asked him, translating the English expression into Spanish for the purpose of getting a laugh out of him.

"What do you mean? I can't see what you're driving at," he asked with a wry smile and looking at me with dark cunning eyes, as if expecting to be caught in a verbal trap. "Does . . . a duck . . . swim?" he repeated slowly to himself, and then suddenly burst out laughing. "Oh, now I see the joke," he exclaimed, once more slapping me on the back.

"*Vamos!* Let's go – a glass of wine will do us good."

As the two of us stood in the shade of a square canvas sheet, beneath which a board placed on two packing-cases did duty for a counter, and wine was served out of a small barrel, the gipsy had another "go" at me about buying a horse from him. Again I assured him that I had not come to buy, and then, seeing that on the stall among a few edibles they sold smoked ham and bread I bought two portions, and whilst we munched our conversation continued.

"Pardon my curiosity, *señor,*" the gipsy said after a while, "of course, I can see that you are not from these parts. When first you spoke to me, your accent made me wonder where you come from, but now, having listened to you for some time, I venture to guess that you come from South America."

When I told him that I had lived in the Argentine for many years, he became quite enthusiastic. "Oh, then you must meet the Guajiro. He knows the Argentine well. I am sure he will be glad to meet you."

To this I replied that friends had given me the mysterious Guajiro's address, and that I knew he had a *picadero* (horse-training school) in a place called "Los Remedios," and that, in fact, it was my intention to go and see him. Now, at last, the gipsy began to believe that I had not come to buy a horse, and when the two of us parted he shook me warmly by the hand. "What was it you said about the duck?" he asked me as I turned to go away. "I have forgotten how your little joke goes."

"Does a duck swim?" I replied.

"Oh yes, that's it . . . Does a duck swim?" he repeated, laughing merrily. "I must remember this *chiste* (joke). *Adios, señor, que le vaya bién,* and with this he made off in the direction where his horses stood, patiently and innocently waiting for a buyer.

Having arranged to meet my friends, Julio and Rosemary, I made my way back to the centre of Seville whence, in their car, we drove back across the river to Los Remedios there to look for the Guajiro. Upon approaching a little hut, near which was an enclosure on the walls of which was painted in large letters; *PICADERO GUAJIRO,* we alighted from the car, soon after to meet the man about whom I had heard so much during the past few hours. About fifty years of age, he was lean and wiry and of medium height. His thin clean-shaven face, with a finely chiselled aquiline nose, penetrating though kindly eyes, and general bearing, gave the man a stamp of distinction. Dressed in the typical horseman's costume of the region, short jacket and grey flat-topped hat, he cut a fine figure, and as he walked towards us, I noticed that he was slightly bandy-legged, and that his gait was that of a man who spends much time on horseback.

Having introduced ourselves to him, upon seeing that, as a sideline to his horse business, he ran a small tavern – which was decorated with flags and bunting to be in keeping with the Fair – we sat down to drink a glass of sherry and to converse. The hut was crudely built, just whitewashed bricks and a corrugated iron roof covered with a layer of straw thatching. The mud floor was more or less levelled, and on the walls hung photographs and pictures of horses, riders, bulls and bull-fighters. Although the Guajiro was remarkably fair-skinned for a gipsy, his wife and aged mother were very dusky, and so were two or three of the several most attractive children who came to peep at us strangers. Two little girls, about ten and eleven years of age, who wore flounced colourful skirts, were introduced to us as nieces, of which, our host told us, he had many. They were about to go to the fairground where their grown-up brothers, sisters and cousins had singing and dancing engage-ments in rich men's *casetas*. How charming and sweet those two little girls looked in their becoming dresses, combed-down raven-black hair, rosy cheeks showing under their alabaster skin, and vivacious eyes sparkling as they smiled shyly, showing rows of teeth which looked snow-white against cherry-red lips.

The Guajiro was greatly interested when Rosemary and I told him that we hailed from the Argentine where, he told us, he had spent several years, acting as horse-trainer and chauffeur to the late President Alvear's sister. Although he earned good money, and enjoyed life in the New World, by degrees the longing to return to Spain became so strong within him that eventually he sailed back to his people, some of whom he had supported with part of his earnings which he regularly sent to them. And so it came about that he settled once more in Triana where, ever since his return home, he carried on with the business of training and buying and selling of horses.

After having chatted for some time, the Guajiro invited us to accompany him to a nearby stable where, with visible pride, he showed us his horses. Fine beasts they were, among them two typical Andalusians, all in excellent condition and well-groomed.

On a large board which was fixed to one of the walls, in large clear lettering was painted the following text, which gave me an insight to the Guajiro's character.

THE HORSE'S SUPPLICATION

MY DEAR MASTER,

Please forgive me for putting before you this my supplication.

After the work and fatigues of the day, give me shelter in a clean stable. Feed me unstintingly, and quench my burning thirst. I can't tell you when I am hungry, thirsty or ill. If I am looked after properly, I can serve you well, for I shall have strength. If I leave the fodder untouched, have my teeth examined. Please don't cut off my tail, for it is my only defence against tormenting flies and other insects. Whilst working me, speak to me, for your voice conveys more to me than the reins and the whip. Pat me, and so encourage me to work with a good will. Don't hurry me up steep inclines, and don't pull on my bit when I'm going downhill. Don't make me carry or pull too heavy a load. I serve you uncomplainingly to the limit of my strength. If you forget this, I might die at any moment whilst doing my best to carry out your will. Treat me with the consideration that is due to a faithful servant, and if I don't understand you immediately, don't get angry, and don't chastise me, for perhaps it's not my fault. Examine my reins, possibly they don't transmit your orders correctly, because they are knotted or twisted. Look at my hooves and shoes, to make sure that they are not hurting me. Dear Master, when old age weakens me, and makes me useless, don't neglect me or let me die of hunger. If you can't keep me any longer, destroy me, but do it yourself, so that my sufferings be less. Above all, when I'm no further use to you, please don't condemn me to the torment of the bullring.

Pardon me for having taken up your time with this my humble supplication, which, I beg you not to forget. This I ask you, invocating the One who was born in a crib . . .

Of course, our conversation was "horses, horses and more horses," all about how to train them, and so on. Several other gipsies joined our little international conference, on the spontaneous agenda of which many important "horsey" matters were brought up, matters which have been discussed ages ago, and which will be discussed long after the deadlock over international control of atomic power has been forgotten, excepting, perhaps, by a few semi-fossilized historians of millennia to come. When I showed my new friends how, by means of a simple trick, a bad-tempered horse can be tamed quickly, the revelation of my secret so pleased the gipsies that the Guajiro invited Rosemary, her husband and me to visit them in their abode that night. He promised that he would produce the best gipsy dancer in the region, as well as several good singers, and that we would enjoy ourselves much more in his little hut than if we went to the fairground.

In Spain at any time, meals are eaten at peculiar but convenient hours, but whilst the Seville Fair lasts, hours do not count. Thus, that day, after having had afternoon tea with friends at 9 p.m., we returned to the Guajiro's abode. Besides his family, several young gipsies were there, waiting for us. The formalities of introducing us to the little assembly having been carried out with a correctness that amounted almost to solemnity, and cigarettes and several bottles of *manzanilla* having been produced, for some time we talked about local events, but mostly about horses, bulls and bullfighters, and all the while the gipsies helped themselves freely to drinks and cigarettes. Upon realizing that we visitors knew nothing or, at the best, but little about *tauromaquia*, as the art of bullfighting is called in Spain – an elderly member of our company – who once upon a time had been a bullfighter – became so enthusiastic that he rose from his seat, and with the help of a table-cloth demonstrated to us some of the mysteries and intricacies of his former vocation. Among other things he gave us a learned and profound lecture on the *psicologia* of bulls. Apparently, once upon a time, our professor of *tauromaquia* was seriously gored because he made a mistake in his psycho-analysis of a bull who, among other mental and physical peculiarities, was ambidextrous, if this term can be applied to a beast which horns in either direction with equal ease and intent. As during my subsequent wanderings through Spain I met several other men highly learned in the art of *tauromaquia,* here I will not go into details about the lecture I heard delivered in the small though select auditorium of my new friend, El Guajiro.

The three young men he had brought to sing to us had so strained their vocal cords in various *casetas* at the Fair that, as they put it, their throats felt as if they had been burnt with a hot iron. Shortly after the "Professor" had resumed his seat in a corner, not forgetting to take with him another big glass of *manzanilla* and a handful of "Looky Streekay" cigarettes, a round wooden platform, about the size of a large manhole lid, was rolled into the hut. After it had been placed flat on the mud floor, levelled and made firm by means of a few stones and sticks, the gipsies who sat near it in a semi-circle began to clap their hands, beating a soft rhythm. The men, women and even the children did this for some time, and every now and again one of the three young men who had come to sing, coughed and spat on the floor to clear his sore throat. As the hand-clapping grew louder, he slightly swayed forwards and backwards, and his face assumed an expression as if he were in pain. Staring at the mud floor, and then raising his head several times, as if trying to look through the ceiling, he would utter an agonized "*Ay . . . ay-ee*" and then, suddenly, begin his weird song. The intricate *cadenzas* of Flamenco songs give evidence of the wanderings of the Spanish gipsy race from their original seat in the Hindu Kush through Asia Minor. Also, a strong North African influence prevails in these *cantos Flamencos: tonas, seguidillas* and others, most of which consist of three or four lines, or *coplas,* as they are called. All the while, the hand-clapping continued, marking the time, and every now and again when the singer finished a particularly intricate *cadenza,* the members of this primitive chorus showed their appreciation by shouting, "*Olé!*"

It was surprising how, despite the state of their throats, the singers who performed in turns were able to produce clear though forced notes, despite the fact that their speaking voices were "thick" and husky.

The African influence is particularly noticeable in the peculiar wailing *cadenzas* which are not improvised. These *cadenzas* are a kind of *appoggiatura,* and are sung in quarter tones, with slight trills, and the high notes are sung in falsetto which ends in normal voice as the *cadenza* is graduated to a lower pitch. These "runs" have time value, in the sense that the tricky embellishments are not added when the singer chooses. They are repeated exactly the same in every verse, and, whilst being sung, the guitar accompaniment ceases, to be resumed at their completion. This is the moment when – if the singer has pleased his audience – enthusiastic *olés* are shouted. Between verses, whilst guitars are being strummed to mark time, and to get ready for the next verse, singers often exchange mumbled remarks with the accompanists and they also use such intervals for clearing their throats.

After short intervals during which the performers in El Guajiro's hut helped themselves liberally to *manzanilla* and cigarettes there followed more singing, and then a lithe, narrow-hipped young man stepped on the round wooden platform. Whilst the hand-clappers beat out a lively rhythm, he stood for a while, staring upwards as if in a trance. "*Si . . . si!* "(Yes, yes), he uttered every now and again, at the same time slowly stretching his body to its maximum height. Then, suddenly, he began to stamp on the boards with such rapidity that it sounded like the loud beating of drums. These were gradations and varied rhythms of this footwork, from faint rippling and purring to loud throbbing as the dancer fairly poured out nervous energy. As he twisted his flexible, narrow-hipped body, spun round and went through abrupt contortions, the hand-clappers urged him on by beating the rhythm louder and louder, and every now and again shouting, "*Olé!*," "*Arre!*" and "*Corre!*" Frowning, sometimes smiling, tossing his head back, or assuming a facial expression of arrogance, defiance or supreme haughtiness, the dancer mimicked what to my inexpert eyes were themes of love, annoyance, defiance, courtship and valour, all these antics being survivals of immemorial Oriental antiquity. The intricate dances were short, and invariably ended with a final stamping of feet, whereafter, leaping off the platform – which acted as sound-board – the narrow-hipped young man laughed and joked whilst his kinsmen rewarded him with loud *olés*.

As our little party warmed up, one by one the gipsies showed us what they could do, until even the Guajiro's wife became so worked up that she, too, gave us a turn. As she stamped, tilted her head, frothed her skirt, flashed her eyes, disdainfully shrugged her shoulders, swayed her hips and twisted her arms and hands, making them resemble snakes responding to the tune of an Indian fakir's pipe, there was nothing old about the woman, and the applause and good-humoured laughter which followed her exhibition almost brought down the hut. Two little girls who had been watching every move and step with such concentration that their large lustrous black eyes looked almost uncanny, also gave us a turn, to the great delight and pride of their elders, who loudly proclaimed that, some day, the youngsters would become the finest dancers in the land.

As the party became merrier and more and more enthusiastic, and my new friends begged of me to give them an imitation of what I considered to be gipsy dancing, eventually I, also, stepped on to the

platform. Apeing some of the previous dancers' mannerisms and atti-
tudes, I stood erect until the hand-clapping, mixed with laughter and
jocular exclamations of *"Olé,"* *"Vamos"* and *"Arre!"* urged me to
begin, and then, to everybody's delight, I gave an exhibition of clumsi-
ness such as surely Triana has never seen. Anyway, we had a grand
evening, and when at about 1 a.m. we returned to the fairground on the
other side of the river, we took with us some of the singers and dancers
who, despite the late hour and their sore throats, hoped to get an
engagement in some *caseta,* and thus to pick up extra money.

On the following day, whilst having a simple lunch in my *pensión,* a
young man whose head was swathed in bandages seated himself at my
table. Though curious to know what had happened to him, I asked no
questions, but after a while, as the two of us conversed about this and
that, my companion told me that by profession he was assistant to a
motion-picture camera-man, and that on the previous day, whilst
carrying out his duties, he had met with a serious accident. Finding a
sympathetic listener in me, he proceeded to recount how, from a
specially rigged-out motor-car, he and his superior had been busy
taking a picture of fighting bulls in the country district, when one of the
animals, infuriated by the disturbance of its peace, charged their
vehicle. Apparently the attack was so sudden and unexpected that the
frightened chauffeur lost his head, and drove into the ditch where the
car turned over, smashing the camera and injuring its occupants. For a
few long seconds the bull horned the wreck, but fortunately a number
of *ganaderos* came galloping up on their horses, and managed to drive
the beast away before it had time to attack the victims of this accident,
who were lying half stunned and injured in the ditch.

There was so much to be seen in Seville, that I was on the move
almost day and night. Many books have been written about the city's
history, ancient buildings and monuments, so here I will relate mainly
personal experiences and a few observations on things which escape
the notice of the vast majority of visitors, especially if they do not
speak Spanish.

"When in Rome, do as the Romans do;" and so, when friends
invited me to accompany them to witness one of Seville's famed bullfights, I went with them, expecting to see something memorable.

Whenever I talk to people about Spain, the first thing they ask me is
to tell them something about bullfights. Even those among my

questioners who abhor this typical Spanish spectacle, many thirst for information about it, and when I tell them what I saw, they act very much like one of the two elderly English ladies who came to a bullfight with me in Barcelona; they listen, shudder and say, "Please, no more about this barbarity." And when I change the subject, they ask me to tell them more about it.

Much has been written about bullfighting, and novels dealing with this subject have been universal best-sellers, though in many cases their authors did not trouble themselves to make a study of this ancient spectacle. Therefore, in order to put readers "wise," in the next chapter I shall endeavour to describe briefly what I saw in the several bullrings I visited, and to give a brief but concise outline of the history of bullfighting, its traditions, fundamental technicalities and general atmosphere connected with it. Readers who are not interested in these subjects will do well to skip the next chapter, and to resume their reading where I continue with personal narrative.

CHAPTER 8

ABOUT BULLFIGHTING

The approaches to Seville's famous bullring were filled with a mass of excited humanity and luxurious cars. It was about 3.30 p.m. when we arrived, and as we looked for the entrance through which to make the shortest cut to our seats – which had been reserved ten days previously – there was a stir among the crowd near us. A large limousine slowly ploughed its way through the crowd, who surged forward to have a close look at the bullfighters who were seated inside. As it happened, the vehicle came to a standstill outside an entrance near us, so I had an excellent view of its occupants as they alighted. Already dressed for the fray, the *toreros* wore their magnificent glittering costumes.

The traditional *traje de luces*[2] consists of a short jacket which is slightly shortened at the back so as to show the silk sash which is wound round the waist. The jacket is richly embroidered with gold and silver braid, and also with silk, and similar designs are worked into the waistcoat. The tight-fitting trousers – known as *talequilla* – are also made of silk which is of the same colour as that of the jacket and waistcoat. There is no rule as far as the main colour of a bullfighter's costume is concerned, but usually it is light-blue, green, lilac or some

---

[2] *Traje:* costume, dress, attire, garb. *Luz:* light, lustre, lucidity. Therefore, perhaps, the most acceptable translation of *traje de luces* is "costume of glitter."

other colour to which the wearer gives preference, in some cases to please his personal taste, but in many cases for reasons of superstition of which there are many among these men whose profession offers so many dangers. The trousers reach to just below the knees, and on either side they have a wide strip of gold, silver and silk embroidery, the patterns of which match those of the jacket and waistcoat. From the lower ends of the trousers dangle tassels which are known as *machos.* Pale-rose silk stockings and light flexible slippers made of black leather complete the costume, which can cost a small fortune. Besides this glittering apparel, bullfighters wear white shorts and neck-ties, the colour of which almost invariably matches that of the sash. According to the inflexible rules of tradition, on their heads *matadores* must wear what is known as a *coleta,* a kind of little pig-tail made of false hair. This holds a small disk, called *castañeta,* to the base of the back of the head. In order to fix the *castañeta* and the *coleta* firmly, a black silk cord is passed through it, the ends being left to hang down two or three inches. Peculiar and superfluous as the wearing of a *castañeta* may seem to casual spectators, it offers protection to the back of the bull-fighter's head, and especially so should he have the misfortune to be thrown backwards against the wooden barrier which surrounds the sandy arena. The traditional hat is of old Andalusian origin. Close-fitting to the head, the *montonera,* as it is called, is always black, covered with a mass of adornments made of silk cord, and with a large perky tuft protruding on either side. The masterpiece of a bullfighter's wearing apparel is his cape, which is only used during the opening parade into the bullring. The *capote de paseo* (parade cape) is made of heavy silk, covered with a profusion of artistic gold and silver braid embroidery, worked on silk of every hue and colour. Successful *matadores* spend enormous sums of money on such capes which are veritable jewels, often destined to become museum pieces.

This, briefly, is what I saw whilst watching two *matadores* arrive at the bullring in Seville. Both were good-looking, lithe and athletic young men, one of them almost fair-skinned, and the other rather dark, and they made great efforts to look calm and serene. The onlookers who were crowded near the side-entrance to the bullring stepped back to let their heroes pass. At that moment I caught sight of two young men whom I recognized at once: Milo and Mila, the precious young things I had seen at the bullfight in Barcelona. Both leaned forward

and, craning their girlish necks, followed the *matadores* with hungry
stares. Taking no notice of the people near them, the *matadores* disappeared in the darkness under the grand-stand, whilst assistants
unloaded wooden boxes and open wicker-work baskets containing
capes, swords and other paraphernalia, whereafter the onlookers dispersed to seek their seats in the stands. These seats being normally of
concrete, at the entrance gate attendants offered spectators little square
cushions for hire.

The bullring and its surrounding stands constituted a sight never to
be forgotten. The balcony-like *gradas* with their pillars and arches,
situated behind the uncovered *tendidos* which slope down towards the
sandy arena *(ruedo)* were packed with people. The ladies were dressed
so gaily that where many sat together, viewed from the distance they
made those parts of the stands resemble sloping beds of multi-coloured
flowers. From ballustrades hung richly-embroidered *mantillas* (shawls),
vibrating in the strong light. On the sunny side vendors sold paper hats
to those who wished to protect themselves against the slanting rays of
the afternoon sun, whilst other vendors who wore white jackets,
wormed their way along the rows of seats, shouting, *"limonada,
caramelos, cigarros!"* Every now and again, recognizing friends among
the crowd, somebody would rise and wave to them, or some witty bird
amused those within earshot of him with amusing remarks and droll
replies. Many of the men smoked cigars, impregnating the air with their
aroma. If the cigars happened to be brittle, and their outer leaves
became unstuck, the smokers wound round them a piece of paper, off
which they tore sections as the cigar was gradually smoked away. As I
am writing these lines, and visualize the scenes I saw in various
Spanish bullrings, I can still smell the smell of those cigars, mixed with
that of bottled scent and of carnations.

Inherently and notoriously unpunctual, when it comes to bullfights
Spaniards demand that these begin on the dot of time. One minute or
even seconds too early or too late would cause an uproar or even a riot.
Therefore, as the hour hand of the big clock over the main stand
approached the little black line which marks the exact time of 4 p.m.,
ever-increasing waves of excitement rose among the crowd, some poor
members of which must have "sold their mattresses to be there", as a
Spanish joke has it. When the hour indicated that the eagerly awaited
moment had arrived, two riders wearing the picturesque costume of

constables *(alguacilillos)* of the reign of Philip IV (roughly 1650) trotted into the ring, the golden sand of which had been so carefully levelled out and raked. Loud applause greeted the appearance of the *alguacilillos,* who were mounted on fairly good horses. They made a fine sight in their black uniforms with short capes fluttering down their backs, and their white ruffs and gay red and yellow plumes waving above black three-cornered hats. Having crossed the ring slowly, they halted before a balcony to doff their hats to the president of the bullfight, whereafter they returned to the main gate *(puerta de caballos,* horse gate), through which they had made their entry into the ring. Upon reaching it, they swung round their mounts and up in the stands the band struck up a lively *pasodoble;* whereupon, to thunderous applause from the excited crowd, the two *alguacilillos* led the parade of the bullfighters into the arena. This *paseo de las cuadrillas,* as the parade is called, is the most colourful part of a bullfight. Marching in wide-apart rows of three or four, the *matadores,* dressed in their glittering costumes, lead the parade, followed by the *banderilleros –* who stick the darts into the bulls – and *picadores,* mounted on horses, with lances in their hands. Behind these chief performers come the *monosabios (matadores'* assistants) and servants, who lead a team of fine mules, bedecked with gaily-coloured tassels and jingling bells. Unlike members of other races who love discipline and regimentation, the men who make up such parades do not walk in step. If they did, it would spoil and take away much of the peculiar charm and psychological interest of these entries. Looking serious, or even scowling – as befits the seriousness of the occasion – every bullfighter walks, struts or swaggers along as he pleases. I observed that most of them, apparently oblivious of the crowd, marched slowly and deliberately, their bent right arms wrapped up in the *capote de paseo,* left arms swinging stiffly, and eyes fixed on the ground. If these men marched in step, and acted according to "officially" set rules and precepts of movement and deportment, such parades would lose much of their character.

Before entering the *ruedo* (bullring) *matadores* usually go to a chapel there to confess and pray to their particular saint or virgin, for possibly they may be dead before the sun sets. Besides a chapel, bullrings have other annexes: first-aid station, rest-rooms for the performers, corrals and in some cases an operating theatre with surgeons standing by to attend to cases of serious injury.

Having saluted the president, the parade breaks up, whilst one of the *alguacilillos,* hat in hand, catches a key thrown to him by the president, and then gallops away towards the gate through which the bulls are let into the arena. Without slowing down, the rider hands or throws the key to an attendant, whereafter both *alguacilillos* retire.

At this point a few words of explanation are necessary. Before a fight, the bulls are moved from the corrals, to be kept undisturbed in the *toril,* a kind of loose-box situated under the stands. When the time comes, one by one they are driven into a chute, whence to be released into the arena through a gate or trap-door. I have heard it said that before this is done a beast is goaded into a state of fury, but as far as my experience and careful observation goes, I have not seen this being done. However, immediately before the bull is released, a little trap-door above the beast is opened by an attendant who, by means of a staff, fixes a rosette with two flowing ribbons to his neck. This is the badge or *divisa* of the animal's breeder. The sudden disturbance and the sharp barbed point of the rosette are sufficient to infuriate the beast.

In the meantime the bullfighters have taken up their positions on the shady side near the five-foot high wooden barrier *(barrera)* which surrounds the ring. Between this barrier and the raised stands is an alley-way *(callejon),* some six or seven feet wide. This is the place where hard-pressed bullfighters can take refuge by leaping over the wooden barrier, inside which, in case of emergency, are four narrow wooden refuges, known as *burladeros.* They are roughly four feet long, and of the same height as the barrier which surrounds the ring.

A fanfare sounded by trumpeters brings excitement to a fever-pitch, and after a few minutes of hushed silence, as the trap-door opens, and the first bull comes tearing into the arena, snorting and sometimes horning the barrier in passing, the crowd greets his appearance with shouts of admiration. If a beast's appearance and behaviour fails to please the knowing and critical spectators, they give vent to their disapproval by hooting, whistling, cat-calling and booing, hoping thus to make the president decide to have the animal withdrawn. In rare cases when this happens, or when a bull suffers an accident which lames him or in some other way incapacitates him from putting up a good fight, the president gives a signal to the trumpeters who play a call which, in its turn, is the signal for two tame steers with large bells dangling from their necks to be let into the arena. Upon seeing these *mansos* (tame ones) as they are called, the bull goes to join them, whereafter it is easy to drive the trio back to the corrals. A bull who has been thus rejected or withdrawn saves his life, for never again will he be put into a ring.

But to go back to the moment when the first *toro* comes tearing into the arena. In order to attract his attention, the *banderilleros* and assistants wave large silk capes, the bright colours of which vary on the inside and the outside. During this *bienvenida* (welcome), as it is called, the cape is held in only one hand, and as the bull makes a vicious charge, it is waved in front of him, or dragged along the ground as the assistant cleverly dodges or runs towards one of the wooden refuges *(burladeros)*. Once behind it, the man is safe, for although part of his chest and the head protrude over it, a bull cannot horn so high. However, in his rage he usually makes a charge at the boards, behind which the objects of his fury watch calmly and unperturbed. After a few such wavings of capes (*capotazos*) the chief bullfighter, called either *matador* or *espada,* steps into the ring to manipulate his cape with both hands. This is one of the opportunities when a *matador* can shine. As the beast charges him he must do as little footwork as possible, and as it passes him he must stand close up, now absolutely motionless, save the movements of his arms, and the position of his body must be statuesque and graceful. During this first stage of a bull-fight, the *matador* watches every movement of the animal; whether he prefers horning to the right or to the left, if his eyesight is correct, or if he had any peculiarity of attack, the oversight of which might prove fatal. There are many such possibilities, besides the psychological aspect, briefly referred to in the previous chapter. No two bulls react alike, and therefore in order to become a first-class *matador,* years have to be spent studying the reactions of fighting bulls, under many conditions and circumstances.

All great *matadores* had their first lessons in the taurine art when they were boys. The ladder to fame is a long, difficult and dangerous one, and many of those who have eventually reached its top, have ended their careers by being carried out of the *ruedo* to be buried by a vast crowd of admirers who had both cheered and booed them, according to how they had performed on certain days. The bullfighting public is not carried away by hero-worship during any *corrida* (fight).

If their hero gives a bad performance, even the staunchest admirers show their disapproval in no uncertain manner, and even if they threaten to mob him, next time he steps into the arena, he does it with a clean sheet. If his display comes up to expectation, or surpasses it, the cheers and the ovation with which he is rewarded could not have been surpassed by the joyous frenzy with which the ancient Romans greeted the return of a conquering hero.

Once the bull has been "fixed" with a few passes at the cape – or, as one might say, when the *matadores* have him "taped" – follows the second and most disagreeable part of the spectacle. Two horses, mounted by *picadores,* enter into the arena. The men's jackets and waistcoats resemble those of the *matadores,* though they are not as ornate and luxuriously embroidered. The *picadores* wear grey, large, wide-brimmed and round-topped hats (called *castorenos)* made of some stiff material, adorned with a cockade of some bright colour, and long leather trousers, and the right leg is protected by a kind of armour which can be bent at the knee. A thick gaiter on the left leg and heavy boots reinforced with steel, completes a *picador's* costume. Like the *matadores,* he also sports a *coleta* and *castafieta,* the pig-tail-like appendices to the back of the head already described. Fortunately, nowadays the horses are protected by strong mattress-like armour, known as the *peto.* The use of this protection was introduced and made compulsory by the late Spanish dictator, Primo de Rivera. Thanks to this ugly and clumsy-looking contraption, which considerably hinders the horses' movements, serious injuries or deaths among them are very rare, and the disgusting spectacle of seeing them ripped open by the bulls' horns is a thing of the past.

Keeping near the barrier, one of the two mounted *picadores* approaches the bull, whilst the other stands by in the distance. Shouting and raising his lance, the rider provokes the bull until he charges, and as he does so, the *picador* endeavours to stick the lance into the slight hump (called *morillo)* fighting bulls have above their shoulders. About three or four inches behind the point of the lance is a ring which makes it impossible to make too deep a thrust which might cripple or even kill the bull. If the *picador* is clever and strong enough to stave off the bull's first onrush, and if the point of his lance is stuck into the right place, the spectators reward the difficult feat with applause, and the horse will not suffer as much as a bump. However, this happens but rarely, and as often as not the *picadores* miss their aim, lancing too far back, or to one side or the other, which infuriates the crowd, and even more so if "boring" is done with the lance. Although the horses get severely bumped and sometimes are lifted off the ground or even knocked over, the *matadores* are always near to entice the bull away with their capes, especially so if the *picador* happens to be unseated and falls to the ground where, owing to the armour on his right leg, he is practically helpless. Although the sight of a blindfolded horse being knocked about by an infuriated bull is revolting, thanks to the *peto* they wear, I do not think that they suffer any more physical pain than a rugby football player does when being brought down by an opponent. After two, three, or at the maximum, four thrusts with the lance, when the president considers that more might disable the bull too much, he makes a signal to the trumpeter who plays a call which orders the *picadores* to betake themselves and the horses out of the ring. If one of them has displeased the crowd – which usually seems to be the case – on his way out he is subjected to a terrible broadside of insults, with every now and again a humorous one thrown in by a wag. Thus, on one occasion, an infuriated man near me finished a long string of abuse by referring to the modern French Blue Beard. "Petiot, Petiot, Petiot!" he yelled, leaning over the barrier below which the *picador* jogged along on his old nag, "Assassin, assassin, I hope a flying saucer will kill you!"

Once, when, just for fun, I also joined in, and shouted two typically Argentine insults, "*Indio!*"and *Atorrante!*" a neighbour of mine who was yelling his head off, turned to me to ask what was the meaning of these words, and when I explained that, more or less, they meant "Brute of an Indian" and "Low-down cad," he said, "*Gracias*" (thanks), and immediately bellowed the words at the *picador* who, despite the storm which raged round him, jogged out of the arena, acting as if he were alone in a tranquil world. How on earth any man can choose to become a *picador* is beyond my comprehension. He has to do most of the really dirty work, gets all the hard knocks and insults, and very little money for it all.

After the *suerte de varas* (feat of the lances) comes the third phrase of a bullfight. This is the *suerte de banderillas;* the feat performed with the gaily decorated darts which are about two feet in length, made of some light wood with barbed steel points at their ends. As far as the vast majority of the spectators – who do not know the intricacies of bullfighting – is concerned, this is the most elegant and apparently dangerous part of the spectacle. The *banderillero* steps into the ring, holding a dart in each hand. I noticed that very often – most likely for superstitious reasons – the performer wets the barbed tips with saliva, whereafter, taking up his position, on tiptoe, with both feet together, he raises his arms, darts pointing towards the bull, and by raising and lowering them slightly, and at the same time uttering short exclamations, attracts the beast's attention. As a rule, for a few moments the bull scratches the ground with his forelegs, throwing sand over his back, and then charges the *banderillero* at full speed. At this moment the man must decide which of two courses to take in order to stick the darts into his assailant's *morillo,* or be it, the little hump at the top of his shoulder. Usually the *banderillero* runs towards the bull to meet his onrush half-way, and during the last fraction of a second, when one thinks that the man is about to be killed, he changes the direction of his race to an oblique one, and, whilst executing a swift evasive movement with his body makes the horns miss him by millimetres, he plants the darts. Infuriated by this new torment, and for having missed the thrust with his horns, the bull turns round rapidly to chase his intended victim, who usually runs towards the barrier over which he nimbly leaps to safety. A few of the best *banderilleros* know the reactions of bulls so well that after having stuck in the darts, they run away from the bull at a leisurely pace, not even bothering to look back. Instead, apparently quite at ease, they almost dance away, calmly zigzagging, and thus obliging their pursuer to change his "lead"; that is to say, his gait, from one foreleg to the other, which causes him to lose speed. The other method of sticking in the darts is called *al quiebro.* It is done by standing perfectly still, feet together, and avoiding the beast's onrush and formidable horns by means of what amounts to a miraculous twist of the body. Occasionally, in order to please his admirers, a *matador* plants a pair of darts, three pairs of which is the maximum per beast. On very rare occasions, if at this stage a bull shows lack of fighting spirit, but yet seems to be too formidable to be sent out of the ring to the disgrace and shame of his breeder, the president orders a pair of *banderillas de fuego* (darts to which are attached small fire-crackers), to be planted. I have never seen this being done, but I am told that this additional form of torment invariably so infuriates the bull that he renews the fight. During this phase of the spectacle the *matador* can be seen standing near the barrier, resting, perhaps in serious consultation with some of his assistants, maybe drinking a few drops of water, or with eagle eyes watching every movement of the bull. He is preparing for the last, and most difficult and dangerous part of the fight; the *suerte de matar,* the killing of the bull.

When the eagerly awaited moment arrives, the *matador* steps into the arena. In his hands he holds a vermilion cloth which is fixed to a wooden rod, about two feet in length, and he also carries his sword *(estoque).* Going to the foot of the balcony in which is the president, he salutes him by taking off his hat *(montonera),* and then proceeds to dedicate his intended kill to the president, perhaps to some celebrity who happens to be present, to the public in general, or to any section of the stands, or person he wishes to honour. If the dedication is made to the public in general, the *matador* walks some little distance out into the ring, there to turn round slowly, at the same time with an elegant gesture to wave his *montonera* in the direction of the surrounding stands. This done, he throws it on the ground, leaving it to be picked up by one of his attendants. Presently, alone with the bull, with the help of the coarsely-woven vermilion cloth (which is much smaller than the gaily-coloured silk capes used during the initial stage of the fight) he proceeds to execute what are known as "passes" *(pases).* Of these there is a great variety, every one having a name, such as a *natural, de pecho, en redondo, molinete, gaonera, manoletina,* and so on. The last two are named after the famous *matadores,* who invented them, Gaona the Mexican, and the ill-fated "Manolete" mentioned in previous chapters. Once the *matador* has taken his position, and the bull charges, the former must not indulge in side-stepping, which would be an acknow-ledgment of having misjudged distance and the animal's homing pro-pensities, or, even worse, of being afraid. Calmly, and as elegantly as possible, the *matador* must stand like a statue, and as the bull rushes past him, sometimes brushing against him, besmearing his glittering costume with blood, he must execute the "pass" with grace. Occasionally, clever and especially daring *matadores* perform such passes kneeling down, on one or both knees, and during "psycho-logical" moments when they guess that for a few seconds the bull is in a bewildered or hesitating state of mind, they perform hair-raising stunts, called *adornos (adornments).* Thus, for instance, standing quite near in front of the animal, the *matador* turns his back on him, and remains standing for a few long moments, with the red cloth *(muleta)* limply hanging down to his (the *matador's)* feet. Again, another dare-devil will kneel down, touch or even kiss the tip of one of the bull's horns, rub his forehead with the palm of an outstretched hand, or, as I saw on one occasion, get down on both knees, and, leaning forward, slowly and very cautiously, kiss the bull's nose. Even uninitiated spectators are so thrilled and impressed by such stunts that they retain them in their minds as lasting imprints. No wonder Spaniards often call bullfighting the "plastic art".

After a number of "passes", when the bull begins to show the first signs of exhaustion, or gives up the fight, realizing that he is van-quished, the *matador* endeavours to manoeuvre him into position so as to make him stand firmly and squarely, with the forelegs as close together as possible. This opens slightly the narrow gap between the shoulder blades between which the sword must be thrust as deeply and at as acute a downward angle as possible. When a *matador* has his intended victim standing as described *(igualado* in taurine jargon), he holds the red cloth *(muleta)* in his left hand slightly lower than his hips, in front of him, and, standing in a sideways position, dead in front of the bull, with his right hand raises the sword to a horizontal position, level with his chest. Taking careful aim, he stands thus, immobile as a statue, not even the point of his sword showing as much as a symptom of a tremor. This is the critical and – as far as the *matador* is concerned – most dangerous moment of the fight. The thrust with the sword must be made in dead-straight line from in front of the bull who may – as is often the case – have a tremendous lot of fight left in him, or who may make one of those unexpected and dangerous last efforts of fury and despair. When one considers the size of a bull's head – even if it is held low – and one adds to it the length of the neck, as well as the distance from its base to the spot *(morillo)* where the sword must be thrust in at a most difficult angle, it seems miraculous that all *matadores* are not maimed or killed when attempting this difficult feat. It can be accomplished in three manners: the *matador* induces the bull to charge him, and to make the fatal thrust whilst standing still. This is called "receiving" *(recibir)* the charge. The second method consists of the reverse: the *matador* leaps forward to kill, *a volapie* as this variation is called. Thirdly, man and beast charge simultaneously, *a un tiempo* in taurine jargon.

Years ago, whilst in Mexico, I tried the first method on a dummy bull made of stuffed sacking, boards and sticks fixed to a wheelbarrow, but all my attempts to make my sword-thrust in the right place failed miserably And it must be borne in mind that, having taken no violent exercise, let alone been in mortal danger previous to making those futile attempts, I was as fresh as the proverbial daisy, and in front of me was only a stationary dummy, instead of a formidable beast with long sharp horns, not to overstress a critical public which forgives no error.

If a *matador* is unlucky (and, incidentally, also the bull), and in missing his aim gives the beast only a prick *(pinchazo),* most likely striking a bone, the public begins to voice its disapproval, and if the failure of killing neatly is repeated, perhaps three or four times, the voice of the people – which, it is said, is the voice of God – becomes so loud and menacing that when I saw bullfighters in such predicaments I could not help feeling sorry for them.

On one occasion, when a *matador* made a mess of the killing, the spectators raised such a storm of howls that I expected worse was about to happen, and all the while the bull charged the victim of this continued fury, whose nose was bleeding profusely. During the next attempt to find the right spot into which to thrust his sword, the bull got him fair and square in the mid-section of his body, but fortunately only with the forehead, with the result that the man was dragged out of the arena, completely "winded." His assistants came to his rescue in the nick of time, to entice away the bull with their capes, as the *matador* was lying prostrate on the ground. A substitute being permitted only in case of serious injury, after a few moments, when the unfortunate one had recovered sufficiently to walk half doubled up, he returned to the fray, eventually, to the accompaniment of cat-calls, booing and whistling to kill the beast.

If a *matador* finds the right place with the first thrust, the bull dies soon after, but often it happens otherwise. In such cases, if the animal is mortally wounded, in order to put it out of its misery, the *matador* asks an assistant to hand him a special kind of sword with which to pierce the spinal marrow at the back of his victim's head. If done properly, this causes instantaneous death. Dying bulls are also destroyed by an assistant (called *puntillero)* who does the same thing with a dagger. As soon as a bull is dead he is dragged out of the arena by a galloping team of mules bedecked with gay tassels and jingling bells. If he has put up a good fight, his last journey is made to the accompaniment of loud applause, the honour and glory going to the man who bred so valiant a beast. If the *matador* has done well, or surpassed himself, the ovation he receives is terrific. Whilst, followed by some of his attendants, he does a round of honour, hats, flowers, often even jackets, ladies' handbags and other articles are thrown into the ring. Keeping the flowers, the smiling *matador,* assisted by his followers, throws back the hats and other tokens of appreciation, and if a wine-skin is flung at his feet, to please his admirer he takes a swig out of it. Such ovations can go on for some time, and if the *matador's* performance has been exceptionally good, the spectators wave thousands of handkerchiefs, thus asking the president to give official recognition for skill and valour. If he agrees with the public, by displaying his handkerchief, he gives the order to present the *matador* with one ear of the bull, and if he merits it, with both ears. On rare occasions, if the *matador* has risen to giddy heights in the taurine art, besides the two ears he also receives the tail.

On an average, from the time a bull dashes into the arena, until he is dragged out, dead, some twenty minutes elapse, whereafter the second victim is let in, to be fought by another *matador.*

Detailed explanations concerning the intricacies, history and traditions connected with bullfighting would fill a volume. Therefore, trusting that the foregoing very much condensed details and descriptions have given the reader a fair and comprehensive idea about this ancient Spanish spectacle, in continuation I will refer briefly to another ancient taurine sport which has survived, and is practised occasionally in Spain, and, with slight variations also, in Portugal. The *rejoneo,* as it is called, dates back to the eighteenth century. (A *rejon* is a kind of poniard which, upon being thrust into the slight hump at the base of the bull's-neck, breaks off the staff to which it is fixed.) Whereas in Spain the few men (and very occasionally a woman) who practise this sport, wear the typical costume of cattle-men *(ganaderos),* i.e. short jackets, leather chaps *(zahones)* and wide-brimmed, flat-topped hats already described, in Portugal *rejoneadores* cling to the eighteenth century costume; three-cornered hat, long, flowing and richly embroidered Louis XI coat, high boots, and so on. Another differrence between the two forms of *rejoneo* is that in Spain the bull is always killed, whereas in Portugal his horns are padded, and there is no bloodshed. After a display of superb horsemanship and skill, when – in the Portuguese variant – the bull begins to tire, eight young men wrestle with him simultaneously, invariably subduing the beast in a few moments whereafter it is released. But to come to the Spanish *rejoneo.*

As a rule this is just an extra – a kind of *hors d'oeuvre* – to an ordinary bullfight, and only one animal is killed before the main show begins. Seated on a fiery highly-trained horse, with no one in the ring, the *rejoneador* begins by giving an exhibition of *haute école* riding, making his mount do fancy steps, glissades, and so on. When the bull is let into the arena, the rider gallops up to him, round him, away from him, and cleverly dodges when the bull charges or chases him, and at opportune moments the rider sticks darts into his antagonist's neck. The horse seems to be familiar with every trick of the dangerous sport, and therefore knows exactly how and when to keep out of harm's way. When the bull begins to tire, the rider dismounts to do the killing afoot, exactly in the same manner as in an ordinary bullfight.

And now a few words about the history of the sport, and a few general remarks concerning it and its evolution up to modern times.

Combats with men and bulls were common in Greece and Rome, and also, it is believed, in ancient Egypt. Nowadays, though bullfights are by no means the essence of Spanish life, they continue to attract large crowds, as is also the case in Mexico where successful *matadores* are public idols and earn vast sums of money. To a much lesser degree, the taurine art is also practised in the south of France and in several South American republics, though in some, such as the Argentine, Uruguay and Chile, bullfights have been prohibited for many years.

In the sixteenth century bulls were fought on horseback, and it was a sport exclusively for noblemen who were assisted by a few servants on foot. Those were the days of lancing *(alanzamiento),* of which the modern *rejoneo* is a modified survival. In the seventeenth century bullfighting became a profession, and during that period the modern style of lancing *(suerte de picar)* came into fashion. *Picadores* were called *varilagueros* (a word derived from *vara,* meaning "staff" or "pole"). Mounted on horseback, these "stars" of bullfights were assisted by lesser luminaries, who, as in the case of the servants in the sixteenth century, did their work afoot. Among them were the *banderilleros* who stuck darts into the bulls' necks, and the *chulos* whose duty it was to make themselves generally useful, especially so when a *varilarguero* was in danger of being hurt or killed. Once a bull was wounded so severely with his lance that but little fight was left in him, then one of the *chulos* had to kill him *(ramatar)*. At a later period, when the use of a small red cloth *(muleta)* came into fashion, and bulls had to be killed afoot with a sword *(espada)* or a rapier *(estoque)*, the new names of *matador* or *espada* came into use for the bullfighters who did the killing and whose general skill surpassed that of the others who acted as their assistants. In modern Spanish the general term for "bullfighter" is *torero*, not *toreador*. When Bizet wrote his opera, *Carmen*, he revived the old four-syllable word, *toreador* (to-re-a-dor), to fit in with the music. For the benefit of readers who know no Spanish, I repeat: in bullfighter's jargon which has come into current use, the words *matador* and *espada* mean the same thing; they stand for the "star" who does the killing of bulls.

As explained previously, fortunately, nowadays, the *picadores'* horses are protected with a kind of armoured mattress *(peto)* which almost eliminates the danger of suffering any other harm than knocks. During the several bullfights I witnessed in Spain, no horse came to any serious harm; in fact, four months after having made my first visit to the bullring in Barcelona, when I returned, the same two horses – a light-grey and a chestnut – were still being used by the *picadores.* The animals looked none the worse for the rough treatment to which they are subjected at least once per week. Formerly the goring of horses was a horrible sight to behold, and exceptionally strong and ferocious bulls frequently killed several. The following figures speak for themselves. In 1896, in 478 fights *(corridas)* 2,118 bulls were killed, and these accounted for 5,730 horses. For having introduced and made compulsory the protective *peto* I bless the memory of Primo de Rivera, and I sincerely hope that one of these days a mechanical device will take the place of the horses used by *picadores.* Unfortunately, as long as bulls must be killed in the manner prescribed by tradition, several pricks with the lance are necessary in order to weaken the strong, agile, and ferocious beasts, and to take some of the thrust out of their necks, for if this were not done, *matadores* would almost invariably be killed. Despite the *picadores'* efforts to make things safer for the *matadores,* accidents occur frequently, every now and again with fatal results. I have heard it said – with how much truth I do not know – that, taking bullfighters *en masse,* often more of them are in hospitals or recuperat-

ing from injuries, knocks and bruises than fit ones are available to go
into a ring at short notice.

Whenever I am asked if bullfighting is likely to be abolished some
day, my reply is a definite "No". For many years this ancient and
primitive sport has received a good deal of attention, both from the
foreign and Spanish press, but if a vote were taken, only a small
minority would vote for its suppression. Before casting stones at Spain
for cruelty, we must remember that in other countries blood-sports are
practised and favoured by many. In my carefully considered opinion,
the hunting of an inoffensive noble stag with a pack of blood-thirsty
hounds is much more cruel than a bullfight, in which the beast, blinded
by fury, does all the attacking until it is killed. *Toros de lidia* (fighting
bulls) are not just any vicious farm bulls, as many people believe. They
have been specially selected and bred for centuries, and to-day a good
one costs between twenty and twenty-five thousand *pesetas,* or between
£200 and £250.

It seems to me that as we "progress" we become more and more
brutal. For instance, I can't imagine thousands of savages flocking to
watch two men punch each other into a bleeding mass of pulp, until one
of them falls down unconscious, and paying considerable sums of
money to see such a spectacle. And yet, whenever an "important"
boxing match takes place in a civilized country, the arena is packed
with men and even women wearing the *dernier cri* of fashion, and the
press gives much space to the bout, which is even broadcast and
televised for the benefit of the masses who are unable to gain admittance to the arena. Such is the commercialized version of the "Noble
Art of Self-Defence," not to go into details about various aspects of
professional all-in wrestling. Whether one agrees with bullfighting or
not, it must be admitted that the commercial side of it does not lend
itself to the trickery, faking, and sometimes even gangsterism which is
often connected with professional boxing. A bull can't be bribed to
"pull" his "punches," or to fake being knocked out by his opponent (to
act as "rosin inspector", as a delightfully descriptive slang expression
calls it.). There is no possibility of betting on bullfights, and there is a
kind of competition only if two distinguished *matadores* perform *mano
a mano* (hand to hand), that is to say, fighting the bulls in turns as they
are let into the ring. And even then, it is only a rivalry of grace and
valour and of *tauromaquian* skill. No fare this for crooks, "twisters,"

"quitters," "framers," and all the other rabble with which modern prize-fighters have to contend. True, successful *matadores* have their hangers-on, but they are of a different type, just *vividores,* individuals who live on them.

At different times I have heard it said that bullfighting is falling into decadence, and that *matadores* are not what they used to be, that bulls are getting smaller and smaller, and that in some cases, prior to a fight, the tips of their horns are cut off and re-sharpened *(afeitado,* meaning "shaved"). I have it from good and reliable authority that this is done occasionally, if horns are exceptionally long and of a shape which would oblige the *matador* to stand back somewhat whilst making "passes."

Regarding decadence, I have an interesting booklet, presented to me by Sir William Davenhill, the British Vice-Consul in Granada. It was written by his father, who spent his boyhood in Seville and who re-visited the city later in life. Among other things, in his booklet, published in 1899, he says:

"*. . . Indeed, Spaniards of the old school speak in loud and unreserved criticism of this falling off in the character of the fiestas and ask contemptuously: Where are the Montes, the Cuchares, the Tatos of other days? Espadas, it is true, are still to be found, they will add, but where are the once-renowned matadores? Where are those men of iron who fought the maddened bulls and did not play merely with the weary, goaded, half-dying animal as nowadays; those bold fellows who entered the plaza after due confession and the making of their testaments in the neighbouring chapel, so conscious and determined were they of the peril they would run, or the victory or death which should await them? And thus extolling themselves with youthful recollections these old connoisseurs will exclaim: 'Que disparate!' What nonsense, we have no longer either bulls or bullfighters! We remember the time when it was no ordinary thing to see a bull rush round the ring with a couple of poor devils pinned to his horns; but nowadays what have we? 'Vaya! no hay toros ni toreros" our friends from behind the Pyrenees have made us chicken-hearted and daunted our old Spanish daring and valour!*"

Thus wrote Sir Charles Davenhill in 1899, and thus spoke old con-noisseurs on matters and conditions connected with *tauromaquia* a century ago. Little did they dream that their idols were to be followed by other *matadores* who surpassed them in skill, and whose daring and valour equalled that of any of their predecessors. Yes, there came the giants, Don Gayetano, the "perfect gentleman of the bullring" and intimate friend of Goya, the painter, "El Califa", "El Gallo," "Carancha," "Bombita" Vicente Pastor, Joselito, Belmonte and several others, and in very recent times the ill-fated Manolete, whose tragic death in 1948 I often heard lamented, and whose glories will be sung by many generations to come. So, where is that decadence some people talk about?

In Spain every year some three hundred bullfights *(Corridas de toros)* and 250 *novilladas* take place, which means that at least three thousand three hundred bulls are killed. In the former, big, strong and fully-grown bulls, between four and seven years old, are used, whereas in *novilladas* the beasts are younger, or perhaps slightly defective. *(Novillo* means a young bull or a steer.) All bullfighters begin their careers as *novilleros,* that is to say, as what might be described as already skilled apprentices who perform in *novilladas,* the ritual, rules and regulations of which are exactly the same as in *corridas de toros.* When a *matador* has distinguished himself in *novilladas,* and has been awarded a certain number of ears and tails, he is promoted: he becomes a *matador de toros* (killer of bulls).

How does a man become a bullfighter? As already explained, *toreros* begin their careers when they are boys. This is how it usually comes about. When a youngster finds himself bitten by the bullfighting "bug," he leaves his home to seek work on a ranch where fighting bulls are being bred. Often they have to walk far and wide until a *ganadero* (breeder) gives them a job, generally with no salary attached to it. Doing odd jobs, and looking after and handling bulls, if the boys are clever and observant, they learn much about the beasts' ways, habits and peculiarities. Sometimes, at night, on the sly, with their jackets or capes they try a few "passes" on a young beast, but their great day comes when during some village feast or celebration a *capea* is held; that is to say, a minor kind of bullfight. During such displays (without horses), mostly young bulls are used, and they are played with capes only, hence the word *capea.* The budding *toreros* have to take on any beast which is let into the barricaded village square in which many of these *capeas* take place, and sometimes it happens that a rather formidable one has to be dealt with. As novices receive no salary for risking their lives in entertaining the spectators, two of the boys, holding an extended cape between them, go among the public to collect money. This is called *pasar el guante* (passing the glove). If the performance has been good, sometimes they reap a fair reward, but as often as not, all the lads get are insults and rude jokes about their ability as bullfighters. If they are lucky, the local mayor or some rich person gives them a present, and, perhaps, a good meal thrown in. Better class *capeas* are run by bullfighters of some renown who perform in them, and if one of those apprentices is allowed to make a few "passes" with a cape, he thinks himself very honoured. The next rung up the long *tauromaquian* ladder is when a youngster qualifies to take part in steer-fights *(novilladas)* which take place at night. Horses are not used during such, nor in those of the next step forward; the minor *novilladas* which are held in daylight, usually in the early evening. Sleeping "rough" and often walking far with tightened belts, these young enthusiasts go from one *capea* or *novillada* to another, frequently to find that there is no room for them on the bill. If a skilful one among them catches the eye of some established bullfighter, and he is taken under his wing, he has a good chance of making his mark. However, two or three successful seasons are necessary before he is allowed to take part in first-class *novilladas,* and even then only as second or third string to the fiddle, in the person of the "star" *matador.* In order to reach these giddy heights, in many cases much "wire-pulling" is necessary; newspaper men who report on taurine matters, critics and others must have their palms "greased" to give the young aspirant good boosts, but, last and most important, the hopeful rising "star" must please the merciless critical public. How very similar to what has to be done by actors, singers and other artists, and not infrequently by playwrights and even authors!

During my conversations with members of the bullfighting fraternity I heard a great deal about the ins and outs connected with their professions; how relatives and friends hang on to a successful *matador,* how they have to hand out free tickets even to the families of the gentlemen of the Press, and how much he is expected to give to all sorts of charities, and so on. It is the old, old story: nothing succeeds like success. When a man succeeds, those who call him lucky expect a great deal from him, and they are the self-same ones who formerly did not care a fig if the "lucky" one starved. Such is human nature.

Until a *novillero* obtains what is called the "alternative" *(alternativa)* to an established *matador,* he continues to depend on the goodwill of those of the spectators who give him money. Obtaining the *alternativa* means when a novice is allowed to take his turn, killing one or possibly two bulls during a fight. Until then, he performs under contract and for a fixed salary, and is called an *aficionado,* meaning an amateur. This is the great moment eagerly awaited by all young *novilleros.* The *matador de toros* under whose wing the lucky one has reached this important stage of his career, steps into the arena to hand over to the youngster the *muleta* (small red cloth fixed to a stick) and the sword. This done, he embraces him midst the applause of the public, whereafter the budding "star" goes up to the bull, in order to make the final "passes" before killing him.

As we have already seen, there is a great difference between a *matador* and a *matador de toros;* and. even when a man qualifies for the latter title, there are several groups before a limited few rise to the very top.

Let us start at the bottom of the bullfighter's ladder.

In the year 1950 there were only forty really recognized and established *matadores* (including *matadores de toros)* in Spain. Here are the figures in their respective groups:

Novilleros (Matadores of young or slightly defective bulls): Group 2 – a great number; Group 1: 10.

Matadores de toros: Group 3: 10; Group 2: 3; Group 1: 8.

Special Group: 9 (these are the "big shots" or, as it were, the *prima donnas* among the bullfighters.)

The *Sindicato de Toreros* – a kind of Bullfighters' Union – in Madrid decides when a candidate is to be given promotion, or when for some reason or other disciplinary action has to be taken against one of its members.

And now; how much does a *matador de toros* earn? If he belongs to the coveted special group, anything between 125,000 and 150,000 *pesetas* per afternoon, and in exceptional cases, such as Manolete, an additional percentage on gate-money.

As mentioned previously, fighting bulls are of a special breed, but apart from this, *ganaderos* (breeders) produce different strains. Though most of the specimens are black, there can be a great variety of colours among which the dark shades predominate. Many of these magnificent though vicious-looking beasts – which are crossbred descendants of the now extinct European aurochs – reminded me of wild boars. With their thick necks and the slight hump *(morillo)* on tremendously powerful shoulders and deep chests, their backs slope down somewhat towards the well-muscled hind-quarters. Their broad foreheads, formidable horns and lustrous eyes are awe-inspiring at any time, and when the beasts are in a fury they become terrifying. The loud vicious snort of a fighting bull, as his rapid charge culminates in a wicked thrust of the horns into which he puts all his weight and strength, is something to weaken even the stoutest of hearts. The fighting of a really fierce and dashing bull is much easier and less dangerous than that of one who, on the surface, shows less ferocity and eagerness to attack. The former charges in a straight line and "through," whereas the apparently tamer one thinks – and therefore hesitates before taking the offensive. This obliges the bullfighter to go close to him in order to induce the beast to charge, and when this happens, the onrush is short, premeditated, and frequently not in straight line, but made at the man, instead of at his cape. Apart from the danger of such a charge – especially so if the animal happens to be one of those rare "ambidextrous" ones which horns sideways in either direction – the *matador* finds it difficult to perform with elegance, or to do fancy work with his cape. In other words, in such cases the man is constantly on the defensive, whereas if he is fighting a really vicious and dashing bull, he can display the best and most showy tricks of his repertoire. Therefore it will be seen that in order to appreciate the art of bullfighting and its many intricacies, the first essential is that a spectator must know something about bulls and their physical and psychological reactions under many circumstances and conditions. Experts in the taurine art have told me that not more than one among a thousand spectators has that knowledge, though many of them pretend to know all about *tauromaquia,* especially so when they assemble in *cafés.* On such occasions young "bloods" can be seen elegantly demonstrating with their overcoats how certain "passes" should be made, and late into the night they vociferate, every one of those gallant *café* bullfighters delighted with the sound of his own voice.

The nervous tension and emotions experienced during bullfights are so many and strong, that when a *corrida* comes to an end, and the spectators rise from their seats to return home, they are utterly exhausted. In connection with this, before concluding this somewhat lengthy chapter, I will recount a Spanish anecdote which gives an excellent idea of how a bullfight affects spectators.

One Sunday afternoon a man strutted down a street, evidently pleased with himself and the world in general. "Hello!" a passing friend shouted, "Where are you going?" "*A los toros!*" ("To the bulls!" meaning bullfight) the happy one replied, waving a hand as he proceeded on his way. Late that evening, another friend of that same man saw him crawl towards his home, as if in a state of collapse. "What's the matter with you? Where have you been?" the friend asked. "At the bullfight," the weary one replied in a mournful tone of voice.

CHAPTER 9

SEVILLE – RETURN TO MADRID

The Seville Fair had already lasted four days, but the animation and merry-making, instead of diminishing, increased. There was so much to be seen and done that I was constantly on the move, and often so tired and sleepy that I almost envied loafers and beggars who dozed in the balmy sunshine, sitting on the ground with their backs against the wall of a church. However, towards evening, my feeling of lassitude always disappeared, and I did not care if I was up and about until the early hours of morning.

The gipsy cattle fair had such an attraction for me that I returned to it to have another good look round, and to listen to the haggling and bartering. A tiny shaggy donkey which had an abnormally big head and long ears, stood, oblivious of its surroundings, half asleep, nodding its head and occasionally blinking at this our crazy world with large philosophical eyes. Its owner was a young. man who evidently had a sense of humour, for on a rusty sheet of tin he had painted with whitewash:

> *Soy el Guerra,*
> *El reldmpago soy,*
> *A donde me llaman voy.*

Perhaps the following is an acceptable translation of this doggerel:

www.aimetschiffely.org

> I am the charger,
> The lightning am I,
> Whencever they call me
> Thither I fly.

With the placard hanging down one of its flanks, the poor little beast looked like a kind of armoured monstrosity, but what amused me even more was what was added beneath the verse: TO BE SOLD OR EXCHANGED FOR A MOTOR-CYCLE.

Of course, during my second visit several cunning gipsies tried to make me buy their animals, which they praised sky-high, all being – according to their respective owners – the finest beasts ever bred in Spain.

On the amusement fairground I saw a little interlude which both surprised and amused me. Leaning against one of the numerous flag-poles, a young gallant was talking to a most attractive *señorita* who was dressed in the becoming costume of the region, with its colourful many-tiered skirt. The pair looked so romantic in this picturesque setting, that I hoped to be able to take a photograph of them on the sly, lest they pose or become self-conscious, and thus spoil the picture, or run away as the three young ladies had done outside the cathedral in Cordova. Whilst preparing my camera, I walked up and down near them, pretending to be interested in a group of young ladies who danced in one of the *casetas* (tents). Encouraged by all the gaiety, music and clicking of castanets that was going on near him, and also by the coquettish manner in which the *señorita* acted, her wooer became so "fresh" that he chucked her under the chin. This playful act so infuriated the fair one that, with flashing eyes and a rude exclamation, she aimed a high kick at the offender, who was fortunate to be able to bend back quickly enough to avoid the tip of her shoe from making contact with his chin. With her flowing flounced skirts flying up, showing a pair of shapely legs and neat ankles, that *Sevillana* gave as neat a high kick as ever I have seen a dancer execute on any stage.

Unknown to me, a friend of mine had also watched this little incident, and when I asked him to which class of Sevillian Society the young virago might belong, he told me that he happened to know her, and that she worked in the famous tobacco factory. Strange coincidence this; for the Carmen of Bizet's opera originated in the self-same establishment, the *fábrica de tabacos* in which hundreds of *cigarreras* are engaged in the manufacture of cigars, cigarettes and snuff.

Another amusing thing happened to me whilst on my way to make one of the several visits I made to the cathedral. As I walked along one of the main thoroughfares which lead to it, a woman came rushing out of a kiosk, screaming murder. Wondering what was amiss, I stopped to see if I could be of assistance. *"Ay, señor, ay, señor* !" the agitated woman shouted to me. "What a horror – a mouse!"

Assisted by a man and several street urchins who appeared, probably hoping that murder was being committed, I entered the kiosk and after having poked among papers with a broomstick, caused the mouse to scurry out of the door where the eager and noisy urchins killed it. Tranquillity having been restored, I continued my way towards the nearby cathedral, in the solemn and impressive mystery of which I soon forgot my recent adventure with poor Mousie. About the cathedral and its marvellous Gothic architecture I will say but little, for detailed descriptions are available in many excellent technical books and even in ordinary guide books for tourists. However, I put on record one peculiar thing I saw in this amazing temple with its cyclopean arches and pillars, beautiful stained glass windows and many other treasures. Who is responsible for it I know not, but at one end of the main nave, high up on the wall, is a huge ugly clock, of the type one sees in some railway stations; just a large dial, black hands, and hours and minutes marked in black. What a horrid defacement of an architectural and artistic masterpiece!

During a drive to several picturesque villages and small towns near Seville we passed a new settlement of prefabricated houses which are very different from any I had seen in England and in other parts of Spain. About ten feet high, they are round, and built in the shape of large igloos, and to make the resemblance more exact, their exteriors are whitewashed. In this region are large symmetrically planted orchards in which the famous Seville oranges are grown.

What enchanted me most in Seville was to stroll through the narrow streets of the old sector of the city where some streets and lanes are so narrow that they have not been desecrated by wheels. There, the life of the south can be seen at its best. Itinerant and noisy vendors of fruit, fish, pots and pans, and household necessities, shout out their wares, and here and there squats or lurks a professional beggar, ready to mumble the stereotype *"Que Dios se la pague"* (May God repay you), if you give him or her alms. In little squares or *plazoletas* are assembled groups of men, talking, talking, talking. If a graceful *señorita* passes by coquettishly, drawing their gaze, after she has disappeared round the corner of some narrow alleyway, they begin an animated conversation regarding her charms.

At night, my favourite walk was through the old Jewry, where, once upon a time, Jews were strictly confined and separated from the Gentiles. In that, nowadays, most picturesque and romantic corner of the town, alongside the walled-in gardens of the old alcazar, is a shady park and two or three small quaint squares. Some of the snow-white houses, with their balconies and artistic wrought-iron grilles in front of windows, are gems of their kind, and the street lights – also with wrought-iron adornments – add to the general atmosphere of romance. Once, when I strolled through that neighbourhood in the moonlight, my footsteps reverberated through the mysterious stillness of the narrow alley which I followed. The gate which gives access to the Jewry was locked, but the night-watchman must have heard me approaching, for just as I reached the gate he appeared on its other side and offered to open it with a huge key he carried. When I apologized for having disturbed him at so late an hour, he replied that it was a pleasure to be of service, and with this unlocked and swung open the heavy iron gate, presently to guide me through the picturesque labyrinth. Naturally, for this service he expected a tip, which he received with the politeness and dignity typical of men of his class in Spain.

Whenever I wandered through the old sector of Seville or sat in one of those quaint *plazoletas,* I pictured famous men of the past who had trodden the self-same cobblestones centuries before me. Among those giants was the great and incomparable Hernan Cortez, who, after having conquered Mexico, lived in Seville, neglected and almost forgotten, until he died in 1547. In my mind's eye I could see him wend his way through the narrow streets, probably thinking about his voyages across the seas in tiny ships, his landing in Mexico with only 110 mariners, 503 soldiers and 16 horses, to attempt to wrest the mighty Aztec empire from Montezuma, its ruler. Many times, whilst perambulating, he must have remembered the time when dissension and all but mutiny broke out among his men, for who can blame them for having considered an attempt to penetrate into that mysterious empire as a reckless adventure amounting to suicide? Sadly, Cortez must have half shaken, half nodded his head, when he recalled how, in order to make retreat impossible for his men, he set fire to five of his ships, leaving only one. Perhaps at such times he repeated to himself the momentous speech he made to his men on that occasion: "If there be any so craven as to shrink from the glorious enterprise, let them go home, in God's name. There is still one vessel left, so let them take that to go and tell how they deserted their commander and their comrades!"

And yet, in spite of his fantastic conquest of Mexico and all the wealth and glory Cortez brought to king and country, as in the case of many other great men who lived before and after him, his services were forgotten by those who reaped the chief benefits from them. Some years after Cortez died, his bones were taken to a convent in a little town named Castilleja de la Cuesta, near Seville, where they were placed in a convent later to be transferred to Mexico.

A century after Cortez died, Murillo, the great painter of scriptural and religious pictures, must often have meditated in the same streets and *plazoletas,* for before painting a divine subject he always fasted to prepare himself for, the task.

Legend has it that Seville was founded by the classic navigator, Hercules, but what we do know definitely is that many centuries ago those regions were occupied by the Venetians, and that the long rivalry between Rome and Carthage was followed by the Moorish conquest and tenure which lasted eight centuries. But lest I weary the reader with too much history and asides concerning great personalities, I will proceed with the story about my travels.

Though it is a great blessing to have friends who are anxious and keen to entertain one, sooner or later their hospitality makes one feel uncomfortable or even embarrassed, especially so when, as was the case with me, it is impossible to reciprocate the many favours received. Therefore, in a way, I was glad when the time came to return to Madrid where I had left my motor-cycle, for it would make me independent, and with it I should be able to go to many places which are difficult or even impossible to reach in a car.

Early one morning, Julio and Rosemary picked me up in their car, and soon after we drove over the same highway we had followed on our journey down to Seville. On our way, as we approached La Guardia – the miserable village with cave dwellings where begging children and women had all but assaulted us – Julio turned round to ask me if I wanted to take another photograph, in which case, he added with a wry smile, he would be glad to stop for a while. Needless to say, he drove through the place at high speed, lest the hordes of starvelings sally forth to make another attack on us. Late that night we reached Madrid, and for the first time in a week I was able to have a good and much needed rest.

When my friends returned to Barcelona in their car, I was left more or less alone, and thus able to have a good look round Madrid, and to visit art galleries and museums. The famous Prado with its wonderful collection of pictures was my first port of call, and whenever I had two or three hours to spare I returned there to gaze at masterpieces, of which there are so many that it would take a lifetime to study them properly. Thanks to letters of introduction I met a number of distinguished people who went out of their way to introduce me to others, and to make my stay in their city as pleasant and interesting as possible. Wherever I went – not only in Madrid but everywhere in that friendly and hospitable land – I found the same eagerness on the part of people to be of assistance to me, to show me little-known places of interest, and to supply me with every kind of information, academic or otherwise, according to the leanings of my willing teachers. In the Anglo-American Club I met several old friends I had not seen for years, and I made new ones, among them two or three who have lived in Madrid so long that they qualify to be called old *Madrileños*. To my surprise I discovered – not only in Madrid, but also in other cities – that among the British and American residents who have lived in Spain for a long time, there are many who have become rabid bullfight enthusiasts. Some of them have made such a study of the taurine art, and have acquired such a knowledge of its intricacies, that even professsional bullfighters recognize them as great experts.

It is remarkable that despite its unfavourable position and general conditions for a country so extensive as Spain (nearly two and a half times the size of the United Kingdom) Madrid is its metropolis, and that the city is one of the finest in Europe. As mentioned previously, it is situated over two thousand feet above sea-level, on a rolling semi-barren plateau. Formerly the small river Manzanares provided the city with water, but nowadays it is brought through a pipe-line from a place about twenty miles distant.

In the tenth century, on the site on which Madrid's royal palace stands to-day, was a Moorish fort, Madjrit. The object of this outpost was to check the advance of the Castilians who were endeavouring to re-conquer those regions. Close on a century after the Moors had been expelled from Spain, and the various kingdoms were united under Philip II, he had to choose a capital for the newly created "Las Españas." Despite the fact that by that time Madjrit (now Madrid) had grown into a small and most unattractive town, in 1560 the king declared it a capital. This he did partly for diplomatic reasons, and also because the place of his choice was situated near the geographical centre of the now united kingdom. It was only in the late eighteenth century that the town began to grow and improve, and even much later it was generally considered to be Europe's dirtiest and most unattractive capital. With the passing of time, however, and thanks to hard work and artistic taste, Madrid grew and developed into a fine modern city.

Owing to its lofty situation, it has a changeable and at times even treacherous climate. In winter it can be bitterly cold, and in summer the heat is often so unbearable that those of the *Madrileños* who have time, and the necessary money, flee to cooler regions, of which there are many in Spain, several of them quite near. The changes in temperature can be so sudden and great that according to an old saying "the air is so keen and subtle that when a north-west wind springs up, it can kill a man, while it will not blow out a candle." The old English saying "never cast a clout until May is out," has a humorous but significant variant in Spain, where people say: "Until the fortieth of May do not take off your overcoat" *(Hasta el citarenta de Mayo no te quites el sayo)*.

During the Civil War, some parts of the city were badly damaged or even completely destroyed, but to-day only a very few traces of that tragedy can be seen, many new houses and huge blocks of modern buildings having replaced the old ones. With visible pride a professor showed me the University City which is nearing completion, and I was amazed by the speed and vigour with which new houses are being built.

Spaniards, especially those who live in cities, would be mystified if one translated for them the old English saying about what "early to bed and early to rise" is supposed to do to a man. Naturally, they are all for being healthy, wealthy and wise, but in addition to these three blessings they want to ENJOY life. Unlike masses of "good" and "industrious" citizens in many other countries I know, who are determined not to let life pass without doing business, the average Spaniard's instinctive urge is not to let life pass without enjoying life. If it is true that sleep is the brother of death, this possibly explains why Spaniards put off going to bed at what we call a "reasonable" hour. In their case, before midnight would be most "unreasonable" and a waste of life, but, being only human, and therefore needing a certain amount of sleep, they very wisely take it in two instalments: a good *siesta* after lunch (which is taken between 2 and 4 p.m.) and the second instalment at any time between midnight and sunrise. It must not be thought that this applies only to the rich or leisured class, for even among working people – tradesmen, clerks and peasants – midnight is *temprano* (early) for retiring to bed for the night. In cities, whilst most of the well-to-do citizens take their time in rising in the morning, their servants, the same as labourers, traders and street vendors, are up and about early, and most of them make up for lost sleep during *siesta* time.

In warm climates much is to be said for the institution of the *siesta.* Labourers rise early to toil hard until they have their midday meal, whereafter they pass the hottest hours sleeping, to resume work refreshed, and to carry on until 8 or 9 p.m. After that, they stay up until well after midnight, enjoying life according to their tastes, inclinations and means.

In connection with *siestas,* in Madrid I saw something that amused me greatly. When London taxi-drivers cover the meters of their vehicles with a glove or a piece of some material, this means that the taxi is not for hire, or that the driver is away, perhaps taking refreshment or having a rest. For the same purpose, in Madrid taxi-drivers have a fair-sized piece of cardboard on which is printed *DESCANSO,* meaning "Rest." Once, as I walked along an avenue, in the shade of a spreading tree a taxi was parked, in the passenger compartment of which lolled the driver, snoring rhythmically, his feet protruding from the open window of the vehicle whilst on the windscreen hung a piece of cardboard on which was printed in large letters, the word *DESCANSO.*

The modest but immaculately clean and very comfortable *pensión* in which I stayed, was situated in a side-street, leading to the Gran Via, the fashionable main thoroughfare of Madrid. Every morning I was awakened by throaty cries of street vendors and hawkers, and, above all, by loud annoying tappings. Wondering what they signified and what caused them, on my second day in the *pensión,* I got out of bed and went to the window to investigate. The mystery was solved almost immediately, for upon looking across the narrow street, I saw maid-servants, busy beating carpets and rugs which were hung over the rails of balconies. Later I was told that according to a municipal regulation this must be done before 8.30 a.m.

After a simple breakfast, consisting of coffee, roll, butter and jam, I usually set out to do what in American slang is so descriptively called "rubber-necking;" to watch people, to indulge in "window-shopping", and to become acquainted with the city, or to gaze at some of its many treasures and things of interest. In the early morning, at many street corners are stands where the ubiquitous hot fritters *(churros)* are sold. Everywhere women can be seen scrubbing the floors of *cafés* or doorsteps, most of them singing as they work. This is the time when maid-servants and cooks return home with baskets filled with food-stuffs they have bought at the market.

One morning, as I strolled along observing things, a female voice coming from behind me made me stop. "Pardon, sir," a servant, who was carrying a basket filled with vegetables and fruit, said to me, "there is a piece of thread on your shoulder." Having picked it off, she unfolded a snow-white handkerchief and with it brushed off the back of my jacket some fluff which must have fallen on me from some window. "Now, that's much better," she said with a smile. "Pardon me, sir, for having disturbed you," and with this she continued on her way.

In the shops people are equally obliging and polite. On several occasions when I went into one to ask for something they had not in stock, the assistant came to show me the way to some other establishment where they had what I wanted. I could give many similar examples of politeness and willingness to oblige; but yet, as will be seen, under different circumstances, the self-same people act very differently. Far be it from me to suggest that only Spaniards have this other side to their characters, and that it is a national characteristic, but as, in their case, the contrast can be so big, I could not help noticing it.

Until about eleven o'clock in the morning there is not much movement in the fashionable centre of Madrid, of which the Gran Via and Calle Alcala (derived from the Moorish *al-Kalah,* "The castle") are the favourites among the *élite*, wealthy and otherwise. Especially in the former avenue, on sunny days, the sidewalks are packed with a throng of slow-moving idlers who chatter away as if the fate of the universe depended on the fluency of their tongues. *Cafés* are filled with men and women sipping *aperitivos* and eating *tapas* (snacks). The usual delicacies are *calamares* (squids), *mariscos* (a kind of shellfish) and *langostinos* (crayfish). The last are favourites among many clients, some of whom devour enormous quantities, throwing the shells on the floor to be swept up by the waiters. These *tapas* are not regular meals, but just a kind of *hors d'oeuvres* before lunch, after which the centre of the city is dead and deserted, even the shops being closed until 4 p.m.

The centre of the city comes to life once more in the evening, but he who is in a hurry does well to keep away from the slow-moving mass of humanity. At such times even the politest *Madrileño* and shop assistant who wishes to get somewhere quickly, will elbow his way through the crowd, or gruffly push one off the sidewalk, without bothering to apologize. When traffic congestion is at its highest and worst, it is a treat to watch and listen to what is going on. At pedestrian crossings of the main streets, people assemble like sheep until the green light and the clanging of automatic bells give the signal to cross. Simultaneously, policemen blow whistles, wave arms and sometimes shout at motorists or pedestrians who have displeased them in some manner. What most of these officers of law and order would do without the aid of their whistles and arms I cannot imagine. "From Madrid to heaven, and in heaven a little window to look at Madrid," an old saying goes *(De Madrid al cielo y en el cielo una ventanica [3]para mirar a Madrid)*. Personally, I feel that it would be much more interesting and entertaining to listen to Madrid, for there the art of conversation continues to flourish. If a person has artistic inclinations, and appreciates pictorial art, he or she can get more than a glimpse of heaven by going to the Prado, and if intelligent or amusing conversation is sought, Madrid's innumerable taverns *(tascas)* are the ideal places to find it. Whereas the *élite*, the wealthy and the ubiquitous swells prefer the expensive *cafés* along the Gran Via, artists,

---

[3] In Castile most diminutives end in "*iea* ", or "*ieo* ", instead of the usual Spanish "*ita*" and "*ito*". Thus *ventanita,* (little window) becomes *ventanica,* and *burro* (little donkey) *burrico.*

intellectuals and others who want full value for their money, and who do not care for "show," assemble in *tascas*.

In English towns and cities, licensing hours, prohibitive taxation on alcoholic drinks, and general conditions of living have done away with the last vestiges of old-fashioned taverns and tavern talk, made immortal by Dickens and other great authors. This, as I see it, will prove to be a great and serious loss to English art and literature. Did not Shakespeare discuss and write some of his plays in a certain tavern?

The *tasca* is the home from home for Spanish artists and authors, for in such places good company is always to be found, and a cheap meal can be obtained at almost any time, day or night. Some of these establishments have the atmosphere of wine cellars about them. Along the walls are lined up huge barrels filled with different kinds of wine, from the ceiling hang hams, smoked sausages and similar foodstuffs. In some *tascas* the wine is kept in stout torpedo-shaped earthenware vats, called *cubos*. Between eight and ten feet in height, they look imposing, standing in a row. Besides various kinds of shellfish, a great variety of *hors d'oeuvre* is served at almost any time, and at much more reasonable prices than in fashionable *cafés* or bars, and the food is less than half the price. In such places I met several famous Spanish artists and writers, with whom I sat conversing over glasses of wine until the early hours of morning. None of them over-indulged in anything, save, perhaps, in one or two cases when a speaker shouted too loudly in trying to drive home some point over which there was some disagreement. When one bears in mind that it is a rare thing for two Spaniards to see eye to eye – especially when it comes to political or artistic matters – it is not surprising that occasionally *tascas* can be noisy places. One of the things that struck me in all of them was the friendliness and good cheer of their owners and of the waiters or servants. Though for willingness to oblige, Spanish – especially Galician – servants are by far the best I have seen during my travels through many parts of the world, in a sense they are not servile. Born democrats, and possessed of a strong feeling of personal pride, they do not feel inferior to those for whom they work, or whom they attend. In spite of this, however, they are not "uppish," but merely behave in a delightful friendly manner. No matter who or how famous regular clients may be, they are treated almost as if they were members of the tavern proprietor's family. It is not uncommon for the boss, the waiters and sometimes even the women or girls who are busy cooking or dealing with plates and dishes, to join in a conversation held by their guests. I often saw the boss or a waiter stand near the circle of talkers, and every now and again make a statement, crack a joke or even vehemently contradict something that was said.

Before I left London to visit Spain, friends – among them several Spaniards – told me terrible stories about concentration camps, dungeons filled with political prisoners, daily executions of anti-Francoites, and about spies lurking everywhere, listening to conversations. Needless to say, my informants were opposed to the Franco regime, and some of them had lived in exile since the Civil War. During my travels I met a great many people – high and low, educated and otherwise – who hate the very name of Franco. Taking a cross-section of what I gathered from them regarding ruthless oppression, I came to the conclusion that what I heard prior to visiting Spain, and also since, is grossly exaggerated. No doubt, immediately after the Civil War, the victors imprisoned thousands of their vanquished enemies, and executed many, and until some sort of law and order was restored, Franco and his men ruled with an iron hand. Laws, especially if they are full of loop-holes, give unscrupulous citizens and "twisters" many excellent opportunities to enrich themselves, and this inevitably leads to corruption, with which Spain has been rife for many generations; in fact, so much so that it has become part of the national life. However, in spite of this, it must be said, nay, emphasized, that as far as corruption and dishonesty are concerned, Spaniards are not hypocritical. The more enterprising among them are much too proud to go in for "under-the-counter" business. They are so sure of themselves and of their friends in high official circles that they operate in broad daylight. *Estraperlo* is a word one hears constantly and everywhere throughout Spain. I do not know if the Spanish Academy has passed it to be added to the rich vocabulary of Cervantes' language. If not, on the merit of its daily use, *estraperlo* richly deserves this honour. The strange-sounding word has an interesting origin and history. It is a kind of compound of three names – *Strauss, Perez* and *Lerous.* Some little time before the Civil War broke out, a new law was passed, prohibiting gambling in casinos. Then, one day, an enterprising man named Strauss arrived in San Sebastian from Holland. The luxurious casinos of the famous seaside resort had been closed for some time, but Herr Strauss had an idea for re-opening them, and at the same time of bringing a steady flow of wealth into his pockets. Instead of roulette and baccarat, he had a new game which did not figure among those prohibited by the new anti-gambling law. Joined by Alejandro Lerous, then the chief of the Republican party, and a certain Perez, he made great efforts to have his new game introduced, but eventually the scheme failed. Spaniards find it difficult or even impossible to pronounce words that begin with two consonants, such as "sp" or "st." Thus, for example, "street" they pronounce "estreet", and "snow" becomes "esno". Therefore, when it came to the foreign name Strauss, it became Estrauss. The first two syllables, "Es-tra" were adopted for the beginning of this new slang word, and the names Perez and Lerous, concocted into "perlo", were added to it, thus making *estraperlo*. To-day this word is the cousin of the American "bootleg" and of its more conventional English "black market goods." Contraband smuggled into Spain also comes under the category of *estraperlo*.

Rationing, though at one time officially introduced, never worked with the proud and undisciplined Spaniards. No regimentation, registration and queues for them. Those who have money buy cars, petrol, tobacco, meat, bread, foreign currency or anything they want *estraperlo*. For instance, although the sale of white flour is prohibited, in windows of high-class cake and pastry shops are displayed rows and stacks of delicacies which are openly advertised as having been made with white flour. How come to be there most of the luxurious cars and limousines one sees in Madrid and in all large Spanish cities? Of course, as in other countries, there is the fair sprinkling of automobiles with the "CD" plate, for diplomats must have their luxuries. According to a Spanish joke "CD" stands for *Contrabandista Distinguido* – Distinguished Smuggler. Then there are the masses of other cars one sees everywhere in Spain; those with the "PMM" and "ET" plates. The former letters stand for *"Parque Militar Motorizado"* (Military Motor Pool) and the latter for *"Ejercito Territorial"* – Territorial Army. There are also jokes about the meaning of the letters of those two plates, "PMM" being said to mean *"Para Mi Mujer"* (For My Wife) and "ET" *"Ella Tambien"* (She – or The Other – as Well). How the mass of official cars come to be there needs no explanation, and in the case of the vast majority of the others the answer is simple: they are *estraperlo*. "Elementary, my dear Watson." And who cares or worries? In Spain, no one. Though petrol is rationed for all save tourists, high-up Government officials and, of course, military "shots" of fair calibre, where do the masses of motorists find the extra petrol which enables them to drive every day, and all day long, if they choose to do so? To this even Dr. Watson would have the answer: they pay the extra, and any filling station or garage supplies them with all the *estraperlo* petrol they wish for.

But to return to Madrid, and to where I side-tracked in mentioning the rumours I heard in London regarding spies who are supposed to lurk everywhere, listening to conversations.

One day a well-known and socially prominent Spaniard invited me to dine with him in a fashionable restaurant. As the two of us sat, talking after the meal, my host told me that although he had fought against the "Reds" before Franco came on the scene, he detested him. As my interlocutor thundered away, I felt hotter and hotter under the collar, expecting that the two of us would be arrested at any moment. "Tell me," I asked during a short lull in this storm of abuse, "don't you ever get yourself into trouble for shouting as you are doing now?"

"Oh, very much so," he replied, roaring with laughter. "I have had to pay three big fines, and once I was locked up for six months; but that was some few years ago. Nowadays they don't take much notice, and, furthermore, since then I have pulled in my horns considerably."

"Heavens!" I exclaimed, "they must have been very long and sharp in those days."

The favourite point of reunion for bullfighters and people connected with the sport is at the crossing of Calle Sevilla and Alcalá. There, every day at noon, and again at night, *matadores, banderilleros, picadores* and others assemble to talk about their business or to seek employment. Almost every man one sees in a *café*, situated at one of the corners, is – or tries to be – in the profession. Then there are the usual hangers-on who come to get a cup of coffee or a cigar for nothing, and besides such mostly witty and pleasant parasites, there are the inevitable hero-worshippers who hover about, hoping to get a close view of their idols, or to listen in to their conversation.

One morning, whilst on my way to the animated market called the *Rastro* where knick-knacks, frippery and many rubbishy articles are sold, I was surprised to see a great number of bookstalls in the streets, including the fashionable Gran Via. Among the books for sale were beautifully bound *de luxe* editions, some of which whetted my appetite. Seeing me gaze at some of the volumes, a well-dressed and intelligent-looking man who ran one of these stalls told me not to be shy, to pick up any book I wished and to examine it more closely.

"Before doing so," I said, "I must warn you that I can't afford to make any purchases."

"Never mind," the man replied, "I see that you are a visitor from abroad, and I quite understand, but since you are interested in books, please pick out and handle any you like. That's what they are here for, though, naturally, I hope to sell as many as possible."

Wondering why on that particular day there were bookstalls in so many streets where formerly I had seen none, I asked the vendor if there was any particular reason for this. "Yes, *señor,*" he replied, "to-day is the *Fiesta del Libro* (Feast of the Book). You see, to-morrow is April 23rd, the day on which Cervantes died, but as the date happens to fall on a Sunday, we are holding the annual *fiesta* to-day." "How strange," he continued, "that England's and Spain's two geniuses should have died on the very same day and in the very same year, namely, one thousand six hundred and sixteen – Cervantes at the age of sixty-nine and Shakespeare at the age of fifty-two."

My memory for dates is lamentably bad, but in order to hide my ignorance, I agreed that, indeed, this was a very strange coincidence, and then began my browsing.

Near the centre of the city, in a side-street through which I often passed, is a day-time shrine, the only one of its kind in Madrid. To judge by the shape of its construction, once upon a time it must have been a small shop, the front part of which was partially demolished to be fitted with an iron grille, through which one sees an altar with its array of burning candles. At night the place is closed, large wooden shutters hiding the interior from the view of passers-by. During the day-time, mostly elderly and middle-aged women of the poor class stop to peep through the grille and to mutter a quick prayer before proceeding on their way. The facial expressions of some of these worshippers, as they gaze at the altar through the iron bars, reminded me of paintings of some of the great masters. Almost invariably the women looked worried or distressed, and some shed tears as they seemed to be asking for divine help.

On one occasion, as I stood nearby, watching the comings and goings of such supplicants, a woman who had stopped for a few moments, resumed her walk, leading a small ragged boy by the hand. "*Mamita,*" he asked her as the two passed near me, "how many gods are there?" "Why ask me again?" the mother said, shaking the boy by the arm with some impatience. "I told you before: one." "What ?Only one for all these people?" the child piped, looking at the crowd of passers-by with big mystified eyes.

The only times I was thoroughly bored in Madrid was when friends invited me to have meals with them in some of the luxurious "first-class" hotels, which were exactly the same as those in London, New York, Mexico City, Paris, Rome, Buenos Aires and all over the world where guests expect and demand the same luxuries! In such places one sees the same people, wearing the same clothes and having identical manners and mannerisms. All sip the same cocktails and eat the same food, all the while acting and looking as if they were about to fall asleep with boredom. Why some people travel all over the globe – most of them for pleasure, I suppose – when they can have the same surroundings and tedium at home, is beyond my comprehension. However, every man to his own tastes. After all, it would be a dull world if all of us had the same, and if I never saw people who appear to be bored with everything life offers to them, perhaps I would not realize how lucky I am in being able to enjoy even little things.

The *pensión* (boarding-house) in which I stayed, offered enough material of human interest to satisfy me, especially so whilst eating meals there. The cooking was excellent, the servants obliging and always cheerful, and the guests a very mixed lot, all very friendly. Of course, there were the inevitable flies in the ointment, especially as far as a few of the more or less permanent guests were concerned, who had had ample time to get on one another's nerves. Thus, for instance, a little group consisting of a young and rather lively Peruvian lady who was supposed to be studying Spanish history and literature at the university, a young "smartie" from Barcelona, who held a post in the Banco de España, and two other young "bloods," annoyed some of the other guests with their shouting and boisterous laughter over mere nothings. Most young Spaniards who are of *buena familia,* have one great ambition, namely, that of getting into the Banco de España. Those who succeed are greatly envied, for their jobs are lucrative and "cushy." The budding genius of high finance who lodged in our *pensión* had a narrow strip of carefully clipped black hair on his upper lip, the kind of facial ornament sported by modern dance-band leaders and one or two Hollywood sheiks, and therefore thought himself to be the complete answer to a maiden's prayer. In both senses of the word, he was the "big noise" of the party, and although he thought himself to be very *gracioso* (witty and amusing), a young Irish-American who claimed to be studying Arabic and Oriental languages, so hated the very guts of the human loud-speaker that every now and again he scowled at him from the far corner of the room where he had taken refuge. As far as the philologist and his profound studies were concerned, I had a shrewd suspicion that they were much deeper than met the eye. As a rule he slept until noon, and occasionally he was invisible until evening, when he disappeared for the night. During two or three nocturnal expeditions I made in his company, he took me to various fashionable *cafés,* in which he seemed to know everybody by sight, what the different people were doing, what were prices for this and that, various rates of exchange, and so on. Prior to coming to Madrid, the student of Oriental languages had spent a couple of years in North Africa where, I was given to understand, marvellous business was being done, thanks chiefly to certain restrictions and regulations in European countries.

In connection with various rates of exchange, and mysterious immigrations caused by their fluctuations, I was astonished at the number of visibly prosperous French tourists who invaded Spain from Morocco. I had occasion to speak to a number, and it was truly surprising how many of them claimed to have been key-men in the underground resistance movement during the second World War. Incidentally, similar claims were made by several of their compatriots whom I met on my way through France. Needless to say, whilst listening to some of those anonymous heroes' stories, I chewed the tip of my tongue.

In my *pensión* in Madrid we also had a small contingent of *citoyens de la belle France;* a married couple, both *très formales et sérieux,* and a real "eye-tonic," a more or less natural blonde of about twenty-five who hailed from Morocco. Like still waters which are apt to run deep, she always sat at a small table on her own, pretending to be reading a book between courses, whilst every now and again *madame* sniffed and cast "clinical" glances at her from the matrimonial table.

My table companion was a middle-aged, short and podgy gentleman who hailed from the Canary Islands, whence he had come to indulge in what seemed to be his favourite pastime and sport, namely, to consult – it seemed – every physician in Madrid, and between consultations to chase after *señoritas*. Swarthy, and with puffy dark-blue lips, he looked like an over-fed Arab, but as he had quite a sense of humour, he thoroughly enjoyed being teased about his weaknesses. Every day he brought bottles containing new medicines, capsules and tubes filled with pills of every size and colour. Before meals, the waitress had to place the whole collection on his table, thus making it resemble the counter of a chemist's shop on stock-taking day. Of course, my new friend the "Canario" (canary) as I called him upon becoming familiar with him, was on every kind of diet, and a different one was being tried after every visit to a new doctor. If ever he arrived late for a meal, and brought with him his latest acquisition in the line of medicines or tonics, he entered the dining-room, flourishing the bottle and beaming like a child showing off with a particularly welcome Christmas present. Between lectures on blood pressure, and glowing accounts of beautiful young ladies he claimed to have met during his latest prowl round the *cafés*, he told me so much about the Canary Islands that I remember but little of his conversations. Besides being a considerable experimental physicist and a lip service Don Juan, he was also a bit of a poet. Of this hidden talent he gave me proof when, after a meal, he laboriously wrote for me on a piece of paper a bit of non-rhyming doggerel concerning what a wise man never ought to do after a meal. Here is a copy of his effort, the original of which I preserve as a treasured souvenir of the first live Canary Islander I met, not in captivity, but on the "loose" in Madrid.

Despues de almorzar,	After breakfast,
Ni un paso dar.	Take not a step.
Despues de comer	After lunch,
Ni cortar papel.	Cut not even paper.
Despues de cenar	After dinner,
Ni un paso dar.	Take not one step.

But the most glorious moment of supreme exaltation in which I saw the "Canario" was when, one day, he came bounding into the dining-room, eyes fairly bulging out, and puffy lips extended up to his ears with an ape-like grin. "Look!" he exclaimed, rolling up one sleeve of his jacket, to show me the upper part of his forearm round which was a gauze bandage. Wondering if by any chance some charming *señorita* had stabbed him, I stared at the bandage, which covered what appeared to be a pad of cotton wool. "Friend!" the "Canario" shouted, at the same time pointing at, the bulge, "I have just been to a marvellous doctor who is going to cure me with amazing injections. Under this protective covering is a *cultivo de hongos* (a cultivation of mushrooms or fungi). Yes, believe it or not, *un CUL-TI-VO de HON-GOS,*" he repeated slowly, loudly and with emphasis, at the same time staring into my eyes. After a dramatic pause he continued, "When these mushrooms are ripe, minute and invisible to the eye as they will be even then, the doctor is going to harvest them, and by means of a syringe he will inject them into my body. Now, do you understand me, my friend?"

"More or less," I replied, rubbing my chin to look as if I were deeply interested in the subject. Then, in order to give the impression that I know a little about injections, I ventured to ask, "Are the injections to be arterial or muscular?"

"*Que se yo?*" (What do I know?), the human guinea-pig shouted, shrugging his shoulders. "This part I leave to the doctor, but in the meantime I must be careful with this *cultivo de hongos.*" Having rolled down his sleeves with great care, he seated himself opposite me, and after having surveyed the rows of bottles, tubes and little cardboard boxes filled with capsules and pills, as a general might survey a group of soldiers who volunteer to carry out an important and highly dangerous task, the "Canario" picked out one of his pets, and asked the smiling waitress to bring him a glass of luke-warm water. "Not too hot, and not too cold; you know, as usual," he shouted after the obliging girl, as, making valiant but futile attempts at suppressing a broad grin from coming over her pretty face, she hurried out through the door which led to the kitchen.

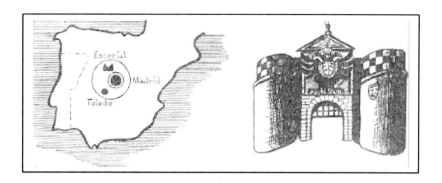

CHAPTER 10

MADRID – TOLEDO – ESCORIAL

From Madrid I made several excursions by train, car and motor-coach. In trains I made a point of travelling third class, partly in order to save *pesetas,* and partly because thus I met all sorts of people, with some of whom I had many interesting and amusing conversations. During railway journeys Spaniards love to talk, and they are so un-reserved that after a while they act as if they had known one for years. Railway carriage companions told me all about their family and other private affairs, and they were quite outspoken when it came to express-ing their opinions on politics and the country's situation in general.

Toledo being situated only a little over forty miles from Madrid, I visited the place twice, once in the delightful company of a well-known Spanish writer whom I had met previously in London, and also of a distinguished American journalist and his charming wife. Our Spanish friend did the driving and acted as guide, and proved to be an excellent and most entertaining host. The landscape reminded me of the Mexican *meseta.* Though fertile in many parts, the region has a "desert" look about it, especially so because the soil of the rolling plain has a peculiar red tint. As it happened to be a Sunday, the streets of little towns and villages through which we passed were thronged with people, most of whom, especially the men, stood in groups, talking. Although our driver made an infernal noise with the claxon horn of his modern American car, and to my consternation raced along at a high speed, the talkers took not the slightest notice of our rapid approach until we were almost on top of them, when, with an elegant twist of their bodies, they side-stepped a trifle, just enough to let the car pass, "shaving" them. "Gee whizz!" our American friend exclaimed over and over again as we fairly shot through such groups. "No wonder Spain produces bull-fighters!" Indeed, some of the young men acted as *matadores* do in making certain "passes" with bulls; just a little step to one side, then feet together, a twist of the waist, back turned towards the car, and one arm and hand making a nonchalant gesture as if to say, "Pass, sir!"

As I found out later, in villages and towns through which highways pass, it is absolutely useless to slow down too much if one wants to get past the crowds which insist on doing their talking in the middle of the main thoroughfare. The thing to do is to make as much noise as possible, and to drive straight ahead, though, naturally, with some caution. If a driver slows down too much – as I did very often – people simply remain standing where they are, and some of the young men are disappointed, being unable to show off with their game of imitating bullfighters. What in other parts of the world is called "road-sense" simply does not exist in happy-go-lucky Spain. In fact, without meaning to be rude or derogatory, I came to the firm conclusion that there only donkeys and mules have real road and traffic sense. If they are left alone by their drivers – who in country districts are often asleep, lying flat on their vehicles – the wise beasts always plod along on the right side of the road, which is rarely the case when the man does the guiding. In towns, if there is no policeman about to control the traffic, as often as not pedestrians cross streets in the most convenient though dangerous manner, namely by meandering across them diagonally, without bothering to look out for possible danger. I vividly remember a little girl who, like so many other youngsters I had seen, was thus crossing a street, walking very slowly and with the dignity of a queen. As it happened, a car approached her from behind, and the driver sounded the horn. Taking not the slightest notice of the repeated sounds of warning, the little girl continued her stately march, obliging the driver to slow down, and to wait until there was room for him to pass. As he did so, evidently annoyed, he tooted at the girl several times, whereupon, turning her head proudly, and talking over her shoulder, she called the driver a badly educated lout. For a moment her black eyes flashed fire, and then, feigning a shudder, in disgust she threw up her little head and walked on, deliberately swaying her hips.

Upon nearing Toledo the land becomes more fertile. Here and there are orchards and olive groves, and on low hills stand summer villas, known as *cigarrales, (cigarra: cicada,* a large insect with transparent wings. The male makes a shrill noise in hot weather). Approaching from the north – or be it from the plain of Castile – one has the first glimpse of this unique town from a narrow isthmus. Built on a granite hill in the form of a horseshoe, with steep inaccessible rocks facing the River Tagus (the natives' "Tajo" – cut or slice), it is a natural and formidable fortification of which men have made use since prehistoric times. Toledo, the Romans' *Toletum* and the Moors' *Toleitola,* is almost surrounded by the deep gorge of the river, and jagged stern-looking mountains make a marvellous background for this rocky pile of history. As far as I am concerned, however, Toledo is a town to be gazed and wondered at, but not one in which I would like to live for long. There is something wild and forbidding about the narrow, Moorish-looking streets with their old churches, monasteries and sombre houses with practically windowless outer walls. These prison-like edifices with their huge gates, most of which are studded with great iron bosses, differ greatly from the cheerful and friendly wrought-iron gates of the *patios* in gay Seville. However, many of Toledo's quad-rangular courtyards are most picturesque and cheerful, once one has passed through stern repelling gates, and one is surprised to find a blaze of flowers, ornamental plants and bushes. In the middle of such *patios* is the inevitable *aljibe* (well) in which rain-water is gathered. In former times, before water was brought to the town by means of pumping and pipes, in a state of emergency or. siege, the *aljibes* provided the only water, unless water carriers made the journey down to the river. The hammer and anvil of many centuries of fighting have forged the city of Toledo into what it is, but great architects and artists have also contributed their share.

As I climbed up one of the steep, roughly cobbled, narrow and tortuous streets, upon coming to a more or less open space, I saw something that made me stop and rub my eyes. There on a little stool sat one of our typical Chelsea painters, busy working at a small canvas. How super-Montparnassien he looked with his frothy moustache and pointed beard, and how "stagy" "Frenchie" his black and white checked baggy trousers, narrow at the ankles. And oh, what an exotic Mexican *sombrero,* one for which the very Pancho Villa would have envied him!

And to think that some four centuries ago Theotocopuli produced his many masterpieces in Toledo. (Or is it Theotocoupoulis? No wonder the Spaniards called him merely "El Greco," meaning "The Greek.")

Some of the churches – especially the cathedral – are, nowadays, to all intents and purposes, as far as tourists are concerned, museums. As we entered into the cathedral by a wooden swing-door, I stopped to examine a certain piece of primitive engineering more closely. A thin rope, which in the course of many years had been knotted together many times, passed over a crudely made iron wheel, and had a counter-weight at one end. This caricaturesque piece of mechanism shut the door more or less automatically every time it was pushed open, and as, apparently, neither the hinges of the door nor the iron wheel had been oiled since they were forged by hand, the groans and squeaks they made brought to my mind the voices of the damned in Dante's *Inferno*. This *leitmotif* suited the gloomy and mysterious atmosphere to perfection, and I could hear the sounds produced by this busy door, even when I was at the far end of the imposing Gothic structure, gazing at the marvels it contains. But then, in Spain a door is not a door unless it squeaks and groans.

The Alcazar overlooks the town, standing on its highest point. No doubt, this must have been a fortification already in prehistoric times, being ideally situated for defence. Later, the Romans made it into a citadel which, at different times, was also used as such by the Moors and Visigoths. Twice it was burned down and restored, and during the recent Civil War a great part of it was destroyed when the Reds besieged the heroic defenders, among whom were even women and a few children. The men who acted as our guides had been among the heroes, and whilst taking us through the different underground galleries, they gave dramatic details about the siege. Among the relics, they showed us the dirty mattresses on which they slept on the stone floor, and a crude operating table on which casualties were attended to. After the Civil War, a large room in the Alcazar was turned into a kind of chapel in which some of its defenders are buried. The centre-piece is the grave of General Jose Moscardo, and there are also a number of niches in which others who withstood the siege will be buried when they die. Although I fairly itched to ask our guide to show us his "reservation," I dared not do so. No doubt, the siege of the Alcazar made history, but yet I could not help feeling that since then it has been somewhat vulgarized, and to a certain extent commercialized. Far be it from me to belittle the heroism of the glorious little garrison of starvelings and of their leader's mental make-up, when the commander of the besiegers rang him up to inform him that his son of seventeen was in his hands as a prisoner, and that he would be shot unless the defenders of the Alcazar surrendered. The telephone conversation which ensued between father and son, as well as other details – pictorial and written – are to be seen in a room in the citadel. "You must get ready to die," the father who refused to surrender told his son over the telephone. "Yes, father, I will," came the reply, whereafter the youth was taken away to be shot.

Hundreds, nay thousands, of similar crimes were committed during that terrible Civil War, not only by the losers but also by the victors. As far as fanaticism and heroism are concerned, the spotlight of the international press fell mainly on the siege of the Alcazar, and even in Spain people are beginning to forget equally heroic episodes of that tragic and horrible upheaval. Not many remember or talk about other tragic and stubborn sieges, or mention the occasion when, in winter, despite adverse weather conditions, several hundred Red volunteers attempted to cross the high mountain ranges near Granada, to relieve a besieged garrison of comrades. The little army of suicides set out into the cold and windswept inferno where every man perished miserably.

To me, it seemed strange that crimes committed during the Civil War should be advertised to tourists, as is being done in the case of the one of the Alcazar of Toledo. After all is said and done, were not these crimes committed by Spaniards? Political and military victories always carry away southern races on a wave of hysterical enthusiasm, often to such an extent that monuments are built to the conquering heroes, and that public squares and streets are named after them. In fact, if it were possible, the two poles, the sun, the moon and some of the stars would be given their names. Of course, following the rise of other military and political heroes, these new names would be changed once more. Naturally, such hero or bread-and-butter worship mortifies the defeated, and constantly kindles the fire of hatred which smoulders in their breasts. In connection with the Alcazar of Toledo I can't refrain from adding that, although I have a tremendous admiration for the little band of heroes who so valiantly and stubbornly defended it, whilst walking through its ruins, I could not help thinking about millions of other heroes, men, women and children, who during the Second World War, and also since its termination, endured – and are enduring – far worse sieges than that of the Alcazar. What about the bombing of cities, night after night? What about starvation, sickness and disease, and many other horrors? What about the effect of modern explosives, one charge of which alone would have reduced not only the Alcazar but almost the whole of Toledo to a heap of rubble? What about sailors in ships and submarines, airmen, and many others who sailed, flew, swam or walked into the jaws of death. And what about the women – on all belligerent sides – who under aerial and other bombardment kept the home fires burning whilst their husbands, sons and in many cases grown-up daughters were away doing their bit? If the names of public squares and streets were to be changed to honour the memory of all the known heroes and heroines among them, there would not be enough in the world to go round.

Whilst pondering over such and similar matters, I stood on a kind of terrace of the Alcazar, looking at the river in the winding gorge below, and beyond it at the rolling reddish plain of Castile. Across the river, on a low hill – whence, during the siege, artillery kept up a sporadic fire which did much damage to the old citadel – I saw a horrid blot on the unforgettable landscape – military barracks. The sight of them shocked me as much as if a caricaturist superimposed a vulgar figure on a landscape painted by a great master. In several regions through which I passed, huge barracks are being built, for it must be remembered that outside Russia, to-day Spain has the largest army in Europe. Though badly equipped, if provided with modern armaments, within a very short time Spain could put a formidable fighting force in the field. Of course, American aid is the dream of every Spanish officer.

Among several interesting excursions I made from Madrid was one to the Escorial, situated near the Guadarrama mountains, some thirty-five miles from the capital. Owing to lack of rain, most of the fields looked dismal, and where wheat grew it was exceedingly thin, with its growth retarded, and the ears contained but little grain. The mountains were still capped with snow which glittered in the bright sunshine. As I proceeded, the country became more and more undulating until I reached the foot-hills of the Guadarramas, where I found myself among rocky hills, with here and there a small clear stream winding its way through depressions in which grew fir trees, pines and gay wild flowers. Everywhere are scattered huge weird-shaped rocks-probably deposited there during the glacial age – and here and there roamed cattle.

Situated on a hilly terrace, with a nearby background of a rocky mountain-range, the Escorial (3,300 feet above sea-level) is situated in ideal country where many *Madrileños* take refuge during the hot summer months. However, in winter it can be bitterly cold, and heavy snowfalls are not uncommon. When Philip II declared Madrid the capital of the united kingdom of Las Españas (1560) and made it his residence, he searched for a suitable place where to build a country residence for himself. The site having been found near the Guadarrama mountains, after forty years of feverish work, the Escorial was completed.

Although the geometrically perfect colossus has been called the World's Eighth Wonder, its whitish-grey walls and gloomy roofs and fabric towers inspired me with a feeling of melancholy. Somehow its colour and the late Renaissance style of northern Italy suit the landscape, but even the large, square swimming-pool-like fountains on a terrace below one of its 680 foot-long-walls fail to counteract the general atmosphere of sadness and severity.

Before entering into the building, I walked through a nearby flower-garden where, among the trees, birds sang merrily, whilst on the barren parade-ground-like square in front of the main entrance, boys shouted whilst playing football. Otherwise the place was deserted, for I had arrived before the hour when sightseers are admitted.

Shortly after the massive door was opened with great noise, a stoutish, middle-aged man acted as guide to the little flock of visitors, together with whom I was herded through rooms, halls, along galleries and passages. Though uncouth, crude and blatantly ignorant, the guide had memorized his "lines" so well that he recited them like a parrot. He spoke in a loud croaky voice and through a corner of his mouth, and judging by his accent, he hailed from the low regions in the south. Despite these shortcomings, our guide was an amusing character, though I doubt that the funny things he said were intentional. He had not taken us far when members of his flock began to laugh and titter behind his back. Even a Frenchman and his wife, who understood not a word of Spanish, had to disappear round corners to laugh to their heart's content, without giving offence to our human gramophone who seemed to have a special liking for tapestries and minor quite unimportant details connected with them. Thus, for instance, when the guide tried to explain to us the finer points of a really amazing tapestry (after a painting by Goya) representing the sausage-maker to one of the Spanish kings, pointing at a ham – which lies on the ground near the *salchichero's* feet – he smacked his lips, and, all but slobbering, said, "*Fijense en el jamon*" (Fix your eyes on the ham). This *chorizero* of Candelario knew his business. He was a master in the art of making hams and sausages. "Look at the grain where the ham has been cut; not too lean, not too fat, and the colour just right. One feels like picking it up and digging one's teeth into it!"

King Philip's humble apartments with their brick floors and general austerity touched within me a chord of admiration mixed with pity. The austerity and utter simplicity of it all, when compared with the magnificence of the rest of the palace, the most beautiful part of which is the main chapel with its *Panteon de los Reyes* (Burial Vault of the Kings) under the main altar. According to ancient chronicles, whilst the king supervised every detail connected with the building of the Escorial, he often said: "*Un palacio para Dios y una choza para el rey*" (A palace for God, and a cabin for the king). From his bed in a tiny room in which for a long time he lay ill and finally died, through a small window in one of the inner walls he could see the altar in the main chapel, which was the last thing he gazed at before passing on.

The litter in which, in the latter part of his life, Philip made his journeys between Madrid and the Escorial is still preserved. The crudely made wooden armchair, fixed to wooden poles which rested on the carriers' shoulders, gives further testimony of the king's simple tastes, as far as luxuries and personal comforts were concerned. It is astonishing to think that towards the end of his life, all Spanish State affairs – including those connected with the newly discovered and conquered territories in the New World – were run from this, in those times, remote place. When one considers the enormous distances and difficulties of transport and communication, not to overstress the fact that many of the small ships which tried to cross the ocean never reached their destination, it seems fantastic that the king's *choza* (cabin) near the Guadarramas, was the spot whence everything under the jurisdiction of the Spanish crown was directed. And to complicate matters further, the Council of the Indies sat in Seville.

Our guide seemed to take a sadistic delight in giving us what evidently were asides to his officially set and memorized repertoire. With great gusto he pointed out bloody details of certain pictures. Perhaps his mental kink was caused by years spent in the sprawling charnel house, the Escorial, beneath the magnificent main chapel of which are vaults in which lie the bones of a number of kings, queens, members of the royal family and of other notabilities. When we finished our round, the guide took me aside and asked if I wanted to see the *pudridero* and one or two other things of interest which, as a rule, are not shown to visitors. Speaking slowly and as if communicating the secrets of the whereabouts of a hidden treasure, he told me that the *pudridero* (rotting vault) is the place where bodies are kept for a number of years, until putrefaction is complete, and the cadaver has dried up *como carton* (like cardboard) whereafter it is removed to its final resting-place. Having thanked the guide for his offer and enlightening information, I gave him a tip and departed.

The little town of Escorial is prettily situated. Among the quaint old houses are a number of modern villas with their respective gardens whence fine views of the hilly country towards the south can be obtained, the jagged outline of the mountains of Toledo making a fine background in the far distance.

Back in Madrid, that night I dined in the company of several acquaintances, among them an elderly gentleman who belongs to a famous aristocratic family. Having been educated in a famous Roman Catholic school in England, his English was perfect, and being an intelligent and widely-travelled person, his conversation on many subjects was illuminating, especially so when we discussed various aspects of Spain and its people. He referred to the commercial superiority and war potential of the Anglo-Saxon and Germanic races, which he attributed to certain fundamental elements in peoples' early education. Southern races, he maintained, have more individualism, and consequently are apt to place their private affairs before those of the State. In cold countries, since the earliest days of dawn, people had to work and hunt together, and think of long winters, whereas in warmer climates there was no need for this team work and forethought. When the religious side of Spanish life was discussed, the same speaker made a statement which has stuck in my mind ever since. "We are not a religious people," he said, "we are religionnaires."

According to what I saw of Spaniards, not only in Spain, but also in South America, they are not pious in the Protestant sense, nor, perhaps, in the sense of English, American, French and other European Roman Catholics. Spaniards of the intellectual middle or lower classes are delightfully superstitious, and they are fatalists and stoics. They cling to certain rituals, feasts and processions which are older than Christianity. Being mystics, they love churches in which the gloom seems to rise round one like a mist, temples in which, once one's eyes become accustomed to the darkness, one sees flickering light of candles, the glitter of gold, silver and jewels, and old velvets hanging from the walls, dusty with their own dust, and faded with their fading, and relics which mould in their own mould. They like to hear their own footsteps echoing through vault-like emptiness, and to see shadows gliding along walls, and they are deeply thrilled by gorgeous priestly vestments, intoxicating incense and other influences which speak directly to the senses. The awe-inspiring mystery of massive constructions with imposing Gothic arches, dark confession boxes and weird throaty chanting holds them spellbound, and, above all, give them consolation.

The prolonged Moorish occupation of the country left behind many traces, physical and mental, and some of the Moorish fanaticism has remained in Spain, especially so in the case of members of the uneducated class, many of whom who have a strong admixture of North African blood. For instance, during the Moorish occupation, a white marble pavement surrounded the great mosque in Cordova. Before entering one of its chapels, in order to show their devotion to Allah, pilgrims made a sevenfold circuit of this pavement, crawling on their hands and knees, in doing so wearing the flesh off their bones, and, with the passing of time, and the crawling of countless pilgrims, wearing out the thick marble slabs. In those days, among Christians – who, incidentally, the tolerant Moors never molested on account of their different religious beliefs – the chapel was known as the *Capilla del Zancarron*, meaning chapel of the leg bone without flesh.

In the south of Spain I met two old ladies – one American and the other English – who had spent two months travelling through the country, but chiefly in the south. Both these ladies were ardent and devout Roman Catholics, and when they spoke to me about the Spaniards' attitude towards religion, and, above all, told me about some of the religious processions they had seen, they described them as being shocking and pagan. It took me quite a while to explain to them that, for many reasons, the mentality of the masses in Spain differs greatly from that of other nations, and that even though strong pagan influences remain, they are – especially in the case of processions – so weird, fanciful, even fantastic, and so picturesque, that I was thrilled by them.

To-day Spanish Society is on the wane, due, in great part, to appropriation of land, begun in Primo de Rivera's time.

Like other countries, Spain has had its famous bandits, whose exploits are being sung to this day; but who has ever heard of a Spanish gangster? Modern gangsterism is a product of Sicily, and is an offshoot of the Italian *Mafia,* which has taken firm root in the United States of America. Spaniards are much too individualistic to join together in organized gangs, and although materialism is strong within them, they are too proud and independent to make *mafiosos.*

With the passing of time, the wounds inflicted by the Civil War continue to heal – perhaps only superficially, for many of them are deep and festering internally – and nowadays people can express themselves more or less freely. The Press is biased and one-sided, and therefore the reading of newspaper and magazines apt to be dull, save in the case of sporting chronicles and special articles which have no connection with politics. A few such articles I read were brilliant, and the humour of some was superb, full of *gracia* as the Spanish variety is called. To give just one example of how certain things have changed since the end of the Civil War, I will give one of something a high-ranking officer said whilst we discussed such and similar subjects in a crowded *café.* Naturally he had fought on Franco's side, for otherwise it is not in the least likely that he would have retained his rank.

Like members of other nationalities, Spaniards love to tell stories against themselves, but, as is the case all over the world, if a foreigner tells them the self-same yarn, they don't like it. On this occasion, when the officer to whom I have referred started telling me a story against Franco's troops, I was frankly surprised, but he did it with such *gracia* that when he finished all his listeners laughed heartily, though, no doubt, some had heard the little anecdote before. Until an underling is "sacked" or "fired" as Americans say, it is highly advisable for him or her to laugh at the stale joke the boss cracks as if it were new and his own.

In the centre of Madrid stands a famous monument, that of Cybele. The goddess of ancient mythology is represented on a chariot drawn by lions, and is surrounded by the water of a round fountain. To *Madrileños* the statue of Cybele is what that of Eros in Piccadilly Circus is to Londoners. As in the case of the latter during the second World War, Cybele was also covered over with sand-bags whilst the Spanish upheaval lasted. According to the anecdote, when Franco's victorious troops were about to march into the city, a female voice was heard calling from beneath the pile of sand-bags which covered the monument, "Oh, please, please, uncover me, I want to see Franco and his glorious troops march past!" The sand-bags having been removed, it was discovered that the voice was that of Cybele, and so she was left to watch the march-past of the troops. After a while, once more the goddess shouted, but this time in an even more pleading voice, "Oh, please, please, cover me again, as quick as you can! I have seen enough!"

Officially, there is no tipping of waiters in Spain, but human nature being what it is, the passing and accepting of *propinas* (gratuities) is not uncommon. According to regulations, hotels, catering establishments and bars add twelve per cent to clients' bills, this extra charge being the tip. From what I saw, Spaniards hardly ever give the waiters any extra money, but foreigners who are not accustomed to the system, usually hand over a tip which is never refused.

One morning I went to a *café* for some refreshment, and when the waiter brought what I had ordered, he presented me with a tiny cardboard shield, on one side of which, on a red background, was printed a kind of boot, as worn in the Middle Ages. On the reverse were a few words about "the honoured and privileged Alonso de Abarca, descendant of a king of Aragon, who in Valencia helped King Jaimé the Conqueror with a cavalry regiment at his own cost." The little cardboard shield was so made that it could be fixed to the button-hole of a jacket's lapel, and when I asked the waiter what was the meaning of it, he explained that it was "Waiters' Day," and that in addition to the normal charge of twelve per cent, which represents the tip, for this shield an extra thirty *centésimos* would be added to my bill. At the same time he recommended that I keep the little shield, which would protect me against being charged a further thirty cents, in case I went to another *café* or restaurant that day. He furthermore explained that "Waiters' Day" was a monthly event, and then, bending down, added in a whisper that it was *un disparate* (nonsense or a blunder) and that he wondered what was being done with the money thus collected. During my subsequent travels I had to pay for other similar tokens for the benefit of waiters.

The typical *Madrileño* is a gay and open-hearted creature whose generosity and willingness to oblige often make him over-enthusiastic, though often only on the spur of the moment. Thus, when excited, he will make all sorts of quite unsolicited promises, only to forget all about them until one meets him again, when he will be full of apologies and excuses for his omissions. As everywhere in Spain, appointments are promises one makes, but only keeps on time when it is a matter of life or death, or to go to a bullfight, or maybe to catch a train of which only one runs per day. If there are several trains, and one is missed, well, then the next one will do just as well.

Whenever I felt like being on my own, I went to the Retiro Park, which is one of the finest I have seen anywhere. As it is situated within a stone's-throw of the centre of the city, I loved to go there to admire the magnificent shady trees, the lake and ponds, gardens full of roses and other flowers, or to rest in some secluded nook where birds entertained me with their song.

Another favourite walk of mine was through the old sector of Madrid, especially at night, when the streets are practically deserted. Once, well after midnight, when the moon was shining brightly, two artists took me there, and explained to me the history of certain ancient buildings. When we came to a modern viaduct which leads over a deep depression, they told me that for a time there was a kind of epidemic of suicides and that so many people flung themselves over the parapet of this viaduct to a road deep down below, that special guards had to be put on duty. As we stood, chatting and looking down, one of them approached, whereupon my friends cracked a number of jokes with him, all of which he took in good humour. Then, for a while, he told us a story about a man who took the big "dive", and miraculously fell on an unfortunate mule which happened to be passing below. According to our enthusiastic informant, the beast – which acted as cushion – broke the would-be suicide's fall to such an extent that he survived with only a number of broken bones. The story seemed so far-fetched that it made me suspect that the guard who told it hailed from Andalusia, where people are gifted with remarkable powers of imagination.

The same friends took me to a *café* which is frequented by young artists, budding *intelectuales,* writers and poets. In several respects the place reminded me of London's Cafe Royal, as it used to be years ago. Along the walls were similar red plush seats, and at marble-topped tables the would-be geniuses sat in groups, talking quietly, holding forth with aplomb, or arguing loudly. Upon seeing us enter, and recognizing my companions as old friends, several patrons who were seated at a table, rose and beckoned us to join them. Introductions over, we sat down, and soon the conversation was in full swing. One of our party, a young man of about twenty-five, appeared to be the accepted "Big Chief" among the members of his circle. Seated on the upholstered bench with his back to the wall, alongside him he had a large brief-case filled with papers, and on the table before him were stacked others, evidently part of a manuscript. Whilst his friends carried on an animated conversation, he scribbled away feverishly, every now and again interrupting his activities for a few moments to make some weighty remark. When I suggested we others move to some other table in order to leave the man of letters alone to do his work undisturbed, the budding Cervantes protested, saying that, whilst writing, he was at his best if people round him talked and made a great deal of noise, which, in his case, acted as a kind of stimulant, and provided him with inspiration.

I happened to be glancing in the direction of the door, when two familiar figures minced their way into the *café*. Yes, there they were again: my old friends from Barcelona and Seville, Milo and Mila! Until that night, as far as I was concerned, they had no names; they were just a couple of precious young men who had evidently come to Spain to enjoy themselves in their own peculiar way. Their elegance was such that a hush fell on our company, and even our busy author looked up from his work to stare in their direction. "*Ça!*" he muttered, thus breaking the almost painful silence, "here comes *la Venus de Milo!*" Suppressed laughter followed this remark, and presently one of our party said, "No, no! not Venus de Milo. Look at the tall one's upper-lip; it somewhat resembles that of a *camello.*" This led to a prolonged debate, and when one of the critics suggested that the subject of our conversation was much too good-looking to be called "Camel," one who evidently knew a little Roman History, proposed we call him

Marcus Furius Camillus. Eventually, it was decided to call the two young men Camilo and Camila, and for the sake of brevity just Milo and Mila. I trust this will explain why in earlier chapters I have referred to them under these nick-names.

Like all good things, my delightful stay in Madrid had to come to an end, but as it happened, I was to return to the city later.

CHAPTER 11

MADRID – VALENCIA

When the time came to leave Madrid I felt like an explorer setting out towards unknown regions. Packing my few belongings did not take long, and when the two panniers and my small suitcase were fixed to the motor-cycle, a friend who rode on another machine showed me the best and shortest way out of the city. Upon reaching the outskirts he put me on the Madrid-Valencia road and after having smoked a cigarette with me, cranked up, and soon after disappeared in the direction whence we had come. Until my cigarette was finished, I sat by the wayside, looking at the skyline of Madrid, then at passing wisps of cloud and the semi-barren rolling country round me, and every now and again I cast sideways glances at my machine which looked rather forlorn in its bleak setting. In the past I had so often seen motor-cyclists having great difficulties in starting off their machines, that I wondered if it would refuse to crank up. Therefore, as a rule, when I stopped for a short rest, I did this at the top of hills where, on the downgrade, I could free-wheel for a while, and then put the motor into gear, thus starting it without the necessity of having to crank up. Although the motor was an easy starter, for some peculiar reason I never trusted it. To me all machines are rather like stubborn mules, with which, for my sins in the past, I have had dealings and a certain amount of trouble. Some of these creatures have the nasty habit of kicking would-be riders, whereas, in the case of motor-cycles, prospective riders have to do the kicking in order to produce the necessary spark to start the motor. As I sat by the wayside on the bleak Castilian plain, I cast several distinctly mulish glances in the direction of my steel and cast-iron mount, for which, despite my quite unwarranted distrust, I had developed quite an affection. Although until then it had done all the hard work, carrying me and my belongings over hill and dale for a great many miles without ever refusing to do what I asked of it, I could not help wondering if sooner or later it would not take it into its explosive head to play a nasty trick on me. Supposing my mount suddenly refused to move? The very thought of spanners, screwdrivers and all the other surgical instruments which were among my first-aid equipment made me shudder. True, I had a kind of hand-book, full of instructions and diagrams, showing how, in cases of emergency, to do this and that, what not to do under any circumstances, what to guard against, and so on. During spare moments I studied the contents of this book, but the more I read, the greater became my confusion in matters relating to the anatomy of a motor-cycle and the functions of its inner organs. No wonder, then, that whilst sitting there, I eyed the two-wheeled enigma near me with suspicion and not a little awe. However, when the time came, and I gave her a vigorous kick in the right place, the engine started off with a loud cough, followed by a steady flow of rhythmic gurgling, and soon after I was off in an easterly direction heading towards Valencia and the yet distant Mediterranean coast.

When the wind dropped, the sun was pleasantly warm. Every now and again large green lizards who were basking on the road scurried to safety at my approach, astonishing me with their speed and agility. The regions through which I travelled are so barren that, according to an ancient local proverb, the lark has to bring his provisions with him if he is foolish enough to visit them. And yet, despite prevailing conditions, somehow a few sheep managed to exist there, and a thin sprinkling of peasants contrive to eke out a bare living.

In some parts of the Castilian plain, rainfall percolates through layers of ground, but thanks to a subsoil of tenacious loam is prevented from sinking deeper. The water thus collected keeps the soil moist by constant process of evaporation, and it is brought up by means of primitive pumps already described. Castilian peasants still use wooden ploughs, and the threshing of wheat is done with a simple roller or by treading out the grain by the feet of oxen.

When I halted in a dismal little village, in order to eat a *chorizo* (sausage seasoned with red pepper) and some brown bread, and to have a glass of wine, soon a number of ill-clad men came slouching into the little store, whilst others, including several young men and boys, were outside, admiring my motor-cycle.

The owner of the *almacén* (store) – in which I ate my food out of a piece of brown paper placed on a little round table, the marble top of which was none too clean – was a young man of about thirty. Though quite polite, he looked rather surly until I started a conversation with him, whereupon he became quite pleasant and talkative. "I see you come from Great Britain," he said, looking through the door at the "GB" plate on my motor-cycle. "What a place to come to, I presume, for amusement."

This remark made the loiterers in the place snigger sarcastically, and when the boss asked me where I had learnt my Spanish, and I gave my usual reply, namely, that I had spent some years in South America, my listeners pricked up their ears. Though my offer of a glass of wine to all those present was refused very politely, the bystanders accepted a cigarette each, and, soon after, we conversed freely. All the men were very depressed owing to the general situation, and about prospects for the future they spoke most gloomily. "If only we had the necessary money, and 'they' (meaning the Government) allowed us to migrate, we'd all get out of this misery, and go to South America," my interlocutors said in chorus, and then proceeded to curse those on whom they laid the blame for making it impossible for them to realize their ambition.

During my travels I often heard the same story and the same complaints, which became so monotonous in their sameness that the recording of them would make dull and weary reading. Judging by the many similar conversations, I came to the conclusion that, given the means and full freedom of movement, a great part of Spain's population would migrate to the New World. I do not suggest that this urge to seek new horizons is entirely due to the political situation. To a large extent, low wages, the rising cost of living, lack of prospects, and, above all, four years with practically no rain, have driven people in many districts to despair. On the other hand, minor internal migrations to fertile regions have caused these to become over-populated, with the result that even there the South-America "drang" is strong. Over and over again people asked me how to set about to go abroad, where permission had to be obtained, where ships sailed from, and how much the cheapest passages cost. Many of the stories I heard were so pathetic, and the people who told them to me so fine and noble, that I grieved deeply at being unable to help them, In several regions the men who spoke to me were in a sullen and ugly mood, and openly admitted to me that they are Communists, and some assured me that if a free election were held, the "Reds" would win it by a large majority. How much truth there is in this, I am unable to judge, but after four months' of travelling and mixing with people in every station of life, I came to the conclusion that if a really free election were held, its result would inevitably lead to another upheaval. Politically and financially, Spain is up the proverbial gum-tree-and a very high one it is. Until recently, ostracized by other nations, and without the benefits of foreign aid – which temporarily helped other countries out of the quagmire – Spain has had to tighten her belt. To make things even worse, four years of drought caused much additional want and misery, for which General Franco is so unjustly blamed by many, not only in Spain, but also by certain interested parties abroad. Considering the horrors and devastation of a long, fierce and bloody civil war and all the subsequent adversities, the recovery made by Spain amazed me. A war with an enemy outside the door, or on the other side of a stretch of water, is one thing, but a civil war quite another. It needs no great stretch of the imagination to appreciate the great difference between the two forms of horror and disaster. If, in a nightmare, I were made to choose in which of the two kinds I would forcibly have to become involved, I am sure that even in such a crazy dream I would say, "Give me war between nations; never mind radio-guided rockets, atomic bombs and other marvellous inventions put to such fiendish use, but God deliver me from a civil war."

Being in no hurry, and finding the company interesting, I spent some time in that store on the Castilian plain, and when the time came to leave, a little crowd of loafers came to see if my machine would start. Fortunately it did on the first kick, which made the bystanders exchange glances of admiration, and made it possible for me to ride away, pleased with myself. Such is vanity.

As I proceeded, by degrees the land became more fertile. In places where patches had been ploughed, the soil was of a peculiar reddish-chocolate colour, almost what the French so aptly describe as *sang de boeuf.* Although the road I followed was quite good, there was very little traffic on it; in fact, during the whole day I did not see more than six or eight cars. Along either side of the road, long stretches were planted with trees, and most of them appeared to have taken root. This, as mentioned previously, has been done along many similar highways I followed.

Towards evening, upon reaching a village named Motilla del Palancar, I decided to spend the night in a wayside inn, and on the following day to proceed to Valencia. There being ample time before dinner, I went for a stroll through the ancient village, the streets of which were fit only for alpinists, sure-footed goats and donkeys. Despite the uneven ground, women walked along briskly and elegantly, balancing huge pitchers on their hips. Upon reaching the sandy main square, under some shady trees I saw the old village fountain, near which were assembled a number of women, all laughing and chattering away like so many excited parakeets. Throughout Spain such fountains are the women's forums, without which social life in country districts would change completely, and lose much of its romance and character.

I can hear some of our city-bred sanitary engineering fiends say, "Why don't they have running water in those Spanish villages?" Now, supposing they had – when and where could the women meet, in order to discuss matters far more important and far-reaching to them than, say, a proposal to amend the law of slander, making it an offence on the level with premeditated murder? And supposing that every little town, village and hamlet in Spain had running water and a silent-flush W.C. in every house, hut and hovel? Quite apart from the matters discussed at the fountains, those wells of knowledge and sources of information, where and when could the graceful water-carriers show their figures at their best? Again I hear some ignorant city-bred heathen say, "Of course, at the *fiestas,* when these beauties are dressed up in their becoming regional costumes." But a fig for those costumes, which can be worn only a few times in the course of a year. True, Spanish women look perfect in them; but then, there is the daily unofficial *fiesta* to be thought of, the routine *fiesta* of going to the fountain where girl meets girl, and woman meets woman. There femininity has it all its own way, though during the hip-swaying walk to and from the source of manifold enlightenment, may be encountered men, who are always ready with some flattery, such as "blessed be the mother who bore such beauty." At such times the water-carrier thus addressed, raises high her head, shrugs her shoulders, and having thrown a glance of assumed indignation at the would-be Don Juan, strides on elegantly with her pitcher. If she happens to be alone, a blush comes over her face, but if there are two or more women or girls together, as they walk away, past the flatterer, suppressed titters can be heard. Occasionally, when a seasoned beauty is thus addressed by a *piropo* – as these street-corner bird-fanciers are called – she shouts back her humorous though stinging personal remark, presently to smile to herself as she continues her journey with added flamboyance. Running water then? No, a thousand times no! Let our mollycoddled and stereotype-minded city dwellers have it in their modern prisons; let them have sanitary engineering luxuries, constant hot and cold water, their radio, television, telephones, and all the rest, but may continue to flourish for ever the good old Spanish village fountains.

As hinted out previously, in every region in Spain, customs, traditions, food, music, and so on, vary greatly. This is also the case with the method of carrying water or loads. In the parts to which I hope to have taken the reader in this chapter, water is carried in pitchers which are held so as to rest on the hips. In some regions pitchers are carried on the head, whereas in other parts this is done on poles which rest on the shoulders, or in square wooden frames, suspended by means of broad straps which also put the weight on the shoulders. In the case of the frames, the pitchers or buckets are held with the hands, one on either side of the carrier, and the frames serve to take half the strain, and to prevent the containers from knocking against the legs, and thus to spill some of the water.

During my wanderings through Motilla del Palancar I came to an open space where little boys were playing a keen and vigorous game of football with a ball made of rags tied together. Though the biggest of them was only some ten years of age, and the smallest about six, all played and acted like grown-up players, taking themselves and the game very seriously. A few old men and women – during whose youth football could not have been played in Spain – watched, and occasionally shouted encouragement or advice to their favourites. As I stood looking on, an old woman who held a baby in her arms, and led a toddler by a hand, came alongside me and said proudly, at the same time pointing at a nipper who was busy showing off, "*Señor*, that's my grandson, and that one over there is another. Don't you think they play well?" "Excellently," I replied, "both have the makings of great *futbolistas.*" After a while, just in order to see what effect my remark would have on the old woman, I turned to her and said, "That grandson of yours, the one over there, has the build and looks of one who, some day, might turn into a good bullfighter." "*Dios me libre!*" (God deliver me !) she croaked, at the same time crossing herself, "A *torero!* No, no. A cousin of mine was a bullfighter. Once he was gored so badly that from that day on, until he died, he had to be kept by his family. No, no, *por amor de Dios,* not a *torero!*" Then, turning to watch the game, she shouted, "That's right, Tito, push him out of the way, gooo, good . . . *goll!*"

At a filling station situated alongside the highway were assembled a number of men, among them several peasants who had bundles tied together with thick coarse string. All were hoping to find room on one of the cars, lorries or buses that passed at long intervals. Whenever one came and stopped in order to fill the fuel tank, the members of the little group of would-be travellers fairly charged the driver, in order to ask him if there was room in his vehicle. Almost invariably the answer was in the negative, whereupon, resigned to their fate, all settled down to another long spell of patient waiting. Although I was very hungry, I had to wait until 9.30 p.m. before dinner was served, and upon going out for a little stroll before turning in for the night, the patient ones were still at the filling station, hoping to get a lift. Next morning I was told that it was 4 a.m. before the last pair found room on a lorry.

The sky was overcast, and a strong wind blew, when I resumed my journey towards Valencia. It being early spring, and the regions through which I travelled high, I was glad to be warmly clad, and even more so when I reached forested mountains where the winding road led up very steep inclines, at the top of which the force of the cold wind was considerable. Fortunately, during the descent I came to more sheltered parts. Upon reaching a small town called Utiel, I went to a small inn to have a peculiar beverage the owner called coffee and milk. The milk must have been quite good before the so-called *café* was added to it, but the brown bread and the smoked ham were excellent. Whilst eating, I studied several excellently drawn posters announcing bullfights, and presently my eyes fell on one which gave me the information that a month before I arrived in Utiel, my old friend, José Iturbi, the famous pianist and conductor, had been there with the

Seville Symphonic Orchestra. As only a few months before, Iturbi had invited me to one of his concerts at the Albert Hall in London, I asked the owner of the little inn if there are enough music-lovers in Utiel to make a concert given by so important an orchestra a paying proposition. To this he replied that whenever Iturbi and his men performed, the concert hall was packed to full capacity, and that after performances the musicians, including the conductor, always assembled in his little inn, where, over cups of coffee, to discuss all sorts of subjects, including Iturbi's travels through different parts of the world.

It was early evening when I reached the outskirts of Valencia, and a heavy downpour obliged me to seek shelter in a garage. Its owner and two assistants were so worried by the fact that my clothes were wet, that they made me sit near an electric fire, and before I knew what was happening, one of the men arrived with a glass of brandy he had fetched from a nearby tavern. When I told the good Samaritans that I did not know Valencia, and that I had no idea. where I was going to stay, the boss rang up an hotel where he made a reservation for me. This done, he proceeded to telephone to a colleague who, as he told me, ran a garage quite near the hotel, where my machine would be in good hands. After about an hour the downpour ceased, and when I made ready to depart, and asked my new friends what I owed them for all their kindness, they were almost offended.

Owing to adverse weather conditions I saw very little of Valencia until next day, when bright sunshine made walking through the ancient town a great delight. There was so much to be seen that I was constantly on the move, looking at ancient monuments, watching people, visiting the Art Gallery and meeting a painter for whom I had a letter of introduction from a friend in Madrid. It was he who solved a riddle for me. During one of my walks I came to a modern kind of triumphal arch, situated in the middle of a vast plaza, and surrounded by well-tended flower beds. On the top of the arch was what I took to be a most peculiar effigy of a neckless eagle with outspread wings, perched on a crown. A plaque below revealed that the monument was erected to the memory of the fallen during the Civil War, so after another look at the peculiar eagle, I went to inspect another monument which stands near by. I liked the second one immensely, for it represents the famous Valencian artist, Pinazo, in the act of painting. For the rest of the day the thought of the neckless eagle kept passing through my mind. That night, when I met the painter, he explained that what puzzled me does not represent an eagle, but a bat. Apparently this insectivorous mammal is the emblem of Valencia, and was adopted owing to a legend connected with King Jaimé I of Aragon. According to it, in 1238, when he and his troops were preparing to wrest the town from the Moors, on the night previous to the attack, the king was in his tent, surrounded by several of his captains. Whilst the plan of attack was being discussed, a bat flew into the tent and perched itself on the monarch's crown. This being taken as a good omen, it was decided to make the attack on the town at once, and so it came about that the Moors were expelled, and hence a crown surmounted by a bat. Two centuries previously Spain's national hero, El Cid, had also captured the town from the Moors who subsequently re-conquered it. The legendary El Cid combines in his person the highest conception of valour and courtesy. "El Cid," a poem about him, has nearly four thousand lines, and scores of ballads still exist about this great fighter who died in the year 1099, after having reached the age of approximately sixty. According to one of the countless legends concerning him, even after his death, when his body was placed on his war-horse, the Moors fled in terror upon seeing the animal and its dead rider come charging towards them.

The general aspect of Valencia is distinctly oriental, though the modern part of the town, with its luxurious shops and wide paved streets, stands out in startling contrast with the narrow winding lanes of the old sector in which I spent most of my time. The ancient churches with their coloured glazed tile domes glittering in the sun, venerable walls and city gates, loafers, laden donkeys, tall palm trees, and general atmosphere, often made me feel that I was in North Africa. Among themselves, the natives of those regions speak Valenciano, which is a softer-sounding version of Catalan, as spoken in the northern regions near Barcelona and the eastern parts of the Pyrenees.

As everywhere else, the markets were a great attraction to me. One of the most characteristic and picturesque I have seen anywhere is the textile market of Valencia. Nothing suggests its presence until one passes through one of three or four archways which lead to a round kind of *plaza,* surrounded by old high houses with balconies, built in a circle. Once upon a time the market place was the scene of jousts, tournaments and bullfights, and from the windows and balconies of the surrounding houses people watched the displays of daring and bravado below. To-day tents and awnings fill the former arena, and instead of the clattering of armour and swords, and the snorting of horses and bulls, the chatter of hundreds of female voices reverberates through it whenever the market is at its peak of activity. In high shrill voices vendors offer their goods; there is haggling and bartering, laughter and gossip, and all the time prospective buyers circulate or push their way through from stall to stall, whilst here and there a man or woman looks down on the busy scene from a window or balcony. Between some of the latter, suspended from strings, clothes hang out in the sun, and on the sunny side Venetian blinds of various bright colours afford shade to the people who are behind them. The eight-sided bell-tower of Miguelete is one of the most famous landmarks of Valencia. The town is, as it were, a man-built island in the *huerta* (vegetable garden) which surrounds it. Thanks to artificial irrigation, and a perfect climate, almost anything grows in those regions where skilful husbandmen succeed in getting the best out of the soil. Apart from horticulture and agriculture, the industrious and thrifty Valencians – like their cousins, the Catalans – are also successful industrialists, and therefore envied by many of their less enterprising and consequently poorer countrymen.

During one of my solitary rambles through the modern section of the town, a foxy-looking young man sidled up to me, and holding before my eyes what appeared to be a gold ring, inset into which was a large diamond, whispered, "*Señor,* I see you are a stranger, and therefore I trust you." Then, almost sobbing, he began to tell me a heart-rending story of a family misfortune, due to which he was driven to part with his treasured heirloom. The diamond alone, he assured me, was worth at least double of what he was prepared to accept from me, a stranger, who would take the ring to a far-away country where no one would recognize it as being the testimony of the fall in fortune of an ancient and once upon a time highly respected Valencian family. Being acquainted with this old confidence trick, I let the young man talk for some time, and when he suggested that the two of us go to any jeweller to have the stone valued, I spoke for the first time, but before I could finish what I had to say, the young man ran away as if some demon were chasing him. Of course, the ring and stone which he showed to me were genuine, and if the two of us had gone to some jeweller, his assessment of the diamond's value would have amounted to double or even more than the price the young man asked for it from me. However, if I had fallen into the trap, my would-be swindler would have taken the ring back from the jeweller, and in the act of doing so, by a sleight of hand he would have "spirited away" the genuine article, and put another ring with a glass replica of the diamond on one of my fingers.

Between about noon and 2 p.m., and then again in the evening, masses of well-dressed men stroll up and down the main street of the new sector of the town, whilst others stand in groups at street corners. The less prosperous-looking members of Valencia's male community sit on benches or hang about on a huge kind of terrace in front of the *Ayuntamiento* (City Hall), making one wonder who keeps the wheels of industry turning.

In my modest hotel I made the acquaintance of several peasants who had come to town on business. All wore dark-grey smocks and black corduroy trousers, and even during meals did not take off their berets (in Spain called *boinas).* They were fine-looking men, two of them rather stout, but the others lean, with clean-shaven faces and finely-chiselled aquiline noses which gave them an aspect of pride and distinction. After meals we sat in a circle, talking about many subjects and cracking jokes. One evening, when one of our circle left in order to return to his *barraca,* as farms are called in those parts, he invited me to visit him. His home being near the town, towards midday I set out on my motor-cycle which took me to my destination in about an hour. How neat the white-washed *barraca* looked, with bright flowers in window-boxes, and its garden in which everything grew in wild profusion. When I arrived, and my friend from the hotel came out to give me his welcome, one would have thought I was a brother whom he had not seen for years. When he introduced me to his wife and family, he did this with a natural grace and elegance for which any marshal of the diplomatic corps might well have envied him. After a simple though excellent meal, my host showed me some of the neighbouring farms, and told me a great deal about conditions in the neighbourhood. Density of population, he explained, is one of the most serious troubles; in the wake of it come many others. In these regions orange-groves can be seen everywhere, and pomegranate, lemon and olive trees thrive also. Most of the peasants wear hempen sandals, called *espardenas* which are both cheap and practical, though far from elegant, especially in cases when the wearer's big knobbly toe overlaps the thick sole.

On my return to the town, I befriended another man in a curious way. I was so thirsty that upon reaching a tiny tavern in a side-street, I parked the cycle against a wall, and went inside to have a glass of wine. Whilst I was sipping some of it, a Galician knife sharpener came along the road, pushing before him his barrow-like workshop, at the same time blowing a shrill tune on his little panpipe. Upon seeing the motor-cycle, he stopped to examine it closely and with great concentration. After a while, evidently intending to ask me some questions about the construction and the mechanism of the machine, he came into the tavern and ordered a glass of wine. In order not to appear to be over-anxious to break the silence, he turned his back towards me, and began to whistle, "It's a long way to Tipperary." Now it was my turn to turn my back on the newcomer, and to pretend that I did not realize that the tune was being whistled for my benefit, and to attract my attention. Just for a little joke I began to whistle "Valencia," and so the little game between the Galician and myself went on for some time, until our eyes happened to meet. "*Señor*," the knife-sharpener asked, smiling bashfully, "do you know Teeperarree ? It is in *Inglaterra,* is it not? Ah, they make fine *motos* in Teeperarree! Yours out there is *muy maja* (very spruce). Would you mind telling me? Is it a two or four stroke?"

The ice having been broken, the two of us conversed for some time. To my surprise the young man knew a great deal about motors, and when we parted he told me that his greatest ambition was to become the owner of a *moto,* exactly the same as mine.

The church of San Juan is situated in the centre of the town, near the central market. One peculiarity about it attracted my attention. In its semi-subterranean vaults, the entrance to which face the street, are junk shops in which only old iron is sold, rusty keys, bolts, rivets, springs of clocks, and masses of similar odds and ends. Here and there street vendors sell liquorice sticks, which brought back memories of days gone by.

Owing to the prolonged drought, the river Turia[4] was only a dirty little stream, and in its wide bed a few cattle were grazing. I crossed it over one of its several long and well-built bridges, on my way to the

---

[4] Also called Guadalaviar, derived from the Arabic *Wadi-al-abyad,* meaning "White River".

port, some two and a half miles distant. This is a trip I do not recommend, for besides the small but quite neat port, nothing attractive is to be seen there.

Before leaving Valencia, one word to green-eyed young ladies who look for a husband. Nearly all the local men with whom I discussed feminine charms simply raved about *ojos verdes* (green eyes). Most likely this was due to the fact that dark skins and black eyes predominate in those regions where people show strong traces of the successive occupation by the Greeks, Carthaginians, Romans and especially of the Moors. The original inhabitants were Iberians, and at a later period some of them intermixed with Visigoths which accounts for the sprinkling of more or less fair-skinned and light-eyed people in those parts. Be this as it may, green eyes are a rarity and therefore greatly admired; so young ladies of this ocular hue, here is a tip for you. Be of good courage, take the jump, and make your battle-cry: "Valencia and green eyes for ever!"

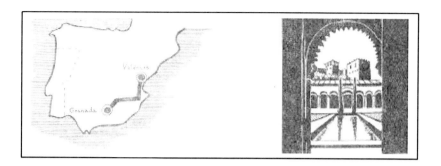

CHAPTER 12

VALENCIA – ALICANTE – BAZA – G UADIX – GRANADA

It was early morning when I left Valencia. Travelling in a southerly direction, for some distance I followed the river Turia which flows into the great lagoon of Albufera. This wide and roughly fifteen-mile-long stretch of fresh water is divided from the sea by a narrow strip of land on which are small forests of sea-pines. The marshy smell was mixed with the scent of these trees and that of wild flowers which grew everywhere in great profusion. The name Albufera is of Arabic origin, *al-buhera,* meaning "the lagoon." The waters are fresh, and though only between ten and twelve feet deep, in them thrive numerous fish and eels. As I was riding along the lagoon's reed-covered bank, fisher-men were making ready to set out in boats with peculiar triangle-shaped sails. The slight haze of early morning, the mirror-like surface of the waters and the border of tall slender bullrushes, made a fine setting as, through a gap in which I caught a glimpse of the boats, I halted, took my camera, and went down to the water's edge whence I photographed the scene, without the fishermen being aware of my presence. As I was to discover later, the picture turned out even better than I expected, and several artists who have seen it think it is a dry-point. Such can be the luck of an amateur photographer.

On the lagoon's western bank are a number of small but interesting villages, near which are extensive paddy-fields. Besides rice, wheat and beans are grown in these regions. A native told me that thanks to favourable climatic conditions and artificial irrigation, some of the fields yield as much as three crops per year. Here I must mention that the Moorish conquerors taught the Spaniards how to convert some of the deserts into fertile land by the help of artificial irrigation, which until then was unknown in Europe. Many of the Moors' admirable works are still to be seen, among them being the lagoon of Albufera which is a converted salt marsh. In some of the marshes, large water-wheels are used to drain the land, and the peasants' *chozas* (huts) have thatched roofs. I was told that in summer mosquitoes are a plague, and that the inhabitants of these "rice-villages" suffer from malarial fever. Here and there, for long stretches, trees planted on either side of the road gave welcome shade, and in open parts I had fine views of serrated mountains ahead. Among them the Sierra de las Agujas (Needle Mountain) with its sharp-pointed peak, was particularly conspicuous. The region offered so much of interest that I decided to stay in a village situated near the southern end of the lagoon.

The little modest *fonda* (inn) of my choice turned out to be spotlessly clean, the food served simple but well-cooked, and the people I met there most interesting and amusing. Shortly after my arrival, whilst I waited for a Spanish omelette to be cooked for me, three elderly men of the peasant class came in to have some wine. The tap-room, in which food was served at a long, crudely-made wooden table with a bench on either side, was low, and its walls and ceiling whitewashed. Of course, table-cloths and napkins were not used in the humble establishment, but the tops of tables, stools and benches were scrubbed snow-white, though here and there could be seen obstinate stains where red wine or hot grease had fallen, or nasty black grooves where careless clients had deposited lighted cigars or cigarettes. In a large rustic cage which hung on one of the walls, a canary divided its time equally between singing its heart out and nibbling at a leaf of lettuce, whilst a cat which sat on the counter licked its coat and occasionally cast a longing sideways glance in the direction of the golden-yellow temptation.

When my omelette was brought in by a buxom woman of about thirty, who looked forty, the boss introduced her to me as his wife, and then seated himself beside me, in order to converse whilst I was eating. He told me all about the region being over-populated, and that he was intending to migrate to Brazil. In order to show me how much red tape is connected with emigration and immigration nowadays, he went to fetch a stack of correspondence he had had with the Spanish and Brazilian authorities, and asked me if I knew of a short cut to overcome some of the obstacles. Whilst the two of us were talking, one of the trio who were drinking their wine at another table, shouted: "Never mind all that *papeleo* (paper business), come here and join us, the two of you. Let's have some more wine and a good laugh."

The man who called us was of a good age, ponderously fat and very jovial, and his two cronies were also well past middle-age, and soon after the five of us sat together, talking, laughing and drinking wine. The stout one revealed himself to be a great character, and a man who had seen quite a bit of the world. In the course of our conversation I discovered that his French was perfect, and when I asked him how and where he had learnt the language, he told me that he had worked for seventeen years in Paris as an engraver, and that during his life, in turns, he had been a bullfighter, variety artist, and that in his old age he had risen to the giddy heights of being, as he put it, "*aunque lo diga yo*" (although I say it) the best baker in the whole region of the Albufera. His fat face which looked like an unshaven full-moon seemed to be made of rubber, for whenever he spoke, cracked a personal joke, or laughed, it twisted itself into all sorts of shapes. When one of the company teased him about the enormous size of his toothless mouth and his practically bald head, the stout one roared with laughter and replied that both these facts went to prove that he was reaching his second childhood, but that this time he would not make the mistake of drinking milk. His two companions, as I had guessed rightly when they arrived at the place, were agriculturists. Between jokes and laughter, when we discussed the local situation, they had a great deal to say about the heavy taxation and interference of Government inspectors, whom they accused of being utterly unscrupulous, and the main go-betweens in the great game of *estraperlo* (black market).

When the three jolly cronies left, they insisted on paying for everything, including the food I had eaten, and late that evening they returned for another long and merry session.

Continuing my journey in a southerly direction, for some time I passed through more or less flat and very fertile regions. Although I was near the sea, only here and there did I get a glimpse of splendid sandy beaches and rocky land-points. The several villages through which I passed were picturesque, but very much alike. Oranges were being harvested, the golden fruit being carried by donkeys in large panniers, or loaded on carts. It was about 2 p.m. when, upon reaching a small town named Gandia, I halted at a modern filling-station. When its owner tried to manipulate the new and beautifully painted pump, and it refused to function, he heaved a deep sigh, and told me to wait a little while whilst a boy went to fetch a mechanic whom he described to me as being a wizard. After some time, when the messenger returned, he reported that the man was just finishing his lunch, and that he would not be long in arriving. Whilst waiting I got into conversation with several men who, guessing that something had gone wrong with the petrol pump, had appeared as if by magic to watch it being mended. Time passed, and still the "wizard" failed to turn up, so the boy was sent once more with an SOS. To make a long story short, the messenger was sent a third time to remind the man that his help was urgently needed, and upon returning he brought the ominous news that the mechanic was just finishing a game of cards, and that he would not be long in coming on his bicycle. Fortunately I was in no hurry, and as my company was pleasant, and the conversation interesting, I enjoyed this interlude. After having kept us waiting for exactly two hours and a quarter, the "wizard" came wobbling down the road on his bicycle. "What's happening?" he asked, upon getting off his machine. "What's all this hurry about? Can't a man be left to have his meal in peace?"

Having cast a glance at the petrol pump, he calmly lit a cigarette, and whilst everybody watched in respectful silence, proceeded to take out of his pockets two or three spanners and screwdrivers, all of which he laid on the ground with great care. This done, he puffed away at his cigarette, and told us all about his recent game of cards. After what seemed an eternity, he took a long last puff, threw away the end, spat on the ground, hitched up his trousers, and then set to work with astonishing speed, unscrewing the cast-iron casing of the pump, and investigating the mechanism within. We onlookers craned our necks to watch cog-wheels, pins and other mysterious objects being taken out of the casing, presently to be put back, one by one. "*Ya está!*" – it's already done – the "wizard" exclaimed. And sure enough, when the boss manipulated a long handle, the glass container above the pump began to fill with petrol, and soon after the tank of my motor-cycle was full. "Many thanks," I said before departing, to which the boss and the "wizard" replied in unison, "For nothing, *señor*."

Shortly after I found myself in beautiful mountainous country. The winding road was quite good, and every now and again below me spread the deep-blue waters of the Mediterranean Sea. Rounding a curve, I came to a spot which made me think that I had arrived in Fairyland. On my right, like a perfect stage setting, were several high jagged mountains, arranged in a semicircle, and between them and the place whence I gazed were a few rolling hills, covered with olive, pomegranate and almond trees, all in full bloom. The delicate pink of the almond blossom and the bright scarlet of that of the pomegranate stood out to perfection against the green background. On my left, like an enormous bowl open at the far end, were steep inclines, all planted with olive trees and patches of pineapple, with here and there a few almond or pomegranate trees to add to the riot of colour. Down below, at the open end of the huge bowl, out of the deep-blue sea rose a gigantic rock, the famous Peñon de Ifach. Alongside the road, among a mass of flowers, stood a whitewashed house, its arcades, balconies and geraniums in pots making an enchanting sight. Upon realizing that the house I looked at was an *albergue* (guest-house), there and then I decided to travel no further that day. On one of the walls, neatly painted in black letters, I read "VENTA DE LA CHATA." In a way, I was lucky to have arrived at the place during the off-season, for upon being shown the interior of the house by the innkeeper, I found that I was the only guest. Never in my life have I seen a neater and more beautifully kept place than the "Venta de la Chata." On tables covered with brightly-coloured and immaculately ironed cloths, stood vases filled with flowers. Everything was spick and span, and the owner of the place and his family quiet and very friendly. His two sons were busy loading earth on a donkey whose condition and trappings spoke highly of their owner. The earth was for making a new flower-bed in the garden, and even the donkey seemed to know exactly what he was doing, going to and fro without having to be guided. What a paradise for a painter this spot, only some forty miles north of Alicante.

I walked about as if in a dream until darkness and the first chill of night made me go indoors to sit down to a meal, served by one of the daughters of the house. Later, I joined the family who sat in the hall, the men doing odd mending jobs, and the women sewing at a round table, fitted with flaps, the ends of which were put on the women's laps. Seeing me look at the table with curiosity, one of the party explained to me that it was a *camilla,* and proceeded to show me a small charcoal burner beneath it. Lifting one of the flaps, I seated myself close to the table, with my legs tucked under it, and within a few moments began to feel comfortably warm.

Brilliant sunshine greeted me upon waking next morning, so after a simple breakfast I made ready to depart. The emerald sea below me made me long to have a swim, but remembering the time of year, I proceeded towards the next town, Alicante.

In a village through which I passed, upon seeing come towards me what appeared to be a religious procession, I halted. At the head of it walked the sacristan, carrying a cross, and immediately behind him came an elderly rather stout and dusky priest, on either side of whom was a choir boy, carrying a lighted incense burner. Walking along slowly in two rows, followed some twenty men, each one holding a lighted candle. As the little procession approached me, the sounds of suppressed wailing reached my ears, and I noticed that two or three of the men were staggering as if overcome by emotion and grief. Then it dawned on me that the priest had given – or was on his way to give – the last sacraments to a dying person. The appearance and demeanour of the men had something distinctly American about them, an atmosphere that was enhanced by a few tall palm trees, the brightly coloured tiles of the church's cupola and the low whitewashed houses. I had not gone far when outside the front door of one of them, I saw a group of people on their knees, men, women and a few children, all praying, and every now and again sobbing or wailing. Evidently, within the humble abode with its shuttered windows and open door, lay the dying person.

Although the road I followed was quite good, and the mostly fertile coastal regions veritable gardens of Eden, there was but little traffic, save every now and again a car or some mule or donkey-drawn vehicle. In most parts of Spain gipsies and peasants train their dogs to walk under the vehicles. This is done by tying them by means of a thin rope to the middle of the axle when the animals are young, often only mere puppies. The first few lessons can be most unpleasant for the learners, for if they refuse to follow, they are dragged along. However, once they become accustomed to walking or jogging along beneath the carts, there is no further need to tie them, for they follow without even going near the wheels, no matter in which direction the carts turn. Being under the vehicles, usually the dogs travel in the shade, which is a great advantage during the hot summer months. Other dogs are trained to keep guard on the top of lorries and wagons, and it is surprising to see how they are able to keep their balance, or even to run from side to side whilst being driven along at speed, often round sharp bends of the road. Most of the dogs I saw seemed to enjoy such rides, and many of them took a delight in barking at people as they were being whisked past them.

After I had passed through a stretch of dreary country, the old Moorish castle of Alicante came in sight, perched on a high rocky hill which overlooks the town. Upon approaching the hill, on the steep slopes of which grow many agave plants, the sight of ugly military barracks being erected near its foot jarred my eyes. Near the harbour is a remarkable double avenue of huge date palms in the shade of which idlers appear to pass most of their time. Whilst I was making preparations to leave the town, the usual circle of motor-cycle enthusiasts collected round me. Among them was an elderly man who detached himself from the others just as I was about to crank up. Pointing at the sky towards the west, and then at swallows which were flying so low that they appeared to be skimming over the ground, he said, "Señor, I hope you have a good raincoat among your baggage, for it looks as if we are in for a. wet spell." Indeed, the clouds in the distance looked very threatening, so I remembered the raincoat I had lost on leaving Barcelona.

"Thanks," I replied, "I shall be quite all right. After all, a little rain doesn't hurt a man."

Striking inland, I rode at a merry pace, and soon left the last white, flat-roofed houses of the town's outskirts behind me. I did not like the look of the clouds ahead, for they appeared to be rolling out of the mountain tops to cover the sky like a gigantic black steel shutter. After a while, just as I was catching up with a two-wheeled cart, the peasant who drove the good-looking mule which pulled it shouted to me, "Don't go further, señor. You'll never reach the next houses before the flood begins. Follow me, I know a place where we can take shelter."

It was a good thing that I took his advice, for by the time we reached a hollow spanned by a bridge over which the road passed, the heavens opened with a vengeance. Beneath the bridge we were well sheltered, so, whilst waiting, we smoked and chatted. An hour passed, and still rain fell in such torrents that by degrees the hollow in which we stood was transformed into a muddy rapidly-flowing stream. As it rose higher and higher, we were obliged to shift our position, and when it looked as if we would be driven from our shelter, during a lull in the downpour we decided to trust to luck, and to hurry to the nearest village. The man climbed on the cart, whipped up his mule, I cranked up the motor-cycle, and after brief farewells we began to make a bolt for it. Naturally, I soon left the cart far behind, but then another deluge started, and within a few moments I was soaked to the skin. Spanish country roads are apt to have deep holes in them where least expected, and as the one I followed now looked like a river, there was no telling when I would run into one of those *vaches*. Consequently, I had to drive slowly and with caution, and even more so because water stream-ing down the mica shield which protected my face impeded my vision. At long last, however, I reached the first houses of the village, and as I passed one of them, from the door several girls shouted to me to proceed no further, but to join them inside. Somehow I did not like the idea of accepting their invitation, so with a very wet wave of one hand I drove on through the water. I had not gone far when the back wheel of my cycle skidded and splashed into a hole, with the result that I almost fell. Upon recovering my balance, the same thing happened again, and then I heard a male voice calling me from a nearby house. "*Señor,* for the love of God, stop, and come inside. You'll drown out there!"

This time I accepted the invitation without thinking twice, and soon after found myself inside a humble abode where I was accorded the reception of a mariner saved from a shipwreck. Before I had time to introduce myself, or even to have a look at my surroundings, an old woman brought me a clean towel wherewith to wipe my face and hands, and whilst I did this, another woman piled up a huge bundle of dry twigs in an open fireplace, and lit them. "You are wet to the bones," the man said, "you must put on dry clothes. I will give you what you need."

Not liking the idea of undressing where I was, I explained that I had a sweater in my small suitcase, as well as a spare shirt, trousers and socks, and that if I changed my wet jacket, shirt and socks for dry ones, I would be quite all right. "No, no," one of the two old women pleaded, "you must change your trousers as well, for otherwise you'll catch a *pulmonia.* Quick, come into this small room, here you can attend to your comforts undisturbed." Saying this, she all but dragged me into an adjoining room where I did as ordered. Upon returning to the other room, a huge fire was roaring up the chimney, and I was made to sit near it on a stool. Before I had time to express my gratitude for such kindness and hospitality, there was another stir and rush, for at that moment a dripping wet boy arrived, carrying a bottle. A glass having been produced and placed on a stool near me, some of the liquid was poured into it, and I was told to drink some of it quickly. "This will warm your guts," the man said, "against the wet and cold there's nothing like a drop of cognac."

I had to argue much, and all but use force to make the women desist from cooking something for me, and when things calmed down a little, at last I was able to talk quietly, and to have a look round the room. Its brick floor was rough and littered with small chips of wood, and the furniture was of the most simple; just a rough deal table, two rustic benches and a few stools. From smoke-blackened beams across the ceiling hung what appeared to be small weird-shaped branches of bushes or trees, which looked rather like stags' horns. When I asked what they were for, the man pointed at a corner of the room where I saw a number of wooden pitch-forks. "Making these, and breeding a few rabbits," the man said, "keeps us alive."

Whilst we conversed, at regular intervals one of the women put more dry twigs on the fire, and all the time the rain beat down incessantly. Outside, the road looked like a slow-flowing muddy river, on the surface of which floated masses of bubbles, large and small, according to the size of the drops of rain which brought them into being for a brief existence. During lulls in the downpour, as wave after wave of black clouds came rolling over the nearby mountains, my host pointed at them and assured me that there would be no change of the weather until after sundown. "Don't worry about it," he said, "here we shall make you comfortable for the night, and to-morrow, God willing, it will be fine, and I hope you will come with me to a nearby hamlet which is very picturesque. I have to go there, partly on business, and partly to visit friends, and to have a change from my work."

All my protests were in vain, but after much pressure on my part, towards evening he took me to a brother-in-law of his who ran a small inn and guesthouse in the village. A few moments after having been introduced to the boss and to a number of peasants who passed away time playing dominoes, one might have thought I had known the people for many years. The bedroom in which I deposited my belongings was clean and neat, and the bed good enough to satisfy even one fussy in such matters. The wife and the daughters of the house hurried off to cook my dinner, and after it I joined a circle of peasants who were busy talking about the weather. The sage among them was an unshaven individual who was introduced to me as the village barber. Later in the evening when the first stars began to twinkle through gaps in the clouds, we waded through mud and water to his establishment where, assisted by his son, he attended to clients. Being shaved, or having a hair-cut, seemed to be only a secondary consideration with them, the main attraction of the primitive place being the conversations held in it. Weather and other conditions having been discussed, a number of other subjects were brought before the meeting, and after a while, when it came to politics, things became more lively. The government, the police force, and all officials having been condemned unanimously, and the last client having been shaved, the barber led the way out into the street, locked the door of his shop, and gave marching orders, whereafter we all returned to the inn, where over cups of evil-tasting *ersatz* coffee to begin a new debate.

Early next morning, my saviour of the previous day came to fetch me with a cart drawn by a mule, and as the sun was shining brightly, I looked forward to an interesting little expedition. Parts of the fertile country through which we passed made me think I was in Africa, and the hamlet in which my guide visited relatives strengthened the illusion. I found those peasants, though poor, to be a happy people, but all complained about the hard and difficult times and the uncertainty of the future. That night, upon returning to our starting point, my host insisted that I go to his house to share a meal with him; and lo and behold, when we got there, the good women were waiting for us with a rabbit stew and a jug of excellent, locally grown wine. This is just one of many similar examples I could give of Spanish hospitality and kindness.

The heavy rain had left stretches of the road in a bad state, and as many holes were filled with water, I had to proceed with caution. Whilst passing through a very Moorish-looking little town named Ori-huela I met with a minor accident. The roughly cobbled street through which I rode was narrow and most of it resembled a muddy stream.

Suddenly the back wheel of my cycle skidded into a deep hole, and in doing so caused me to lose balance, and to turn the accelerator of the motor, with the result that the machine leapt forward like a horse taking a jump. Before I had time to brake, I struck the side of a donkey-cart, and ignominiously fell into the slimy water. Within a few seconds, men and women came out of houses and little shops, and whilst one of the latter wiped my clothes and hands with a rag, the others stood, looking on and saying that it was a shame and a disgrace to allow the road to remain in such a shocking state, and that they hoped I would accept their apologies on behalf of the town. Quite unperturbed by what had happened, the donkey stood, looking as if bored. As my shoes had filled with water, I decided not to ride the cycle, but to push it until I should reach a less treacherous road.

The regions through which I passed a little later were hilly, with picturesque mountains quite near. Everywhere oranges, lemons, pomegranate, wheat and potatoes were being cultivated, and along the road I followed moved a regular procession of mule and donkey carts.

In a little wayside inn, where I stopped to have a snack, a number of peasants were assembled. When they finished discussing the prices of lemons and oranges and the prospects of the wheat and potato crops, they teased an elderly braggart who claimed to be a hundred years old. Eventually he came up to me and said, "*Señor*, you are the only intelligent-looking person in here. Please tell me how old you think I am." "Oh," I said after having had a good look at him, "I should say about seventy." This led to more teasing, whereupon my interrogator began to swear in perfect French and Italian, which greatly amused his listeners, though they did not understand any of the insults hurled at them, not in a temper, but in good fun. To finish with, the orator turned to me, and said, "Thirty years ago, when I was forty . . . oh, I mean seventy . . . I used to ride a motor-cycle, not just like you, but in important races, of which I won so many that I only remember those during which I broke world's records." This led to more teasing, but when the man began to tell some remarkably good anecdotes, everybody listened to him in silence.

Near a place called Puerto Lumbreras I stopped in an excellent *albergue*, run by the Spanish Tourist Office. In the evening, whilst I went for a walk among the nearby hills, a fine-looking young man drove a herd of black goats towards his humble abode, all the while singing Flamenco songs, the weird *cadenzas* of which suited the surroundings to perfection.

Leaving the main road, I followed a bad one which wound over hill and through dale, and here and there through a ravine, an amazing old village, or past a ruined castle, arrogantly and defiantly perched on a hill. It happened to be a Saturday when I arrived in an interesting town named Baza, situated on the slope of a hill. The *fonda* (inn) in which I stopped, was situated on a large *plaza* in the upper sector of the historic place which Isabella of Castille captured from the Moors in 1489. Over some of the stone entrance gates to old houses are to be seen the coats-of-arms of ancient hidalgos and grandees. In some of the taverns, wine is kept in huge earthenware containers, in those regions called *quintajas*. The young "bloods" who, like foxes and other nocturnal prowlers, only sally forth late in the evening, were assembled in a more or less modem *café* in the steep main street. With their light gabardine raincoats carelessly slung over their shoulders, they sauntered towards their favourite meeting place, there to spend hours, talking, talking and talking. When I asked my inn-keeper what kind of work those young men were doing, he looked at me with surprise. "Work?" he gasped. "Work? They don't even know what the word means. They just live at home, sleep practically all day, and are out all night. Their parents, sisters and servants do all the work for them."

I loved watching men ride on their donkeys and little mules on which they almost invariably sit sideways. In many cases, besides the riders, the beasts carry enormous loads. Sometimes, when two riders meet and begin a long conversation, the animals stand patiently, every now and again putting the main weight from one hind-leg to the other.

After dinner, two or three of the guests and several local know-alls sat on a low wall outside the inn. When they called to me to join them, I seated myself on the wall, the top stones of which had been polished by countless posteriors of babblers who in the course of centuries have held forth there. The main topic of our conversation was a football match which was to take place on the morrow. The visiting team was described to me as being formidable, and the forecast was that the struggle would be titanic. Accordingly, when the great hour approached, in the company of several new friends, I went to the nearby *cancha de futbol*. Situated on the gentle slope of a hill, its surface and levelling-out were the result of much hard labour, and, no doubt, considerable expense. Upon entering through a small door in an old wall, we seated ourselves on some roughly made steps which were the grand-stand. The balconies of several houses which faced the sun-baked grassless field were crowded with people, among them a number of young and middle-aged ladies whose brightly-coloured dresses, and here and there a *mantilla,* were more suggestive of a bullfight than of a football match. Those of the spectators who could not afford the luxury of a seat stood on the far side of the field, whilst others made themselves comfortable on a steep slope behind one of the goals. Immediately behind the other, the field came to an abrupt end, a drop of some eight or nine feet ending in a road below, where stood many who had come to listen. Until a spoil-sport policeman intervened, a number of boys and young men had made themselves as comfortable as circumstances permitted on various trees, and whenever the vigilant eye of the representative of law and order was turned in some other direction, agile and enterprising youngsters made acrobatic and cunning infiltrations, quickly to mingle with the spectators, and to look as if butter would not melt in their mouths.

The match was billed to begin at 4 p.m., but this being a football match, and not a bullfight, it was a quarter to five before there was a stir among the spectators, and presently loud cheers as, one by one, some of the players ran, danced or solemnly walked onto the field. By the time the last straggler made his appearance, the atmosphere among the little crowd of onlookers was electric, and even the three or four stolid members of the Civil Guard adjusted their shiny three-cornered hats. When the referee appeared, he was greeted with a great ovation. And well he merited it, for in his spotless white shoes, reddish-brown and marvellously creased trousers and lilac-coloured buck-skin pullover, he was as startling as the brightest and weirdest creation by Picasso. The game which followed was played at a great pace, and every time one side or the other scored a goal, on a huge board at one end of the field, a number was put up under LOCAL or VISITANTE, according to who had put the ball into the net. Evidently, in matches of the type I watched with great delight, so many goals are expected to be scored that only human adding machines can keep pace with them. Be this as it may, this was the first time I had seen a score-board at a football match, and the game I witnessed was keen and played in the right spirit. After its termination, when the victorious visitors made ready to depart to their home town, a swarm of young men and boys ran after the charabanc, cheering them wildly, whereafter the little town of Baza became tranquil once more.

Sitting in our little forum outside the inn, we were discussing the recent match, when suddenly there started quite a commotion among the many children who had come to watch the *futbolistas* depart. Boys cheered and laughed, little girls screamed and ran away, as out of the inn came the middle-aged handy-man, guiding a huge rat which he held subjected with a long piece of string firmly tied to the middle of its tail. Apparently he had caught the horrid rodent in one of the several ingenious traps of his manufacture, and now was bent on showing off to the populace. As the unfortunate rat tried to struggle away, he guided it towards the youngsters, who greatly enjoyed this peculiar game. After a while, when the excitement began to subside, the cause of all this commotion was taken to the nearby fountain where it was made to swim until it drowned.

Guadix, the next town through which I passed, is situated in a fertile basin in a large steppe, the semi-barren parts of which are tertiary deposits of debris. The hilly sectors are furrowed where during rainy periods water causes erosion, which, in its turn, has produced weird rock formations. Here and there I came to small settlements of cave-dwellers, and I was surprised to see that several of the comfortable dwellings on the outskirts of Guadix have electric light, and one even a telephone. Their entrance doors are well made, and in most cases painted in bright colours. But more about cave dwellings later.

From some of the heights in this region I had excellent views of the weird winding arid depressions below, or of stretches of *vega,* as fertile parts are called. Ahead, dark clouds were gathering, so like a young lady in a capricious mood, only every now and again did the snowed *sierras* ahead give me a glimpse of their wild beauty.

At intervals I passed peasants who were seated on donkeys, or who drove the beasts before them. "*Arré, burro!*" (Gee up, donkey) was the cry I heard almost continuously as they passed me, the "r's sounding like the rolling of a drum. The Spanish word *arriero,* meaning a man who drives animals (horses, mules, donkeys or cattle) is derived from the call "*arré,*" gee up!

Upon reaching the top of a pass, a sharp shower made me take refuge in a shallow cave which, most likely, had been hewn out of the soft rock by road builders. I had not been there long when a few gipsies and peasants joined me. A jolly little gathering it turned out to be, especially so when one of the peasants, a typical Andelusian, tried his repartee on a middle-aged gipsy woman whose quick wit and sharp tongue was more than a match for the man's friendly jibes. As the two indulged in their verbal duel, the rest of the company listened and watched facial expressions, disdainful glances of twinkling eyes, shrugging of shoulders and tilting of the head by the woman, as the pair jousted, and every now and again a particularly witty or biting reply brought forth roars of laughter. After a cutting remark made by the woman, her antagonist turned to me, and through the corner of his mouth said, "You see, señor, this gipsy is *salada*" (salted). As it happened, I knew the meaning of this expression which is a great compliment in Andalusia where wit and quick repartee is more appreciated in a woman than even beauty. By the time the shower passed, and we made ready to proceed in our respective directions, I fully realized that the gipsy virago was a well-"salted" specimen. "*Arré, burro!*" she shouted to me as I made ready to depart, and then added quickly, "*Por amor de Dios, rubio* (fair-skinned and fair-haired one), don't think I am speaking to you. I am addressing your *moto*. Beware of the kick, and beware of the *morenas!*" (dark ladies).

At different times I had heard a great deal about banditry in the mountains which loomed ahead of me, but guessing that these reports were based more on imagination than on fact, I rode alone enjoying the wild scenery. Between the sea-coast, whence I had come, and the summits of the Sierra Nevada, every zone of vegetation is represented, from the tropics to the Arctic Circle. In the low regions thrive palms, oranges, lemon, pomegranate trees, pineapple and other hot climate fruits, then come maize and wheat fields, chestnuts and oaks, and higher up *borreguiles* (sheep pastures), and above them tower regions of eternal snow.

As the twisting and winding road took me higher and higher, then down into wild desolate valleys, every now and again through a small settlement or past a solitary shepherd's hut, to begin another long climb, I found it difficult to believe that I was in Spain. In high places, cold winds swept over the beautiful rocky desolation, making me long to reach more sheltered parts.

Among these mountains, during the Civil War a whole relief

column of "Red" volunteers perished. When the news reached them that some of their comrades were beleaguered on the other side, despite adverse weather conditions and warnings by those who realized that an attempt to cross the *sierras* during the winter amounted to suicide, they set out into the mountain fastness where all perished in a snow-storm, and where their remains lie unburied to this day.

In olden times some of the *sierras* in different parts of Spain were the strongholds and hiding places of bandits.   Among them were several Robin Hoods, whose exploits are being recounted and sung to this day. In Andalusia especially, *bandoleros* and some of their feats of daring, appeal to the imagination of people who, with the passing of time, have enlarged on fact. As I was to learn after having crossed the mountains, a few bands of so-called bandits are still active there, but as the main highways are well patrolled by the Civil Guard, travellers are perfectly safe. I have it from good authority that a few bands of poor mountaineers make occasional raids on remote villages or on travellers who venture into the mountain fastness, but that such attacks or kidnappings are directed almost exclusively against people – mostly government officials – against whom the desperadoes have a grievance.

At this point I must interrupt my narrative with an aside connected with banditry in Spain. When I sent the manuscript of this book to be typed out neatly by the lady who has done this work for me during the past few years, she returned it to me with a letter, part of which reads as follows: " . . . A friend of mine used to carry around with him a pocket-knife the size of a miniature sabre with a wicked-looking blade. He used it to sharpen his pencils. The knife was given him by a priest who had acquired it in Spain – he had come upon a Spanish brigand. dying in solitude and extreme poverty. The brigand had repented his bri-gandry and received absolution, etc.; but as he was at the point of death he murmured something and pushed the knife into the padre's hand. 'My thanks and dying gratitude, Father. This is my greatest treasure, and remember my advice always – Your thumb on the blade, and strike upwards.' "

Another letter, written to me by the same lady, reads as follows:

"I am so pleased you liked the story of the brigand's knife. There was an amusing sequel. My friend who was given the knife was sent to Ireland in 1921 just after the 'rebellion' as unofficial liaison mediator (he was not a politician but a writer, very much beloved both in Ireland and England – an Englishman with Irish sympathies). He was debating in the Abbey Theatre and while his opponent was speaking, he drew out the knife absent-mindedly to sharpen his pencil in order to make a note. He was startled by a roar from the Irish audience (who were not in sympathy with the opponent): the whole Abbey Theatre (which was packed to capacity) rose as one man and shouted, 'By God – have at him!' . . . . It then dawned on my friend that they thought (being Irishmen) that the knife was being kept 'at the ready' for practical and immediate use and attack!!! It was quite a few minutes before he was able to restore some sort of order!'"

Thanks for these stories, Miss Nicholl. I am sure readers will enjoy them as much as I did.

But to continue with my travels. I was glad when a long winding descent took me to lower regions, and when, at last, I came to a number of modern-built little villas with flower gardens, and a few neat cottages. Upon seeing that one of the latter was a humble wayside inn, I stopped to drink a glass of brandy, for during the high crossing I got chilled to the marrow, so a little alcohol would do me good. After a short conversation with the pleasant and healthy-looking young inn-keeper, I went out into the bright sunshine, and continued my downhill journey. The gay Andalusian sky and flowers seemed to smile at me, and after a few more twists and turns of the road, at the base of the mountain spur on which I found myself, Granada came in sight. Though the town is situated some 2,000 feet above sea-level, viewed from the spot whence I caught my first sight of it, it suggested no such altitude. The Sierra Nevada with its perpetual snow, and the fruitful hills and plain below, made an unforgettable picture, but what most attracted my gaze were the walls and towers of the Alhambra. Whilst the motor of my cycle ticked over slowly, I sat in the saddle, both feet resting on the ground, feasting my eyes and wondering if it really was true that after years of longing, at last I was beholding Granada.

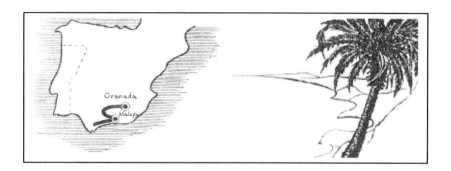

CHAPTER 13

GRANADA – ANTEQUERA – MALAGA – GIBRALTAR

A good friend of mine, who knew all about my financial standing, had invited me to stay in an excellent hotel. Accordingly, upon arriving there I was given a luxurious room, and after a welcome hot bath went out for a walk through the modern part of the town. It was late in the evening when I retraced my steps towards the hotel. As I passed through an old archway which leads into the park, I felt as if I were in a trance. The steep hill before me was beneath a high roof of stately elms, originally brought there by Wellington in 1812. Beside the cobbled road and its sidewalks streams gurgled, bubbled and cascaded down, and among the greenery above me nightingales were engaged in a veritable musical free-for-all. As I slowly ascended the steep incline, listening to the birds and looking at moss-covered rockeries, ferns and bushes, I made mental pictures of the Alhambra above, and what I expected to see on the morrow when I would visit that great masterpiece of Moorish architecture and art. Back in the hotel, after a sumptuous dinner, together with many other guests, I watched a performance given by gipsies who entertained us with some of their typical songs and abandoned dances. My day had been a long and strenuous one, so by the time the hour of midnight approached I was ready to go to bed. Whilst I lay, reading bits out of a newspaper, and thinking over this and that, suddenly it dawned on me that I was in the wrong hotel. What was I to do? Get up, pack my few belongings, go and explain the situation to the management, pay my bill, and ride over to the other hotel? No: I did not like the idea, for various obvious reasons. Having taken counsel with myself, I decided that I might just as well hang for a sheep as for a lamb. After all, I had come to Granada to enjoy myself, and even if I over-spent on my limited budget, surely things would sort themselves out, and, perhaps, in some town along my route, a lecture or two could be arranged for me at short notice, and thus I would be able to pick up some *pesetas*. Accordingly, from my comfortable bed I telephoned to the other hotel, informing the reception clerk that owing to unforeseen happenings I was obliged to cancel my reservation. This done, in order to calm my shaken nerves, I telephoned for a large brandy and soda, and by the time I finished drinking it I saw the humour of my situation, so after having chuckled to myself I fell into a deep sleep.

It would take up far too much space if I attempted to describe – even if only briefly – all the marvels I saw in Granada. Therefore, a few personal experiences will have to suffice, but, for the sake of readers who may not be acquainted with the intricacies of early Spanish history, I will give a few superficial pointers which may be of interest to them.

No doubt, in the remote past, Iberians had settlements on the two-ridged hill, where – roughly in the seventh century – the Moors built their imposing fortress and amazing palaces. The old and original town of Granada lay to the north of the hill of the Alhambra, on the other side of a deep gorge of the river Darro, an Alpine torrent which is fed by the melted snows of the nearby Sierra Nevada. The waters of this river are diverted in great part for purposes of irrigation, and the rivulets on the said hill are the legacies of Moorish skill and enterprise. The modern sector of the town extends to the east where the river Darro joins the Genil. The old part is known as Albaicin, a name derived from the Moorish *Rabad-el-bayyacin,* meaning "quarter of the falconers." Once upon a time, the Albaicin was inhabited by members of the Moorish aristocracy, but to-day it is occupied by many gipsies, of which there are estimated to be some three thousand in greater Granada. In the heyday of Moorish domination, Granada had a population of about half a million, but after its downfall – caused indirectly and to a large extent by dissension and strife among Moorish noblemen – expulsion and migration reduced the population to a little over thirty thousand. To-day this has grown to over 150,000.

The name "Moors" is of Latin, Greek and Spanish origin; *maurus,* Latin, *mauros,* Greek and *moros,* Spanish. The members of this composite North African race were dark-skinned, and were a mixture of Numidians, Phoenicians, Arabs, Berbers, Saracens (the name given by Greek writers of the first century to the Bedouin Arabs) and of various tribes. Conquered and subdued by the Arabs, most of them embraced the Mohammedan religion. It is believed that in the seventh century, following an invitation by certain factions of the Christian Church party in southern Spain, to assist in the suppression of the Visigothic aristocracy, Tarik, the Mohammedan general, crossed the straits of Gibraltar with a large army. Even though, in the opinion of certain historians, there is a doubt as to whether or not the Moors landed in Spain by invitation, the fact remains that, having gained a foothold in regions which were to their liking, this led to an invasion of the whole Iberian peninsula, and even as far as to the river Loire where Charles Martel defeated the Moors at Poitiers (732). As a result of the prolonged occupation of their country by the Romans and Visigoths, and the overrunning of it by the Vandals, among most of the Spaniards there was an indifference to the new rule by the Moors who, besides being more lenient and tolerant than had been the former conquerors, initiated many improvements, such as distribution and artificial irrigation of land. Though the Moors over-ran the whole of the Iberian peninsula, they never really conquered the North, including the Basque country, Asturias and parts of Galicia. Cordova and Granada became the centres of their dominion, but as there was a great rivalry between two Moorish dynasties – chiefly between those of Arab and Berb blood – this led to disruption. Of this the Christians – who by that time had rallied together – took full advantage, and eventually it led to the expulsion of the Moors who had held sway in Spain for seven centuries. Like all the mighty and conquerors who establish themselves in lands of their desire, the Moors indulged in luxuries, but, being a highly cultivated race, excesses among them were rare. In the study of mathematics, science and philosophy they were far ahead of other European countries, and later their culture and civilization became a great influence on the modern world. Naturally, many Moors intermarried with natives of the Iberian peninsula, especially so in the south where their blood and character remain in strong evidence. Thanks to the Moorish invasion, and later to the Crusades, sugar, cotton and many other articles were introduced into Europe, and it was from the Saracens that we first heard the meaning of the word "chivalry." And now, after these brief and superficial explanations, back to Granada.

The first visit I made to the Alhambra remains so clearly and deeply engraved in my memory that whenever I wish I can return there, almost as if in the flesh. As I ascended the road which leads steeply towards a massive tower-gateway, I was assailed by several quite well-dressed men who offered to act for me as guides. All claimed to speak French perfectly, and one-assured me that "espeaking el Eenglis ees da semm to me as el Espahnis." Having shaken off my would-be guides, I had to run the gauntlet between a row of photograph and picture postcard sellers, but, taking no notice of them I passed through the gateway, and after another short climb reached the top of the hill where I emerged into a small square. From under an archway on my immediate right, several gipsy women and little girls came hurrying towards me to offer baskets filled with strawberries, more picture postcards, various trinkets and what appeared to be amulets and lucky charms. When I refused the various offers, one of the women insisted on telling my fortune, and when I managed to shake her off, I proceeded towards a rampart in order to look at the ravine deep down below, and beyond at the gaily-coloured houses which extend along a sweeping hill. My peace was disturbed by a gipsy boot-black who suddenly appeared as if from nowhere, carrying the wooden box of his trade from a strap slung over one of his shoulders. He was a nice-looking fellow, between seventeen and eighteen years of age, and when I told him to be gone, half pleading, half smiling, he said that all he asked for as good a shine as I could get anywhere in Granada, was two *pesetas*. "I have come here to be alone, and to walk about undisturbed, so please go away and leave me in peace," I replied. "But, *señor*," the gipsy came back, in a humble tone of voice, "it won't take long, and if you can't afford two *pesetas,* I shall shine your shoes for one *peseta* and fifty *centesimos*." "No," I shouted, feigning annoyance, "even if you offer to do it for nothing, I will not waste my time, so, *anda!*" (go away). Despite this, wherever I went, the young rogue followed me, and whenever his and my eyes happened to meet, he smiled and beckoned to me to be seated on some bench or low wall.

The tourist season had not yet begun, so very few visitors were to be seen, and sometimes, for long spells, I was left entirely alone, but whenever I came out of a door or passed through a gate, there was the boot-black, smiling at me, and now asking only one *peseta,* and eventually a mere fifty *centesimos,* "Just to be able to buy myself something to eat."

When I decided that for a first visit I had seen enough of this amazing testimony of the Moors' genius, and my brain was in a whirl with the mass of delicate marble columns and riot of intricate yet harmonious geometrical patterns, brilliant coloured tiles, stalactite arabesque arches, Arabic inscriptions, towers, and turrets with marvellously carved larch-wood domes, resembling lacework, imposing walls and battlements of the fortifications, fountains, sunken gardens with square marble-lined pools at the bottom, flowers, stately old elms, cypresses, palms, orange and lemon trees, upon coming out of a gate, there, again, was the gipsy boot-black, smiling and beckoning to me. Admiring his perseverance, and feeling sorry for him, I said, "Let's go, *picarón* (cunning one). Show me the way to a bench where you may shine my shoes."

Beaming with delight, he led the way towards an archway, in the shade of which I seated myself in a kind of alcove, on a stone ledge on which thousands of long-departed people must have sat before me. Whilst the young man cleaned my shoes as if he were giving the same attention to a precious old vase, the two of us began a friendly conversation. This, however, was interrupted by gipsy women and girls who again came to offer me their strawberries, picture postcards and trinkets, and when I begged my shadow of the day to tell them that, having but little money to spend, I was no buyer, he told them something in Caló, which, I was given to understand, is a dialect of the Spanish gipsy language. Whatever it was, and whatever he said, his few words produced the desired effect, for after that the dusky and cunning-looking fortune-tellers and vendors left us alone. When it came to paying for service rendered, I made a great mistake, which, however, as it happened, led to something I would not have missed for a hundred times the five *pesetas* I gave to the boot-black for his work.

Gipsies are always on the "make", and, as in the case of the proverbial devil who, when he is given one inch, wants the ell, the *simpático* young rogue was bent on squeezing more money out of me. "*Señor,*" he said, "if you want to see something interesting, come home with me, for there my people will entertain you with song and dance." Saying this he pointed towards the Albaicin on the other side of the gorge which separated the towering Alhambra from a long-stretched hill on the other side.

"Oh yes?" was my sarcastic reply. "I know you gipsies. If I accepted your invitation, you and your people would *desplumarme*" (pluck all the feathers off me).

"Please don't tell me that," the young man pleaded. "You've been very good to me. I am inviting you to come home with me because I want to show my gratitude for your generosity, that's all."

After a great deal of teasing on my part, and much persuasion on that of the gipsy, eventually I gave in, and on the following day the two of us met, and he guided me to a colony of cave-dwellers. On the way, when I told my companion that I had seen gipsy dancers perform in my hotel, with a "Bah!" of derision and a look of disgust on his face, he said, "Oh, those! I know them well. Yes, they are gipsies, and they are good performers, but what they do is *de teatro* and *de hotel,* calculated to appeal to tourists, who don't know any better. Just wait until you see my people, they'll do the legitimate stuff for you."

After a long but most entertaining walk, and a steep climb, we reached our destination, where I was introduced as an *amigo* (friend) to my guide's family. Evidently they had been expecting me, for the women and even the little girls were dressed in many-tiered flounced skirts, but the men wore ordinary dark lounge suits, some of which were rather tight-fitting and showed distinct signs of wear. The cave was clean and cosy, and its walls decorated with pictures of gipsy dancers and bullfighters, and on a ledge was a small and brightly coloured statuette of the Virgin, in front of which, in a small red glass container filled with oil, floated a lighted wick. Introductions over, wooden chairs were arranged in a small semicircle, and, of course, *manzanilla* (sherry) was produced. Whilst glasses were being filled, I handed out American cigarettes, of which I had brought a good supply, and then placed three or four packets on a table. For the children I had brought sweets, and so everybody was happy. Our party consisted of about twelve, but it soon became evident to me that all the gipsies were not members of the same family, and that reinforcements had been brought in from some neighbouring cave. The dusky and rather stout old woman who had taken it upon herself to act as waitress, saw to it that glasses were never empty, and that the men did not have to wait until I should offer them more cigarettes. After having conversed for some time, when the party warmed up, two guitars were produced and tuned in, a slow and seemingly difficult and tiring task which called for more cigarettes and *manzanilla*. A *tablón* (small round wooden board) having been put into place, the boot-black was the first to make the boards purr and throb with his footwork, and as the dancing and singing that followed was more or less the same as I had seen in Seville, here I will not repeat what is described in a previous chapter. As time passed, the gipsies got more and more warmed up to their work, not to please me, but quite evidently because the varied rhythm gripped them. As if by magic, bread, smoked ham, sausages and a big jug of wine appeared, and between songs and solo dances we ate like so many wolves. Taking the boot-black aside, I whispered to him that I could not afford to let the party become a kind of banquet, to which he replied that I need not worry, that he had fixed everything, and that no one expected to make any profit out of me. Despite these assurances, I felt very uneasy about things until the time came for me to depart. When I asked the old woman what I owed for the food and enter-tainment, she told me that this matter was entirely in the hands of her son (my guide), and that he would let me know the amount on the way back to the hotel whither he insisted on guiding me. Thinking that in having come to this den of gipsies I had been led up the garden path (in this case the cave path), I was expecting the worst, especially so when the people and even the children gave me a farewell so warm and affectionate that any onlooker might have thought he was witnessing the departure to a distant land of a beloved relative. All the way back to the ancient archway which leads into the park of the Alhambra, my companion never mentioned money. Instead, over and over again he told me how he had enjoyed the party and my company, and that he hoped that if ever I returned to Granada "*Vd. sabe en donde tiene su casa*" (literally translated: You know where you have your house, meaning: you know where there is a home for you). This formal Spanish phrase did not help to allay my fears; but then, I thought to myself, if my companion intended to over-charge me, why had he insisted on showing me the way home? After all, if he meant to rook me, I could flatly refuse to pay, and where we found ourselves there would be very little he could do about it.

When the moment came to part, and again I asked what I owed, the gipsy looked at me with lustrous enquiring eyes, scratched his glossy black hair, and after some hesitation said, softly, "Would eighty *pesetas* be asking for too much?" When I gave him a hundred, or be it roughly one pound, he beamed with delight, and after a warm hand-shake hurried off in the direction whence we had come.

An unexpected pleasure awaited me when I was invited to have tea with the British Vice-Consul in Granada, Sir William Davenhill, whose quaint house is situated in the park of the Alhambra, on the southern slope of the hill. In his day, Sir William was a great walker, and he enjoys local fame as being the man who knows the vast *sierras* and their remotest corners better than any person in the region. After my travels, it felt quite strange to be in a drawing-room of the Victorian type, having a typically English tea served by my host's two sisters.

Before leaving Granada with its many relics of past ages, interesting churches, and tombs of kings and queens, just another few words about the fortifications and palaces of the Alhambra. Early in the eighteenth century, owing to various circumstances, there began a period of neglect, and in 1812 the evacuating French troops did further serious damage. In fact, they would have blown up the fortress, had it not been for a Spanish soldier who cut the fuse-line at the last moment. Later the Alhambra (the Moors' *Medinat al-hambra,* "Red Town", so named owing to the colour of the stone used in building) became a refuge for vagrants and a great many gipsies. The fountains were used by washerwomen, and the gipsies' chieftain – who happened to be a blacksmith – used one of the beautiful tiled towers with a priceless carved wood dome as his forge. Upon inspecting the place, I was astonished to see how little damage the gipsy blacksmith had done, but, unfortunately, the same thing cannot be said for other sections of the palace. Towards the middle of the nineteenth century, restorations were begun half-heartedly, and subsequently the gipsies were expelled from their veritable stronghold, whereafter they moved to the other side of the gorge of the river Darro. Though the work of restoration con-tinues under expert guidance, one great eye-sore remains, namely the Charles V Palace, which was never properly finished. As I looked at the huge dark-red quadrangular edifice, built in the Renaissance style of Rome – for which parts of the old Alhambra were sacrificed, and for the building of which the conquered Moors had to pay – I thought of the old Arabic motto which recurs with frequency on walls I had admired, *"Wala ghaliba ill Allah"* (There is no conqueror but Allah), and I pondered over the equally conspicuous inscription there, that of the motto coined by Charles V (1500-1558), *Plus Ultra.*

Though I could have spent weeks in Granada, so rich in treasures, history and legend, I had to move on, so after having had a final look at the town and the snow-clad Sierra Nevada in the background, I rode away in a westerly direction, towards hills and mountains which rose at the horizon ahead of me, with sinister dark clouds creeping over them.

Being in no hurry, whenever I came to a high spot whence a good view of the countryside could be obtained, I stopped to look at the rolling fields below, and to admire the wild flowers which grew everywhere in great profusion. It was about noon when I reached a little town named Loja, situated at the foot of reddish-grey hills. I was about to pass a little inn, when a man who stood at the door, talking to another, suddenly came running towards me. "Well, well," he shouted, "fancy meeting you here, and riding a *moto!*" No sooner had I stopped than he embraced me, and it was only when he said, "Don't you remember our meeting in Seville?" that it dawned on me that the one who gave me such a warm welcome had lived in the same boarding-house with me. When I explained whither I was bound that day, my old acquaintance laughed and told me to be in no such hurry, and added that as it looked as if it were going to rain at any moment, I had better come inside and have a glass of wine with him. He had hardly spoken when a few rain-drops began to fall, so I was glad to accept his invitation, and even more so when I saw that food could be obtained in the inn, for I had eaten nothing solid since the previous evening. To begin with, I was introduced as an "old and dear" friend to the boss of the establishment and then to several patrons, and whilst it rained heavily, a number of us were assembled at a table, talking and laughing. An old fellow among us was a jolly soul, whose wit and repertoire of proverbs seemed to be inexhaustible. No matter what was said, like a card manipulator who can produce ace after ace, seemingly out of the air, this sage always capped the conversation with a joke or a suitable proverb, of which there are countless in the Spanish language. He had several peculiar mannerisms, among them that of raising his right leg to scratch his calf every time he made a point, at the same time laughing stentorously, showing a row of tobacco-stained teeth, his bulging paunch shaking and quivering, which brought to my mind a half-inflated captive balloon I had seen in Chelsea during the blitzes, when gusts of wind struck it, making it heave, bulge and quiver. I longed to chip in with a proverb as other members of the company did every now and again, but somehow I could never think of a suitable one. When the witty conversation veered to a certain man who, ever since he had become a high-up Government official, had given up frequenting the establishment in which we sat, at last I had a chance. Interrupting the speakers, I said, "This *caballero* must be like the monkey climbing up a flag-pole." "What do you mean?" the stout one asked, looking at me with a grin of anticipation. "The higher he climbs, the more of his backside you see," was my reply, and whilst my listeners roared with laughter, I was proud to have scored one point in this competition of repartee and of quoting proverbs.

Fortunately the rain did not last long, so after having eaten well, and spent some two hours in delightful company, I made ready to depart. It was no easy matter to get away, for by this time I was on such friendly terms with several members of our newly-formed little gang, that they wanted me to stay on, and to make their homes mine for as long as I might wish.

Leaving Loja, I proceeded through hilly and mountainous country, until, towards evening, I came to Antequera, a most picturesque little town, the ancient houses of which are clustered together on the slopes of a hill, on the top of which are the ruins of a Moorish castle. A little beyond the outskirts of Antequera is the remarkable cave of Mengal, and another impressive sight is what the natives call the "Stone Forest," a mass of weird-shaped red marble rocks. Coats-of-arms over some of the entrances to sprawling old houses indicate that once upon a time they were inhabited by grandees or hidalgos. Nearby towards the east, jagged mountains make a fine background to the town, and in the distance, below it, spread irrigated stretches of fertile land.

It was late in the evening when I sat in the garden outside the *albergue,* one of the excellent kinds of inns run by the Spanish Tourist Department. Whilst looking at the nearby town in its beautiful setting, and watching and listening to the swallows playing their evening game, circling, wheeling and screaming through the still air, I had my musing interrupted by the arrival of a motor-car with a "GB" plate on it. The driver was a man of about thirty-five, and his companions, a man and a woman, were considerably older. Wondering if I could be of assistance,

I rose from my seat, and went to speak to the driver. "No, thanks," he said, "we're O.K., just stopped to have a bit to eat and to let the engine cool down a little, and then we shall shoot on to Granada, and next day up to Barcelona and then back into France." "Heavens," I replied, "you are fast travellers. And may I ask you, where did you start from this morning?" "Oh," my interlocutor said, stroking his "graspable" moustache, "actually we left Madrid at five this morning, and on the way here visited Cordova and Seville, not bad places, actually, very Spanish, you know. I'm glad to have seen them."

Having supplied me with this illuminating "actual" information, he went inside the *albergue* to join his two companions, and about half an hour later, when it was beginning to get dusk, the car and its occupants disappeared down the hill as if they were taking part in an exciting race.

The last afterglow of the sun flung the Spanish flag across the horizon, and as it got darker this changed into lines of dark-red and purplish-green. When the last wisps of cloud put out their fairy lights, one by one, like bright stars, electric bulbs in the town on the nearby hill began to twinkle. Sheep and goats on their way home bleated and blethered, the merry voices of children playing reached my ears, boys and girls shouting and laughing, crickets began to chirp, and every now and again I heard the familiar cry of "*Arré, burro!*" as a peasant urged on his donkey. More and more electric lights began to twinkle, and when the moon rose over the jagged mountain peaks, the houses and the Moorish castle above them were turned into silver. The cool air was impregnated with the scent of flowers, and as I sat, giving free play to my imagination, suddenly a. horrible question flashed through my mind; the three English tourists who had departed not so long ago, by what time could they reach Granada?

Instead of following the main road that leads from Antequera to Malaga, I decided to explore the mountainous regions in the southwest. Although some of the roads I followed were exceedingly rough in parts, and many of the inclines long and steep, and certain high parts uninhabited, save here and there for the humble abode of some shepherd, I greatly enjoyed the marvellous panoramas. The sun was shining brightly, and in high places the cold wind was penetrating, but as I approached Malaga, and descended into deep wooded valleys, the atmosphere became pleasantly warm. In such places masses of red anemones, dwarf iris, marigold, large marguerites, and many other wild flowers grew, and oleander bushes seemed to be afire with their bright flowers.

The outskirts of Malaga, though some of the houses are modern-built, I found to be rather dreary, but upon nearing the centre of the town, the picture changed completely. There I came to wide shaded avenues of palm and plane trees, and the hustle and bustle of a modem Spanish town, cars of American vintage, mule-drawn carts, laden donkeys and women carrying baskets, and masses of men strolling about or sitting outside *cafés*.

Owing to its ideal climate and general atmosphere, during recent years Malaga has become a favourite haunt with foreign painters and others who have made their homes there. Among them are quite a number of Englishmen and Americans, but as I had come to meet Spaniards, I kept away from foreign residents and visitors.

From the Moorish fortress which stands on a hill rising above the town, one has a splendid view of the houses and towers below, and of the large harbour, originally used by the Phoenicians. The district of Malaga is famed for its wine, but in modern times the textile industry, iron foundries and sugar mills play a great part in the town's economic life.

It was here that I had my first real taste of southern professional begging. Of course, I had seen beggars in other parts, but those who molested me between Malaga and Algeciras differed greatly from the others. Most of those of the southern variety seemed to be either Moorish or gipsy blood, and they had their own technique of approach. Often, as I walked along, suddenly I would feel a slight tapping on one of my arms, and upon turning round, would discover that I was being touched lightly with a forefinger. Owing to this habit, in those parts beggars are popularly known as *telegrafistas* (telegraphists).

I do not think that even the most liberal public assistance would ever change any typical Spanish *limosnero* (beggar) into anything else but what he was born and educated to be. Among many of them, begging is an old family tradition, in the same way as, among certain gipsies, generations have been horse, mule and donkey traders, or in some cases, thieving nomads. In England and in most other European countries, every step is taken to suppress vagrancy. Compulsory schools and modem legislation have caused the gipsies as such to deteriorate, having made them change their main racial characteristics. Spain without gipsies would lose much of its colour, and Spain without beggars and bullfights simply would not be Spain.

Among the many stories I heard about Spanish beggars is one which was told to me by my friend, Roy Campbell, the South African poet and Bohemian who, among other unexpected occupations, for several years earned his living as a horse and mule dealer in Spain. Regularly, once per week, an old beggar called for his alms at Campbell's house in Toledo, but one day upon having collected it, the old man explained that advancing years and infirmity made it very difficult for him to make the long journey every week, and that, therefore, in future he would have to limit his calls to one per fortnight. To this he added that for his bi-weekly trip to Campbell's house, henceforward he would expect his alms to be doubled, or be it, to receive the amount corresponding to two weeks.

As pointed out previously, in southern Spain, especially so as I approached the regions near Gibraltar, Moorish influence remains strong. Many of the barefooted ragamuffins who swarmed round me whenever I stopped in small towns or villages, made me think I was among North-Africans. Dark-skinned, and in many cases spindle-legged, most of the boys' heads with their far-protruding backs, had the hair clipped short, with only a tuft left in the middle of the forehead. Whenever I was foolish enough to give some of those imps a few coins, hordes of them would come to molest me, for among these beggars the news that an easy victim has arrived goes round quickly.

One day, when I was having something to eat outside a little restaurant, where I could keep an eye on my motor-cycle, youthful beggars so worried me that the waiter came to shoo and chase them away. However, no matter what he did, and what threats he uttered, every time my defender went away for a while, or turned his back, the youngsters renewed their assaults on me. Eventually I had an idea. Calling the biggest and strongest-looking boy to my side, I told him that if he kept all the other beggars away from me I would give him a big sandwich, and, before departing, one *peseta*. This worked miracles, for within a few moments my bodyguard cleared the field of assailants, whereafter he patrolled up and down near me, at the same time munching his sandwich. What happened to him after I left I do not know, but I guess that by the time the other ragamuffins and, perhaps, their parents finished with my *capataz* (over-seer or foreman), as I called him, he must have thought that one *peseta* was inadequate remuneration for the job he had done for me, and for what, most likely, he had to endure and suffer after I had gone.

Most foreign visitors who make a quick inland trip from Gibraltar make Ronda their Mecca. Standing on an isolated hill which rises abruptly from fertile land, and in a setting of mountains, in olden times, this town was a kind of Aladdin's cave for smugglers. With its deep precipices and a wide chasm, formed by the river Guatalevin, the Ronda impresses people who arrive from Gibraltar, and who have not seen any of the many other romantic towns in other parts of Spain.

My journey along the coast, from Malaga to the shores of the Straits of Gibraltar, was a sheer delight. The road I followed was excellent, and the views from many points enchanting. Flowers, shrubs and trees of every clime thrive in this coastal paradise with its white houses, many of which have balconies and windows with wrought-iron work and flowers, the bright colours of which vibrated in the brilliant sunshine. Here and there, as I passed through shaded avenues, I smelt the strong scent of pines, then of eucalyptus, and for long stretches that of masses of wild flowers, and the brine of the sea. Whilst riding along, it almost saddened me to think that very soon I would have to say good-bye to the smiling deep-blue Mediterranean, but at the same time I was thrilled by the prospect of getting my first view of Gibraltar, and of rounding the corner, as it were, before seeing more of that fascinating land, Spain. And so I proceeded slowly until, suddenly, upon reaching the top of a slight incline, ahead of me, to the south-west, appeared the Rock of Gibraltar, not unlike a crouching monster of ancient mythology, looking in the direction of Africa.

CHAPTER 14

CADIZ – JEREZ DE LA FRONTERA – SEVILLE

Fearing that a visit to Gibraltar would mean getting entangled in a mass of red tape, permits and rubber stamps, for myself and the motor-cycle, and then the same again on my return to Spanish territory, I made up my mind to give the place a miss.

Upon reaching the land end of the narrow promontory – which is less than two miles long and about half a mile wide – I came to a Spanish frontier post, outside which a number of workers and other people who had come from Gibraltar were being examined by the guards. I arrived so quietly that an officer of the Civil Guard only realized that I was behind him when he turned round. Surprised by my appearance as if from nowhere, he looked at me, and then at my machine, round which he began to walk slowly, like a judge examining an animal at a horse-show. Upon seeing my "GB" plate, he asked me where I had come from, and when I replied "from Barcelona", he looked at me in blank astonishment. "From Barcelona?" he asked after a pause, the tone of his voice expressing incredulity. "But how do you come from there with an English registration number?" "Because I have come from London, and I am on my way round Spain on this machine," I replied. It was quite evident that the officer did not believe me, but presently, pointing at one of the panniers which were fixed to the back of the machine, he asked, "And what is this sticking out of here?" "A bottle of excellent wine, presented to me by a friend near Malaga. Good stuff this. Would you like to taste some of it?"

When the officer asked me for my documents, in order to save bother and time, from my pocket I produced a special letter of recommendation to the military and civil authorities, given to me in Madrid. He read it with great interest, and then shook me warmly by the hand, and asked me if he could be of any assistance. "Excuse my curiosity," he went on, "but would you mind telling me where you intend to go from here?" "Oh," I said, putting on an air of nonchalance, "first of all to Algeciras, then to Cadiz, Seville, and from there north through Extremadura, over the mountains of Gredos to Salamanca, then more or less along the Portuguese border into Galicia, to Vigo, Cape Finisterre, and then in and out along the shores of the Bay of Biscay, and over the Cantabrian mountains to the French border near San Sebastian, through the Basque country, along the southern slopes of the Pyrenees back to Barcelona, my starting point, only about another three or four thousand kilometres, that's all."

"What a journey!" my listener exclaimed, passing a hand over his forehead and scratching the back of his neck. For a few moments I was very pleased with the effect my words had on the officer, but then he took all the swank and bravado out of me by asking, almost in a whisper, "Pardon me, *señor,* but aren't you a little old for this kind of thing?"

Having had to reply to the same rather annoying question before – and, incidentally, several times later – I used the time-worn stock phrase about a man being as old as he feels, and then cranked up, giving the machine a particularly vigorous kick, and shortly after rode into Algeciras.

My first impressions of the people there were unfavourable. As I cruised about slowly, looking for a suitable place where to stay, out of several hotels and guest houses came dark, oily individuals who evidently acted as "whippers-in." Two or three of them spoke English and French quite well, and stuck to me like glue. This, as well as the general atmosphere, was not Spanish, but that of a sea-port, spoilt by sailors and visitors from abroad. After some looking round, near the port I found an hotel where prices were reasonable, and where they even allowed me to put my motor-cycle in a corner of the entrance hall. In order to make quite sure, I took the precaution of fastening it to an iron pillar with a chain and padlock I had with me for the purpose. This done, I went for a walk to the nearby port area where I seated myself at a table under one of the many large parasols which afford clients shade outside *cafés*. Having ordered a glass of sherry, I looked forward to watching the people and scenes near me, when the first of many impudent beggar boys, shoe-blacks, vendors of contraband watches and fountain-pens, and *souteneurs,* from mere little boys to grown-up men, came to pester me. Seeing me smoke, in quick succession several quite well-dressed and healthy-looking boys came to beg for cigarettes, and when I asked them what they would give me in return for one, some gave stupid grins, but others were so taken aback and bewildered by my question that they retired, evidently thinking they had bumped into some sort of madman.   When the ferry-boat returned from Gibraltar across the bay, masses of workmen landed on the wharf, where officials searched a few of the arrivals for contraband.   This, of course, amounted to a farce, for even to me it was blatantly evident that, some-how and somewhere near, smuggling is done openly and on a large scale.   Incidentally, in Algeciras American cigarettes cost only. eight *pesetas* per packet of twenty, whereas in Madrid and in other inland towns vendors charged anything up to fifteen *pesetas,* transport and the "squaring" of officials *en route* increasing the cost.

With the approach of night, fishermen were preparing their boats, for in those parts most of the fishing is done in the dark, with bright lights burning in the boats to attract the fish.

Upon returning to my hotel for dinner, there I met a French naval officer with whom I had become acquainted in Malaga. Together with his wife and four remarkably good-looking and well-behaved children, he was on his way to Morocco. The family had travelled from France by car, and on the way south had spent a few days with friends in Malaga. Having greeted me at the entrance to the hotel in Algeciras, the French officer apologized for having to ask me for a cigarette. He explained that, having gone without a smoke all day, he craved for a cigarette. As it happened, I had bought several packets of Camels and Chesterfields from the hotel porter, so when I gave one of them to the Frenchman, he was delighted, and whilst puffing away in ecstasy, he told me a story about how he had been swindled in Malaga. Appa-rently, a young man had sold him a packet of cigarettes, and whilst the transaction was being made, the vendor acted as if he were afraid of being seen by the police selling contraband. However, upon opening the packet, and taking out of it a cigarette, the buyer discovered that, instead of American tobacco, it was filled with saw-dust, for which he had given the young rogue fifteen *pesetas*. *"Mais c'était très bien fait,"* the Frenchman told me, "I can't help admiring that bounder for the way he acted his part, pretending to be afraid of the police, and for the way he whispered to me to hide my purchase from spying eyes. *Oui, c'était très bien fait, très bien."*

After dinner I went to have another look round the town, and eventually seated myself in a secluded spot which overlooks the Bay of Algeciras, on the opposite side of which loomed the Rock of Gibraltar with masses of bright lights twinkling at its foot. Stars glittered in the dark-purple velvety sky, and a few ships lying at anchor in the bay looked black and mysterious in the pale-blue light. After a long day I felt somewhat drowsy, so I sat, looking and thinking about nothing in particular, but by degrees I began to feel as if I were dreaming a dream extending over many, many centuries.

Here was I, in a place which once upon a time the Phoenicians thought to be the world's end, a narrow passage between two continents, with nothing but water and sky beyond it. According to ancient Greek and Roman legends, it was believed that in the remote past the African and European continents were united, and that it was Hercules who tore asunder the rocks in order to make a passage between the Mediterranean Sea and the Atlantic Ocean. The rock of Gibraltar– some 1,400 feet at its highest point – was called Calpe and the other – only eighteen miles distant – which rises some 2,700 feet from a promontory near Ceuta, on the African side, was known as Abila. It is said that many centuries ago the Phoenicians erected a huge silver pillar on each of these rocks, and that for a long time no ship ventured beyond these marks of warning, which became known as the "Pillars of Hercules" *(Columnae Herculis).*

According to another legend, once upon a time the Straits of Gibraltar were much wider than they are now, but after several colossal sea monsters had passed through, coming from the North Sea, Hercules narrowed the Straits, and so prevented others from passing through it to infest the Mediterranean Sea.

Another fascinating legend tells us that when Hercules undertook the tenth of his twelve labours, he went to the island of Gades (hence Cadiz to-day) where lived Geryon, who had three bodies and three heads. This monster kept many red cattle who fed upon human flesh.

They were guarded by a centaur named Eurythion and a two-headed dog, Orthos. Having killed Geryon, Hercules placed the rocks of Calpe and Abila where they are to-day, in order to make a bridge over which to drive the terrible cattle.

As I sat in that secluded spot on the outskirts of Algeciras, looking across the glittering sheet of silver that was the bay, and on the other side of it I beheld the rock of Gibraltar, I pictured Hercules performing some of his labours. Then I imagined seeing many phases of history being re-enacted at this vital gateway. I saw primitive ancient warriors arrive in sailing vessels and galleons, then soldiers and sailors wearing the uniforms of several European nations, I remembered international intrigues and even "double-crossings" caused by the ambition to occupy the short, narrow promontory with the mighty rock at its end.

Most likely, the rock of Gibraltar was used as a stronghold since prehistoric times, and we know definitely that after the Phoenicians, the Carthaginians and the Romans had settlements there. In A.D. 711 an Arab general named Tarik ibm Zijad landed at a place which was given the name of al-Gezira al-Khadra, meaning "Green Island," to-day Algeciras, and that subsequently he built a fortress on the rock which became known as Jebel-al-Tarik (Hill of Tarik), from which the name Gibraltar is derived.

Following the discovery of the New World, Spanish coins struck in the Spanish colonies bore the figure of the pillars of Hercules, and beneath them several wavy lines, representing the sea. Across, behind the pillars, were two lines, between which lettering gave the initials of the reigning king, and the reverse of these crudely, made coins bore the arms of Spain. (I have in my possession such a crudely made coin, struck in Potosé – Bolivia – in 1585. It was given to me by a primitive Bolivian Aymara Indian, in lieu of modern money.) These coins became known as Spanish pieces of eight (eight *reales)* or "'pillar dollars." It is believed that with the passing of time and political changes in the New World, the original design of Spanish colonial coins was changed, in the sense that the figures of the two pillars of Hercules were retained, and that the wavy lines beneath them were raised to replace the former straight lines, thus making the symbol of the dollar, the familiar sign. The word "dollar" is of German origin, being a derivation of the Joachimstaler (gulden) of Joachimsthal in Bohemia, where they were coined in 1519, from a silver mine opened there in 1516. In England, in 1600, the word "thaler," "daller," dalder," "doler" or "dolor" was modified to "dollar," and in 1785, at the Continent Congress in America, it was resolved that the money unit of the U.S.A. be one silver dollar. Later, a gold coin of similar value was struck, and in South America the $ sign came into use to denote the *peso,* though in this case with only one downward stroke to the "S" shape. Be the origin of the $ sign what it may, to-day the U.S.A. dollar is the undisputed Hercules among the monetary currencies of the world, and therefore frantically sought after to prop up shaky and creaking pillars of bankruptcy. In English slang the term "dollar" was used for five shillings, and to this day many people call the half crown[5] "half dollar."

And now, after this aside, which makes me feel very poor indeed, back to Algeciras Bay, and in a north-westerly direction, on towards Cadiz.

Most of the hills which overlook the Bay of Algeciras and the waters immediately east of Gibraltar, as well as the heights which dominate the Strait, have been heavily fortified by the Spaniards. Here and there, where roads branch off the main highway which I followed, are sign-posts on which is written in large letters CAMINO MILITAR (Military Road). If the Spanish fortifications and their equipment are strong and up to date (which I venture to guess they are not), they would neutralize Gibraltar and make it useless as a naval base. This, as I see it, means that in the event of war it would be essential that Spain be on England's side, or remain neutral, lest much fighting would have to be done on the Spanish mainland, in order to try to put the Spanish forts out of action.

Leaving such and similar problems to strategists and diplomatists, in bright sunshine I rode through beautiful hilly country, covered with grass and here and there patches of small fir trees. The waters of the North Sea were of a much paler blue than those of the Mediterranean. Grazing cattle and little white farm houses looked very picturesque in their setting of green. When a cow tried to cross the road, just as I approached her, and she suddenly changed her mind, and turned to face me in a menacing manner, I had a fright, but thanks to a quick man-oeuvre – which, I guess, surprised me more than it did the cow – I

---

[5] *Editor's note*: Half a crown was two shillings and sixpence.

managed to dodge her horns by a hair's breadth. Accelerating my speed, I thanked my lucky stars that my antagonist was only a cow, and not one of the formidable fighting bulls I had seen in other parts.

As a rule, whilst passing through picturesque or interesting parts, I cruised along at speeds varying between fifteen and eighteen miles per hour, but if there was nothing worthwhile to be seen, or the region happened to be monotonous, and the road I followed safe, I travelled faster.

Shortly after my interlude with the cow, something on the road attracted my attention. It was a large wasp-like, bright electric blue insect which went through some peculiar antics, half flying and half walking on a dry, perfectly round seed, about the size of a marble. Wondering what the insect was doing, I stopped to watch it for some time, rolling the seed hither and thither, and sometimes in circles, as if enjoying the feat of equilibrium.

Upon coming to a long narrow strip of low-lying land, which juts out into the sea in a north-westerly direction, I knew that another six miles or so would take me to Cadiz which is built on a low rock of shell limestone at the spreading end of this peculiar promontory. For some distance I rode along a dead-straight road with salt marshes on either side, and beyond them, on my left, the pale-blue waters of the Atlantic, and on my right those of the nearly closed-in Bay of Cadiz. Some three miles further along, the promontory widened slightly, and after having passed through a small town, ahead of me Cadiz came in sight. With its flat-roofed white houses shimmering in the brilliant sunlight, and standing on a low circular rocky ledge, it reminded me of an iced cake. My first impressions of this town were dazzling whiteness, promenades winding along the sea-front, palm groves, stately trees of various kinds, and flowers.

Few towns in the world can have had so many changes of fortune as Cadiz. As far back as 500 B.C. *Gadir* (meaning "stronghold") was a Phoenician trading centre, and under the Romans, *Gades* became the terminus of the "Via Augusta" which began in northern France. The influx of wealth, and its situation, soon turned Gades into a gay spot which rivalled Rome for high and fast living, and made it famous for its alluring dancing girls. Later, the Moorish invasion all but wrote "Finis" to the importance of Cadiz, but yet the town recovered, only to be subjected to many raids by corsairs from Barbary, and later to others by

Drake and Lord Essex, whose men sacked and plundered the town. However, with the arrival of gold and silver from the Americas, Cadiz recovered once more, only to be ruined again when Spain lost her colonies. Then came the siege by the French, which Wellington helped to raise, and from that time on, once more Cadiz began to thrive, though it is not in the least likely that ever again it will have the importance and wealth it had in the heyday of Rome, and subsequently for some time after the discovery of the New World.

In the same way as, throughout the English-speaking world, Aberdeen is jocularly accused of being the cradle and home of the most tight-wad people among the "careful" Scots, so, for some to me unknown reason, in Spain modern Cadiz has the unenviable reputation of being the favourite hunting-ground for effeminate men. If I had believed the many stories I heard before reaching the fabled city, I would have expected Lot himself to be sitting at its gate to give me a welcome, bowing himself with his face to the ground, and before lying down to sleep in the hotel in which I stayed, "the men of the city, even the men of Sodom, to compass the house round, both old and young, all the people from every quarter," to quote from the Book of Genesis. During my subsequent travels, often when I mentioned my visit to Cadiz, my interlocutors smiled sarcastically, or even laughed outright, and jokingly asked me all sorts of rude and very personal questions. After my sojourn of three days in Cadiz, when, upon resuming my travels, I turned to have a final look at its white houses, unlike Lot's wife of the biblical story, I did not become a pillar of salt, and there and then I decided to take up the sword (in my case a feeble pen) to defend the honour of the ancient city. Therefore, ever since then, whenever some mischievous tongue has told me the usual joke about the habits of some members of its male population, my reply has been – and is – "a fig for idle and malignant talk!"

True, the typical inhabitant of that much maligned city is inclined to be rather showy, tawdry and, when excited, loud; but in this respect they do not differ much from their brothers and sisters in Andalusia who often refer to natives of Cadiz as *curros,* meaning gaudy "swank-pots."

The greater part of Cadiz was rebuilt after the catastrophe when Lord Essex sacked and plundered it, but the heart of the city, with its narrow curved streets, retains its old character. The semi-circular sea-front, with high stone walls against which break the waves of the Atlantic Ocean, wide shady avenues and botanic garden, is a delightful place for a walk.

During my many perambulations, near the unattractive port, in the middle of a big square, a high monument fairly hit my eyes. Though the gardens round it were well tended, not a soul was to be seen in them. With equestrian statues, oxen, Dame Liberty, men and women harvesting wheat, a high pillar on the top of which several human figures raise a book towards heaven, the encyclopaedic monument reminded me of the much derided Albert Memorial in London, so I went to investigate what it might commemorate. "1812 ARGUELLES CONSTITUCION," I read, whereupon I realized that this monument had been erected to commemorate Spain's liberal constitution, drawn up and issued during the French siege of Cadiz. For some peculiar reason, the monument, instead of facing the town – as one might expect – faces the sea, and I was amused to see that two storks had made the top of the high column their nesting-place. As I thought over the practical results of the constitutions of various countries I know, and the value of words, decrees, charters, codes, statutes and similar human instructions, the storks looked down at me from on high, and clapped their beaks, which, I take it, is their way of communicating thoughts, and, perhaps, of laughing.

In an avenue near the docks I saw a sight which amused me greatly. A dilapidated old cab stood in a shady spot, its owner busy dusting it, as well as the skinny old nag, with a duster made of fluffy palm fibres affixed to a stick. This was the first time in my life that I had seen a horse being dusted; and what a museum piece the poor old crock was.

I have already mentioned Spanish street photographers who cater for children who want to have their pictures taken, sitting on wooden horses. In a *plaza* near the dock area, when I seated myself outside a *café* to have a rest and some refreshment, near me I saw such a photographer with two of the finest wooden horses I had beheld until then. One was so big and high that a low step-ladder was placed alongside it, ready for clients to mount. Both horses were painted in bright colours, and looked fit to be ridden by the Valkyrie, and to add to the effigies' attraction, both had tails made of real horse-hair. For a joke, I longed to have my photograph taken on such a horse, and as I looked at the two magnificent effigies, this longing grew stronger and stronger, but I had not the courage to mount, and to expose myself to ridicule. What would all those people who sat outside the *café* think – and perhaps shout – if I bestrode the object of my admiration? No; I dared not give way to my longing.

Children must have been making their first Communion in one of. the many churches in the town. Little girls, dressed in white, with little wreaths of white flowers on their heads and wearing white veils, walked along self-consciously, their parents following behind them, beaming with pride. Boys who had gone through the same religious ceremony wore white armlets with gold fringes, and one or two of the youngsters I saw strutting past, with gold epaulettes and white silk sashes with gold tassels dangling from them, looked like miniature princes in Viennese operettas. In contrast with these young peacocks, the urchins who raided tables outside *cafés* to snatch up sugar, olives and snacks left behind by departing clients, wore clothes, the patching-up of which spoke highly of the urchins' mothers' or sisters' skill with needle and thread. A fat old vendor of lottery tickets who tried to make me buy one from him turned out to be a most amusing character. He had a face like a bulldog, his greasy jacket was so patched up that but little of the original cloth could have remained, but its lapels and collar-piece were made of fur. Perched on his big head at a saucy angle was a filthy old trilby hat, which its wearer doffed with a flourish and elegance Beau Brummell would have envied. Smiling continually, in so doing showing his toothless gums, the man began by trying to recommend to me what he called his "favourite winning number," and when I refused to buy, in a voice that sounded like the loud croaking of a toad, he began to tell me his life story, interspersed with many wise proverbs and witty asides. When he told me that his wife contributed towards the family budget, washing and mending clothes, and that, as a needle worker, she was second to none in Cadiz, I told the man that I had a little work for her, and that if he met me in the same place later in the evening, I would hand over to him two pairs of socks which needed mending. In due time, when I gave them to him, he hurried away as fast as his weight permitted, and in less than an hour returned with my socks, mended beautifully. When I gave him a few *pesetas* for his wife, and bought a lottery ticket off him, he took his leave with a deep bow and an elegant flourish of his battered and greasy old hat.

Arabs wearing fezes and selling cheap jewellery, water-carriers and vendors of newspapers, shouting their throaty "agua!" and "*diario!*" added to the exotic atmosphere of the town. The water is carried in big earthenware jars, and the glasses from which buyers drink are kept in a kind of rack tied to the vendor's belt. At the busy central market, women gossiped, chattered and bartered, and here and there, standing on a platform and shaded by a huge coloured parasol, glib-tongued vendors of cheap crockery, kitchen utensils and a variety of other articles, shouted that the prices at which they offered their goods to the public amounted to making a present of them.

Alongside a shady avenue, near the Atlantic sea-front, stand the prison-like old-fashioned military barracks. As in the case of all such in Spain, over the main entrance, in large letters are written the words TODO POR LA PATRIA (All for the fatherland). After sundown, when a cool breeze blew in from the sea, soldiers and a few officers could be seen sitting on benches and chairs outside the gate, smoking and chatting. At such times, democratic Spaniards know no ranks, and officers lose no status in mixing with their subordinates on level terms.

During the night before I left Cadiz, a "levanter" sprang up, blowing from the sea. Locally this wind is sometimes called *virazón*. That night, as usual, it brought rain, the downpour lasting some two hours, but fortunately in the morning the sky was clear once more, though the air had cooled down considerably.

Leaving the city, I rode back along the narrow promontory towards the mainland, and on the way, upon coming to a railway crossing, I found the barrier down, and presently appeared an antiquated train, pulled along laboriously by a kind of "Puffing Billy." From the open windows of the box-like carriages leaned passengers and as the convoy came to a halt at the level crossing, the sounds which emanated from within the carriages brought to my mind a travelling menagerie. I was wondering why the train had stopped where there was no station, when a minor commotion in one of the carriages attracted my attention. Two women and several children were helped down the steps to the track by obliging passengers, and after several bundles and baskets filled with vegetables and fruit had been handed down to them through a window, the engine driver waved a friendly *adios* in the direction of his erst-while passengers, who responded in a like manner, the tooter of the engine gave a few wheezy blasts, passengers waved their hands from windows, last words of farewell were shouted, and then, with much puffing on the part of the engine, and more waving of hands on the part of the driver, with many jerks and much noise, the convoy started and slowly gathered speed, if this word can be applied to the maximum rate of movement of the Jerez de la Frontera-Cadiz railway. When, at last, the barrier was raised by a woman, I proceeded in the direction of the mainland, happy in our age of hurry and scurry to have witnessed such a romantic interlude.

As mentioned in a previous chapter, the Andalusians, among whom I was once more, are gay light-hearted people. In other parts of Spain they are often laughed at for their boastfulness and bragging, but, above all, for their bad pronunciation of the Castilian language. The letters "C" and "Z" instead of being pronounced with a slight lisp, are made to sound the same as "S," as also is the case in South America where many Andalusians settled, introducing and spreading their dialect. All South-American dialects can be traced back to certain regions in Spain, though, particularly in the Argentine and in Uruguay, Italian has had a slight influence on pronunciation. In the Americas, certain pure Spanish words have different meanings, new ones having been adopted from various languages. For instance, in the Argentine and in Uruguay, the Spanish *andén* (meaning railway platform) has become *plataforma,* and the Castilian *traviesas* for railway sleepers had become *durmientes.* No doubt this is due to the fact that English engineers built most of the South American railways, and that they translated the English terms directly into what they thought was Spanish. In Argentina and Uruguay particularly, the liquid Spanish "ll" and "y" are pronounced as "sh." Thus, the word *calle* (street) becomes "cahshe" and *yo* (I) "sheo". Typical Andalusians are so lazy in pronouncing certain words that with them, to give one example, "Cadiz" becomes "Cahee." Among the vast majority of Spaniards and South Americans alike, the pronouncing of the letters "V" and "B" are such a problem that they are always being mixed up. "*Vaca*" (cow) and "*vino*" (wine) become "*baca*" and "*bino*", and, on the other hand, *burro* (donkey) and *basura* (refuse) are pronounced "*vurro*" and "*vasura.*" In South America, certain quite ordinary pure Spanish words must be substituted for others, lest the speaker be misunderstood by his listener, or shock him or her with rudeness. However, quite apart from such shortcomings, South America has enriched her version of the Spanish language with a number of new words, and as I am writing this, one of them comes to

my mind, one which deserves to be added to the rich Castilian
dictionary. I am referring to the South American word *yuyo,* meaning
"weed." *Yuyo* is a slight corruption of the Quichua Indian *yuyu.* (The
Incas of Peru spoke Quichua.) In Spain a weed is called *yerba mala*
(bad herb), on which, to my mind, *yuyo* is an improvement.

And now, after this aside, back to the road which leads from Cadiz
to Jerez. The fertile rolling country through which I passed did not
suggest that the wine industry is the life and soul of these regions, for
the extensive vineyards are not visible from the road. Like many other
good things, they are hidden away from the view of the profane, and
therefore, in order to see them, it is necessary to follow some of the
many lanes which lead towards the sacred places where grow the plants
nature created for man to provide him with the liquid gold a poetic
Andalusian once called "sweat of eternity."

Whilst riding along some of the byways, looking at the region, I was
annoyed with myself, for somehow and somewhere I had lost a letter of
introduction I had been given to the owners of a famous *bodega* (wine
cellar) in Jerez. In due time, upon arriving in the quaint old town, I did
a little sight-seeing and then decided to move on to Seville. Before
setting out, I went to a petrol pump, situated near the main square, and
whilst I waited for the owner to appear, a group of young men collected
round me to have a look at my motor-cycle. Naturally, this led to
conversation, and when one of the bystanders heard where I came from,
and what I was doing in Spain, he asked me if I had visited any of the
famous *bodegas* in the town. When I told him about the loss of my
letter of introduction, he and several of my listeners spoke together,
telling me that this did not matter, that people in Jerez were friendly,
and that if I went to any *bodega,* the people there would be delighted to
show me round. Despite these assurances, I maintained that without a
letter of introduction I preferred not to present myself anywhere,
whereupon one of my listeners told me that, in any event, if I left the
town, taking the road towards Seville, I would have to pass quite near a
bodega run by the British Vice-Consul. "No, no, *señor,* you must not
leave Jerez without looking over a *bodega,*" several voices shouted.
"Go and call on the *consul ingles,* he is a very nice person, one of us, a
real *jerezano.*"

Taking their advice, I halted at the gate in a white-washed wall, and
when a caretaker appeared and asked me what he could do for me, I

gave him a card, and asked him to be good enough to take it to his
patrón. Great was my surprise when, a little while after, a tall English-
looking gentleman appeared, holding my card, slightly bent, between
the thumb and middle finger of his left hand. "Excuse me, are you by
any chance the author of one of my favourite books, *Don Roberto,* the
biography of the late R. B. Cunninghame Graham, and of other books I
have in my house?" When I replied that, for my sins, I was the pen-
pusher to whom he referred, he shook me warmly by the hand, and
shortly after, under his expert guidance, I wandered through his *bodega*
where, in the space of about two hours, I learnt a great deal.

The first thing that struck me about the huge storing places for the
famous wine was that they are not cellars, but that they are level with
the ground, and that their interiors are constructed rather like
cathedrals, with rows of high arches and lofty roofs above them. Jerez
is built on rock, and therefore the making of deep cellars would be very
costly, so ever since wine has been made there, it was left to ferment
and mature in *bodegas* of the type I have described.

The old name of the town is Jerez de la Frontera (of the frontier),
because, like a number of other Spanish towns which are also called *de
la frontera,* it was on the border which separated territory held by the
Moors from that of the Christians.   Shakespeare's Falstaff sings the
glories of "Sherries," a name derived from "Jerez." "Sherries sack"
means "dry sherry," "sack" being a corruption of the Spanish word
"*seco*" (dry) or the French "*sec*". Therefore, the modern "Dry Sack"
really is a repetition of statement.

In the regions of Jerez, wine has been made since time immemorial,
and even during the Moorish occupation vines were cultivated with
great care, though some were uprooted to make room for olive trees.
For religious reasons, the conquerors from Africa were not allowed to
drink alcoholic beverages, but as they were very fond of raisins, the
vineyards were carefully tended. However, despite this prohibition on
religious grounds, we have it from reliable ancient sources that this did
not prevent some of the Moorish potentates from drinking freely, and
often to great excess, of what an old Arab-Andalusian poet was first to
call "bottled sunshine." No doubt, during such carousals in luxurious
and well-stocked harems, the merry-makers forgot all about the Koran,
mosques and muezzins, leaving these to their faithful underlings, who
sought happiness in after-life. It is to be doubted, though, if even the

greatest bacchanalian champion among the merry caliphs could ever have competed with the redoubtable Roman, Novellius Torquatus, who in one session "sank" three *"congii"* – or a little more than forty-five pints – of wine. When we compare this feat of elbow-bending and capacity of bodily expansion with what Montaigne tells us in one of his essays, namely that in the Middle Ages "any gentleman adorned with the highest virtues" drank ten bottles of wine with one meal, these knights and esquires were mere sucklings.   In more recent times, Flammarion once confessed that he had never drunk water, and in his *Handbook of Gastronomy,* the great and incomparable gourmet, Brillat Savarin, makes the witty statement that he did not like eating grapes because he, hated taking his wine "in capsules."

It must not be thought that after the Moors were expelled from the Iberian peninsula, all was wine, song and castanets in Jerez, for there followed other invasions and incursions. In the time of Charles I of England, Lord Wimbledon landed successfully with 10,000 men at Cadiz, but on the way up to Jerez they found so much wine that very soon the whole army was drunk. This led to insubordination, followed by retreat, and the loss of 1,000 men and thirty ships. However, as far as Jerez and other wine-growing districts in Europe are concerned, the most disastrous invasion was that of the phylloxera, an insect belonging to the family of plant lice. Of American origin, in Europe the plague first broke out in England, in 1863, and soon spread over the continent, and finally reached Jerez in 1894. Century-old vines – some of the patriarchs' trunks as thick as a man's body – had to be uprooted and burned, until vineyards became deserts. Eventually, scientists discovered – in America, of all places in the world – a wild vine which resisted the attacks of the phylloxera. Masses of these were shipped across the Atlantic, and shoots of European vines were grafted on them. Though in their original state, the American wild vines bore only small and sour grapes, the grafting on of European shoots produced wonderful results, and thus, in time, the wine industry began to flourish once more. Few people who drink French champagne realize that the original plants from which the grapes are harvested were brought from Texas, and that many of the vines in the district of Jerez were imported from the Rhineland where one or two small regions escaped the ravages of the phylloxera.

Prior to the invasion of this pest, there were quite a number of famous old vines in Jerez, and most of these Methuselahs had names. One of them, in the season of the year 1836, gave 365 bottles of wine, and its proud owner used to sit in its shade where, every day, he drank solemnly one bottle of the liquid the venerable plant had produced for him.

It would take up far too much space if I attempted to give a full account of how sherry wine is made. Suffice it to say that when the grapes have been cut and selected, and have been left to dry in the sun for one day, they are trodden by men who wear heavy special boots, the soles of which are studded with hob-nails. For some unaccountable reason, if the grapes are pressed by a machine, the juice thus extracted from them will not make sherry wine. The experiment has been made, but always with unsatisfactory results.

As my excellent host and guide, Mr. G. D. Williams, took me through his cathedral-like *bodegas* with avenues of barrels on either side of us, here and there he halted, and dipped into one of them a long cane with a section of bamboo fixed to its end. The section of bamboo is closed at the bottom end, and open at the other, and is, as it were, a kind of test-tube, used for taking a measure of wine out of the barrel. For this reason, in some parts of Spain, when people ask for a glass of sherry, they call it *una caña,* a cane. As we walked along, my host carried several glasses in one hand, holding them upside down by their stems, and whenever he poured a little wine into one of them, he made me smell it. In bewildering succession I was told about *soleras,* these being three basic types, classified as *fino, oloroso* and *dulce,* and between these are other categories, such as *amontillado, amoroso, dulce de rayos* and so on. The effort of trying to memorize all this, and to learn to recognize the difference between samples by smelling them, made me long to have a good swig, but after short halts my guide wandered on, along rows of huge barrels, then through beautiful gardens with a riot of flowers and fruit trees in them, into laboratories where experts sampled wine, spitting the liquid into basins such as modem dentists use; next I saw how the famous sherry casks are made, then more smelling of samples, but all this time not a drop of sherry to drink. Surely Tantalus himself would have squirmed. Still, I knew that if I swallowed some of the wine, my sense of taste and smell would be blunted, so I followed, listening intently, and every now and again sniffing or inhaling slowly and deeply. I felt quite proud when my instructor told me that I was an exceptionally good pupil, and that my sense of smell was well above the average. The reason for this was that I had been in the fresh air ever since early morning, and that I had smoked but little, and that, in consequence, my sense of smell was unimpaired.

In connection with sherry casks, here I must add that out of the innumerable made in – and exported from – Jerez, not a single one has been returned. When emptied of their contents, all, save a very few, are bought by Scottish distilleries, where they are used for maturing whisky, to which the wood, impregnated with what might be described as the essence of sherry wine, gives a golden colour and a certain "bouquet."

When at last we came to the Valhalla of the *bodega,* where there were several barrels, specially painted to commemorate the visits of several famous people, we seated ourselves at a small table, biscuits and cheese were brought, and then, glory be . . . a decanter filled with "liquid sunshine" was placed before us. No wonder that once, when a witty Andalusian was asked why wine is called *vino,* he replied, "*Porque vino del cielo*" (because it *came* from heaven). *(Vino* can mean either "wine" or "came.")

After a delightful little luncheon party in my host's beautiful old home, I resumed my northward journey. When I approached Seville, like heavenly searchlights, rays of the evening sun stabbed through heavy billowing clouds, throwing their beams athwart the fertile plain, illuminating the city's domes and towers, among which that of my old friend, the Giralda, rose proudly, as if to welcome me back, and to tell me to remember the Moorish conquerors who called Andalusia their earthly paradise. Whilst I stopped for a while to gaze at what looked like an almost supernatural stage-setting, I imagined muezzins calling the faithful to evening prayer from the Giralda's delicately arched *ajimezes* (windows). Riding on, I soon reached an old bridge which spans the river Guadalquivir, and immediately after having crossed it I found myself in a part of the old section of the town I remembered well.

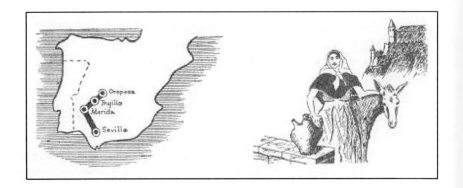

CHAPTER 15

SEVILLE – MÉRIDA – TRUJILLO – OROPESA

It was a pleasant sensation to be back in a place I knew, and where I did not have to ask policemen or passers-by to guide me. A friend and his charming Galician wife, who had entertained me during my previous visit to Seville, had invited me to stay with them, so after having crossed over the bridge, I halted in a nearby little *plaza* in order to have a short rest and to shake the dust off. Whilst I was busy doing this, a dark sleek-haired young man came up to greet me most warmly. It was not until he told me that he was one of the gipsies who, during the Fair, had danced in the Guajiro's hut, that I recognized him. No sooner had I reciprocated his greeting, than one of the inmates of the little *pensión* (guest house) in which I had stayed appeared to hug me as if I were a long-lost brother. As it happened, the *pensión* was quite near the place where I had halted, in one of the narrow winding lanes which in old Seville are called *calles* (streets). Of course, such an unexpected reunion called for a drink, so, soon after, the three of us were in a quaint little *tasca* and, upon recognizing me as a former client, the *patrón* gave me a hearty welcome back to his home-town. Shortly after, whilst riding towards my destination, I felt like an old *Sevillano* for, apart from being familiar with almost everything I saw, the unexpected welcome extended to me upon my return to the town pleased me more than if red carpets had been rolled out for me, and if the blaring of a brass band and thumping of drums, the mayor and a reception committee had been there to extend an official welcome, and to give me the freedom of the city.

My hosts and their two delightful children were pleased to see me back, and did everything to make my stay with them a happy one. How Seville had changed since my previous visit! The formerly gay, colourful and animated fairground with its mass of *casetas* (tents), flags, bunting, and thousands of electric lights, now was an empty space. The streets and avenues, which had been packed with luxurious cars and carriages drawn by teams of magnificent high-stepping horses and mules, now were so empty that one could have run motor-car races through them without endangering other human lives, save, perhaps, those of the contestants. Yes, Seville had "folded up" until the next *Semana Santa* (Holy Week) and *feria* (fair). Still, in most respects I preferred the town as I found it now, for it had the right atmosphere; no artificiality, and no cadging from pleasure-bent tourists and visitors.

One night, whilst walking about with my host, a friend told him not to miss seeing a troupe of gipsies who performed in one of the hotels, so the two of us went to see their show. During the Fair I had witnessed much excellent and fascinating dancing, but what I saw the gipsies do in this hotel was of a higher order. When, between typical *flamenco* (gipsy) dancing, the performers executed some of those short *sevillanas*, the speed, vim, grace and precision with which they did it was simply amazing, in short, it was dancing brought to the highest pitch.

Before setting out again, I crossed over the river to Triana, there to pay my respects to my friend, the gipsy Guajiro, but unfortunately he was not at home, having gone somewhere on business connected with horses.

Shortly after having left Seville, riding in a northerly direction, I came to rolling country, with here and there wooded hills, and green fields with cattle grazing in them. Many of these fields are surrounded by stone walls, and in some of them peasants were busy harvesting wheat, oats and barley. In the woods pigs nosed about, and goats appeared to think that the most succulent leaves were those which grew so high up that the animals had to stand on their hind-legs to reach them. The antics of some of these acrobatic goats amused me, though not nearly as much as a solitary donkey who happened to be sleeping peacefully in the middle of the road when I approached him. He only woke up just as I passed him, and with such a start that, to my amazement, he leapt to his feet with the agility of a cat, immediately to bolt as if he were being chased by some asinine demon. Never before, and never since, have I seen a donkey move so quickly, for as a rule these sagacious animals are imperturbable and not easily thrown into a panic.

After having passed through a number of picturesque villages and small towns, towards evening, at the foot of an incline, on the other side of the river Guadiana, the ancient town of Mérida came in sight, situated partly on the steep slope of a hill, and partly on a high rocky eminence which overlooks the river below. Towers and bastions indicated that, once upon a time, Mérida had been a strong fortress. The massive half-mile-long stone bridge with its sixty-four arches, was built by the Romans, but since those times has been reconstructed in several parts, for some of its arches were blown up, in 1812, to hinder the progress of a French army which advanced from the regions through which I had passed that day.

Though, undoubtedly, the site on which Mérida stands to-day was used as a stronghold and ideal place for settlement since prehistoric days, shortly before the Christian era the Romans founded the town, which later became the capital of Lusitania, one of the three provinces into which Augustus divided Hispania. (The Lusitani were a tribe.) From a structural point of view, Mérida must have been the Romans' masterpiece in Spain, for after the original builders and their successors in power, the Visigoths, had gone, and the Moors took possession, one Rasis wrote: "No man on earth can describe the wonders of Mérida." This boastful statement must be taken with a big pinch of salt, for even among the Moors there was jealousy, and since Mérida was occupied by Berbers who were at loggerheads with the caliphs of marvellous Cordova, most likely the smaller dog did most of the barking.

Unfortunately, after the expulsion of the Moors by the Christians, the town sank into a state of decay, and to-day, apart from the remarkable Roman bridge, amphitheatre, imposing remains of an aqueduct, and sections of the original fortifications, very little remains to bear testimony of the "wonders" of Mérida.

The amphitheatre – which has been slightly restored in recent times – gives one an excellent idea of what it must have been like in the heyday of the Roman occupation. The different entrances, circular tiers for seating spectators, passages which led from rooms to the arena, and even enclosures in which wild beasts were kept, remain in an excellent state of preservation. The aqueduct at the outskirts of the town was of great interest to me for various reasons. Between 80 and 90 feet high, those of the arches which remain standing are made of granite and brick. Under one of the high arches a gipsy family lived in a miserable hut, made of sticks, bits of board and tin, and a few sheets of rusty corrugated iron served as roof.

On the top of the arches, on ledges, and where parts of the actual conduit remain, storks had built their nests. As it was evening when I wandered about there, the birds returned to their roosting place after a day's hunting for food. As they approached, soaring through the air with outspread wings, their legs held close together, stretched out horizontally beneath the tail feathers, they reminded me of some of the early monoplanes. A few moments before landing on or near their nests, their legs came forward like landing gear, and a second or so later flapping wings acted as brakes, and then the birds came to a smooth standstill in perfect equilibrium. Above me, at intervals, there was much clapping of beaks as the storks conversed with one another in their peculiar Ciconian language. But what mystified and surprised me more than the cyclopean arches and the behaviour of the storks, was to see that beneath their huge nests – made of high piles of dry sticks and twigs – hawks had theirs, the latter birds being, as it were, "squatters" or intruders in the storks' homes. This extraordinary co-habitation of the two species of bird is general throughout southern Spain, and I am told that the hawks never interfere with the storks, not even with their young.

Whenever I looked at and admired some of the many cyclopean constructions left behind by the Romans, I made mental pictures of how the work was done. I saw the ghosts of architects directing opera-tions, others of master-masons measuring huge blocks of stone, then others of centurions, armed with terrible whips, driving along squirming slaves, urging them to lift or pull harder until some of the poor wretches fell down exhausted; for such was the cruelty and oppression that went with the building of aqueducts, bridges, amphitheatres, forts and palaces.

I was now in Estremadura, in a part of Spain I had longed to visit for many years. For some strange reason – probably due to the fact that I had read books written by authors who did not know the region – I imagined those parts to be a rocky semi-desert. Instead, I found fair, hilly and gently rolling country, stretches of which were shaded by Barbary oaks which provide the sweet acorns on which pigs feed, eventually to provide the famous Estremadura hams. Rock roses (gum cistus) with their white flowers, with a yellow mark at the base of each petal, grew in great abundance, and patches of fertile land in which grain, vegetables, vines, olives, figs and almonds were cultivated. True, some of the pasture-land is poor and rocky, but it provides sufficient grass for thousands of sheep which in the autumn descend from the plateau of Castile and Leon. These flocks are guarded by shepherds with their powerful wolf hounds; for among the nearby mountains wolves occasionally attack sheep. As I passed through Estremadura in early summer, the sheep were far away, on the other side of the mountains, which stood like a dark-blue serrated line in the distance. The name of this province is derived from the Romans' *Extrema Terra,* and it is in these regions that the most famous *conquistadores* were born.

Many centuries ago, the indiscriminate felling of forests played havoc with the arid soil of certain parts of Spain, but it was also due to the expulsion of the Moors, and, immediately following it, to the discovery of the New World and subsequent emigration, that some regions, hitherto made fertile by sheer hard work, were neglected, and became semi-deserts.

Since the most famous and successful of the *conquistadores* were natives of Estremadura, naturally, when they returned home with many tales about the wonders they had seen in the newly discovered lands across the seas, and brought with them more than ample proof of the wealth that waited there, to be amassed by the brave and enterprising, their listeners abandoned the plough and the spade, and hurried to the nearest port to enlist as members of expeditions preparing for another voyage to the Americas. With the passing of time, whole families migrated to join their relatives in the colonies, and thus, by degrees, Estremadura lost much of its population.

Upon reaching Trujillo – the native town of Pizarro, the conqueror of Peru – I was thrilled to think that after having travelled over many trails he had blazed and trodden in South America, at last I found myself where his cradle had stood, and where he had played as a boy. On the top of the steep hill on which the old town stands, I went to see the shell of what, more than four centuries ago, had been the Pizarro family's house. Further down the steep slope, I peeped in through several doors over which remain the coat-of-arms of other *conquistadores*. As I explored some of the narrow streets and alleys, I felt the shadowy presence of these long-dead men vibrate through the air. I pictured them in armour, or in doublet and hose, ruffled shoes and high-peaked hats, with swords clanking against the rough cobble-stones, or cloaked to the eyes, dark, sombre, as if a love intrigue might mean a swift passage of swords glinting in the moonlight. Again, I stopped to look at the old Moorish castle which dominates the town, or to study gratings which twist their variously wrought and pierced scrolls of iron-work, or to admire the carnations and geraniums which flashed their brilliancy against the walls of the opposite houses. As the town is situated close on 1600 feet above sea-level, the air was keen and invigorating, but I well imagined what the heat could be in summer, when the rays of the sun blaze down on rocky patches in the surrounding country.

I do not think that any of the world's brave and noble men have been vilified as much as the Spanish *conquistadores*. Of course, this campaign of slander originated in European countries where everybody envied Spain for the new lands she had discovered, and for the wealth she derived from them. But is there any country which has not its black legend? As I have written in a book dealing with the discovery and the conquest of Peru[6], Spain has always been a singular contradiction, but instead of attempting utterly to explain this, many writers have found it much easier to invent dark legends against this peculiarly democratic land. As far as physical courage and disregard for suffering are con-cerned, the world has never produced men more remarkable than the Spaniards who sailed to the New World. Greed for gold was not their only driving power, for had it not been for deep religious conviction and the belief that they had a holy mission to fulfil, these amazing men could never have accomplished what they did. The fact that Indians were robbed, and on occasions ruthlessly massacred, is not sufficient reason to point at the *conquistador* with a finger of horror and scorn. Before casting stones, let us remember what we ourselves are doing in

---

[6] *Editor's note: Coricancha, Garden of Gold,* first published by Messrs. Hodder & Stoughton, London, 1942, reissued by The Long Riders' Guild Press in 2008.

our modern and "enlightened" times, not only in war, but also during so-called times of peace. Even the richest treasures taken home by Spaniards from the New World are insignificant and puny when one takes into consideration what, alone materially, they gave the newly discovered lands. Among cereals, fruits, vegetables, shrubs, trees and an infinity of plants imported into the Americas by the "wicked and destructive" *conquistadores* were wheat, oats, barley, oranges, lemons, grapes, figs, melons, bananas, pears, etc., etc., as well as sugar cane, rice, flax, flowers and so on. Until they introduced cows and goats, only Indian sucklings consumed milk of the human variety, no domestic animals having been available. Apart from the llama, the only domestic animals kept by the Peruvian Indians was a kind of duck. People who to this day curse the *conquistadores* are ignorant of these facts, and some do not know – deliberately and stubbornly refusing to learn – that Europe in general benefited greatly by the discovery of the new lands across the ocean. Thanks to Spanish vision and thought for the future, to mention just a few items, maize, potatoes, tomatoes, many varieties of flowers, shrubs, vegetables, certain important medicines, etc., were brought to Europe. No doubt the Spaniards had learnt much from their erstwhile conquerors, the Romans and the Moors, but their constructive and civilizing activities in the New World, and what they brought to Europe from there, has no parallel in the history of the world. True, Spain made many bad mistakes during the time of her colony, but then it must be remembered that this was the first experiment of its kind ever made in the world, and that nations who embarked on colonization later could be guided by those mistakes.

All said and done, even though some of the *conquistadores* raped the Inca's Virgins of the Sun and looted temples, have not conquering modern armies done the same during the recent World War? Let us not be hypocritical, but face facts; this was not done to vanquished heathen, but in most cases to fellow-Christians, though the modern word for "loot" is "booty" or "reparations." As I see it, the dividing line between these terms is so slender that only so-called statesmen of a certain mentality, and "learned friends" in international law, pretend that it is otherwise. And as for rape, had not the great Clodius himself been accused of seducing one of Rome's vestal virgins? Evidently, in the case of Clodius the crime is called "seduction," but in the case of the *conquistadores* it is "rape."

Book-happy, stay-at-home historians tell us that Pizarro started life as a swine-herd, and that he ran away from home after having let some of his father's animals go astray. This story may be perfectly true, but in the case of the region in which this is supposed to have happened, the word "swine-herd" needs some explanation. To this day most of the fields in Estremadura are not fenced in, and therefore, when pigs, sheep or cows are driven out to graze on wide strips of no-man's-land by the wayside, a guardian has to watch over them, lest they invade nearby cultivated fields. This task is often carried out by elderly people or children, usually early in the morning and then again towards evening when the animals are taken out for an extra feed to supplement their ordinary ration, given to them in suitable enclosures at home.

The fact that the Pizarros had a coat-of-arms – which can still be seen over the door of the ruined house situated near the highest point of the town – indicates that the family had some tradition behind it, but whether or not Francisco Pizarro, the conqueror of Peru, could read and write, is more difficult to decide. Even if it is true that he could only sign his name, it must be remembered that in those days literacy was not widespread, and throughout Europe, even among noblemen, there were many who could barely sign their names.

A passing shower made me seek shelter under an ancient gateway which is said to have been built by the Romans, and as I looked down the steep roughly cobbled street which leads to the lower and more modern part of the town, I observed the low houses with their heavily tiled roofs. The massively built, and in some cases dilapidated, abodes, escutchioned and forbidding from the exterior, had heavy entrance gates and walls which had been polished by many generations of inhabitants who had rubbed against them, and they seemed to hold the secrets of centuries. Among some of these fortress-like constructions are several of men who felt the irresistible attraction of the Americas, and who, after successful campaigns and constructive activities, returned home to build their minor palaces with gold they brought from the newly discovered and conquered lands. Thus, in Trujillo can be seen the palace of the "Marquis of the Conquest" (Pizarro), that of the Duque of San Carlos and the one in which lived Cortez, the conqueror of Mexico.

From this historic town, a ride of some fifty miles through undulating agricultural country took me to Oropesa, an ancient town situated on a hill. Heavy dark clouds had been gathering for some time, and shortly before I reached my journey's end, a strong wind began to blow, smacking the first heavy drops of rain against me. Driving at full speed, I raced uphill towards the now-nearby town, through an old gate, then along a narrow street paved with huge blocks of granite, and after another short climb reached a castle I had wanted to see for some years. In its massive walls I came to a huge entrance gate, with an archway, and just as I entered into its gloom, rain began to fall in torrents. I had arrived at the old castle of the Dukes of Frias, about whom I knew a great deal, having known the last member of that ancient family. As will be seen presently, the proud lineage came to a sad end, and the lives of its last members were more colourful and stranger than fiction.

The castle in which I found myself sheltering from the heavy downpour had fallen into a state of decay and neglect until, during very recent years, the Spanish State Tourist Department bought it, and at great expense made it into a *parador,* as these luxurious hotels are called. The castle, its big sandy courtyard – in which, occasionally, minor bullfights are held – arcades and balconies facing it, remain exactly as they were in olden times. The interior, with its vast banqueting hall, wide staircases and spacious rooms, is most impressive.

Having washed and generally cleaned myself, I went to sit near a large fireplace to warm myself, for the atmosphere had become raw and cold. As I looked at the massive wooden furniture, artistic wrought-iron gratings, and ancestral pictures on the walls, and observed the enormous thickness of the walls, I thought about the past glories of one of the most noble families of Spain. Whilst listening to the crackling of the logs, and watching flames and smoke make grotesque patterns, spirals and sometimes weird figures resembling men, monsters and beasts, I thought over the adventures and wanderings of Bernardino de Velasco, the last of the Duques of Frias, Hereditary Constables of Castile, Counts of Oropesa and of Haro, and Grandees of Spain, and I remembered what my friend, the late Mr. R. B. Cunninghame Graham, wrote about the family in one of his masterful sketches, entitled *Fin de Race*[7]. Bernardino's father had been a legendary aristocrat, such as Balzac might well have seized upon for the hero of one of his minor studies of mankind, for he appeared to have walked straight from his

---

[7] *Writ in Sand,* published by Messrs. William Heinemann, London, 1932

novels, or, rather, never to have emerged from them. He married the daughter of Michael William Balfe, the celebrated Dublin-born musician and composer of *Bohemian Girl, Rose of Castile* and of many melodies which are still popular. Their son, Bernardino, was educated at Eton, and therefore spoke Spanish and English perfectly, as well as French, Portuguese and a little Arabic. The duke started life the owner of great estates that stretched half over Spain, but being a high and fast liver, and, above all, an inveterate and reckless gambler, he proceeded to get rid of his possessions, chiefly at gaming tables all over Europe. He died, as befitted a Spanish nobleman of his kidney, greatly impoverished, leaving his son, Bernardino, but a relatively small part of his vast properties. What he could not help bequeathing to him was his handsome figure and quick wit, and his mother left him her blue eyes and her father's (M. W. Balfe's) musical talent. Bernardino was an accomplished all-round musician, but he excelled in the playing of the violin. The great Spanish violinist, Pablo Sarasate, said of him that had he but the spur of poverty, he would have made him one of the first violinists of the world. However, Bernardino, the musical genius, was a great performer in every branch of life for, besides many other attributes, he was a perfect horseman, a good shot, fencer and tireless walker. Although Nature had blessed him with many gifts, she omitted to endow him with a sense of responsibility and perseverance. After leaving Eton he drifted to Tangiers as an unpaid secretary to the Spanish minister. He had not the least shadow of pose, and, like most Spaniards, had the same manner whether he addressed a pauper or a prince. In free-and-easy Tangiers he found himself at home, and had a whale of a time. Together with the hard-drinking Crawhall, the great English painter and Bohemian, and a nondescript youth from Gibraltar, the duke entered into a partnership to hunt the Tangier hounds, which must have been the most original ones the world has seen. The pack was a collection of three mangy-looking foxhounds brought over from "Gib," and a few half-bred fox terriers, and their ponies were as original and picturesque as the clothes the merry huntsmen wore when they sallied forth with their pack, to which they always referred as the "bastards."

It was in Tangiers that the duke met his wife, an English lady who was almost as irresponsible as himself, and who did not care one iota about the innumerable love-affairs he had in his villa in Biarritz, or during visits to gaming tables all over Europe. A daughter, Maria Victoria (whom I knew as "Lala"), was born to this marriage. Later the duchess and her daughter took up more or less permanent residence in England, where the duke saw them occasionally during hurricane visits. Every now and again, when the spirit moved him, he wiped the dust off his violin case and took from it the fine Amati to play to his friends, or at High Mass in a Franciscan chapel. One by one, the remaining family estates were sold, and, slowly but steadily, debts began to pile up. Money-lenders and anyone who asked the duke for assistance spoke highly of him, and so things went from bad to worse, until he went to live on his one remaining estate, situated some ten miles from the mediaeval castle of Oropesa, the ancestral home of the Frias family. There, a girl inappropriately called Modesta – whom he had met in Madrid at a street corner one night after the theatre – looked after him, assisted by a gipsy-looking woman who did the cooking. Always on horseback in all weathers, after a hectic visit to the capital, the duke caught a cold which turned into pneumonia.

Although, besides many other blessings and gifts, Nature had endowed him with an iron constitution, years of dissipation had undermined his health, and so died Bernardino de Velasco, the last Duke of Frias, Hereditary Grand Constable of Castile, Count of Oropesa and of Haro.

For some years after the loss of her mother, the daughter, Maria Victoria, continued to live in England, where she was educated. At the time, she was the Marchioness of Flachilla, but with her father's death she inherited the title of Duchess of Frias. Like her parents, she was a light-hearted, rather "wild" and totally irresponsible young woman. Once, when she tried to raise some much-needed money, and put her father's valuable Amati violin up for sale, it was discovered that the case contained only an imitation, the authentic old instrument having, no doubt, been sold by her father. I do not know how much truth there is in a rumour I heard about the violin, but I have it from a fairly reliable source that it was bought by the brother of Guglielmo Marconi (of wireless telegraphy fame) who was a great collector of fine violins.

Trying to save some flotsam and jetsam of the wrecked family fortune, "Lala" returned to Spain where, after a prolonged spell of gay living, she hooked up with a third-rate bullfighter, with whom she lived for some time. Dissipation took her lower and lower, until she disappeared, no one knew or cared whither, until, one day a wealthy lady found her, emaciated, starved and half demented, in an attic in a poor quarter of Madrid. Taking compassion on the wretched creature, the lady took her to a nursing home where, despite every care that was taken of the patient, "Lala" left the turbulent world into which she was born.

As I sat in front of the roaring fire in the mediaeval castle of Oropesa, listening to the crackling of the logs and to the beating of the rain against the windows, I reconstructed the history of the last two generations of the Frias, and I saw "Lala" in London, light-hearted, gay and most entertaining, laughing and joking in drawing-rooms, before setting out with friends to go to another party.

The arrival of two charabancs filled with Mexicans who had been to a pilgrimage in Rome, and who that day had visited the monastery of Guadalupe (about 60 miles from Oropesa) brought my reverie to an abrupt end. Led by a stout middle-aged priest who must have been a pure Mexican Indian, the pilgrims invaded the castle, shouting, chattering, their footsteps sounding like the trampling of hoofs on the floor boards. Servants appeared, seemingly from nowhere, tables were laid in great haste, and there was a general hustle and bustle.

The history and legends attached to the Monastery of Guadalupe are interesting. A figure of the Madonna, said to have been carved by Saint Luke, was hidden during the Moorish occupation, and with the passing of time its existence and whereabouts were forgotten. After seven centuries, when the invaders from Africa were expelled, according to a legend, a shepherd lost a cow, and when, after a long search, he found her, she was dead. He was about to remove the skin when the Virgin appeared, and told him that under the spot where he stood was buried her long-lost image. The vision having vanished, the shepherd hurried to inform a priest about the strange happening, and upon digging at the indicated spot, Saint Luke's carving was found, and subsequently a chapel was built there. Soon after, the cult of Guadalupe spread throughout Spain and through parts of the Americas, particularly Mexico. The Virgin was so named because the image was discovered near the river Guadalupe, a name derived from the Arabic meaning "Hidden River."

The arrival of the Mexican pilgrims in the castle of Oropesa created such a commotion that as soon as the sky had cleared somewhat, I left in order to have a look round the town, but before I had gone far, another downpour made me seek shelter under an archway, whence I watched the street being transformed into a swift-flowing stream. To my relief, upon returning to the castle, I found that the noisy Mexicans were making ready to depart, and I was about to pass them when one came towards me, after a short preamble of apologies for speaking to me to ask if by any chance I happened to be the Tschiffely who, many years ago, had ridden on horseback through Mexico, on the way from the Argentine to the U.S.A. When I told him that, indeed, I was the man, he embraced me warmly, and then proceeded to inform me that the two of us had met in Mexico City during one of the official recaptions they had given me there. When I asked him how on earth he remembered me after all these years, he replied that he had seen my name on a note-book I had inadvertently left by the fireside, and that, it being such an uncommon and difficult name, he had recognized it at once.

When I woke up in the morning, the sky was clear, and bright sunshine warmed up the chilly atmosphere. Going to the window, I had a marvellous view of a vast fertile plain below me, and beyond it, to the south-east, of the Mountains of Toledo, and to the north, stretching from east to west, of the Sierra of Gredos, the high parts of which were covered with a glittering mantle of white. In the course of the previous afternoon, and also during the night, it must have snowed heavily in the mountains, and as it was my intention to cross the Sierra of Gredos that day, I looked forward to an adventurous ride, for its highest peaks are between eight and nine thousand feet above sea-level.

CHAPTER 16

OROPESA – AVILA – MADRID – SALAMANCA

Having had a last look at the stern-looking castle of Oropesa from the foot of the rock on which it stands, I set out in a northerly direction towards the Sierra de Gredos with its serrated snow-covered peaks. The fertile plain over which I rode is a veritable Garden of Eden, and the narrow road I followed, though sandy in parts, was quite good. Here and there were small well-tended fields, fruit trees of every kind, oak woods alternating with olive and cork trees, picturesque farm-houses with storks' nests above their roofs, and all the time bright sunshine. Driving at a moderate speed, I was able to see and observe things, and thus it came about that a large black beetle on the road attracted my attention. About an inch and a half long, and encased in glossy armour, the insect had two horny back legs, not unlike the nippers of a lobster. In the same manner as the wasp-like electric blue insect whose peculiar antics I had watched near Gibraltar, the black beetle was busy pushing along what appeared to be a little ball made of sand. The little fellow's capers and the feverish haste with which he moved so puzzled me that I stopped to watch him. After a while, curious to find out what the little ball he pushed along was made of, I lifted the beetle away from it, and then gently trod on the little ball. To my surprise I discovered that it contained damp manure of either a horse or a mule, and that, evidently, whilst being rolled along, it had become covered with a thin layer of sand. Quite unperturbed by my interference, the beetle immediately returned to the ball, and finding it slightly flattened out, proceeded to re-shape it with its horny back legs. This done, it resumed its pushing, going through antics which were amusing to behold. Whilst watching, I came to the conclusion that the insect was not playing a game, but that it wanted the manure for a more practical purpose, most likely to roll it to some little hole where to let it ferment, or to allow some minute fungus to grow on it, something the beetle could feed on later.

As I proceeded, the country became hilly, and the vegetation more luxuriant. Huge chestnut, mulberry and other trees shaded quaint old farm-houses, and crystal clear streams seethed and bubbled through their rocky beds, here and there leaping into pools below. Having passed through one or two ancient hamlets and small villages, the road led me up to pine forests, past waterfalls, twisting and turning higher and higher. The strong fragrant smell of pine, rosemary and of wild flowers made me inhale deeply, and the silence was broken only by the swishing and whispering of the wind among the lofty tree-tops, and occasionally by the call of some bird, the sound echoing through the wild and mysterious mountain woods. Suddenly the appearance of a tall, lean, ill-clad but good-looking young man startled me. He came from behind some tall trees, and upon reaching the middle of the road, held up a hand, giving me the sign to stop. Accordingly, I slowed down, and, without stopping the engine, halted.

The young man had a tired and haggard look about him, and when he spoke, his Spanish was broken and halting; and was spoken with a strong accent which I immediately recognized as French. When, in the latter language, I asked him what he wanted, an expression of surprise came over his face, and for a brief moment his eyes lit up with joy. He told me that he had come all the way from France on foot, that, on the previous evening, he had lost his way, and that he had spent the night in the woods. When I asked him what he was doing in Spain, he replied that he was looking for work, and went on to say that, being ravenously hungry, he was looking for the nearest village or farmhouse.

Somehow, I found it difficult to believe that he could have come all the way from France on foot, and I wondered why he had left the road to get lost in this mountain wilderness. Having no weapons of any kind on me, I kept a sharp eye on the wild-looking young man, and watched his every move, for I could not help wondering if, perhaps, other men were hidden somewhere near, in the dusk of the dense forest. I told him that I had no food with me and that, being a stranger to these parts, I could only tell him that if he followed the road in the direction whence I had come, in about an hour or so he would reach a hamlet where, I hoped, he would have luck. And with this I bade him *adieu,* and resumed my journey, ready to let the engine go full out, if necessary. However, nothing happened, and after having descended into a deep mountain valley, a steep climb brought me to an amazing ancient village, situated in a kind of wide ravine. In the middle of it, on a rocky eminence, stood an ancient castle and fortress combined, and the small houses near it were stone-built, and had crude wooden balconies. After this came the longest and most difficult climb I had during my travels through Spain, but one I would not have missed for anything. Soon I found myself above the timber-line, on the slope of a steep rocky mountainside, with a similar one facing it across a gully, which grew narrower towards the top of the *sierra.*

Despite the fact that there was no sign of life anywhere within sight, for some strange reason I began to feel that somebody or something alive was near me, and although I turned to look in every direction, I could not understand the reason for the peculiar feeling which had assailed me, until I heard a faint swishing noise above me. And lo, there hovered an eagle, with outspread wings as if suspended from the sky by an invisible string. The bird was not more than fifteen feet above me, turning its head from side to side, as if trying to get a better view of me with one eye and then with the other. Most likely, it wondered what kind of strange being it was that made its way uphill along the road, cut out of the mountain-side, for to eagles in the Sierras de Gredos a motor-cycle must have been a sensational novelty, and so, perhaps, one of those feathered kings of the heights had volunteered to go and investigate the mystery, and in due time to return to its eyrie, with a detailed report. Be this as it may, the eagle remained directly above me for some time, and then, banking sharply into an air-current, turned round and glided away as silently as it had come, leaving me alone to make my way up to higher regions.

Zigzagging, sometimes along one mountain-side, then along the other, across the gully and then back again, more and more zigzags, and then more, higher and higher, at last I reached the top of the pass where I halted to gaze at the regions through which I had passed that morning. Owing to recent adverse weather conditions, where I stood, shivering in the strong icy wind, the road and the nearby rocks were covered with snow, and as far as the eye could reach, serrated peaks glittered like diamonds. Below me, the zigzagging road I had followed, looked as if a long thin paper-streamer or ticker-tape had been thrown on the barren mountain-sides. The crazy pattern lost itself in the wooded parts, deep down below, only to re-appear further down, and finally to fade away in the distance. Far away, through the open end of the "V" shaped gap in the mountain whence I gazed, I could see the fertile plain through which I had passed that morning, though now it seemed that those parts belonged to another world. Temporarily, mine was up in the cold windswept heights fit only for eagles. As my eyes swept along the wild mountain ranges, I remembered that those are the haunts of the *capra hispanica,* a large species of wild goat resembling the ibex of the Swiss and Tyrolean Alps, known as *steinbock,* and the *markhor* of the Himalayas. The male of the *capra hispanica* – with his long, flattish and slightly twisted horns that curve backwards from the head in an open spiral – is locally called *macho montés,* and in some regions as *bucardo.* Until recent years the species was threatened with extinction, but since it came under government protection, it has increased in numbers. Mountaineers whose sport and glory it was to hunt this shy and elusive animal were made paid guards to see that the new law is respected, a clever trick that has had excellent results. The wild forests and glades are the haunts of deer, wild cats, wolves, even bears. No wonder, then, that the hardy shepherds who take their flocks to and fro over these mountains from the Castilian plateau to Estremadura, keep formidable hounds, known as *perros de presa.*

Though I could have feasted my eyes on this unforgettable panorama for hours, the wind was so strong and cold that I moved on, shivering and my teeth chattering. Upon having rounded a nearby rock, another wonderful vista opened before me, now towards the north. Suddenly it seemed that, as if by magic, I had reached an entirely different mountain world, for there the northern slopes of the mountain on which I stood were much more gentle, and overgrown with grass and clumps of Spanish broom, *retama,* with their mass of golden flowers, the brilliancy of which contrasted marvellously with the severe landscape I had beheld only a few moments before. Longing to reach warmer and more sheltered parts, without loss of time I started on the down-grade, and, after a while, upon reaching a comfortable spot, I halted to take a short rest. Complete silence reigned; and whilst I admired the colours and shapes of a few small wild flowers near me, suddenly I heard a familiar sound, and then, again, there was silence. Presently, once more I heard, "Cuckoo, cuckoo!" . . . or was it "Cuco, cuco!" seeing that the bird was a native of Spain, and therefore, presumably, sang in *cuclillo* or *cuco?* As if mocking the cuckoo for his vocal efforts among the heather, some other bird chirped and twittered, and whilst I listened to this counterpoint, a little bright-green lizard appeared on a nearby rock to inspect me with tiny eyes which resembled two minute highly-polished black diamonds. Remembering something a shepherd had told me about lizards liking music, I began to whistle softly. This made the pretty little reptile turn and jerk its head from side to side, as if trying to ascertain whence came the sounds, but when a magpie flew past, so low that I heard the beating of its wings, my listener quickly disappeared into a crack in the rock.

Winding down, down and down, after having passed through two villages, eventually I reached a fertile but almost treeless upland plain, surrounded by mountains, except ahead of me to the north. For several miles I rode along a dead-straight road, on which, for once, I let my machine go full out. Ever since having set out from Oropesa in the early morning, I had not seen a single vehicle, and even when I reached a main road near Avila, I had it practically to myself. The fortified mediaeval town is enclosed within mighty walls with many towers, and stands on a flat-topped ridge which rises abruptly from the plain.

A bitterly cold wind continued to blow down from the heights; so upon reaching an extremely modest wayside store, I went inside for a little refreshment. The rather dirty and primitive establishment was run by a woman who, together with two little girls, was sitting at a *camilla* (one of the round tables with cloth flaps and a charcoal brazier under it, described in a previous chapter) busy sewing, whilst her children were doing their school homework. Having greeted the woman, I asked if she could prepare me something to eat; an omelette, or anything she could produce. Before going to the kitchen, she told me, "*Par Dios, señor,* you must be feeling cold, come, sit down here at the *camilla* and warm yourself whilst I prepare something for you to eat. In the meantime, I think, a *traguito* (little drink) would do you good. What do you say, *señor?*"

Whilst sitting at the *camilla* sipping a brandy, I talked to the two little girls, who very soon lost their shyness, and told me much about their school, and about other things which were of great importance and interest to them.   They informed me that trade was slack, except on market days, when peasants stopped for a while to buy something whilst on their way to and from the nearby town.   Their father, they told me, was busy working in a field, and then they had a great deal to say about the few chickens, ducks and pigs they kept, and, of course, much about their schoolmates, and, above all, about the peculiar ways and mannerisms of a nun who was one of their teachers.

I thoroughly enjoyed the simple meal, and when the time came to depart, and I offered the little girls a few pesetas as a little present, it was only after much persuasion on my part that they accepted it.

The walled-in town of Avila, with its nine gates, narrow streets, squares, shaded gardens, old houses and Romanesque churches, was enchanting.   The massive high outer-walls are about one and a half miles long, and have eighty-eight towers.   In parts, some of these walls and towers have undergone a certain amount of restoration, but this has been done so skilfully that it has not marred what is considered to be the most complete military edifice of the Middle Ages in Europe.   As almost everywhere in southern Spain, storks' nests were to be seen on some of the high towers and turrets.   Evidently, these friendly birds like to be near human habitations, and they revel in being in draughty spots, the higher the better, without protection against the elements, fierce sun, storm, wet or dry.

I was fortunate to be in Avila during two market days, which. are held on Fridays, when the old town fairly hums with activity.   Most of the farmers, cattlemen, shepherds and countrymen who flock there from afar, wear black smocks, and some cling to the Castilian dress; large black or brown broad-brimmed hats, short breeches, and, thrown over their shoulder, a cape.   Those of the women who refuse to deviate from tradition, wear short wide skirts made of wool, brightly coloured scarves which come to a point at the back, and their hair is combed down tightly, with a broad pin piercing a plaited knot, low down at the back of the head.   The market square is surrounded by arcades whence I watched the busy scenes.   Among the many things sold there were stacks of sections of old motor-car tyres, which are used for making sandals.   The cattle market is held outside the city walls, on a more or less flat piece of ground which I reached by walking through a huge gateway with a semi-ruined, stork-inhabited tower near it. Peasants passing through that gate, driving laden donkeys and mules before them, made a fine picture, and so did the shepherds beyond it, watching over the sheep which stood in little groups in the shadow of the city wall. At the foot of a nearby slope, in the bright sunshine, viewed from a distance, the cattle looked like a bed of animated tulips. Between the potential buyers and those who offered them animals for sale, there was much bartering, haggling and occasionally loud laughter when a particularly witty though invariably good-humoured jibe found its mark.

In Avila I suffered a minor shock. My coupons for petrol were almost exhausted, and when I mentioned this to the proprietor of a filling station, he informed me that tourists can buy new coupons only with foreign currency. Ignorant of this official regulation, I had changed my remaining traveller's cheques into pesetas, so it was suddenly brought home to me that I was "up a gum tree." Of course, a little "wangling" would have provided me with the necessary fuel, but as I did not like the idea of having to rely on getting mine as *estraperlo* (commodity sold on the black market) for the rest of my tour, I decided to make a quick trip to Madrid, there to explain my situation to a friend who was in a position to help me out of my predicament.

For a change, and in order to see another side of Spanish life, I decided to leave my motor-cycle in Avila, and to make the seventy-mile journey to the capital by train, travelling third class.

When I arrived at the ramshackle station, situated close on a mile to the east of the town, it was early evening, and as the market was over, the place was crowded with peasants, people from nearby regions, and a sprinkling of gipsies. Farmers who had bought wooden pitch-forks, yokes for oxen, earthenware jars and similar things, piled them up on the platform. Other travellers brought parcels tied up with coarse fibre string, crates and baskets containing live poultry, rabbits and even puppies, so very soon the station looked as if a wholesale evacuation were in progress. This impression was strengthened by all the shouting, pushing and scrambling to obtain tickets, which were issued with tantalizing slowness. A few soldiers, policemen and civil guards, with their three-cornered hats, were among the crowd on the platform, as well as a number of local residents who had come to see friends off, or just to pass the time away. Although a subway led to platform 2, and a male voice repeatedly droned on a screechy loud-speaker, politely asking people to make use of it, and informing them that it was strictly *prohibido* to cross the line, no one took the slightest notice of these requests and warnings. Men in uniform, passengers, women and children who could and would not be bothered to go down and up the steps of the subway, crossed over the line in flocks, and sometimes stopped between them to hold lively conversations. Officials – who evidently knew better than to attempt to enforce regulations, or who simply did not care about what was going on – just went on with their business, which appeared to be talking to acquaintances and friends.

At last, a train approached, and even before it came to a standstill, people scrambled up high steps leading into carriages. Packages, parcels, bundles, hand-bags, agricultural implements and so on were lifted and passed in through windows, stout women and children were assisted up the high steps, tight-fitting blouses and skirts were strained to ripping-open point, good-humoured piquant remarks were made about one or two of the portly matrons who were not slow in retaliating with jibes, and so a mass of sweating, puffing and panting humanity squeezed itself into carriages. The train being only a local one, and bound for rural districts, its rolling stock was of the most antiquated, and some of the carriages so dilapidated that they looked more like huge rabbit hutches on wheels. There was much shouting from crowded windows to the onlookers on the platform, and by the latter to friends or relatives on the train, until, at long last last, whistles were blown, warnings were yelled by the station master and porters telling people to stand clear of the train; presently the antiquated engine gave several bronchial hoots, and then, to the accompaniment of much clanging and banging, the convoy began to move, many hands were waved, there was a tirade of *adios, buen viaje* and other stereotyped words of parting, as the train slowly gathered speed. When it had disappeared round a curve, people settled down to waiting for the Vigo-Madrid express, which, by some miracle, arrived only twenty minutes late. This time, instead of being a mere spectator, I took a very active part in the mêlée to get into a carriage, and after Herculean efforts succeeded in occupying the last available seat in a compartment, where I slumped down, out of breath as if I had just finished a fierce all-in wrestling bout. When luggage racks and every available space were piled up with parcels and hand-bags, and passengers stood in the corridor, squeezed together like dried figs, the train began to move. The high, leather-backed seats were so slippery that with every jerk people who sat in a row with me, slid from side to side, causing us to be pressed together closely, until, with a great deal of wriggling, we managed to slide back to our original seats, thus getting a little more breathing-space. However, like chickens going to roost, after a while we settled down, some of us to talk, a fat, rather loudly-dressed woman and her seventeen-year-old son to reading comic magazines, one woman to breast-feeding her baby, and a peasant who was seated next to me to unwrapping a paper parcel which contained brown bread, an apple and two *chorizos* (sausages seasoned with red pepper). As is customary throughout Spain, before beginning his meal, he offered some to all the other passengers, and when they declined with thanks, finishing by saying "*que aproveche*" (may you profit by your meal), he set to work eating. Again, when he produced a *bota* (wine skin), he politely held it out, and when I thanked him for the offer, he insisted that I take some of the wine which, he assured me, was good, being the produce of his own vineyard. Accordingly, I took the wine-skin, unscrewed the stopper from its little beak, and then, raising the *bota* above my slightly held-back head, pressed on the pouch, thus squirting a thin jet of the liquid into my mouth, without touching the beak with my lips. This is a feat which requires some practice, let alone when the wobbling of the train makes one's hands unsteady, so I opened my mouth wide, and held the beak of the wine-skin as near as possible. Though experts can drink thus with barely parted lips, and holding the *bota* as far from their mouths as the length of their arms permit, the peasant complimented me on my performance, and added that this was the first time he had seen a foreigner drink from a *bota*.

The first stage of our journey took us through flat country, but soon we began to climb up low mountains, with thin forests above and below us, and eventually reached the plateau of Castile, where it gave me quite a thrill to view my old friend, the palace of the Escorial, from the window of a train.

When the railway guard came to collect the tickets, I was surprised to see that half of the people who travelled with me had official or free passes, and even more so when the fat woman and her well-dressed and groomed son told me that his father was a sergeant in the army. Seeing how little a Spanish sergeant earns, and the manner in which his wife and son were dressed, I could not help wondering how many other kinds of free passes and profitable things the military man knew how to wangle. Furthermore, I came to the conclusion that if Spanish railways went out of State control, and investors were sought to form a company to run them, even if I had unlimited sums of money at my disposal, I would not invest as much as one *peseta* in such a hopeless venture. However, Spanish, British, and other state-run railways, roll on, the tax-payer makes up for deficits, whilst other "patriots" who are in official positions live on whatever fat comes out of a lean land. Such are conditions in most modern States; giants which grow more and more top-heavy, giants with feet of clay.

Back in Madrid once more, I went to the *pensión* where I had stayed during my previous visits. Most of the more or less permanent guests were still there, among them the young Peruvian lady who was supposed to be studying some subject or other at the university. As formerly, at meal-times the same little group assembled at her table, one of its members being the loud-mouthed young sheik from Barcelona who held a post at the *Banco de España.* As usual, when this human loudspeaker held forth or roared with laughter at his own feeble jokes, the young Irish-American, who claimed to be studying Arabic and Oriental languages, scowled at his pet-aversion from the far corner of the dining-room.

The final football match for the championship of Spain was about to be played in Madrid between the "Atlético" team of Bilbao and Valladolid, and consequently the city was invaded by supporters of both teams who had made the long journey from the coast hoping to see their respective favourites carry away with them the coveted cup. A number of Basques who had come from Bilbao, took lodgings in my *pensión,* and whenever these lively and eminently tough-looking but very nice *futbol entusiastas* came in for a meal, the noise they made was terrific, for invariably they had made merry in taverns, and, being good and typical Basques, this meant that they had been drinking freely of something stronger than coffee or lemonade. On such occasions I found it highly amusing to watch the effect the arrival of the merry Basques had on the little group seated at the young Peruvian lady's table, particularly so on the sheik of the *Banco de España,* for invariably he shut up like an oyster, and with downcast eyes finished his meal, whereafter he slunk out of the dining-room, like a dog expecting to be chastized for having attempted to steal meat off a table. In order to make quite sure that with their meals the Basques had the right kind of wine, they had brought with them several formidable-looking demi-johns, which were attacked with great vigour. On the great day, when the match was played, the members of our contingent from Bilbao sported jerseys with red and white stripes, these being the colours of "Atlético." As it happened, their team won by four goals to one, so for the next two days the roof was nearly blown off my *pensión*. Despite their high spirits and the unearthly din the Basques made whenever they rolled in for a meal, they were very nice fellows, and otherwise well-behaved. When I told one of them that I was touring the country, and that, most likely, within a few weeks I would be in the Basque country, he became most enthusiastic, and told me on no account to pass through Bilbao without looking him up. Having scribbled his telephone number on a card, he handed it to me, with the remark that he would ask taxi-drivers and policemen to be on the look-out for me, and that if by any chance I tried to dodge him, he would soon track me down. With this we parted, but, as will be seen later, this chance meeting in Madrid was to lead to many adventures and to a great deal of fun.

In connection with noisy behaviour in Spanish hotels and inns, here I must add an aside. Of course, I am not referring to first-class hotels, which are practically the same all over the world, and in which guests, servants, waiters and members of the administrative staff, act in an identical manner. In the Spanish hotels and guest houses to which I refer, people can make all the noise they want, late in the evening, and throughout the night, until the early hours of morning. Though, naturally, this is not quite in order, no objections are raised, but if even the slightest noise is made, say between the hours of 4 and 10 a.m., or during the sacred *siesta* time, such an offence raises a storm of com-plaints or even worse. During the above-mentioned hours, servants converse in whispers, and they take great care to do their work as silently as possible, and if a guest is a stranger to these customs, or forgets himself to the extent of speaking in a loud tone of voice, or in some other manner disturbs sleepers, one of them is sure to appear immediately to complain in no uncertain terms.

My business connected with petrol coupons having been settled I returned to Avila. This time the train was not crowded and so, after a pleasant journey which lasted about three hours, I was back in the old walled-in town, and on the following morning I set out towards Salamanca.

After a ride through partly flat and partly rolling agricultural country, on a gentle slope the famous old university city came in sight. After crossing the river Tormes, which is spanned by a Roman bridge, a short uphill climb brought me to the vast *Plaza Mayor* (main square), surrounded with symmetrically-built four-storied houses with colonnades facing the square. Thanks to an obliging policeman, I found a modest hotel, and after having deposited my belongings there, I set out, afoot, to have a look round the town, and to call on several people to whom I had letters of introduction.

Throughout Spain, whenever I presented such a letter, I was received with such enthusiasm and kindness that I felt quite embarrassed. However, to be quite frank, as a rule I preferred to be on my own, without having to make, and listen to, conversation for hours on end, and, sometimes, having to go to places which were of little interest to me.

Founded in 1230, in the sixteenth century Salamanca became one of the four most famous universities in Europe, chiefly because it was from there that the learning of Arabia was introduced to the civilized world.[8] Cervantes, who in his *Don Quixote* put chivalry to sublime ridicule, had many "digs" at Salamanca and its professors. There, in a small way I, too, had one whilst conversing with several learned men, and this is how it came about. Cervantes, like Shakespeare, is discussed infinitely more than he is read. Even among the people who claim to have studied all his works thoroughly, only a very few remember what they have read. Although in this respect my memory leaves much to be desired, for some peculiar reason, whilst conversing with newly made friends in Salamanca, I recalled the gist of a conversation between Don Quixote and Sancho Panza. We happened to be talking about the Spanish language, and when I said that all words which begin with "al" are of Moorish origin, my listeners disagreed with me, and even more so when I maintained that "al" is an abbreviation standing

---

[8] The word "university" did not at that time exist in the Spanish language. A college was defined as: *a body of professors and students, which is set up in any place with the desire and the understanding to acquire knowledge.*

for "Allah." When I maintained that, somewhere in *Don Quixote* this is mentioned, in order to prove to me that I was mistaken, two bulky volumes of Cervantes' work were produced, but although I sought the passage, it proved to be a veritable needle in a haystack, and I failed to find it. For the time being, I had to hold my peace, but, being a stickler in such matters, weeks later; upon returning to my home in London, I renewed my search among the thousand pages of a two-volume edition I have of *Don Quixote*, until with the help of a friend I found the passage, which I copied out, and, filled with pride and satisfaction, mailed to my friends in Salamanca. The passage out of *Don Quixote* reads as follows: " . . . and this name *albogues* (pastoral lute) is Moorish, as are all those in our Castilian tongue which commence with *al* . . ."[9]

Quite apart from this little personal boast, I mention the matter of language because it is of interest. Are Spaniards of the Latin race? The aboriginal inhabitants of the Iberian peninsula were Iberians who later intermarried with the Celtic invaders from Gaul, and long before the Christian era became the powerful warlike Celtiberi whom the Roman conquerors called *Hispaniensis,* and whom they characterized as being "fierce, haughty, proud and restless." Though during the Roman occupation of the country, the greater part of the Celtiberi became more or less Roman in language, religion, customs and legislation, in the north of the peninsula, Roman civilization was only a thin veneer. It is remarkable that the Goths, and, to a lesser degree, the Vandals, did not enrich the Spanish language, but that, on the other hand, the Moors influenced it greatly, and that Arabic learning spread through Europe from Spain.

There was so much to be seen in Salamanca that I was ever on the move. The venerable old buildings are made of sandstone which age has turned into beautiful shades of golden-brown. Whilst I sat in a little shaded square, watching the evening sun paint the spires and domes,

---

[9] " . . . Y este nombre *albogues* es morisco, como lo son todos aquellos que en nuestra lengua castellana comienzan en *al*, conviene saber: *almohaza, almorzar, alfombra, alguacil, alhucema, almacen, alcancia* y otros semejantes, que deben ser pocos mas; y solo tres tiene nuestra lengua que son moriscos y acaban en i, y son *borcegui, zaquizami,* y *maravedi; alheli* y *alfaqui,* tanto por el *al* primero como et *i* en que acaban son conocidos por arabigos."

boys on their way home from school played a running game with marbles, here and there sat old people, two or three nurses, wearing snow-white neatly-ironed aprons with lace borders, looked after infants, birds sang among the trees, and then, suddenly, the peaceful quiet was disturbed by the beating of drums, as soldiers marched past, the jarring sound echoing off the wall of a nearby church. Moving on, I went to the *Plaza Mayor* (main square) where many people sat in open-air *cafés* or under the colonnades, talking and taking refreshment. A female voice shouting my name, made me turn to one side, and lo, there, sitting at a table, waving and smiling at me, was a young woman whom I recognized as none other than the Peruvian student from the *pensión* in Madrid. During our ensuing conversation she told me that she had come to Salamanca in order to study for two or three months, whereafter, thanks to an influential member of her family, she hoped to obtain a highly paid job in the U.N.E.S.C.O., with her quarters in gay Paris. When I asked her in which branch of learning she specialized, her reply was that, so far, she had not been able to make up her mind, but that, in the meantime, she was enjoying herself thoroughly. Wishing her good luck, and happy hunting, I departed to resume my ramblings, and late that night went to sit outside a deserted *café* on the other side of a massive archway which leads into the *Plaza Mayor*. In the semi-darkness, the nearby church of San Martin, with its strange balconies, heavy portal, and relief of the saint on horseback, made a fine picture, especially so where a few street lights threw shadows on its walls, and on the arcades and balconies of nearby houses. From where I sat I had an excellent view of shadowy figures which passed every now and again, on their way to and from the Main Square. Two elderly men, coming from opposite directions, pushing along wheel-barrows, stopped upon recognizing each other, and then settled down to talking. When a motor-car came on the scene, and the driver tooted the horn, asking for a passage, without even turning round the two talkers uttered an expletive and waved him on.

Expletives, swear-words and blasphemy vary greatly in different parts of Spain; in fact, I could make an instructive map, based on experience, showing the various regions and their inhabitants' particular and favourite ways of expressing annoyance, anger, affection or surprise, mental and verbal reactions to happenings which, in the case of some individuals, seem to recur at amazingly short intervals. In *cafés* and taverns, I saw notices, printed in large letters, SE PROHIBE LA BLASFEMIA (Blasphemy is Prohibited). Needless to say, patrons take as little heed of such placards as typical English sailors would if their skippers put up similar ones in their ships.

A friend told me not to miss going to a village named Hurdes, for there, he assured me, I would see something remarkable, many of the *Hurdanos* (people of Hurdes) having six fingers and toes. However, there was so much to be seen in Salamanca, that I did not bother to make a side-trip in order to see human freaks, and to ascertain how much truth is in the story which, incidentally, I heard from several other sources. During my subsequent travels I did meet a man who had six fingers on both hands, though the extra "fingers" were merely a kind of double first joint of the thumbs, with perfectly shaped nails.

Leaving the *Hurdanos* to anthropologists or students of ortho-paedics who might feel like investigating the origin of six fingers and toes, I resumed my northward journey, along the nearby Portuguese border on my left, or be it, to the west of me. I was in the province of Leon, which, near Salamanca, is a little more than 2,500 feet above sea-level. Though *leon* means "lion," the name of the province has nothing to do with the largest and most handsome of carnivora, but was derived from the Seventh Roman Legion *(Legio Septima)* which was stationed in this part of the ancients' Lusitania, which, as mentioned previously, extended from the river Tagus to the Sea of Cantabria (now called Bay of Biscay), and included what is now Portugal.

CHAPTER 17

SALAMANCA – ZAMORA – PUEBLA DE SANABRIA – ORENSE – PUENTE AREAS

Between Salamanca and Zamora, the country changed completely. Plains and valleys between ranges of hills were green, and almost anything grew there. Zamora, with its ancient fort on a rocky hump that overlooks the river Douro (or Duero) is a small though picturesque town. As it happened to be Sunday, and rather hot when I arrived there, I waited until evening before calling on a resident whom I had met and befriended in Madrid. Despite the heat, a football match was being played, and supporters of the teams marched through the streets, singing and shouting *estribillos,* short verses boosting their respective teams, or making fun of the other. The little hotel in which I stayed was situated facing a square, and from a window of the dining-room, which was on the first floor, one would have had a good view of what was going on below, had it not been for a smartly-dressed young Beau Brummel who had made himself comfortable in an armchair at this point of vantage. With a small portable radio set beside him, he lounged there, apparently thinking of nothing. At long last, when, after a programme of popular Spanish music, there followed a "talk," during which a broadcaster made violent attacks on Freemasons, the young man switched off his infernal machine and haughtily asked a servant to bring him a glass of water. Having drunk it with elegance, he rose and departed, and when I observed that several of the guests heaved deep breaths of relief, I asked the waiter who the young smartie might be.

"Oh," he replied, "he is just one of those, the son of a prominent lawyer, a good-for-nothing who regularly comes here to sit at the window, and to see if any interesting guests have arrived. He has done this for several years, but in all this time he has never spent as much as a *centésimo* in this place. You see, his father is an important man, so what are we to do about it?"

In the evening, people were parading down the main street, and nuns shepherded along a troop of schoolgirls who walked slowly in two rows, dressed in black, and looking thoroughly bored, meek and oppressed.

Until well after midnight my friend and I strolled through the town, and when we had seen enough, went to join a group of men who were assembled in a cosy old tavern. When asked what I would like to drink, and I replied that I was not in the mood to take anything alcoholic, one of the company laughed and said, "Come on, friend, a glass of our good wine will do you no harm. Remember, a man without vices is like a plant without flowers."

The company was so interesting and amusing, and the wine so good, that time passed quickly. Another funny remark that was made during that session was when a bachelor was being teased about not getting married. "Get married? . . . Get married?" the target of the jibes asked, and then went on, "The young ladies don't look at me. They wouldn't even if I were shown to them in the shape of an oil painting done by the greatest and most flattering portrait painter alive."

Following a route which took me along a big bend of the Portuguese border, I rode almost due west, now no longer on the plateau of Old Castile, but through undulating country, with here and there high hills to negotiate. Ahead were mountains, the tops of which were flecked with white, and the houses in villages and hamlets through which I passed were small, stone-built, mostly whitewashed, and had dark wooden beams and quaint little wooden balconies. The fields were of every shade of green, and here and there oxen, guided by sturdy sunburnt peasants, pulled ploughs. In one place I passed, a gang of men and women were busy repairing the road, and I was astonished to see with what speed and good cheer they did their heavy work, probably for a mere pittance. This was the first time – except among South American Indians – that I had seen women employed in the construction and maintenance of roads. In this part of Spain and throughout

Galicia, women are remarkably strong, but yet, despite the heavy physical work they do, the vast majority of them are good-looking and full of feminine charm.

In one village in which I halted for a while, a donkey fair was being held. Peasants and dealers had come from afar with their little beasts, who stood about in groups, looking as indifferent and dreamy as only donkeys can. The little place, which normally must be asleep, was now wide awake, and the little wooden balconies seemed to look down with scorn on the bargaining and chaffering sons of the soil. A pair of oxen, with their yoke and sheep-skins adorned with gay tassels to protect the head and eyes, was drawn up against a wall, munched slowly at a bundle of grass, and contemplated the busy scene with philosophic eyes. The women who passed, laughing and talking, carrying earthen-ware jars upon their heads, or great baskets filled with vegetables and eggs which shone like pearls against the green leaves, swung their gaily coloured shawls and flowing skirts as they walked with unparalleled grace and litheness, with necks and cheeks like ripening maize stalks, were survivals of an ancient race, and typical of Galician country districts.

Puebla de Sanabria, situated very close to the Portuguese border, is an ancient little town with an aspect and atmosphere all its own. Upon reaching a stone bridge which leads over the clear waters of the river Tera (a tributary of the Douro which flows into the Atlantic near Oporto in Portugal) ahead of me, on the top of a steep rocky hill, the walls and towers of a citadel and of a Romanesque church rose into the deep-blue sky. On the banks of the river, women were washing clothes and linen, and on the parapet of the bridge sat two Civil Guards, watching my approach with interest. I always made a point of waving a hand to such officers of law and order, and invariably, in their turn, they returned my greeting. Often, also, I stopped to converse with them, and thus made many pleasant and interesting acquaintances, from some of whom I gathered much interesting information. Without exception, I found them to be polite and obliging, and all were pleased to meet a tourist who spoke to them on level terms. Naturally, when I told them where I came from, what I had seen of their country, and which parts I intended to visit before returning to London, they were both surprised and pleased.

Puebla de Sanabria and its surrounding hills appealed to me so much that I spent a day there. A steep climb took me up to the little town, most of the old houses of which are clustered together on a rocky slope which terminates on an uneven square, cobbled with stones the size of sucking-pigs. The narrow main street is so steep that stone blocks are laid so as to make steps for pedestrians, and the houses, with their dark wooden balconies, rise, one above the other, built in rows which describe irregular curves. This is no place for ladies with high-heeled shoes, but rather for foot-wear studded with hobnails, for many generations of inhabitants and the shod hoofs of innumerable donkeys and mules have polished the cobble stones, making them exceedingly slippery. The forbidding-looking mediaeval fort dominates the valley, and on two sides is made inaccessible by precipitous rocky walls. I was told that it was being used as a prison, but although I passed quite near its heavy wooden gate, not a sound came from within. From a little shaded green I had a splendid view of the river below, and of the beautiful green and hilly country which stretches towards the north and west. On a long wooden balcony of the municipal building which overlooks the square, a young man walked up and down, reading a book; otherwise the place was deserted, but whilst carefully treading my way through a little curved lane, I came to two young women who were busy picking and spreading out in the sun the woollen stuffing of mattresses. When I was about to take a photograph of them, a middle-aged woman spied me from a balcony above, and presently came running out of the door to greet me, and to ask to be included in the picture. The two good-looking young women – whom she introduced to me as her daughters – became very excited at the prospect of being photographed, and giggled as the mother took great pains to make them pose to her liking and taste. It took quite a while before the trio was ready to be "shot", and when I made ready to leave, the mother asked me if by any chance I knew Mexico, where, she informed me, lived members of her family who were prospering. Despite my protests, the woman sent one of her daughters to fetch a glass of wine for me, and whilst I drank, she told me a great deal about the good old days, when money circulated freely and when *fiestas* went with a swing which her daughters could not even imagine.

Retracing my steps downhill, I came to a stone fountain where girls were busy filling pitchers, which they loaded on donkeys who waited patiently until gossip and laughter should cease. A little further down, upon reaching the road which leads into Portugal, I saw several houses with crude wooden arcades. Among them were two *paraderos,* wayside inns with accommodation for beasts in courtyards. When, over one I read written "MANUEL CHARRO," I could not resist going in, for the name reminded me of my friends, the *charros,* as cowboys arc called in Mexico.

The tap-room, with its rough wooden floor, a few stools, benches, tables and a counter, all made of pinewood, was untidy, to put it mildly, but yet the place had its charms. Near the door a mongrel dog divided his time equally, scratching himself and snapping at flies, and at a table four peasants were playing cards, grains of maize being used to keep the score of points won or lost. When a ragged man came in to sell a number of trout he swore to have caught that very evening, there ensued much haggling, until, finally, a compromise was reached by splitting the difference, as well as giving the vendor a glass of wine.

About ten miles from Puebla de Sanabria is a large and beautiful lake. Natives say that at its bottom is a sunken village, with its houses and church still intact, and that, once every year, on the day of St. John, the sounds of church bells being rung can be heard coming from the depths.

The *albergue* in which I stayed is situated below the little town, on the north side of the river, and from it I had a fine view of the fort on the precipitous hill. Late that night, as I slowly walked up and down, enjoying a cool breeze which carried with it the smell of flowers and of aromatic trees, the sight of countless stars twinkling in the dark-purple sky, and a solitary light in the faintly outlined silhouette of the old fort attracted my attention, and made me wonder . . . wonder if it was true that prisoners were behind those dark scowling walls, and if so, how many lingered there, for what crimes they were imprisoned, and if, perhaps, some were in the darkness of that grim mediaeval edifice, through heavily-barred slits in those walls gazing at the stars of hope above.

Shortly after having left Puebla de Sanabria I found myself in mountainous country where the tortuous road took me up to high passes where the wind was cold, and then down, past sloping heaths with gorse bushes and Spanish broom in all their golden glory, heather, bright wild flowers, here and there a waterfall, cuckoos calling, birds singing, large green lizards basking in the sun and scuttling away at my approach, herds of goats grazing; then, further down, I came to fertile valleys and clear streams that teem with trout, salmon and other varieties of fish. In a hamlet where I halted to take some food and refreshment, as I sat in the low-roofed tavern, through the window floated all the odorous suggestions of the garden, and the homely sounds of happy pastoral life; the cackling of hens, the bleating of a goat tied to a nearby tree, the mooing of a cow, the distant noise of a sickle being whetted, the heehaw of a donkey, the laughter and joyous shouting of children playing, a woman singing in the kitchen, and the incessant hum of bees who were buzzing in and out of a wisteria which overhung the front door and windows.

After the meal, in order to stretch my legs, and to pass away time, I went to chat with the inn-keeper's wife and daughter who were busy tidying up the kitchen. Whilst complimenting them on the excellence of the omelette they had prepared for me, and on the quality of their home-made cheese, I noticed how spotlessly clean was a stone table, so clean that a single rose left there unheeded, blushed against the polished surface. Going out through a back-door to have a look at the vegetable garden, I was just in time to see an old woman feeding the chickens. As the maize fell in specks of glittering gold on large age-worn stone slabs with which the back of the house was paved, I could not help but compare the aged woman with an old apple-tree, knotted and gnarled. Yet, despite the years of rough house- and field-work and child-bearing, she moved quickly as she jabbered something to the hens, which pecked away about her feet with fierce eyes, their necks askew, cackling with greedy desire as they watched every handful of grain being flung into the dazzling sunlight. Then there was a rush forward, a flutter, a rustle of feathers, a clapping of wings, as gold, silver, white, brown, crimson, yellow and every shade of colour flamed and changed in vivid gleams in the eye of the sun. A hen, more valiant and greedy than the rest, would secure the booty, hold guard over it, frightening away the others with fierce pecks, whilst more timid ones, for all the world like women at a sale or men at the Stock Exchange, made a quick rush at grains which bounced further away. The old woman clucked, scolded and objurgated in a language the fowls seemed to understand, as she dashed forward to rescue some defence-less hen from the aggression of her fellows.

Similar little happenings and interludes made my short halts by the wayside interesting, and I often wished I had the ability and time to paint such colourful scenes, quaint nooks and corners, wonderful land-scapes, charming farm-houses, and humble cottages in their variegated settings.

In another wayside inn where I stopped to eat something, the middle-aged proprietor, after having cast repeated searching glances in my direction, came to ask me if by any chance I knew the Argentine. When I replied that, indeed, I knew that country very well, having resided there for many years, the man shouted, "Say no more. I am sure I know who you are. You are the man who once rode two Argentine Criollo horses, named Mancha and Gato, from Buenos Aires to New York." Surprised by this feat of memory and recognition, I hesitated for a few moments before replying, and when I said that I was the person to whom he referred, the man almost flung himself at me, to slap my back whilst hugging me. Then, running to the foot of a wooden staircase which led to an upper floor, he shouted, "Emilio, Emilio! Come down quickly to meet an old friend of mine from the Argentine!"

The word "friend", though I liked to hear it spoken, amused me, coming from the lips of a man who was a perfect stranger to me. Immediately after this call, a boy of about sixteen came hurrying down the stairs, and after I had been introduced to him, as well as to all the women who were busy cooking in what was tavern, dining-room and kitchen combined, the mystery of the inn-keeper's identity was solved for me. Apparently, he had been waiter in a lively, at one time quite fashionable, *café* I had visited occasionally years before, in Buenos Aires, and on one occasion he had waited on me during a banquet given in my honour by the authorities of the city of Buenos Aires. Of course, this recognition, and for me delightful recollection, called for a drink, and later, whilst my old "friend" from the Argentine, several of his cronies, and I sat together, eating, the ex-waiter told me quite a lot about his various activities in South America. Among other reminis-cences and jokes about bygone times, he told us that "out there" one of his side-lines used to be the selling of narcotics to clients in the *café* in which he worked. This made me remember that, years before, I had heard rumours about this clandestine traffic in drugs, and when I mentioned a minor kind of riot, during which that certain *café* was wrecked, and subsequently closed down by the police for several weeks, my old "friend" roared with laughter, and, thumping the table with two fists, shouted, "Yes, yes, I remember! It was a great to-do! What fun we had in those times!"

When I made ready to depart, he insisted on my staying with him for a day or two, or for as long as I might wish, but after much arguing between the two of us, eventually I managed to take my leave, and when I asked how much I owed for food and wine consumed, I was all but thrown out of the inn. "Get on your steel horse, and out of my sight!" the ex-waiter shouted. "But if ever you return to these parts, remember that a hearty welcome awaits you here."

Continuing my ride across beautiful mountainous country, through picturesque hamlets shaded by stately chestnut, walnut and other trees, past orchards with fig, orange, lemon, apple, pear and other trees, and along narrow valleys with bubbling crystal-clear rivulets and streams, I gradually approached the Atlantic Ocean.

Once, as I free-wheeled down a steep winding incline, ahead of me, round a bend of the road, the squealing of what I took to be pigs being killed resounded through the woods. Then, suddenly, the horrid noise changed to the roaring of hungry lions, and in rapid succession this changed to unearthly moans, the loud twittering of birds and to what sounded like the ear-piercing screeching of many parrots, and the screaming of women and children in agony. Great was my surprise when I discovered that these frightful noises were caused by the massive wooden wheels of a heavy cart being pulled along slowly by a team of oxen. Later I saw several similar vehicles which made me think of remote times when the wheel was in its infancy. Yes, the wheel, the Frankenstein monster which is responsible for all our mechanical progress, which now threatens the world with a catastrophe that may well end in the downfall of our civilization.

The peasants who drove along these heavy carts were sturdy mountaineers. Men and women wore clumsy boots, leather-topped, with thick wooden soles, heavily studded with hobnails. Some came from remote farms and hamlets which it would be impossible to reach in motor vehicles, the roads and tracks leading to them being merely two deep ruts which often wind through narrow hollows. The wind, the sun and the mountain air had chiselled the faces of some of the elderly among these people into a mass of seams and wrinkles which made a veritable network round the corners of the eyes, extending down to the cheek-bone. Elderly men, with grizzly hair growing close about their mahogany-coloured temples, had wonderful character faces I longed to photograph.

In Orense – the Romans' *Aquae Urentes*, because of its hot mineral springs – I climbed up one of the steep streets which lead to the top of the hill. On its slopes the houses are clustered together, and I had to walk over slippery granite stone blocks, some as much as eight feet wide and eleven or twelve in length. A fine view of the river Minó (Minho in Portuguese) and of the surrounding hilly country amply rewarded my efforts.

Upon returning to the main street below, in one place a little crowd attracted my attention. Curious to know what was happening, I approached to investigate, and to my amusement discovered that everybody was watching a man put up a step-ladder, in order to re-paint the faded silver lettering, DENTISTA, on a board fixed to the railing of a balcony on the first floor of a house. As it happened, the ladder proved to be too short, so many of the onlookers wondered what would happen, whilst a few know-alls and more practical among them obliged the sign-painter with advice. Instead of fetching a longer ladder, the man decided to do an acrobatic feat, hanging on to the railing of the balcony with one hand, and painting with the other, whilst a boy dipped the brush in a can containing the paint, and handed it to the "artist" every time he required more. Whilst this was going on, the crowd watched from below, and, whilst working, the sign painter held an animated conversation with two or three good Samaritans who stood below, with outstretched arms, ready to catch him, should he lose his precarious hold.

Late that evening an elderly doctor took me for a walk through the old part of the town, and eventually, when we seated ourselves on a bench to converse, a peasant of my companion's acquaintance joined us. As it happened, the doctor was a keen historian, and when the two of us started to talk about the conquest of Peru and of Mexico, and the names of Cortez and Pizarro were mentioned, the peasant suddenly turned to me and said, "*Señor,* I have never heard about the two *caballeros,* but judging by what you say about them, they must be interesting persons, Do you know them personally?" When I explained briefly who they were, and that they had lived some four centuries ago, the peasant screwed up his face, and waving a gnarled hand as if to shoo away an invisible fly, said, "Bah, bah! If that's the case, then let's talk about somebody we all know."

Early next morning, when I left Orense, the atmosphere was cool and the sky cloudy. Farmers and a few gipsies were driving cattle to the market, and I passed groups of women who carried baskets filled with vegetables and fruit on their heads. When the clouds lifted, and the warm rays of the sun made the air balmy, I sat down by the wayside for a short rest. After a while, a peasant whom I had watched coming towards me, leading a cow by a rope, stopped to greet me with a cheerful "Good morning," whereafter he seated himself beside me for a friendly chat. When he told me that he was on his way to the cattle fair in Orense, where he hoped to sell the cow, I asked him if he was not rather late, seeing that I had passed the last stragglers with their animals a good half hour before. "Too late?" he came back. "Oh no. I'm not too late. Let me tell you, *señor,* I've had many years of experience with markets, and I know what I'm doing. You see, if I arrived early with the old cow, as I have done before, taking her all the way to the. town would be wasting my time, and make the *pobrecita* (poor dear) walk all that way for nothing. Yes, I know what I'm doing, *señor,* let me give you one word of advice which might well be useful to you: people do their buying when the market is nearly over." With this, he rose, shook me by the hand, at the same time saying that he was pleased to have made my acquaintance, and with an *adios* to me, and a *vamos!,* coupled with a rude though kindly-meant epithet to the old cow – who refused to move until she had filled her mouth with a particularly juicy tuft of grass she had found – resumed his peregrination towards the market in Orense.

Shortly after this meeting I came to glorious mountains where the road wound up hill and down dale, through aromatic pine forests, past little cascades tumbling down mountain sides, here and there a saw-mill where the air was impregnated with the fragrant smell of newly-cut pinewood, stone-cutters quarrying and splitting up blocks of granite, near hamlets the joyful voices of children playing, the calls of cuckoos and the song of birds echoing through the shade and coolness of the woods, then up to the summits of high passes where amazing panoramas spread before me. No wonder that, at different times, ever since I had arrived in Spain, I had heard the praises of Galicia being sung. The mountain chains which run in every direction are beautiful and a

few of the higher peaks are covered with snow for the greater part of
the year. In the low parts, owing to the Gulf Stream and the Canaries
Current, the climate is moist, which makes it ideal for raising cattle,
and a favourite haunt for innumerable birds of many varieties. During
the past century, over-population and high taxation caused – and continue to cause – much migration from these parts. On my way I met
many middle-aged and elderly Galicians who had been to different
parts of the Americas, whence they returned to their homeland after.
having saved enough money wherewith to retire or to run a small store,
inn or farm. The mass of migrants, however, stayed to populate the
New World, particularly South America. Some of these enterprising,
courageous and vigorous people landed in the New World, as the
saying goes, "on their feet," whereas many of the less fortunate ones
did it "on their posteriors." During the days of the Spanish colony in
the newly discovered lands, countless sons and daughters of Spain fell
victims to the Indians, disease, and quarrels among themselves.

Of Celtic origin, Galicians have a strong admixture of their erst-
while conquerors running in their veins: Romans, Moorish, Vandal,
Suevi, Gothic and Castilian. The language they speak is *Gallego,*
which is akin to Portuguese, but any patriotic Galician will tell you that
his language is much older than that of the neighbouring republic, and
that, in fact, Portuguese is merely an off-shoot from *Gallego.* Centuries
of subjugation to different invaders left their mark on the character of
the Galicians, especially so among the peasants who are inclined to be
servile, and who, being hard-working, thrifty and trustworthy, make
excellent servants. The more intelligent among them are inclined to be
volatile, very talkative and harum-scarum. Cervantes and many of
Spain's most prominent men were of Galician origin, but yet, throughout the Iberian peninsula and also in South America, the often crude,
slow and in many cases illogical Galician is the target of much derision
and popular jokes. Possibly this is due to the fact that many of the poor
migrants are satisfied with any kind of easy job, and that, apart from the
failings already mentioned, their outlook on life is that of Sancho
Panza. Nowhere during all my travels through different parts of the
world have I seen people who enjoy life as much as Galicians, rich and
poor alike. Many of the peasants are superstitious and full of weird
mysticism, and therefore easily led by the priests, but yet, in a peculiar
roundabout way they are most independent, and fond of having "digs"

at the priests, especially so in some popular and rather "spicy" songs about them. Owing to such contradictions and inconsistencies of character, it often happens that the Galicians' actions strike one as being incongruous and comical, and that their verbal outbursts have to be heard to be believed. However, in fairness to Galician migrants – especially to those who hail from country districts – it must be said that despite their crudeness, and often ignorance, they adapt themselves much more readily to new conditions than stay-at-home yokels of other countries ever could, if they ventured abroad.

Once, during a religious procession I was watching, a sturdy peasant who was heading it, carrying a large wooden cross, was told by a woman bystander that his deportment left much to be desired. The man stopped, and whilst thumping the ground with the base of the cross, let forth a stream of insults and blasphemy, whereafter, as if nothing had happened, he continued his slow march. This was a typical ignorant Galician in a quick fit of temper. And, strangely, not one person among the many who heard what was shouted appeared to be in the least shocked by it.

Whilst riding downhill from a high mountain pass, a nasty jolt caused two supports of my front mudguard to snap, whereafter a rattling noise annoyed me constantly. When I reached an ancient little town, called Puente Areas, upon seeing a small workshop outside which a man was busy reconditioning old bicycles, I stopped to ask if my mudguard could be repaired without much loss of time. Having examined the minor breakage, the man said that he would attend to it at once. Accordingly, I told him to get busy right away, and whilst he worked, a little group of boys and young men assembled to watch him. As usual, I was asked many questions about the motor-cycle, but a nice-looking young man of about twenty was particularly inquisitive. When the mechanic finished his job, and I was making ready to resume my journey, the young man who had asked so many questions told me that it would be a pity if I did not spend another day in the little town, and he went on informing me that on the morrow was the *fiesta* of Corpus Christi, and that, if I stayed, I would see a wonderful sight. What he told me sounded so interesting that I asked him where I could find accommodation, whereupon he replied that he was the son of the local *panadero* (baker), and that, besides this business, his family also ran an inn, situated just across the road, only a few paces from where we stood. There and then I unstrapped the luggage from my motor-cycle, and, following the young man, went to be introduced to his parents and sisters, who received me as if I were an old and honoured guest.

CHAPTER 18

PUENTE AREAS (FIESTA OF CORPUS CHRISTI) –
SANTA TECLA – VIGO –
SANTIAGO DE COMPOSTELA – CORUNNA

Outwardly, the little town of Puente Areas seemed to be almost lifeless. At long intervals a woman would walk up the steep roughly cobbled streets, carrying a basket on her head; a cart, drawn by a mule or donkey, passed slowly; or men, coming from opposite directions, would stop to converse for a while. Like a volcano which has been inactive for a long time, but is about to erupt, there was nothing to suggest that within the walls of the sleepy-looking houses there was feverish activity, and that something had been brewing for a week or even longer, all day and late into the night.

The little room I was given in the inn was on the first floor, and from the window I had a good view of gardens, orchards and fields, and of hills in the distance. Though modestly furnished, my habitation was spotlessly clean, and even though for purposes of personal cleanliness there was only a rickety tin wash-stand and two earthenware pitchers filled with water, and sanitary arrangements were primitive, I took an instant liking to the place. Below, a long room had a large kitchen range at one end, and this was separated from the dining-room by a counter on which food and plates were placed. Two long wooden tables, with benches alongside, were for the guests, and at the other end of the room, steps led down to a space where all manner of things were stored, and whence a door led down to the cellar, and another into a little shop, alongside which, in a large kind of shed, the baking of bread was being done. Smoked sausages, hams, strings of onions and garlic hung down from beams, and the smell of food being cooked whetted the appetite. The woman of the house, her sister and an elderly brother did the cooking, assisted by three or four daughters who thoroughly enjoyed their work, joking, laughing and singing all the time. When the mother asked me what I fancied to eat, and I told her that, seeing that they were busy preparing food for the morrow, I could wait until night-time to have a good meal, she almost ordered me to sit down at once, and, whilst waiting for her to cook something for me, to have a *chica* (a small one) of wine which she recommended highly. The words were hardly out of the woman's mouth, when one of the daughters hurried down into the cellar, whence she returned with a small jug filled with wine, which she placed on the table before me, together with what looked like a white enamelled tea-cup without a handle. This was a Galician *taza*, out of which wine is drunk throughout these regions. I had been sitting for only a little while, when the *patrón* and two friends of his came to introduce themselves to me and to have a chat. After the meal, the son – whom I had met in the bicycle shop – came to ask me to accompany him on a tour of inspection, in order to see what was going on behind the scenes in the seemingly deserted town.

Our first port of call was only a few doors away. From the outside, the house we entered looked like any of the other two-storied old buildings in the narrow street, with their balconies and tiled roofs. However, upon entering through a heavy wooden door with a step which had been worn hollow towards the middle by the footsteps of many generations, to my astonishment I found myself in a large kind of hall, filled with flowers, mosses and twigs of shrubs of many kinds. The perfume of these was almost overpowering, but so pleasant that for a moment I hardly noticed that near me a number of women and girls were sitting on chairs or stools. All were busy plucking the petals off flowers, and dropping them into tubs filled with water, whilst other busy fingers tore leaves off twigs, or sorted and fluffed out moss. On the floor, in one section of the hall, were piled up huge paper and cardboard stencils, rolls of string, wooden pegs, planks, buckets and so on. The women and girls were much too busy to do more than to return my greetings, and whilst my guide explained to me what this scene of activity signified, the workers never ceased to pluck, pluck and pluck. I was told that the same thing was being done in many houses, and that the masses of flowers, mosses, ferns and leaves I saw were the result of several days gathering them in gardens, fields and glens. The stencils, I was informed, had been designed and made in the course of months, by the men who worked in great secrecy, lest rivals in another street or square get to know the design to be used. For the time being, the workers in the different streets and *plazas* were hardly on speaking terms, for such is the rivalry to spring a surprise on the inhabitants of the town. After darkness had fallen, the men sallied forth, armed with stencils, pegs, long lines of string, chalk, brushes and buckets filled with sand. Working like beavers, they spread it out, marked designs and patterns with finger-tips and chalk, and when this was done, women of all ages, girls and boys, came out of houses with baskets filled with petals of flowers, mosses and aromatic leaves, which they proceeded to sprinkle or arrange wherever the designers had marked the areas to be covered with red, blue, yellow, green, purple and other colours, thick layers of petals here, leaves there, and mosses or ferns to make borders. Early in the evening, dark clouds had appeared on the horizon over the hills in the west, and at night, after the work had been going on for some time, suddenly a strong wind began to blow, and after a first loud thunderclap, it began to rain in torrents. During the storm, the electric current failed, and whilst a group of us took refuge in my inn, at short intervals people sighed, and there were exclamations of "*Es una pena*" (It is a sorrow), "*Que fatalidad!*" (What a fatality or ill-chance), "*Que lástima!*" (What a pity), or "*Paciencia!*" (Patience). Two ambulant vendors of toy balloons who had come all the way from Vigo, hoping to do good business next day, sat dejectedly in a corner, smoking, spitting and, after every thunderclap, muttering curses.

After about half an hour, when the storm passed over, and the lights came on again, we trooped out to discover that the rain had washed away all the result of work done previously; but instead of being dis-heartened by this setback, once more everybody set to work with great vigour to make amends for time and labour lost. After a while, another cut of the electric current interrupted work, but soon candles and lanterns appeared everywhere and, in their light, work continued. Sud-denly, out of the darkness appeared what seemed to be some monster, but it turned out to be a man on a bicycle, carrying a large brass trumpet. Soon after the apparition had vanished through the door of a nearby hall, other shadows carrying different instruments passed in the same direction, and presently I heard the strains of a lively *paso doble,* as the town-band rehearsed for the great show.

Returning to the inn, I joined a group of elderly men who, leaving all the hard work to the women and to the youngsters, sat at a table, smoking, and over cups of wine talking about what was being done outside to make the *fiesta* a success. When the electric current failed again, these stalwarts were the first to moan and sigh, and to exclaim what a sorrow, fatality and pity it was, but after having taken a little more wine, conversation was resumed. Perhaps it was due to the flickering light of candles, which threw strong weird shadows against the white-washed walls, that after some time the conversation veered to bandits of olden times. When one of the talkers said that his father had known intimately a very famous one, by name of "Pepe el Barbudo" (Pepe the Bearded, a kind of Robin Hood who was active between 1840 and 1850), and said that he remembered many stories his father had told him about the redoubtable Pepe, all eyes were fixed on the speaker.

Until long after midnight I listened to fascinating yarns about the remarkable bandit, and when the electric light functioned again, I went upstairs to rest after a long and eventful day. Despite the sounds of voices of the talkers in the room below me, and the loud singing of many nightingales on the trees outside my window, I soon fell into a heavy dreamless sleep.

In the morning, when I stepped out into the street, a marvellous sight greeted my eyes. Despite the storm and heavy rain of the previous night, and four cuts of the electric power, the good people of Puente Areas had worked incessantly whilst I had slept. And now, their task nearly completed, they proudly surveyed the results of their art and labour, and here and there added a few finishing touches. And ample reason they had to be proud and satisfied. About one mile and a half of streets, straight or curved, and *plazas,* were heavily carpeted with petals of roses of every shade and colour, of snow-white marguerites, geraniums, golden cotula, flaming poppies and so on. Every street had its own pattern or design, one more breath-taking than the other, all perfect and of distinct artistic merit. Borders and empty spaces between all kinds of designs were filled in with fine mosses and ferns, leaves of myrtle, thyme, arnica, box, fennel and other greenery, which made the different colours of flower petals stand out and vibrate in the bright light.

There were no designs of crosses, human figures, animals or any of religious nature. This tends to prove the correctness of what I was told about the origin of this flower festival, which is said to be lost in antiquity, when it was a pagan feast to celebrate the season of Spring. A scholarly old gentleman with whom I spoke, claimed that similar flower festivals in Genzano (Italy) and in Orotava in the Canary Islands, were copied from Puente Areas.

Among the artists, jealousy was still strong, and spies who sneaked to peep at the design of a section further along the street were given haughty looks by their rivals. Strangers who wish to take photographs being at liberty to enter into any house, I took advantage of this golden though unwritten rule, and thus from a balcony obtained several excellent photographs.

Though dogs are kept strictly at home, lest they walk over the delicate flower carpets and in doing so spoil them, one yellow mongrel, who was about the size of a large fox-terrier, had the misfortune to be wandering abroad. Wherever the hapless creature went, people shouted and yelled at him, missiles were thrown in his direction, and when, with tail between his legs he fled, terrified and visibly perplexed by this to him unaccountable hostility, people tried to head him back whence he had come. I saw the same wretched dog in different parts of the town, and everywhere he was received with the same antagonism. My sympathies were divided equally between the mongrel and the good people who wanted to protect their masterpieces, for, after all, if animals must be protected, so must art.

A group of bagpipers in their picturesque regional costumes, several rather corpulent priests, evidently from country districts, with faces like brown leather, and cassocks rusty and shining at the seams, and a few bashful nuns mingled with the crowd of sightseers, until, as the hour of noon approached, everybody got ready to watch the procession. One of the nuns, alongside whom I took my place by the roadside, fascinated me with her waxen face, shrivelled and eaten into masses of fine wrinkles, and staring eyes, deeply set in their orbits. I had forgotten all about the yellow mongrel, when he appeared again, now shut in by rows of people, who had lined up on both sides of the streets, up and down which the dog raced, desperately looking for an avenue of escape. With his tongue lolling out, he ran like the ubiquitous Derby dog until he disappeared from my view round a bend on the downward course. The novena and triduum over, in the church tower, situated on the main *plaza,* unmelodious bells began to clang, and presently the religious procession approached slowly.   Petals of flowers were showered down from balconies, and at two or three street altars, specially erected and decorated for the occasion, the procession halted whilst some sixty Franciscan monks of the *schola cantorum* of a nearby monastery sang.

With the passing of the procession, the glory of the flower carpets vanished, rivalry and jealousies among the artists of the various streets ceased, and now it was the urchins' turn to have some fun, throwing flower petals at one another, and with their feet scattering the last vestiges of patterns and designs.   According to the official printed programme, the *programa religioso* came to an end, and now the *programa profano* began: brass band, bag-pipes, loud-speakers blaring, and people making merry.

When, in the company of several acquaintances, I went to a little establishment where the only drinkable *ersatz* coffee was to be had in Puente Areas, there, under a table, utterly exhausted, lay the yellow mongrel dog, sleeping, if not the sleep of the just, the sleep of a canine martyr.   After many sore trials and tribulations, the prodigal was back in his peaceful home, sweet home.

During the afternoon, my new friend, the inn-keeper's son, and several other young men took me for a walk through the surrounding country.   Having visited a Roman bridge and a ruined castle of the same period, towards evening we went to have a swim in a large pool of the crystal-clear river Tea, and later watched a football match which was being played nearby.   The field was fenced in entirely with narrow granite slabs, some ten feet high, and solidly planted in the ground, close together.   It was explained to me that in these regions stone is much cheaper than wood, the greatest expense being the transportation by bullock cart.   Quarry-men and stone-cutters are so deft at their work, that with one stroke of a heavy hammer they split a rock into slabs, and these with a few more strokes into sections.   Thanks to the abundance of suitable stone, and to the high standard of craftsmanship among stone-cutters – among whom those of Pontevedra enjoy special fame – in some regions of Galicia it is cheaper to build houses with stone than with wood.   I was shown several beautiful modern chalets, and when I was told what was the cost of their construction, I considered the price tantamount to a gift. In those parts *canteros* (stone-cutters) do a long day's highly skilled work for twenty-five *pesetas,* (say five shillings) and in many cases for less.

The football match over, we returned to the town, and late into the night watched a dense crowd dance in the main square. When I returned to my inn to eat something before going to bed, only a few guests were there, among them the two vendors of toy balloons, who had arrived on the previous day. Both wore surprisingly neat dark jackets and black corduroy trousers, and the taller of the two was so handsome that any judge of masculine form would have agreed with me that he was a kind of very much improved edition of the film star, Ronald Coleman. His companion was stocky, fat and jovial, and both were in good humour, having had a good day. Whilst devouring a roast chicken, and drinking wine, they told me much about their trade; how they travelled from *fiesta* to *fiesta* all over the country, independent and free as birds of the air. Of course, sometimes business was slack, but the two companions were healthy, and always able to turn to some other work, most forms of which, they admitted frankly, were loathsome to them. As a rule, transportation from place to place offered no serious problems, and involved little or no expense, drivers of vans or lorries usually giving them a lift, even if it had to be on the top of the load they carried on their vehicles. Occasionally, they stole a ride in a goods wagon, or wangled a cheap third-class fare by bribing the guard of a passenger train. The two had so many amusing and interesting yarns to tell that I listened to them until my eyelids began to droop.

Early next morning, when the time came to say *adios* to my hosts, I felt like a young man departing from his home to face life in a distant land. The whole family and a number of their friends and guests were there to see me off, and soon after I rode through beautiful country with hills covered with pines. In some parts, I saw wild rabbits, which reminded me that, many centuries ago, great regions of Spain were over-run by these rodents, and that in the Roman times the rabbit was used as a design on the coat-of-arms representing Spain. It is even believed that the name *España* or *Hispania* is derived from the Phoenician *pahan,* meaning "rabbit."

Ugly black clouds threatened me from behind, like a stampede of weird celestial monsters, so, making my machine go full out, I raced the storm, over wooded hills, through fertile little plains and two or three picturesque villages situated near the river Minó, on the opposite bank of which is Portugal.   Upon reaching a little town named La Guardia, situated near the shores of the Atlantic Ocean, it looked as if I had won the exciting and exhilarating race, so I decided to climb to the top of the nearby Mount Santa Tecla, about which I had heard many glowing reports.   A steep road zigzagged up through the forests, and when I emerged from them near the summit, I beheld a marvellous panorama.   Below, to the west, spread the light-blue waters of the Atlantic, and upon turning towards the south, a twisting band of silver, that was the river Minó, I saw the green hills of Portugal.   Viewed from the heights, two or three fishermen's boats looked like tiny beetles crawling over a mirror, and on the Portuguese side a small golden beach and the gaily painted houses and chalets of a village resembled miniature toys.   The black clouds from which I had fled appeared to be drifting away towards the north, when, suddenly, the wind changed, making them roll towards me. I had just finished examining a number of prehistoric stone relics, among them several crosses – which resembled the Maltese and Manx type – when the sky darkened, and soon after a terrific storm began to rain.   Fortunately, a modem stone-built restaurant stood on the precipitous mountain side, so whilst sheltering there, from a long, covered-in verandah, I watched the heavenly turmoil.   Flashes of lightning were followed by thunder which shook the very rocks, gusts of wind drove before them torrents of rain which struck pines horizontally, bending them to breaking point. Occasionally, deep down below I had a glimpse of the wide mouth of the river, or of the ocean, now no longer mirror-like, but whipped up into a mass of frothy white.

After about half an hour, when the centre of the storm shifted towards the north, and thunder sounded like loud growls in the distance, the first sunrays began to pierce through the clouds, illuminating the hills and waters in the distance like the beams of spot-lights shifting over the scenery of a stage.

Continuing my journey, I splashed through puddles and pools which had not yet had time to drain off depressions in the uneven surface of the road. Rain had fallen in such torrents that the hilly countryside and rocky land-points jutting out into the sea seemed to have emerged from it after a dip.

Apart from being cheap to run, a motor-cycle is an exhilarating and delightful means of transportation, provided the weather is good, but when the surface of a road is wet, or it rains, unless a rider is well protected, within a few moments he is thoroughly soaked. As I had lost my rain-coat early on during my travels, and my limited funds made it impossible for me to buy a new one, within an hour of having left Mount Santa Tecla, the splashing from the front wheel filled my shoes with muddy water, and the legs of my trousers were so filthy and wet that upon coming to a stream I went to wade in it, in order to clean them. Despite this seemingly drastic measure, by the time I reached Vigo my trousers were perfectly dry, though in the case of my shoes it was a very different matter.

Some of the fishing villages and one or two small seaside resorts through which I passed were most attractive, but as the summer season had not yet begun, most of the small yachts and pleasure boats were still drawn up on ramps and beaches. These are the ports from which anglers set out to do their deep-sea fishing, for in the nearby waters of the Atlantic, mighty tunny and swordfish provide them with exciting sport.

Among the wooded hills, towards the east, roam many semi-wild horses, which are rounded up every year in the month of May. This round-up is a great regional event, known as the *Curro de Mougas*. Unfortunately I arrived after it had taken place, but judging by reports, it must be a sight well worth seeing.

After a journey, partly along the picturesque coast, and partly through hilly farm country, from a height I got my first view of the beautiful estuary of Vigo, and of the town which stands on the slope of a hill. The recent cloudburst had washed away parts of the road, but already squads of workers were busy making repairs.

Thirty years had passed since I had been in Vigo, and during that time the general aspect of the town has changed completely. The main streets with their modem shops and buildings, and even a skyscraper which is nearing completion, made me blink my eyes, and gave me a feeling of being a kind of Methuselah. Besides these innovations and vast improvements, I saw well-kept parks – in the middle of one a rather out-of-placc-looking though life-like snow-white stone effigy of a polar bear – the port modernized, with the fine building of the Yacht Club near it, and so on. The fish market is a scene of great activity, for it is from there that Madrid and several inland towns are supplied with fish, lobsters, prawns and many varieties of shell-fish. These are rushed across the country by a fleet of lorries which, despite the difficult mountainous terrain to be traversed, are driven at break-neck speed, and to the danger of villagers and their children, many of whom have been killed for the sake of delivering the food fresh at its destination. The fisherwomen at the central market are picturesque with their dark, ankle-long spreading skirts and aprons. All wear peculiar, rather Japanese-looking clogs, with high heels and a piece of wood across under the ball of the foot. The soles are carved out of one piece, and the small stilt-like excrescences serve to wade through the water without wetting the feet.

On a steep street which leads up to the centre of Vigo from the port, I saw the only case of gross ill-treatment of an animal during my whole tour through Spain. A mule was struggling hard to pull a heavily-laden cart up the steep incline which was paved with slippery granite cobble-stones, and all the time, as the willing beast made great efforts, the driver cursed and shouted, and lashed it with his whip, or prodded it in the ribs with its handle. Eventually, terrified and exhausted, the mule stopped, whereupon the infuriated driver took to kicking its belly, until, to his blank astonishment, I intervened, showering upon him my considerable vocabulary of swear-words and epithets, some of which, being of South-American corral and gutter origin, made him stare at me with an open mouth, and most likely wondering what kind of peculiar foreigner it could be who was interfering with him. Before he had time to recover from the shock, I threatened to have him arrested and locked up forthwith, and in order to give weight to my statement and to impress the scoundrel, I pointed at an impressive badge I wore in the buttonhole of my lapel. This worked such wonders that a few men, who had stopped to listen to the row, came forward and with strong arms turned the wheels of the cart, whilst others put their shoulders against its back, to push with all their might. For a few yards I led the mule, whereafter I handed it over to the driver, with the threat that if ever again I caught him ill-treating the animal, or, for the matter of that, any other, I would report him to all the authorities up to General Franco himself, or eyen to the very Pope. Meekly the driver took over the reins, his eyes not fixed on mine, but on my crown-surrounded badge, with which I had been presented, some weeks before, by the president of the . . . Royal Polo Club of Barcelona!

Having had a great deal of experience with the ignorant type of Galician in South America, I did not utter my threats in a quiet tone of voice, but, instead, bellowed and roared them like an enraged bull and an infuriated lion combined, for had I done otherwise, what I said would have had no more effect than an ordinary friendly conversation.

Among Mediterranean and southern people ill-treatment of animals is a common occurrence, partly due to ignorance and lack of feeling, but also, to a great extent, because people are told that animals have no souls. As pointed out already, the carter in Vigo was the only man I saw ill-treat an animal during my whole tour through Spain, though in making this assertion I am not including bullfights which are not part and parcel of Spanish life, as many people seem to think. Most likely, the offender of my story was not the owner of the mule, but being in the employ of some firm of carters, he had no financial interest in his charge. This brings me to an important point, for had it not been as I venture to guess, surely he would have acted otherwise; for nowadays mules, donkeys and horses are costly in Spain. A good mule fetches between eight and ten thousand *pesetas,* or even more, and a donkey between three and eight thousand *pesetas.* Therefore, when one considers that labourers earn only between eight and twelve *pesetas* for a long day's hard work, it will be seen that a donkey or a mule represents a great deal of money, and a capital but few labourers can amass by saving from their wages. The shortage – and consequently high prices – of cattle, mules, horses and donkeys, is due to the Civil War, when cattle were slaughtered ruthlessly for meat, without an eye on the future, and when masses of beasts of burden lost their lives. Since the Civil War ended, much has been done to remedy the shortage of live stock, and in certain regions, such as Galicia, things have greatly improved in this respect.

The beautiful estuary of Vigo was the scene of a number of famous naval actions and raids, among the latter that by Sir Francis Drake and, later, the combined Anglo-Dutch attack on the Spanish "Silver Fleet". Near a picturesque place called Redondela, situated on a little bay with a narrow entrance at the northern end of the estuary, efforts are being made to salvage some of the treasure which was sunk by Drake.

In this neighbourhood, whilst taking a rest, I watched two men unload firewood from a big cart which had halted on a street that led up a steep incline. Wood was piled up high on the vehicle, and on the top of the load were three empty barrels. As the men filled baskets with wood, taking it from the open back of the cart, I wondered how long this undermining of the barrels could continue before the load would collapse, and cause the barrels to roll off. And sure enough, after a little while it occurred, and whilst the men looked on helplessly, the barrels began to career downhill, causing a great commotion among passers-by and dogs. Fortunately, no harm was done, but when it came to deciding as to whether the men should go down the hill, afoot, to retrieve the barrels, and to roll them back to where the cart stood, or to make an about-turn with the cart, and drive it downhill in order to pick up the three barrels, this led to much discussion and debate, in which bystanders joined wholeheartedly. After much vociferation, pointing and waving about of arms, despite lively opposition on the part of several self-appointed technical experts, it was decided to finish unloading and delivering the wood, then to take the cart down the street, load the barrels on it, and then to make the return trip uphill, in order to deliver the rest of the wood at a house situated near its top. Even after this important decision had been reached, whilst the little crowd of onlookers and advisers dispersed, a policeman in his white tropical helmet could be seen walking downhill, every now and again stopping to argue and gesticulate with two ill-clad delegates who followed him. And all the while, at the bottom of the incline, dogs circled round and round, and inspected the barrels which had caused this Galician interlude.

I was about to resume my journey when a tall, lean, and quite well-dressed and good-looking man of about forty came to introduce himself to me in his best English, of which I understood only a few words. Although I told him to speak to me in Spanish, he kept on repeating, "I am sorree, I onderstand verree well. I am an interpretay, sometime work Eenglis ship come Vigo. I am sorree, verree sorree. You have Eenglis cigarette for me? Yes? No? Thank you verree moch. You shentleman, I know."

I am mentioning this trivial incident because it goes to show what influence seaports can have on people who live near them. Algeciras was another example;. and I could cite many others in different parts of the world. No Spaniard, let alone a proud Castilian, would ask a perfect stranger for a cigarette. Unfortunately, visitors from abroad, who call at ports, are apt to go away with very wrong impressions if they judge national character by what they hear and see there.

Leaving the interpreter smoking my gift cigarette, I headed towards ancient Pontevedra, situated at the head of an estuary by the same name. The winding road skirted blue waters, led through pine forests, past carefully tended fields, and through a number of quaint villages and hamlets. Near every peasant's abode, built upon mushroom-like pillars, stand granaries which resemble small narrow chapels, especially so because most of them have a cross on their roofs. These are the typical Galician *hórreos* in which maize is stored. The pillars or stilts prevent mice, rats, and other vermin from gaining access to the maize, stored in the granaries which are ventilated through narrow slats in the walls, made either of stone or of wood. In these regions, maize is the basic diet of peasants who rely, to a large extent, on the contents of their *hórreos* to make their *borrona,* a kind of bread which is their staple diet. In those parts, there are so many *hórreos* that they can be said to be part of the landscape, and to be, together with the bag-pipes, the symbols of Galicia.

On a hilly plateau which is surrounded by mountains, I came to Santiago de Compostela, a wonderful town steeped in ancient history. With its mostly narrow streets, paved with huge blocks of granite, balconies, massive arcades under which are shops and *cafés,* splendid monuments everywhere, and, above all, the superb Romanesque cathedral, the town is one of the finest and most interesting in Spain. The Cathedral Square is a masterpiece of architecture and design, and with St. Jerome's College on one side, and the Constitutional Palace on the other, it must be unique. It would take up far too much space if I tried to describe the glories of the Cathedral (locally called the *Obradoiro),* archaeological museum and the university, but I must mention that the foundation of the town is connected with the story of the discovery of the body of the apostle St. James, the patron saint of Spain. According to popular belief, the apostle had preached the Gospel in Spain, and after he had been beheaded in Palestine, his remains were brought to be buried in Galicia. Legend has it that with the passing of time the whereabouts of the grave were forgotten, but that, several centuries later, a brilliant light, in the shape of a star, guided a bishop to the spot where the remains of the Apostle were discovered. The sanctuary which was built over the grave was destroyed by the Moorish conquerors in A.D. 997, but later the Cathedral was built on the spot where it had stood. At one time, this place of pilgrimage attracted so many people from all over Europe that the main road which led towards Santiago de Compostela became known as the "Milky Way".

During my only-too-short stay in the town I had some interesting conversations in quaint old taverns where old and young, learned and otherwise, talk and argue on level terms. The truly democratic atmosphere in such places impressed me greatly, and during such friendly sessions I was never made to feel that I was a stranger, or, worse still, a foreigner.

Between Santiago de Compostela – situated close on two thousand feet above sea-level – and La Coruna (Corunna in English and the old sailors' "The Groin"), the country is very hilly, green and fertile, with stretches of forest here and there. The weather was very unsettled, and shortly before I reached my destination, a regular deluge made me seek shelter in a tiny country store, where a stout woman who ran it amused me with the peculiar dialect in which she spoke to me. It was a mixture of what – to me – sounded like bad Portuguese and worse Spanish, but when she became angry with two of her children who insisted on carrying about and hugging a long-suffering and miauling cat, she shouted in broad Galician, of which, perhaps fortunately, I understood only a few words. As the atmosphere had turned rather chilly, and my clothes were wet, the good woman was quite worried about me, and insisted on my taking a glass of *aguardiente,* a strong spirit – rather like French *eau-de-vie* – which is extracted from the husks of grapes. She assured me that the stuff was excellent, having been distilled locally, and that it would prevent me from clutching a cold or perhaps even pneumonia. There was no arguing with my medical adviser, so after she had filled a small glass with the liquor of her prescription, I sampled it cautiously, but, finding it agreeable to the taste, and very warming, I drank the rest in one gulp. The woman beamed with pride when I complimented her on the quality of the stuff, and about an hour later, when the downpour ceased, and before departing I asked her to re-fill my glass, she exclaimed, "Ah, there you are! See, I told you you would like my *aguardiente!*"

Feeling warm inside, and at peace with a very wet world, I rode over hill and through dale, and after about an hour, upon reaching a height, saw Corunna below me, and beyond, towards the north, the now blue-grey waters of the Atlantic Ocean, over which rolled heavy rain clouds.

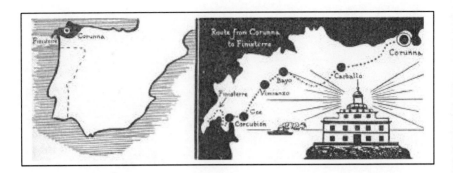

CHAPTER 19

CORUNNA – FINISTERRE

A friend of mine, in whose house I had stayed early on during my tour, hailed from Corunna. As his brother lives in this city, he wrote to him, asking him to take me in hand as soon as I should turn up. When, upon arrival, I presented myself at the address I had on me, the kindness with which I was met knew no bounds. Within a few minutes I was taken to a small but very nice and comfortable *pensión* where I was given a room which overlooked the busy central market-place. Later I was introduced to several doctors, professional men, and to members of the Press and Motorcycle Clubs. The president of the latter was a dentist by profession, and an out-and-out Galician who had the surprising name of Guillermo Mitchell Thomson. True to type, he could not speak a word of English, and when I asked him about the origin of his family, he told me that though, no doubt, his remote ancestors must have been English, the Mitchell Thomsons were an old Galician family, and that he was proud to be a *Gallego*.

It was just as well that I had not come to Corunna with the intention of having a rest, for from the time of my arrival until, several days later when I resumed my lone travels, every hour of the day, and usually half the night, were taken up making merry and seeing interesting things. Many private houses were open to me at any time. I was taken for rides to nearby places in cars, and together with the members of the Motor-cycle Club made several excursions to neighbouring estuaries and highlands with their ancient villages and pine forests.

As in the case of Vigo, many years had passed since I had visited Corunna, and during that time the town has undergone such tremendous changes that, had it not been for its surrounding hills, bays and other permanent landmarks, I would not have recognized it.

Where, close on forty years ago, had been an unattractive sea-front with open spaces and uneven streets, now I saw wide avenues, gardens and parks with rows of palm trees, flowers, kiosks, huge modern hotels and docks, clean spacious beaches, fine shops and many beautifully built edifices. The streets presented a continuous spectacle of life and activity, and at certain hours of day and night, *cafés,* homely taverns and eating houses were crowded with patrons.

The town is finely situated on a tongue of land between an inner and outer bay. The long row of several-storied buildings which face the inner bay have glass galleries which are so characteristic of Corunna that it is often called "the Glass City". Formerly, the entrance to this bay was protected by Fort San Antonio, built on a little rocky island, now used as a military prison. Throughout the ages, from those rocks and from others on the mainland close to them, people witnessed many momentous events; the arrival of the first Phoenician ships, later to be followed by Roman vessels, the arrival of John of Gaunt to claim the throne of Castile, the departure of Philip II for England to marry Queen Mary, the sailing of the "Invincible Armada" to conquer England, and raids by corsairs from different countries. The stone arch and the steps where Philip II embarked are still to be seen as they were in 1554, and so is the house in which Sir John Moore died in 1809, after having been wounded during his calamitous retreat caused by overwhelming French forces. His remains lie buried in a little shady garden on a rocky eminence overlooking the entrance to the inner bay; a fitting resting place for the gallant warrior. Among the feats of heroism enacted in this theatre of many bloody fights, that of Maria Pita is, perhaps, the most outstanding. After the defeat of the Armada, when Drake carried the war into the enemy's country, and laid waste several towns, he also attacked Corunna with 140 ships and 14,000 men. After several days of fierce fighting, when victory seemed to be certain for the attacking forces, whilst fighting gallantly beside her husband, this heroic woman killed the English standard-bearer, a deed which proved to be the turning-point of the battle, for after having fired the city, Drake and his men beat a hasty retreat, leaving behind many dead.

Like other towns on the coast of the Bay of Biscay, Corunna consists of an old town on the heights, and a modern town below, usually near the sea-front. The former has narrow tortuous streets, fortress-like houses with doors emblazoned with coats-of-arms, rough granite paving stones, archways and quiet nooks and corners where the wanderer can rest and meditate. Here and there one comes to a tiny shop, or one sees a donkey carrying a load of foodstuffs, firewood, charcoal or earthenware jars. If a wanderer peeps through an age-worn door into the dimness of a small vault-like workshop, he may see a craftsman making furniture, or perhaps another carving wood, hammering into shape copper, iron or tin, manufacturing pots and pans, perhaps a cobbler making or mending boots, or a saddler making harness. Though such places may appear to be sleepy, with only the occasional throaty call of an ambulant vendor resounding through the narrow streets and alleys, behind the walls of houses there is much unostentatious activity, and if a passer-by chooses to listen, he will hear sounds made by busy craftsmen, or of women singing whilst doing their domestic work. Alongside shady little squares are convents and churches, some of which are built on foundations and walls, which, ages ago, were heathen temples, and further along there are remains of city walls, every big stone block of which is a mute witness of ancient history. Whereas the Old Town is romantic beauty, its modern appendix is commerce, hotels, *cafés,* restaurants, luxurious shops, tramways, railway stations, motor cars, cinematographs with neon lights and vulgar inartistic posters, theatres, parks, warehouses, docks and often discordant noises, jarring to the ear; in fact, the Modern Town is the response to Aladdin's call of "New lamps for old!"

A spell of bad weather made me decide to stay in Corunna, and from there to make excursions whenever it did not rain. Every morning I was awakened by the chattering of many women, when they arrived at the market-place below my window. Most of them brought their vegetables and fruit on mules or donkeys, but others carried their produce in huge baskets which they balanced on their heads. A few came with carts, the unloading of which was done to the accompaniment of much shouting and laughter. When the market was in full swing, the effect of hundreds of female voices talking at the same time might have been a combination of sounds emanating from an aviary, and of water tumbling down a rocky mountainside.

Rain, dust and splashes of mud and oil had so soiled my sports jacket and grey flannel trousers that I decided it was high time to have them cleaned. When I asked one of the servants in the *pensión* where I could have this done as quickly as possible, she told me that if I handed her the clothes in the evening, she would see to it that I had them back first thing next morning. And, lo and behold, when they were returned to me, and I put them on, they looked as good as new, and made me feel like a millionaire. For the work done I was charged a mere pittance, and when I gave the servant a few extra *pesetas,* she was delighted. Spain is one of the few countries I know where servants and inn-keepers are willing to oblige one at any time, and where they do this with genuine pleasure.

Whilst I was in Corunna, a liner filled with tourists arrived from Havana, and soon after there followed a regular invasion of loudly dressed people, armed with cameras, guide-books and parasols of bright colours. One middle-aged woman whose hair was platinum-blonded, and who tried to look and act like a flapper, wore a dirndl skirt of every colour of the rainbow, but above the waist only a small brassiere which matched the skirt. As, in the company of two men who sported silk shirts with crazy patterns all over them, she swept down one of the main streets, Galician women, who carried baskets on their heads, were in such fits of laughter that they had to deposit their loads on the ground. However, the startled and amused ones were much too polite to laugh when the tourists could see them, so whilst giving vent to their merriment, they turned round, stooped down, and pretended to be arranging the contents of their baskets.

On a rocky hill of a land-point which juts out into the open sea, stands the Tower of Hercules, which is said to be the oldest lighthouse in the world. About 170 feet high, according to tradition, the tower was built by the Romans in the second century, and before it was restored in 1785 it was surrounded by a sloping ramp, for the passage of carts laden with wood to feed the fire that served as the beacon.

During a short spell of fine weather I mounted my motor-cycle and rode out to have a close look at this relic of old times, and on my way back, as I drove slowly and cautiously through a narrow street of the Old Town, the sound of a police whistle made me stop. Although I looked round, wondering if the whistling was meant for me, all I could see consisted of people walking down the street, and a few carts being driven along.   Accordingly, I resumed my journey, but I had barely started when, again, I heard two or three frantic blasts of what sounded like the same police whistle, but upon looking for the custodian of law and order, I could see no sign of him.   I was beginning to wonder if some mischievous boy was playing a trick on me, when, behind my back, the whistle was blown again.   Turning round, there I saw a man with a big leather bag slung over his shoulder, looking up at a window. It was a postman delivering letters, blowing his whistle, once for recipients who live on the first floor, twice for those who live on the second, and three times for those on the third, calling them down into the street to collect their mail.

As mentioned in a previous chapter, in Spain the names of streets and squares often change with the vicissitudes of governments.   During the wave of nationalism that followed the Civil War, names of even some hotels and theatres were altered, and thus it came about that, for instance, in Corunna, "Palace Hotel" was changed to "Palas Hotel," "Savoy" (a cinematograph) became "Avoy," and in Vigo the lettering of "Hotel de Paris" was turned into "Hotel del Pais."   I could not help wondering what would happen if throughout England and the U.S.A. cinematographs, theatres, hotels and restaurants would have to change their foreign names, such as, to mention only a few of the legion in Britain alone, "Granada," "Alhambra," "Tivoli," "Odeon," "Plaza," "Rialto," "Frascati," "Bagatelles," "Mayorca," "Martinez."

Apart from other friends, the members of the Corunna Motor-cycle Club went out of their way to entertain me.   In the company of the latter I made several long excursions, which were merely excuses for eating all kinds of dishes of the region, oysters straight out of the sea, shell-fish, smoked farm ham and so on, in old-fashioned establishments where the *motociclistas* were well known.   I was amazed to see how often and how much some of my companions could eat, and how much wine they could drink without turning a hair.   Invariably, after meals they sang some of their gay tuneful Galician songs, the theme of many of which is about the priest and his housekeeper or "niece."   Galician music differs greatly from that of other parts of Spain.   It is of Celtic origin, and as the songs were sung in Gallego, the words had to be translated for me, which was done with great gusto when they were on the piquant side.

Late one night, when we returned to Corunna after one of our outings through beautiful hilly country, along enchanting estuaries, through ancient villages and past farms with rich smells of flowers and manure mixed, we assembled in a little *tasca* (tavern) where, before going home, to have a final cup of wine, and, of course, to sing. Like moths attracted by light, several passers-by came in to join us and, as they had good voices, the singing continued until the early hours of morning. On the following day, at about noon, I returned to the tavern, and there I met an elderly lawyer who lived in a house opposite. When I apologized for having been one of the party which must have made him pass a sleepless night, he smiled and replied, "Oh, that's nothing, friend, I thoroughly enjoyed the singing. Now I'll tell you what I did. Finding that it was impossible to sleep, I propped myself up with my pillows and sang with you. And, incidentally, last night our mutual friends sang many beautiful songs I had not heard for years. Please don't apologize, it was a great treat, and, after all, you didn't do the singing."

In Galicia, and, in fact, throughout Spain, there is no such thing as a favourite wine tavern *(tasca)* in a town. If a certain establishment obtains a barrel of specially good wine, within a day "the voice runs" *(corre la voz)* to every quarter, and men hurry to sample it. If it is to their liking, both in quality and price, they return to the place until the barrel is empty. Everywhere in Spain wine is cheap, and, as the saying goes, "there is no bad wine, only good and better." Most kinds have more "body" than French wine, though this varies according to the region where it is grown. In Galicia a *taza* (cup) costs between fifty *centesimos* and one *peseta,* or be it, at the present rate of exchange, for one English pound one could drink one hundred and ten *tazas* of the best wine.

Despite the abundance and cheapness of alcoholic drinks, drunkenness is extremely rare in Spain, though, as we shall see later, in the Basque provinces things are different in this respect.

Galicia is the region *par excellence* for *fiestas,* especially after harvest-time, when, almost every day, there is merry-making some-where, at *ferias* (fairs), *romerias* (rural feasts of saints), *verbenas* (dances held in streets), *ruadas* (semi-public dances held in country houses), *fiestas tradicionales, fiestas patrónales, fiestas regionales,* and others; in fact, after the harvest is in, Galicia is one continuous *fiesta.*

Despite adverse weather conditions, I decided to go to a *romeria* which was held in a small town, some forty miles from Corunna. For a change, and to do the thing properly, I travelled by motor bus, but as the vehicle was filled to bursting point, I climbed up on the roof, where I was joined by several other merry-makers. It was a rough and uncomfortable journey, and often, when the rather reckless but otherwise excellent driver rounded a curve at speed, I had to lie flat, lest I fall off and roll down some steep hillside. However, the *romeria* was great fun, and when, at 3 a.m., we started on our return journey I was apprehensive, but fortunately we reached the home garage in safety, though battered, shaken and weary.

From Corunna I made a side-trip which is one of the highlights of my whole tour, and an experience I shall always treasure in my memory. This time, also, I decided to travel by motor coach, so after having booked my passage first class (which meant that I could sit inside the vehicle), for a change I went to bed early – in this case shortly after midnight. Early next morning, to my astonishment I was called by an employee of the transport company. How on earth he knew my name and where to find me I do not know, but thanks to his kindness, soon after having been made to leave my comfortable bed, I was installed in the bus bound for Finisterre, the last little town, situated on the western-most promontory, which ends at the cape after which it is named, the ancient Romans' *Finis Terrae:* the southern Land's End of the continent of Europe. Only twice per week do buses run as far as Finisterre, a distance of a little over sixty miles, through hilly and fertile country which reminded me of parts of Scotland. Contrary to rumours I had heard, the road was quite fair, and so our packed conveyance travelled along merrily. In two or three little towns along our route we stopped for long spells, in order to get rid of passengers and to take others on board, or to have refreshment and food. Whilst conversing with a well-dressed old man who sat next to me on the bus, he told me that he was eighty-seven years of age, and that he had spent sixty of them in the Argentine, including the last forty, during which he never left the small town of Rio Gallegos in Patagonia, near the Strait of Magellan, where he had run a store. When I told him that I knew the place, and that I have a number of friends down there, his joy knew no bounds, and whilst we discussed some of them, I noticed that the old man's eyes filled with tears. He told me that he had retired a few years ago, and that although he was happy to be back in his homeland, his greatest remaining wish in life was to go and have another look at Rio Gallegos, and to be reunited with the many good friends he had left down there.

Although the radiator of the bus had sprung a bad leak, which obliged us after every few miles to stop near streams, in order to replace the water lost, we made good progress. Despite these delays, towards evening we arrived at a pretty little place called Cee, situated at the end of a beautiful estuary which is framed in on three sides by wooded hills. Most of the passengers alighted in Cee, and then we proceeded towards nearby Corcubión, and thence a drive of about eight miles took us to the tiny old town of Finisterre. The last two stages of our journey took us over low hills, covered with ferns, bracken, heather and gorse, and here and there patches of pine forest, and along near a marvellous sweeping beach with golden sands.

Alighting from the bus, suddenly I felt as if I were dreaming a weird though delightful dream, and that I was living in the Middle Ages, for after the bus with its steaming radiator had been driven into a kind of barn, and the heavy wooden double door had been closed with much creaking of its rusty hinges, I found myself in a different world, a world I do not recommend to travellers who place comfort and luxurious food before the beauties of nature, and who are not interested in honest, simple and mostly poor people. The rough cobble-stoned roads which I had seen and walked over in many parts of Spain were almost skating rinks when compared with the one along which I now made my way towards an address I had on me: the *Casa Sendón,* a guest-house run by two old women, the one and only place where rare travellers who come to Finisterre can find lodgings. Despite the state of the narrow winding road, and the neglected appearance of the stone-built old houses with their tiny wooden balconies, there was something peculiar, perhaps fundamental – though impossible to fathom, let alone to explain – which appealed to me about these crude abodes to which clung the brine of centuries. Out of doors and tiny windows people watched me pass, carrying my small suitcase, and barefooted children peeped at me as if I were the man in the moon come down to this earth. Nowhere have I seen so many good-looking children as I did in Finisterre, where they abound like the proverbial rabbits. Many of them were blue-eyed, fair-skinned and had curly light-coloured hair, a fact which has caused mischievous tongues to say that it is due to visits of Nordic sailors, and to others who were rescued after the countless shipwrecks which occurred on this to navigators dangerous headland. Though, most likely, Cape Finisterre is the world's greatest graveyard of ships, and masses of sailors were saved there, the stories about the blue-eyed and fair-skinned children must be dismissed as mere inventions of irresponsible babblers who tell them as jokes.

In a narrow alley which leads up a short steep incline I found the guest-house, where the two elderly ladies who run it gave me a warm welcome. On the first floor of the old house I was shown my room in which stood an enormous four-poster bed. The wooden floor was uneven, and in a corner was a wash-stand with earthenware jars filled with water near it. The bed-covers, linen, face-towels and lace curtains were spotlessly clean, but, as fully expected, sanitary arrangements were primitive.

Having deposited my belongings and washed myself, I went to have a look round the immediate neighbourhood. A narrow curved road led to a little *plaza* with a chapel which looked as if it had been closed for years. Bordering it were a few low stone-built houses, among them one rather larger than the others, which must have remained uninhabited for many years. Though dilapidated, with an ancient coat-of-arms over its door, it had great charm, as had the other houses with their mouldering doors and age-worn steps. Behind the chapel I caught glimpses of gardens and tiny fields and of a number of the chapel-like *hórreos* (granaries for storing maize), described in the previous chapter. Close by was a large stone trough, fed by the water of a stream, where a number of young girls were busy washing. Upon seeing me they tittered and giggled, and the boldest among them shouted a jocular remark in my direction. However, when I went up to her and pretended that I thought little of her skill as a washer-woman, she and the other girls blushed and scrubbed away with downcast eyes, all the time making great efforts to suppress giggles.

During my subsequent wanderings through the village, upon peeping into a tiny shop, I saw something which made me stare, wondering if my eyes were deceiving me. Sitting on a low stool, a woman was sucking something through a thin metal tube stuck into a small gourd. Near her, on the floor, was placed a kettle, and whilst I watched her, she picked it up to re-fill the gourd with hot water. Surely it could not be . . .

"*Señor,*" a male voice came out of the dusky interior of the shop, "I bet you don't know what my wife is drinking." Taking a step forward, behind a crude wooden counter I saw that it was a young man who had spoken.

"I am puzzled," I replied, "but if just now I were in South America, instead of being in Spain, I'd say it is *maté* your wife is sipping." For a few moments my two listeners showed great surprise, and then the young man said, "You are right, it is *maté*. How do you know? Have you been in South America?" And when I explained that I had lived in the Argentine for many years, the young man became very enthusiastic, and went on to say that *maté* is the favourite drink in Finisterre. He explained that quite a number of people in the place, including his wife, had lived in South America, and that many others had migrated thither, and that they regularly sent home little sacks of *yerba maté (maté* leaves). When I told him what had brought me to Finisterre, he immediately offered to show me the surroundings, and so the two of us set out on foot.

Cape Finisterre is a continuation of mountains, the highest of which rise some two thousand feet above sea-level, but the long promontory tapers down towards its end, and could be described as having the shape of an enormous whale's back. Jutting out into the Atlantic, it has a vast beach on its outer shore, called *Praia do mar fora,* Galician meaning "shore of the outer sea." The vast inner bay is named after the cape: Bay of Finisterre. Along the shore of this bay there are several small beaches, and one of golden sands, which extend for several miles. To my surprise this bathers' paradise was deserted. I was told that the outer beach, though most inviting in appearance, can be treacherous, currents making swimming dangerous. On the other hand, the inner beaches are safe, and one or two of the smaller ones seem as if they had been made purposely for children.

First of all, my guide took me down to the shore of the inner bay, where, at the foot of the slope on which the village stands, is a little harbour where fishermen anchor their boats. The catching of sardines is the chief means of earning a livelihood in Finisterre, but of late years, for reasons unknown, the immense shoals of *sardinhas* have kept far out at sea, with the result that people in these regions have suffered great privations. Fortunately, when I was there things looked more promising in the bay, which, as the Sea of Galilee of old, gives the fisherman his daily bread. The Bay of Finisterre is these hardy men's orchard, or the liquid field which they plough with their sturdy boats. In the far distance, across the unrestrained space and freedom, I discerned miles of hills and coastline, and near me, on the beach, a number of boats were drawn up, some turned upside-down for the purpose of being painted or mended. A number of workmen were busy constructing a new breakwater, and the gay voices of children playing floated across the little harbour.

Having feasted our eyes on this peaceful scene, we retraced our steps uphill and, after having walked along a steep winding lane between quaint old houses, outside some of which men and women mended nets, we came to vegetable gardens and orchards, little colonies of granaries, perched on their mushroom-shaped stone stilts. Gradually, as we followed a footpath, and climbed higher and higher, threading our way across intricacies of tiny patches of cultivation, the scenery and vegetation changed. Men, women and children worked among the fresh green of young maize stalks which nearly overtopped their heads, exchanged salutes with my guide, and every now and again we passed women or girls, browned by the sun, walking with hands on their hips, or arms swinging elegantly and rhythmically as they balanced baskets filled with newly harvested potatoes on their heads. The greenery and wild flowers shone against the blue of the bay which seemed to laugh up and mingle with that of the sky, as if Earth and Ocean met in gladness to renew their world-long pact.

On our way my guide took me to a barn in which several female members of his family were busy sorting out potatoes and tidying the place, the floor of which was strewn with implements of husbandry and odds and ends. Whilst I was being introduced to the busy women as a "friend from South America," for a while all activity ceased, but presently another attack was made on litter and on spider webs which hung from beams in festoons, like cloudy lace.

When we reached the top of the hill, a new amazing panorama spread before us. Towards the north, at the end of a long and deserted beach, high hills sprang up into the sky like billows, and the rest was the immense expanse of the Atlantic Ocean, which, at the western horizon, seemed to be melting into one behind a faint haze. The golden sands of the beach sloped down gently to the water's edge, as if to feel its cool caresses, and below us, towards the land's end, blue-green waves danced blithely in the glitter of the sunlight against the rocky barrier. As we stood gazing at this glorious scene, I saw a solitary man walking along the beach below, followed by a little dog. The footprints he left behind remained as witnesses of his passing, and there was something so incongruous about the apparition in this setting, that I asked my guide who this man might be, and whither he might be going. "The man you see down there," came the reply, "is an aged schoolmaster, who, for many years, every day, wet or dry, even during storms, has walked to the rocky land-point you see over there, there to seat himself and watch the sun set."

As I was to see a little later, a sunset watched from Cape Finisterre is a sight never to be forgotten, and, evidently, the man who walked those three or four miles every day had the eyes of an artist and the heart of a romantic.

As we climbed up another short incline, in the direction of land's end, the soil became poor, and plantations gave way to semi-moorland covered with grass, heather, bracken and tiny wild flowers. A few sheep were grazing there, and as we approached an old woman who kept watch over a little flock, she called to us. Soon I was to realize that she was nearly blind, and that she was merely curious to know who two wanderers she had heard talking might be. After having held a conversation with my guide, about the state of health of his family, and the prospects of crops, we resumed our ramble, leaving the old woman to drive her sheep towards their fold.

When the first shadows of evening began to creep up the flanks of the hills, and a faint purplish-grey gauze began to veil the most distant from sight, but their tops and clouds above them were still stained with the glory of sunset, we seated ourselves on a slope which faced the Atlantic. During the prolonged silence which ensued, I was overcome by a feeling that something weighed on the mind of my companion, and when, at last, he spoke, his hitherto cheerful voice sounded sad. He told me that the few fields he possessed were much too small to yield sufficient food for his family of three, besides a number of relatives who depended on him. His shop, he went on to say, brought in but little, and therefore he had made plans to leave for the Argentine, where he hoped to pave the way for his wife and two children to follow him. He added that it was strange that I should have arrived in Finisterre only a few days prior to his departure, and when I offered to give him the addresses of friends I have in Buenos Aires, he cheered up a great deal.

Whilst the two of us sat, bars of gold and crimson lashed against the aether plains of the sky, suffused with the pale-greens and yellows of rarely coloured precious stones. Below us, a small low reef of rocks jutted out into the water, and reflections seemed to be tossing it from one smooth wave to another of the now-tranquil giant, the Atlantic Ocean. Further along, towards the north, the foot-prints could still be seen where the old schoolmaster and his little dog had walked along the beach, and whilst I pictured him sitting on a rock, watching the same heavenly fireworks, I sleepily gazed at the sparkling facets where the sun-rays struck the sand glittering with receding waves.

As we returned slowly towards the village, far away I could see two tiny specks on the beach, now coming towards us. Once more we sat down to talk about the far-away land to which my companion was about to migrate, leaving behind him what he loved and treasured most in life. Then darkness fell; a hushed repose, a mysterious silence. Sky, ocean and earth seemed to float together, forming one; Nature seemed to be falling asleep, leaving Night to veil the fickle and often cruel world in her mantle.

Dinner at the guest-house was a friendly affair. There were only three of us at a fair-sized table: a lean, elderly and grey-haired man who hailed from Pontevedra, famed for its stone-cutters, mentioned in the previous chapter. He was the foreman who supervised the building of the new breakwater at the little port, and the other, a middle-aged and rather stout individual, was an electrical engineer who was doing something to the radio installations at the light-house, situated at the end of the promontory, some two miles from Finisterre. The former liked his work and his surroundings, but the engineer made no bones about it that he did not like these what he called "God-forsaken" parts, and that he longed for the day to arrive when he could pack up and go home where "just to stay in bed for three days, only to get up to eat and drink something."

Two large dressers in the dining-room were filled with crockery; plates, cups and saucers, some of which had on them the crests and names of various shipping companies. These articles, I was told, had been salvaged from shipwrecks, but besides them there were other souvenirs and trophies; cheap gaudy vases, fruit dishes, and two or three horrid statuettes, won in raffles at different fairs.

After the meal we went to join the women in the spacious kitchen, and during the conversation which ensued, I heard about various shipwrecks, and a great deal about an English sea-captain and his crew who had been saved, and who subsequently lived in the guesthouse for several days. The captain, I was told, slept in the room I occupied, and the first engineer in a smaller one alongside. Apparently, whenever the skipper was away, the engineer got roaring drunk, and on one occasion he became so obstreperous that the former gave him a sound hiding. Besides such information and mild local gossip, I was told about a remarkable rookery of every kind of sea bird, about five miles distant, on a rocky headland. When the potato crop came to be discussed, and I expressed my admiration for the elegant manner and apparent ease with which women and girls carry heavy loads on their heads, my female listeners became enthusiastic. Taking me to a large kind of store-room, I was shown an enormous heap of potatoes, and with pride I was informed that all of them had been carried to the place in the course of the day, by a girl of fourteen, who on every trip brought a load weighing some forty kilos[10]. When I expressed my amazement at such a feat of strength and endurance, a middle-aged woman told me that only very recently she had carried a packing-case weighing 116 kilos[11] from the guest-house to the bus terminus. Several of the women who heard her say this to me corroborated the statement, and told me that the two commercial travellers who owned the packing-case were not strong enough to carry it between them. "That's nothing," an old woman chimed in, "many years ago when I was in America my defunct husband, God rest his soul, laid a wager that if several men lifted a grand piano on my head, I would carry it round the hall in which a *fiesta* was being held. Bets were made, and after I had run home to fetch the head-pad I had taken across the sea with me, the piano was lifted, and after balancing it carefully on my head, I started off." At this point of her story, the woman rose from her seat and, holding herself erect, began to walk across the kitchen, taking quick short steps. "That's the way I carried the piano. And, watch, just for a little swank, and to show the onlookers what we can do in Galicia, I moved my arms

---

[10] *Editor's note:* Approximately 88 pounds.
[11] *Editor's note:* Approximately 255 pounds.

thus." Saying this she swung them forwards and backwards with every step, her wrists and hands moving somewhat like a swan's feet whilst propelling itself through the water.

Next morning, following a winding road that is cut out of the steep hill-side, I walked towards the lighthouse, situated on the rocky point at the very *Finis Terrae*. It was a wonderful sunny morning, not a cloud in the sky, and the sea looking like a vast grey-blue mirror. About half-way I came to a stream which runs down the hill in little cascades, and there, women who had come from the village were busy washing clothes and linen which they spread out over the heather and bracken to let them dry and bleach in the sun. Whilst I was talking to one whom I had met in the barn on the previous day, the old woman of the grand piano story appeared, carrying on her head a basket covered with a snow-white cloth. Having greeted me, she said that she was on her way to the lighthouse, in order to take the mid-day meal to the *ingeniero*, who stayed in my guest-house, a job she did every day. And so the two of us walked along, chatting about this and that until we reached our goal. Despite her age – which, she told me, was eighty-six – the woman walked like one many years her junior, which made me think that there must be some vital power in the sun, the sea and the air which acts like a tonic on all the people I saw in those parts.

Near the lighthouse is a wireless telegraphy station, and about a quarter of a mile from the land's end there is a low rock, locally called *O'Centoyo*, the name of a kind of large crab, which makes excellent eating. The lighthouse, together with its accommodation for engineers and their families, is much higher and more spacious than if viewed from a passing ship out at sea. One of the engineers for whom I had brought a letter of introduction went out of his way to show and explain everything to me. All the huge machinery was put into motion, and although it was a perfect day, even the mighty fog-horn was made to send its ear-shattering blasts out to sea and across the bay of Finisterre. Although the distance to the mountain is close on forty miles, the echo came back clearly. It was a wonderful experience to inspect the reflectors and the powerful electric bulbs, the light of which, during voyages to South America, I had seen from far out at sea, and as I looked at many ships which passed in the distance, I wondered whither they were bound, and if any friends of mine happened to be on board. The engineer told me about some of the many aerial battles between

German and Allied planes he had witnessed during the second World War, and about the terrific storms which often rage in the sea, which I saw now on its best behaviour.

When the time came to leave the village of Finisterre, it took quite a time to call on different friends I had met there, and to say good-bye to them. Among them was an elderly bachelor, one of the two local doctors, whose hobby is archaeology and the history connected with the parts in which he has practised for many years, and where he is loved and revered as a great benefactor. On the journey back to Corunna we passed a bus which had broken down hopelessly, though, fortunately, in a little town where the stranded passengers could find sleeping accommodation. Luck had been with me during my visit to Finisterre, for the weather had been ideal, but as we approached our destination, heavy black clouds came rolling over the hills, and in one place a peculiar short and misshapen rainbow made a rugged mountain look like a volcano emitting multicoloured fire. Back in Corunna, whilst I hurried towards the boarding-house in which I had kept my reservation, heavy drops of rain began to fall, smacking the pavement as if whips were being cracked, people ran for shelter, and carters urged on their mules and horses as if the end of the world were at hand.

CHAPTER 20

CORUNNA – BETANZOS – LUARCA – OVIEDO – GIJON – SANTILLANA

When on a beautiful Sunday I left Corunna, several members of the Motor-cycle Club accompanied me. Viewed from the top of a hill, the town, bay and beaches looked most attractive. After a halt at the end of the bay where we had some fresh oysters and a cup of white wine, we proceeded through country with which I was familiar, having been through much of it during some of our excursions. The few clouds which drifted across the otherwise clear sky were typical of Galicia, being of a peculiar colour – a kind of blend between light indigo, light burnt sienna and light grey – which natives call *panza de burra,* meaning "belly of a jenny ass," a term that is applied only to clouds. The road led over wooded hills, past neat farm-houses and along beautiful estuaries. At the end of the last one I had visited previously is the neat and to-day prospering town of El Ferrol. It was there that thousands of workers and shipwrights built the ships which met with disaster at Trafalgar, whereafter, for many years, the town was plunged into misery, all industry having ceased. Having passed through Betanzos (the Romans' Brigantium Flavium), an old town picturesquely situated on a low hill between the rivers Mendó and Mandeo, on a nearby hill we had a gargantuan lunch in an ancient house that was half farm, half inn. As usual, after the meal Galician songs were sung, and when the inn-keeper told us that at the end of his big vegetable garden there were several trees laden with ripe cherries for which there was hardly a market, we went to eat as many as our already full stomachs could hold. This done, we sat down on the cool grass to do more singing, but soon two or three of the biggest gluttons among us stretched themselves out to snore melodiously. Towards evening, after another cup of the excellent white wine of the region, my friends made ready to return to Corunna, and I to proceed inland towards higher regions, to any village or small town where to spend the night. Alone once more, I rode through high rolling country, with mountains in the distance on all sides of me. The evening sun illuminated the tops of forests, and the vivid green fields and bright flowers seemed to smile up at the golden clouds. Rustic peace floated over the countryside and farmhouses like a halo.

The sun had set when I came to a little town by name of Guitirez. The main street was crowded with people, petards[12] and rockets were fired into the air, bunting, flags and garlands were hung out, and when I asked what all this signified, I was told that the *fiesta* of San Juan (St. John) was being celebrated. Hung across one street was a wide strip of canvas on which I read: "STRANGER, GUITIREZ WELCOMES YOU." This made me decide to look for a "shake-down" for the night, so after having asked a passer-by where there might be accommodation for me, he pointed to the entrance of a street which ran downhill, in the direction of a tiny railway station, as I was to discover presently. The *fonda* (inn) which I found close by, grandly called itself "hotel," but liking the cut of the jib of the place, I pushed my way through a crowd to look for the *patrón*. When, at last, I found the veritable needle in a haystack, though he was exceedingly busy, and, as the Irish would say, "on fire," I was received with great courtesy. Brief introductions over,

---

[12] *Editor's note:* Not a spear, as most people believe, but an explosive device formerly used in warfare to blow in a door, breach a wall, etc. Here are the relevant lines from Shakespeare's *Hamlet*:

> There's letters seal'd: and my two schoolfellows
> Whom I will trust as I will adders fang'd,
> They bear the mandate; they must sweep my way
> And marshal me to knavery. Let it work;
> For 'tis the sport to have the engineer
> Hoist with his own petard; and 't shall go hard
> But I will delve one yard below their mines
> And blow them at the moon:

the elderly grey-haired man held out a hand as a stud-groom might when trying to make a lively hackney pony stand still, and saying, "Just one little moment," hurried away, soon to return with a little ink-pot, a pen and a sheet of paper, which I recognized as the *tríptico* form, one of those horrid inflictions travellers are supposed to fill in whenever they arrive at a new place. Law and regulations having been complied with, I handed the document back to the *patrón,* who proceeded to glance through the entries I had made. "I seem to know your name," he said; "haven't you been in the Argentine?" When I told him that, indeed, I had, and who I was, he was delighted, and informed me that a few years previously, after having made good out there, he had returned to Galicia, hoping to retire, but that, owing to rising prices and the depreciation of the purchasing value of the *peseta,* he found himself forced to work once more. However, his business prospered, and, in a way, he was glad to have plenty to do, instead of just waiting to die of old age or boredom.

Whilst my host spoke to me, a radio set which had been placed outside the entrance door on a chair blared, screeched, drummed, twittered, droned, whistled, snarled and chirped away, and round it stood a crowd of men and boys, listening intently. Upon enquiring what was being broadcast, I was told that within a few minutes I would hear a transmission, direct from Rio de Janeiro in Brazil, giving a running commentary on the association football match between the teams representing Spain and U.S.A., and that this was one of the matches for the world championship. No wonder, then, that by the time Rio came through with much grating and noises which sounded like the distant breaking of waves on a beach, the crowd – now greatly increased in numbers – listened intently, and that some of its members trembled with excitement. When the match ended with a 3 to 1 victory for Spain, and the announcer in Brazil seemed to be beside himself with joy, and finished with *"Viva España! Viva Franco!"* the crowd of listeners in the little old town of Guitirez in Galicia gave vent to its feelings by cheering, jumping with delight, and men and boys hugging each other. Even two far from athletic-looking priests joined in this frenzied jubilation, and when things calmed down a little, the tap-room of the inn was invaded, glasses were filled with wine, and whilst the know-alls in football technique demonstrated how some of their heroes out in Brazil played and controlled the ball, all eyes were fixed on them.

Guitirez enjoys a certain fame for its mineral waters, which are reputed to be good for liver trouble, and therefore a number of semi-invalids stayed in the little hotel. Among them were an elderly, stout, red-faced gentleman, with imposing, rather aggressive moustachios, who might have been a retired ringmaster of a circus or a general, and a most affable middle-aged lady who, during dinner, insisted on telling me all about her husband, grown-up son, family history and affairs but, above all, about the sorry state of her liver.

Many Spaniards, and also their South American cousins, seem to revel in talking about their livers, kidneys and other internal organs, about the respective functions and ailments of which they know just enough to make them feel doubly bad if something goes wrong with them. As far as I am concerned, I prefer to remain abysmally ignorant in such matters, and therefore, whilst the good *señora* delivered her scientific lecture, and told me all about her ailment and its effects, my thoughts wandered afar, though every now and again, as if understand-ing, I nodded my head, or in order to show sympathy, made clicking noises with my tongue.

In certain parts of Galicia, on the eve of the feast of St. John, maidens and spinsters who hope to catch their man act according to an old superstition. They pluck three unopened thistle buds off a plant, and after having written on little pieces of paper the names of their three favourite men, and these have been attached to the buds, they are placed under the pillow for one night. Next morning the charms are put into water, and the bud which opens first is believed to indicate which of the three candidates to single out to be enticed into the matrimonial net.

Leaving Guitirez, with its semi-invalids and football enthusiasts, I headed for the coast, following a road which led through picturesque farm country, and over wooded mountains, below which wound rush-ing streams and rivers. In villages, stores reminded me of their counter-parts in South America, for in such establishments almost anything needed by people of the region can be obtained: foodstuffs, wine, harness, yokes, wooden clogs, cloth and so on, and if it is information on any subject a caller requires, the *almacén* is the place to obtain it.

After having descended from a high pass, halting at such a store in order to eat a slice of smoked ham and some brown bread, I found a little group of men engaged in serious conversation. In chorus they all replied to my "good day", and before I had time to ask for what I wanted, the man behind the counter said to me, "*Señor,* do you know war has broken out?" "What, where?" I gasped, feeling apprehensive. "In Korea," came the reply, "the news has just come over the wireless." For a moment I stood, wondering if this was really true, and if it meant that I would be stranded in Spain. However, there being nothing I could do about it, I shrugged my shoulders and said, "Well, if the report is correct, *paciencia.*" "Yes, *señor, paciencia,*" several voices sighed.

Beautiful mountain scenery and peaceful farm houses with flowers and golden mimosa in little gardens, helped to cheer me up as I proceeded towards the now nearby coast.   Whilst riding along, I remembered what happened to me when the second World War broke out. At the time, I was touring Ireland with a pony and trap, and I was on the Aran Islands off Galway when the terrible news was broadcast from London. I remembered my return journey to London in the black-out, things that happened after, and that the book I intended to write on my tour through Ireland was never written.

Galicia was behind me, and now I found myself in Asturias, among the Cantabrian mountains, but towards evening I reached a quaint old town called Luarca, situated in a hollow, behind two high land-points which shut it off from the sea, save a narrow entrance which connects the picturesque fishing port with the waters of the Bay of Biscay.

As I was to discover within the next few days, like Galicia, Asturias is alpine in character, and those two parts are the most fertile and possibly beautiful in Spain. Galicia has a softer climate than Asturias, and therefore its pastures are more succulent, and mountain sides and hills more thickly wooded. Also, Galicia has her wonderful estuaries, whereas the general aspect of Asturias is sterner, mountains and ravines being more broken. These conditions have affected the character of the people, for whereas the Galician is light-hearted and gay, his neigh-bour, the Asturian, is more rugged. Both have to struggle hard to eke out a living from the land, especially so on account of over-population, which, as already explained, has been responsible for mass migrations, especially to South America, which is the Mecca of Galicians and Asturians. The latter have more the character of the typical moun-taineer, for, like the Basques and mountain dwellers all over the world, they are independent and "solid." Asturians who live along the coast are great mariners, and both they and their brothers, the mountaineers, are formidable fighters when roused.

Luarca, with its entrancing little fishing port and old houses clustered together on the precipitous side of the high hill which hides the sea from view, appealed to me greatly. After a climb up the steep hill, I was rewarded with a fine view of the little town below, and a walk across fields took me to a hamlet consisting of several old wooden farm houses and their adjoining fields. Asturian *hórreos* (granaries for storing maize) differ from those in Galicia. With their slate-tiled roofs, many of which are weighed down with rocks, they resemble Swiss chalets, though like the Galician *hórreos,* they also stand on mushroom-like stilts. Furthermore, the Asturian type has wooden balconies, called *corredores,* where the maize is hung out to dry before storing it.

Whilst sitting on the high rocky promontory, which makes a natural port of Luarca, and shuts in the town, I had a splendid view of the boats and houses below. The evening sun lit up a sandy beach which faces the open sea, and a few cottony clouds drifted across the sky, casting purple shadows which crept over the nearby mountains and green hills. Near a rocky headland, two fishermen's vessels ploughed through the blue-green waters, and below me the houses and churches of the town, looked like miniature toys, which seemed to beckon to me as an old friend. The gently heaving sea made white patterns like animated lace-work on the wet sand, and the voices of children playing there came floating up to me.

Whilst I was sitting enjoying these scenes, an old peasant approached, and after having greeted me, began a conversation. When I offered him a cigarette, he gladly accepted it, whereafter, between puffs, he recounted some episodes of recent local history. He told me that when he was a young man, two of his brothers asked him to emigrate to South America with them, but that he felt it was his duty to remain with his ageing parents who needed his assistance. Both his brothers made their mark in the New World where they became the owners of prospering *estancias* (ranches). Then, pointing at a clump of trees on a hill, he went on to tell me that a rich man's huge modern house which stood behind them had burnt down, and that a modern construction near the ruin was the hospital, built with the money given by one who had migrated to the Americas where he had amassed a great fortune. Then, of course, I heard a great deal about the situation and local life in general, and after about an hour when the two of us rose to go in opposite directions, the peasant shook me warmly by the hand, and at the same time told me his name, adding that he was my *servidor* (servant), and that a certain modest farm house towards which he pointed was his property, and that it was at my disposal at any time.

"Tell me," I said before turning round to go on my way, "have you any regrets for not having gone to South America with your two brothers?"

"Occasionally, when times are hard and difficult, yes," the old man replied, and after a pause added, "However, on the whole, no. Although I have worked hard all my life, and continue to do so to help my son and his family, I have no regrets. My forefathers' little farm has remained in the hands of the family, and although it would have been interesting to see something of this world, besides those regions beyond which I have never gone, I am quite happy. Why chase after wealth, especially so when it means leaving behind the happiness a simple life offers? My brothers succeeded. I am happy for them, and happy to think that when I am called out of this world, my bones will lie alongside those of members of my family who have tilled this soil before me. No, sir, I have no regrets for having stayed at home, though most of my life has been passed in poverty."

Those were the parting words of an old Asturian peasant, a descendant of a race of men it took the mighty Romans two centuries to subdue, and whom the Moors found too tough a nut to crack.

Sometimes following the beautiful coast, and then again heading inland, where I found myself in the labyrinth of the Cantabrian mountains, I made a short stop in the city of Oviedo with its fine Gothic cathedral and other ancient buildings of great artistic merit, and thence descended to Gijon, the gay seaside resort and busy industrial centre where, for the first time on my whole tour, I saw more modern factory chimneys than church towers. There, quite by accident, I had the good fortune to be re-united with a friend from Madrid, Manuel de Ortueta, the champion motor-cycle racer of Spain, a dare-devil who races merely because he likes speed and all the skill and thrills that go with his favourite sport.

At night, whilst the two of us strolled about, he suggested we go to a *chigre* where he had arranged to meet his mechanic. The word *chigre* being new to me, I asked what it meant, whereupon my companion became quite enthusiastic, and told me that if I had never been to a *chigre* I had missed something typical of Asturias. Wondering what kind of a peculiar place he was taking me to, I followed him through the semi-dusk of a badly lighted side-street, and presently entered into what, to me, looked like an ordinary though rather primitive tavern, in which were assembled a number of men. In a corner, at the end of a long bench, with papers before him on a deal-topped table, a man of about thirty sat, busy writing. Of serious demeanour, and wearing heavy horn-rimmed spectacles, there was something distinctly profes-sorial about him, and when my friend introduced him to me as his mechanic, for a moment I thought he was joking. The young man explained that he was writing letters to his family and friends, and that if we gave him a couple of minutes, he would join us at the counter, where drinks were being despatched. The stuff everybody in the place consumed was apple cider, of a kind which is a speciality in certain regions in Asturias. The liquid is poured out of stout bottles, into thick glasses which hold about a pint. When a *patrón* asks for a *culín,* the boss or one of his assistants raises the bottle high above his head with one hand, and, whilst holding the glass in the other, as low as possible, pours out the cider until the glass is about one-third full, when he hands it to the client who drinks as quickly as possible, whilst the liquid froths and bubbles. When the glass is nearly empty, its remaining contents are swirled round and spilt on the stone floor, or into a low tub, of which there were several in the *chigre* of my description. In spite of these repositories for dregs, the floor was so wet with cider that if my shoes had leaked my feet would have got wet. It was explained to me that this particular kind of Asturian cider must be drunk at once, lest it go "flat" and turn a dark colour, as happens in the case of an apple when it is dissected, and the pieces are left to stand for a while. Naturally, thanks to long practice, some of the patrons in the *chigre* were experts at pouring out the cider. When the boss saw me watch them with admiration, just to do one better he poured out the next *culín* holding the glass behind his back, a clever trick he performed without looking at the bottle or glass, and without spilling a drop.

Between Gijon and Santander I rode more or less along the coast, on the way passing through two or three pretty little towns with fine beaches. About twenty miles from Santander I spent several days in

Santillana, a romantic little town which, until the eighteenth century, was a kind of retreat for *hidalgos* whose escutcheoned houses with their fine balconies remain as mute witnesses of past glories. It is in places such as Santillana that one can feel the pulse of time, for they are, as it were, back-waters of bygone times. Some of the ground-floor halls in which grandees of old held their banquets, to-day house cattle and even pigs. Once upon a time, Santillana was the capital of Asturias, and between the fifteenth and eighteenth centuries, when Spanish aristocracy was on thin ice, it was a favourite place of retreat and a rallying point. Among the *hidalgos* – who in those days wore black clothes and ruffs – rivalry was such that fanciful verses were concocted by rhymesters to enhance the names of famous families. These boastful verses were not necessarily produced by the families themselves, but most likely by hangers-on who wished to ingratiate themselves with the rich and powerful.

In a foregoing chapter I mentioned the tragic end of the succession of the title of the Dukes of Frias of the ancient family of Velasco. Among the many vast properties they owned was a mansion in Santillana. A saying about the Velascos has it that, "Before God was God, and the mountains, mountains, the Quiros were Quiros, and the Velascos, Velascos."[13] This was capped by a verse even more boastful about the family of Estrada: "I am the house of Estrada, founded on this rock, older in the highlands than the house of Velasco, and to the King it owes nothing."[14] About the coat-of-arms of the Estrada family (a black eagle on a field of gold) there is an interesting verse which goes as follows: "The Goth from Germany, cousin of the emperor, brought

---

[13] *Antes que Dios fuera Dios*
y los peitascos, peitascos,
los Quiros eran Quiros
y los Velascos, Velacos

[14] *Yo soy la casa de Estrada*
fundada en este peitasco,
mds antigua en la Montaña
que la casa de Velasco,
y al rey no le debe nada

to Spain the black eagle which bathes in a field of gold."[15]

A few of Santillana's splendid old houses, with their *patios* and quiet gardens, remain more or less as they were before the town's glory began to ebb. One such house, which contains splendid old furniture and many beautiful things, belongs to Archduchess Margaret of Hapsburg-Lorraine and Bourbon, sister of the late Prince, Don Jaime. When I visited the place, the Archduchess – who is said to be an artist of talent – had been absent for several years, being detained in Italy where, for political reasons, she was under a cloud. Despite her prolonged absence, the caretaker – an old woman – kept everything spick and span, and even vases filled with flowers, as if expecting her mistress to return at any moment.

In the romantic and comfortable *parador* (hostel run by the State Tourist Department) in which I stayed, there were only a very few guests besides myself, for the tourist season had not yet begun. Two of the visitors whom I befriended were an old Uruguayan doctor and his wife, who were about to end their first tour through Europe. Whilst talking about their experiences in different countries, the old doctor told me that in Rome some boot-blacks have such amazing throne-like seats for clients, that when he sat in a particularly big and ornate one, he wished someone had been there to photograph him. This changed our conversation to the wooden horses I had seen in several Spanish towns, where street photographers take pictures of children sitting on them. When I told my new acquaintances that on several occasions I had longed to be photographed on such a horse, both he and his wife laughed heartily, and the doctor admitted that one of his latest childish ambitions happened to be the same as mine, but that, so far, he had been unable to screw up sufficient courage to pose on such a wooden horse.

As it happened, that day a *fiesta* was being held in the little town, and early in the morning, whilst strolling about near the little fairground, I had seen a photographer who had the very thing we wanted.

---

[15] *El Gótico de Alemania*
   primo del Emperador,
   el aguila trajo a España,
   que en el campo de oro se bañai
   siendo negro su colo

When I told the doctor about it, his wife chimed in, "Go on, you two. Let me see if you have the courage to have your pictures taken." After much teasing on her part, the three of us set out, but upon reaching the fair-ground where, by that time, many people were making merry, the doctor's and my courage failed, and so our mutual ambition remained unfulfilled.

On one side of the roughly cobbled main square of Santillana is an old fountain where women and girls go to fill jars and buckets with water. Unlike in other parts of Spain, in those regions of Asturias, water is not carried on the head, or supported on the hips. Water-carriers have a square wooden frame which is suspended from the shoulders by means of two straps, and made to hang down to about the level of the hands, when arms are outstretched downwards. Buckets and jars are held outside the frame which prevents them from knocking against the carrier's legs, and the straps distribute the weight equally between shoulders and arms.

One evening, whilst I was watching and listening to the women at the fountain, a ponderously fat wench waddled towards them, as fast as her abnormally thick legs and ankles permitted, and when she reached the chatterers, one of them turned round to greet the newcomer with an affectionate, "How are you, *Camión?*" (A *camión* is a heavy motor truck.)

About one mile south of Santillana stands a high green hill, near the rounded top of which is a famous cave, discovered by chance in 1876. And yet, before that time, according to ancient legends and superstitious stories, it was believed that a mysterious bewitched cave existed somewhere in that hill, but although the natives were familiar with a small aperture, they were much too afraid to investigate its depth, until, one day, a peasant sought a trap he had set for a rodent which had done damage to his maize crop. The man's little dog followed the scent to the aperture where he stopped to bark, until his master caught up with him. Seeing traces which indicated that his trap had been dragged into what looked like a large hole, the man crept into it on all fours; soon, however, to find himself in what seemed to be a large subterranean chamber, which, with the help of a torch, he proceeded to explore. To his amazement, he discovered that on the low ceiling of one of the two large chambers of which the cave consists were a number of remarkable paintings of animals. Fortunately the peasant was intelligent enough to report his discovery to the authorities, who lost no time in summoning experts to make a scientific investigation. In due time they came to the conclusion that the amazing life-like paintings of bison, deer, boar and horses, were made by a troglodyte artist, between twenty and thirty thousand years ago. Thanks to atmospheric and other conditions in the cave, their colouring remains so bright and vivid that they might have been made yesterday. Most of the pictures are done in semi-relief, the shapes having been hewn out of the rock, and, rough edges having polished off, the animals were painted in bright colours ranging between grey, light-red and burnt sienna, but a few were done in black. Geological investigations prove that, ages ago, the valleys below were part of the Cantabrian Sea, and that besides meat of bison, deer and wild boar, the ancient troglodytes also lived on sea food.

At night, instead of wasting my time sitting in the luxurious hostel, I strolled through the roughly cobbled streets, or went to some humble tavern there over a glass of wine to talk with peasants, all of whom were friendly and, in some cases, possessed of a grand sense of humour and wit. Once, after such a session, when I stepped out into the open, a full moon was shining so brightly that I decided to roam up the hill of the caves, and thence to have a look at the surrounding country. About half an hour later, I sat on the grassy slope, making mental pictures of the troglodytes, as I imagined them to have been many thousands of years ago. In my mind's eye I saw ape-like, long-haired men digging pitfalls for bison, others driving wild boar and deer into concealed enclosures there to kill them with spears and clubs, whilst near the mouth of the cave, women, their bodies partly covered with skins of wild animals, roasted meat, and naked children played near them. I had a vision of the artist working at his pictures on the low ceiling in the cave, the light in which he did this being provided by a small flickering fire, which threw dancing shadows that made the semi-relief pictures move. The magic of imagination made me see and hear many strange things; the joys and sorrows of those long-departed people, jealousies among them, and fierce battles fought between *my* cave-dwellers and marauding tribes. It fascinated me to think that, many a time, thousands of years ago, those troglodytes must have looked up at the same mysterious moon at which I gazed for a long time before rising to descend to where dwells modern man. I watched its beams quivering on the white sand and fine gravel of the road near me, and faint ripples of light playing on the grassy slopes, which fairly shimmered. One might have thought that the moonbeams drew their arms about the whole countryside, as if struggling with the moon for its possession. A soft breeze rustled the leaves of a nearby clump of trees, making them whisper some of Nature's secrets, and down in the valley it seemed as if some fairy had waved a magic wand that had transmuted all the prosaic detail of day into a sublime dreamland. How subtle is the gamut of beauty, and what strange and opposite symphonies she plays in our minds. The rising sun gives us the note of the cymbal and of the clarion: loud, triumphant, joyous, thrilling us with its life-giving and all-conquering power. And then, again, a night such as this: a fantastic compound of moonshine and shadow, wondrous dimensions, peace, restfulness, evasive beauty, muted violins, harp, lute and softly-played reed instruments.

Delightful Santander was my next port of call, and thence a short ride took me into the country of the Basques. Asturias, with its alpine scenery, prospering farms in the highlands, fishing ports on the beautiful coast, and friendly people, had given me much joy. In some regions there are significant iron, lead and coal mines, and the cutting of peat is another important industry. Among the wooded mountains, game abounds, deer, wild boar and chamois and in some of the remote parts bears roam about. Rivers and streams offer fine fishing, salmon and trout abounding. The coastal regions near Santander are a joy in any season, but it is during the hot summer months that many visitors flock to the ideal beaches and restful little towns.

Whilst riding merrily towards Bilbao, I remembered the Basque football enthusiasts I had met in Madrid, where they had gone in order to witness the final match for the championship of Spain. The name and telephone number of one of these merry "he-men" was in my pocket, and as I had been warned on no account to pass through Bilbao without calling on him, I was ready to make the promised telephone call. As will be seen, this led to many things I never expected to happen or to see. Long before I reached the parts in which I now found myself, whenever I told friends or people that I was timing my travels carefully, in order to be in Pamplona on July 7th, when the famous *fiesta* of Saint Fermin begins, they laughingly said *adios* to me, and some even shook me by the hand, as if to wish me success on a difficult or dangerous enterprise.

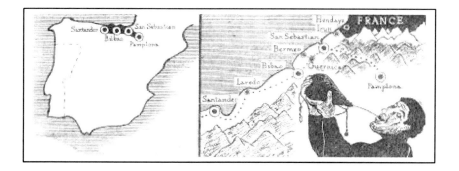

CHAPTER 21

BILBAO – GUERNICA – SAN SEBASTIAN – PAMPLONA

Thanks to the guidance of an obliging policeman, about half an hour after my arrival in Bilbao I was installed in a modest though quite nice hotel, so after having washed myself, and donned my best suit, i.e. a pair of grey flannel "bags", a clean polo shirt and a sports jacket, I rang up the number one of the football enthusiasts had given me in Madrid. I had hardly told the man at the other end of the line who was speaking to him, when he shouted excitedly, "Stay where you are! I shall be with you within a few minutes!" With this he hung up the receiver, and soon after a taxi drew up outside the door, and a young man alighted, dressed in a neat palm beach suit. I was wondering if this could be the same man whom I had met in Madrid, wearing a red and white striped football jersey, when he rushed towards me, to hug me, and at the same time to slap my back with such vigour that it nearly made me cough. These affectionate though rather too virile greetings over, he asked me to jump into the taxi, and then, whilst we were being driven towards his home, my friend, the Herculean Basque, explained to me the reason for all this hurry; the football match between England and Spain was about to commence in Rio de Janeiro, and he was anxious not to miss a word of the broadcast.

In a pretty chalet, which was surrounded by a shady garden, I was introduced to members of his family and a few friends who were assembled in a large room, waiting to hear the broadcast from Brazil.

From the moment of stepping into the house, I felt at home, for the people there were simple, natural and friendly. Wine and a variety of snacks were placed before me, and despite my protests, I was made to eat as if I were Gargantua himself. When Rio came through with many weird incidental noises – "statics", as I believe radio experts call them – a hush fell on the assembly, and old and young began to listen with bated breath. Though a description of what I saw and heard would be most entertaining, it would take up too much space for me to relate it here, so suffice it to say that when Spain scored a goal, both the Spanish broadcaster in Rio and his little audience in the chalet in Bilbao went crazy with joy. At our end, glasses were filled quickly, and trembling hands toasted the scorer of the goal, who happened to be a Basque. When the match ended in a one goal to nil victory for Spain, and, on the part of the frenzied commentator in Brazil, several high-pitched shouts of *"Viva España!"* and *"Viva Franco!"* enthusiasm was such among those present, that I must have been the only one there who heard the final commentaries, for as soon as the broadcaster said that the referee had blown the final whistle, at our end a veritable all-in hugging match began. Once more, glasses were filled, the Basque players were toasted – those of other parts of Spain being clean forgotten – and when nerves became steadier, and the effects of abandoned exaltation calmed down, gradually conversation simmered down to more or less normal. Spain's totally unexpected victory over England gave everybody great hopes that their favourites would return home with the *campeonato mundial de futbol,* but when they asked me what I thought of their chances of doing so, and I said that, judging by what I had seen of South American football, I ventured to forecast that either Uruguay or Brazil would win the series, my friends fairly bombarded me with details regarding the tactics their favourites had up their sleeves – or, maybe, football pants – for the next games. I was told so much about the devastating technique of certain Spanish players that, as far as my informants were concerned, the world championship was as good as in Spain's bag. Incidentally, as it happened, Brazil beat Spain by six goals to one, and in the final Uruguay defeated Brazil, thus winning the coveted title. However, by that time I was far from Bilbao.

I am mentioning these happenings because they go to show the tremendous interest Spaniards take in football, a sport which attracts infinitely more spectators than any bullfight.

Whilst we men talked about the game in Rio, the women were busy in the kitchen, and after a while the table was laid, and, to my consternation, enormous quantities of food were placed on it. All my pleadings that I was already as full as the proverbial tick were in vain. I was told that I was in the Basque country now, that Basques believe in eating and drinking plenty, that another meal would do me good, and therefore, that I was to do as I was ordered, to get busy with knife and fork, and to stop arguing. To this day I marvel at the quantity of food and wine I managed to pack away that evening, but when I compare my performance with that of some of the other men, I come to the conclusion that I was a mere canary, nibbling and pecking at this and that.

The gastronomic battle over, three of us men set out to see the town and certain aspects of its life. Little did I dream at the time that our tour would last until the early hours of morning, and that for the next ten days I was to have practically no sleep, except a few snatches at odd hours.

Bilbao – the Basques' *Ibaizabal* – is situated some six or eight miles from the sea. Though the river Nervión has been dredged and harnessed, most of the big ships anchor at the outer harbour. The New Town, with its fine buildings, avenues and squares, is the centre of activity, and it is there that people like to promenade in the cool of evening, or to sit outside *cafés,* to talk and to watch passers-by. Whilst we were in such a place, sipping cups of excellent coffee of the *estraperlo* (contraband) type, my companions pointed out to me a young lady who strolled about with several others. With an admiration that bordered on awe, they whispered to me that the young lady was the fiancée of the Basques' football idol who that day had played in Rio. They went on telling me that for the sake of convenience and brevity, this player's surname had been changed from Zarraonaindia to Zarra, which, apart from other considerations, made it sound more Spanish. They explained that many Basque names are long and very com-plicated, being, as it were, veritable dossiers of a person's identity, whence an individual hails, who were his parents, situation and description of the family's home, and so on.

Several bridges, including two quaint ones made of steel, take one across the river Nervión to the Old Town, which is situated between the river and hills. I liked the atmosphere of this sector, and when the mass of taverns we passed were pointed out to me, I was astonished. When I told my companions that during my long tour I had seen remarkably little drunkenness, they laughed and said, "Remember you are in the Basque country now, and, above all, in Bilbao. Come, follow us, we'll show you more drunks than you will care to count." With this they led the way towards a badly-lit but crowded street, on either side of which were rows of smelly taverns, all packed with patrons who wasted no time between drinks. A great many of the tipplers were in high spirits, and some had indulged so freely that their faculty of speech and of balance were affected. In dark narrow side-streets, in doorways and along walls, sat or lay inebriates, among them two or three women who looked degenerated and revolting. Vices going hand-in-hand, in some of the "skid-rows" were filthy "honky tonks"[16] and brothels, in and out of which slouched a regular stream of mostly ill-clad men. In connection with this low quarter of Bilbao, I must make it quite clear that it is only a small sector of the town, and that besides filth of various descriptions, the visitor who strays or deliberately goes there is in no danger of being molested in any way. Bilbao being an industrial, but, above all, a port town, its quarter roughly described above, caters for the tastes and needs of a certain very common type of man, for where there is a demand for vice there will always be a supply.

In two nearby streets, *verbenas* (street night festivals) were being held. Squeezed together like sardines, couples danced to music supplied by gramophones and amplifiers, and vendors of food, sweets and cheap delicacies did a great trade, as also did the proprietors of taverns which were filled to capacity. At such *verbenas* people are very well behaved, and old and young alike enjoy themselves.

During the next two days, my friends were so keen on showing me as much of their home-town as possible that it was only when we sat down to eat or drink something that I had a rest. In their company I made several delightful excursions to nearby towns and ports, including picturesque Bermeo, famed for its sardines. There, fishermen who were about to have their midday meal, invited us to join them and to eat a *cocido* (a kind of stew) out of a pot, round which we squatted on the wharf. There was much joking as we dipped our spoons into the tasty stew, and when the inevitable wineskin was handed round the circle,

---

[16] *Editor's note:* A type of bar with musical entertainment.

and I used it more or less expertly, the jolly fishermen were very pleased. They were good-looking, hardy fellows, most of them young, and from them I gathered that their voyages out to sea often take them to southern Ireland, the Aran Islands, and occasionally as far as Newfoundland.

My guides being patriotic Basques, they took me to a pilgrimage to Guernica, there to show me the ancient seat of the diet of Viscaya, known as the *Casa de Juntas,* near which stands an oak tree which is venerated as the symbol of Basque political institutions.   Under its shade, since time immemorial, deputies have met every two years at assemblies called *batzarre.*   It was there that, in 1371, the Infante Don Juan – who later became Juan I, King of Castile – swore the *fueros,* special privileges which gave the Basques immunity from taxes and military service.   The *fueros* were almost wholly abrogated in 1876, by Alfonso XII, a measure which continues to be resented strongly to this day by all Basque nationalists, among whom there are strong anti-Castilian feelings which are encouraged by the majority of Basque priests, in many cases Jesuits who exert a great influence.

Most of the Basques whom I met made no bones about it that they do not like Franco, partly because he is a Galician, and when I was in Galicia, many people told me that they do not like him because he is a native of their home region.   The fact of the matter is that Spaniards – especially the Basques – hate to be bossed.   Every man feels that he is a king, and Spain being a country of twenty-eight million people, who can dictate to so many kings?   The old Spanish saying about royal orders still holds good, "I obey, but I do not comply."   The Basques, who run most of Spain's banks, and whose industries flourish, resent incompetence, the maze of controls, favouritism among high-up officials, and the behind-the-scenes that go on to obtain lucrative Government jobs.

During the Civil War, Guernica was almost entirely destroyed; but who was responsible for this ruthless devastation remains a matter of dispute, as are most *post mortems* of excesses during wars.   When I visited the town, it had been completely reconstructed with fine houses, but during the ruthless aerial bombardment – against which the hapless inhabitants had no defence of any kind – fortunately the low-flying planes avoided hitting the historic *Casa de Juntas* and its adjacent buildings which remained unscarred.   The old oak tree, under which assemblies had sat for many centuries, dried up in 1892, but an off-shoot of it thrives to-day. The trunk of the original tree is preserved under a temple-like circular colonnade. Some two hundred years ago a large assembly hall was constructed near the oak tree, and ever since then the *batzarre* has been held in it. The walls are lined with many fine paintings, and adjacent archives are filled with ancient documents, including the genealogical charts of all old Basque families, branches of which have spread to the four corners of the world. Among the relics kept in the almost sacred *Casa de Juntas* – the construction and general atmosphere of which is as solid and simple as the character of the Basques – is the guitar used by Iparraguirre, the composer of *Guernica-Arbola,* the to-day prohibited – but still much sung – national anthem of the Basques. These rugged and strong people, the most typical among whom often are lantern-jawed, aquiline-nosed, and brown-haired, claim proudly to be the oldest race in Europe, being pure descendants of pre-Aryan aborigines of the Iberian Peninsula. Their soft and melodious language is Euscara, which is totally unintelligible to Spaniards and all foreigners, a peculiar tongue which has not the slightest resemblance to any other, and which remains a riddle to all students of philology. Basque dances, also, differ from any in Spain, and. the traditional instrument is the *dulzaina,* a kind of flageolet which is played to the beating of a small drum.

Leaving industrial Bilbao with its iron ore, steel and other manufacture, accompanied by several friends, I headed for gay San Sebastian. On the way the landscape was hilly, green and smiling, and the farm-houses were mostly stone-built, and had broad flat-tiled roofs. Clear mountain streams and rivers are harnessed to supply power to industry, for wherever nature offers something to be exploited, the thrifty hard-working Basques take full advantage of it. Here and there we passed colonies of blast furnaces, paper mills, foundries, and all kinds of factories which bring prosperity to these parts.

In San Sebastian – the most luxurious and fashionable seaside resort in Spain – we had another hectic time. The beautiful little bay – on account of its shape known as the *Concha* (meaning sea-shell) – is bounded on the north-east by Mount Urgull, and on the opposite side by Mount Igueldo, close on 800 feet above sea-level. A number of years ago the once-famous gaming tables in splendid *casinos* were closed, and it was then that, as explained in a foregoing chapter, the word *estraperlo* was concocted. For beauty, climatic conditions, and luxury, San Sebastian is unrivalled in Spain, and during the summer season tourists from many parts of the world assemble there.

My companions never gave me a moment's rest, for when they did not take me to see this or that, it was a trip up Mount Igueldo on the funicular railway, to meet some of their friends, or just to walk about in order to shake down the mass of food they had eaten, or to work up a thirst for another bottle of wine. One evening, whilst strolling about in the old sector of the town, near the port, at the base of precipitous Mount Urgull, we halted to watch men play a game of *pelota*. The *frontón*, or court in which it was being played, was picturesquely situated alongside the golden-brown wall of an old church, and all the immediate surroundings were so quiet and peaceful that occasional shouts of warning or of advice, uttered by the players, and the sharp smacking sound made by the ball against the wall, echoed through the stillness. A number of men and boys sat or half lay on the ground, watching the vicissitudes of the hard-fought game, and whenever the players stopped for a short while, in order to regain their breath, a looker-on would hand them his wine-skin, out of which the recipient squirted a fine stream, in order to moisten his parched lips and mouth.

Pelota is the Basques' game *par excellence,* and is, I dare say, the most strenuous and intricate of all ball games. There are several varieties of it, such as *cesta* (played with a narrow curved basket which is fixed to a leathern gauntlet, attached to the right hand), *pelota a paleta* (played with a wooden bat), *pelota a mano* (played with bare hands), and others. The construction of the courts also varies, especially so if games which resemble the *jeu de paume* (real tennis) are played in complicated *frontones* (courts) with various hazards and traps built in. Hand ball is the favourite among players in their native region, but professionals who perform in large cities throughout Spain, and also in South America, usually play with bats. *Frontones* are between 30 and 40 feet wide, and between 200 and 300 feet long. The ball weighs a shade over four ounces, and is made of India-rubber, covered with leather. As in the case of lawn tennis, the game is played as "singles" or "doubles." It is amazing to see how hard players can hit the ball with bare hands, though after hard-contested points, hands sometimes swell up to such an extent that, in order to reduce their puffiness, a man lies down on the concrete floor, whilst his partner treads on them to reduce the swelling. No game this for a dental surgeon or a pianist. *Pelota* players must be ambidextrous and, apart from having to be very agile and physically fit, they must be possessed of a special gift of anticipation, which, in the case of good players, is quite uncanny. One of the complaints among the Basques and Navarrese is that all their best players go to cities, or even abroad, to become professional *pelotaris*. There are several systems of betting on the games they play in *frontones* which attract many spectators, though owing to the con-struction of such ball courts, there is a limit to seating accommodation. Unless a man begins to play the game in his infancy, he will never attain proficiency.

In San Sebastian, my friends took me to the premises of a society where I was given an insight into an important side of the Basque character, namely, that of honesty. As already pointed out, Basques are great eaters, and therefore it is not surprising that their women are great cooks, and that they take both pleasure and pride in their work. A Basque woman's kitchen is her kingdom, and woe betide the man who is foolish and reckless enough to try to interfere in its running. However, as not all men have the luck to be looked after by one of these culinary artists, or, perhaps, want an occasional change, the unattached ones clubbed together and formed eating societies.

The premises of one I visited resembled an ordinary restaurant, with a spacious kitchen and store-rooms at the back, but except for a cashier near the entrance nobody was there to attend to members, save, of course, a small kitchen staff.

Proceedings in such eating clubs are simple. At the door, the cashier hands members a sheet of paper, on which is printed a list of foods, wines and other beverages, with a margin opposite each item. This is to be filled in by the consumer who is at liberty to help himself to anything that is available, even a clean table cloth and a napkin, if he does not want to eat at a long, kind of communal, wooden-topped table, which most of the members seemed to prefer.

If a man happens to have with him a nice piece of meat, or perhaps an extra fine fish, and wishes to cook it himself, there is a special section in the kitchen, where he can do so, the materials, extras and ingredients – such as oil, butter, flour or eggs – being kept in the store-room. If it is wine he wants, all he has to do is to go to any barrel he fancies, from it fill a jug, or if he prefers bottled wine, he can pick a bottle of the vintage he likes from well-stocked racks. Nobody is there to supervise or to watch what, or how much, a member takes, and it is entirely up to him to see to it that his chit is duly filled in. When he leaves the premises, the cashier takes whatever sum of money is put down as due, and a member of the kitchen staff clears the table, and removes plates and cutlery to be washed. The most amazing thing about these Basque eating societies is that they more than pay their way, and that, not infrequently, at the end of the financial year, they show a profit which is distributed among members as a bonus.

The great day, the 7th of July, was at hand. The *fiesta* of Saint Fermin[17] was about to begin in Pamplona, one of the most ancient towns in northern Spain, situated up among the hills, about eighty miles from San Sebastian where we still had our headquarters. My companions had so many friends along the route that I did not quite fancy the idea of our making the trip on motor-cycles, for besides the hospitality we were sure to encounter on the way, I knew that the road we would have to follow was of the mountainous type. The saying "an old dog for a hard road" is all very well if it means that the old tail-wagger, or growler, as the case may be, has only the road to cope with, but if he does his travelling in the company of lively doggies who are considerably younger than he, and they are out for any fun and devilment, it is a very different matter. Long experience and not a few hard knocks taught me to be cautious, and to see accidents before they happen, so I put it to my friends that, in my opinion, it would be wiser and safer if we made the trip to Pamplona by train. After some arguing, it was unanimously decided that I was right and so, in order to celebrate the momentous decision, a round of drinks was ordered. My companions were so happy at the thought that on the morrow the big spree of Saint Fermin would begin, that they broke into a favourite song, the words of which are something about the 1st of January, 2nd of February, 3rd of March, and so on, until the 7th of July is reached. At this point they cheered so heartily that even the boss of the establish-

---

[17] Saint Fermin lived in the first century A.D. The Diocese *Pampelonensis* dates from Apostolic times. Saint Saturninus (a personal friend and disciple of St. Peter) sent Honestus as a missionary from Toulouse to Pamplona. There he met and converted the son of the Roman Senator Firminus. His son, Firminus, became the first Bishop of Pamplona. He was later martyred at Amiens in France.

ment, and some of the clients assembled there, joined in. This song was followed by other favourites, and as the party warmed up, I all but shook hands with myself for having made my merry companions agree to travel up to Pamplona by train. Summer had begun, and as it was a hot day, somebody suggested we go and eat something in a place with an "atmosphere" which, he felt sure, would appeal to me. Accordingly, we went to a side-street, near the ramshackle railway station, and upon coming to a door and a rickety wooden staircase which led down into a vast cellar, descended into it. The high, somewhat dungeon-like place was dimly lit by two or three small electric bulbs, and besides these, high up on the solid stone walls, through two or three slats narrow beams of sunlight shone like glittering swords. All along the walls were huge barrels, all filled with cider, and at one end of the cellar was a kitchen range behind which several elderly women were busy cooking. Two long wooden tables with benches alongside them, and a few stools completed the furniture of the establishment, in which, incidentally, no alcoholic drinks were sold. The smell of cider and of food being cooked was most appetizing, and so, shortly after having ordered the dishes of our fancy, we set to work, eating with such gusto that the women smiled with pride and satisfaction. Besides ourselves, a few workmen had their mid-day meal in the place, and after they had departed, I began to feel so sleepy that I yawned and stretched myself. "*Señor,* why not push together two benches, and stretch yourself out on them?" one of the women shouted, "It is nice and cool down here, and a little *siesta* would do you good before the long railway journey to Pamplona." No sooner suggested than done, and soon after my companions and I dozed off.

About two hours later, much refreshed, we departed with the good wishes and thanks of our excellent hostesses. In the street, a solitary well-dressed man who wore a Panama hat, came up to me, and with a strong American accent said, in halting Spanish, "Pardon me. Can you tell me the way to the railway station?" "Just over there," I replied in English, at the same time pointing at what looked like a small, low wooden shed. "No kiddin'," came the reply, accompanied by a wry smile showing suspicion. "Yes, that's the station," I reassured the stranger. "As it happens we are going there ourselves, so come along with us, perhaps I can be of assistance to you."

As it turned out, the American hailed from California, where his

Basque parents had settled before he was born, and now he was on his way to Pamplona, near which town lived some of his relatives whom he was about to visit for the first time. Our respective tickets having been bought, and porters having taken charge of our motorcycles, we made ready to board the train. As we walked towards what looked like a row of rabbit hutches, the American asked, "Tell me, where is the train?" "That's it," I replied, hitting the side of the last carriage with the flat of a hand. For a few moments the American stood, speechless, staring and smiling faintly, whilst all of us watched him, wondering what his next reaction would be. "Gee!" he said softly after a dramatic pause, "So that's a train. Wal, wal, I never. Just wait till I get home and tell my friends about it. They'll never believe me."

If, at the time of saying this, our new friend had been told what was to happen on the journey we were about to begin, he, too, would never have believed it. In fact, as far as I was concerned, the same thing would have held good, for even in my wildest dreams I could never have imagined such an amusing and original railway journey.

Most of the passengers, old and young, were on their way to the feast of Saint Fermin, and although it was to begin at midnight, as far as our convoy was concerned, it started at the ramshackle station in San Sebastian. Before the train left, demijohns, bottles and wine-skins were put on board by passengers, and baskets filled with food were placed on luggage racks or on the floor, and when, at last, we began to move with a few jolts, there was much cheering, followed by unorganized singing of different songs. After a while, as self-appointed conductors took the singers in hand, and players of *dulzainas* (Basque flageolets), *txistú* (pronounced "chistoo", a flute played with one hand, whilst the other beats a *tamboril,* a small drum), guitars and accordions began to perform in turns, things became more entertaining. During lulls, wine was handed round, jokes were cracked, and visits were made to other carriages, and soon even the most sedate and reserved among the elderly passengers joined in the fun.

How the small museum piece of an engine managed to pull the train is still a mystery to me, but yet, though slowly and with difficulty, our train wound its way through green valleys, up long steep inclines, and through mountain country which looked like artists' fantasies in books for children. The mountain sides along which our crazy singing and music academy crawled were covered with pine and other woods, and along the bottoms of deep ravines tumbled wild streams. Whenever we emerged from tunnels – of which there were many – so much smoke belched from their mouths that one might have thought fires were smouldering inside the mountains. Whenever we stopped at tiny stations, in order to take more passengers on the already overcrowded train, or to fill the steaming engine's tank with water, people alighted to dance on the platform, whilst a few of the men rushed off in order to replenish their dwindling supplies of wine. When the engine cooled down sufficiently to face the next lap, the driver blew its tooter, the guards their whistles, the stationmaster shouted, and when the dancers and songsters felt like it, they boarded the train, and when the officials were quite satisfied that no stragglers were left behind, after more tooting on the part of the engine, and blowing of whistles on that of the guards, we chugged off. New passengers were made as comfortable as circumstances permitted, and soon they became one with the merry party. Basques being true democrats who never recognized nobility among themselves, and among whom one man and woman is as good as the other, we were like a large family, all having a grand time, and looking forward to joining the merry throng in Pamplona.

Our American friend made a great hit when he went through his limited vocabulary of Basque words his parents had taught him in California, and when he suggested that a song be sung – of which he only remembered the tune and a few words – everybody sang so lustily that it was a miracle the walls and roof of our carriage withstood the blast of so many powerful lungs. Many times during that memorable journey, the American came to me to say, "Gee, when I get home and tell my friends about this trip, they'll never believe me."

When night fell on the beautiful mountainous country, old-fashioned oil lamps provided us with light, but although it would have been a strain on the eyes to read in it, no one had time or inclination to waste time on literature. We were LIVING and enjoying ourselves to the full, so song followed song, and every now and again *dulzainas, txistú, tamboriles,* guitars and accordions provided us with a change. After a few hours of travelling in such friendly company, I knew everybody in the carriage, and quite a number in others, where they hailed from, what was their business, and even what were their hopes and ambitions for the future.

Naturally, our train did not run according to the time-table, and it must have been about 11 p.m. when a shout went up, many voices announcing that in the distance, on what seemed to be a little plain, the lights of Pamplona had come in sight. This called for more wine, and another repetition of the song about the 1st of January, the 2nd of February, and so on, until the seventh verse brought us to the 7th of July and the *fiesta* de San Fermin, which was cheered so loudly that even the half deaf in yet distant Pamplona must have heard the din.

It was a large, happy though tired contingent that alighted eventually from the train. After having taken almost affectionate leave of our travelling companions, together with the members of my little gang, I made for the main square where more adventures awaited us. The town was packed with visitors from far and near, hotels, guesthouses and inns were so overcrowded that many guests were glad to be given any corner to sleep in. My companions being typical happy-go-lucky young Basques, they had not bothered to make reservations, with the result that we had no idea when and where we would get a little much-needed sleep. However, this did not bother them in the least, and whenever I brought up the subject of sleeping accommodation, I was told, "Don't worry, things will sort themselves out. After all, we did not come here to sleep, but to have a good time. Remember, the fun begins on the dot of 6.45 a.m., and there will be plenty of time after to look for a bed, if you really insist on finding one."

There being nothing I could do about lodgings at so late an hour, resigned to my fate I adopted my friends' mental attitude, and after having found an old-fashioned inn, together with them settled down to eating an enormous meal. In a back-room, between wine barrels we parked our motor-cycles, and when this was done, and before going away I had a final look at my machine, I envied it heartily for the luxury of a good rest, for by that time I was dog-tired, though happy to have reached Pamplona in time to see the great *fiesta* begin.

CHAPTER 22

PAMPLONA (FIESTA OF ST. FERMIN) – TRAIN JOURNEY TO BARCELONA

The annual Fair of Seville is refined art and beauty: it is the *fiesta* for ladies, but its counterpart in Pamplona is a rumpus for he-men, spelt with capital letters.   True, on the first day there is a religious procession, followed by a solemn Mass, and later there are diversions for children, theatrical shows, and, of course, dancing, but the bulk of the entertainment and fun is for men, though the women enjoy it as spectators.

Homeless, and without a place to rest my tired and weary limbs, I wandered about with my companions throughout the night. Fortunately some of the inns remained open, and in them were assembled crowds of men, all making merry whilst waiting for reveille which is given every day during the week of the *fiesta,* at 6.45 a.m., when brass bands, bagpipes[18] and *dulzainas* strike up, calling people out to see the daily rough-and-tumble which begins with a bang sharp at 7 a.m.

The streets and squares which lead from the river Arga to the bullring were strongly barricaded, and the cobble stones carefully covered with a thin layer of sand. Long before the eagerly awaited moment, every available point of vantage, balconies and windows which faced the barricaded streets, was crowded with people, and

---

[18] Bagpipes, though played in the Basque country, are not typical of those regions. They are the instruments of Galicia and Asturias.

thousands more had taken their places in the bullring where, for the morning's entertainment, admittance was free. Thanks to the invitation of a friendly inn-keeper, several members of my little gang, including myself, were given room on a balcony, whence we had a splendid view of the narrow street below us. There, every fifty yards or so, masses of men and even boys were assembled, all ready to begin what looked like a peculiar kind of relay race. With the passing of minutes, excitement grew, watches were consulted, and on the dot of 7 a.m. when, somewhere in the direction of the river, a rocket was fired into the air, a tremendous shout of joy of thousands of voices rolled and reverberated through the town. At the same instant, the runners in the street began to trot off in the direction of the bullring, and, shortly after, a kind of tidal wave of shouts and screams approached me from the opposite direction, growing louder and louder until it reached a bend, beyond which I could not see. As men came running round it, they raced as if for dear life, and then, suddenly, six or eight formidable fighting bulls followed them, tearing along at full speed, horning to the right and to the left as they overtook the runners, most of whom threw themselves flat on the ground as the leading animals caught up with them. Further along, men – who until then had only trotted at a leisurely pace – began to race as fast as they could, but very soon the bulls overtook them also, leaving many scattered on the ground, though, fortunately, none seriously hurt. Within a few moments the wild mêlée passed, and, shortly after, a rocket announced that the fearsome animals had reached the bullring. What I had witnessed – and was to witness again from different points of vantage every morning, sharp at seven, for a whole week – was the *encierro de los toros,* the shutting in of the bulls. During a tour of inspection, I was told a great deal about the technique of running in front of the beasts, and I was taken to a corral near the river where the wild stampede begins. Apparently, until recent years, local butchers reserved the right to run the first hundred yards or so, and after that the other men were at liberty to choose their own starting points. I was told that the most dangerous stretch is that which leads into the bullring where is a bottle-neck in which runners fairly pile up, and where the bulls sometimes trample on them, and horn the fallen. The distance between starting and finishing point is not quite half a mile, and therefore the animals cover it at a great pace, and, sand having been sprinkled over the cobble-stones, without slipping, and thus possibly injuring themselves. It must be borne in mind that good fighting bulls are expensive, and that those who have run through the streets in the morning are fought by professional bullfighters at half past five in the evening. Therefore, as soon as the beasts reach the bullring, they are taken to secluded quiet corrals behind it, there to rest until their turn arrives to be killed. The running before the bulls is a dangerous sport, and although fatal accidents have happened, and cuts, bruises and hard knocks are common, it is a form of amusement and bravado which but few local men would miss. The streets and alleyways between barricades are narrow, and along the entire length of the course there is not as much as a lamp-post behind which a runner can take refuge. Shallow doorways offer protection, provided the bulls charge past them, but should one turn and single out a man who fled into one, he would find himself in a very serious situation.

In order to miss nothing of this barbarous though thrilling and entertaining spectacle, every morning I took up a different position along the route, but I found that by far the best is inside the bullring where the wild race comes to a climax. There, some of the more daring runners who really want to show off, wave their jackets at the bulls, and if the would-be *toreros* can make a pass or two, they are not likely to forget the thunderous applause with which the public rewards them. One morning when one such dare-devil made a slight mistake, the bull knocked him down, and then proceeded to gore him, but fortunately a particularly courageous man was there to divert on to himself the beast's attention and rage, thus saving the man's life.

The real fun comes when the bulls have been driven into the corrals, and, one at a time, four wild cows are let into the ring, in which men swarm about like ants. The cows' horns are made more or less harmless with rubber balls affixed to their tips, but despite this the agile and infuriated beasts knock over men like ninepins, making them tumble in every direction, to the intense amusement of thousands of spectators, among whom, judging by the wild, almost hysterical screams, the women seem to be the most thrilled. As a *gran finale* to this extraordinary entertainment, two wild cows are let into the crowded ring together, and as they rush hither and thither, the con-fusion becomes such that the performers do not know whence the next attack will come, and that, consequently, there ensue most amusing situations and bouts of wholesale knocking-over. When this turbulent spectacle comes to an end, bands strike up, behind them their respective gangs line up, and then they begin to dance their way through the town. Women do not take part in this, and the men do their dancing and hopping about singly, with bent arms raised above their heads, and much pirouetting and kicking. Here and there, halts are made at inns, where wine flows in streams, and then on go the bands and merry dancers.

Having had no sleep, by eleven o'clock in the morning I began to feel so tired that I insisted on finding a bed or, failing this, at least a quiet corner where to sleep. My young and hardy companions were so amused by my lack of guts that from that time they jokingly called me "*Tio*" (Uncle), and later they went one better by changing this to "*Abuelo*" (Grandfather). After a long search, when we found a double bed on the fifth floor of an old house, without further ado I stretched myself out on the welcome softness, and within a few seconds fell into a deep sleep.

Normally, the room was occupied by a pleasant young couple who had a lovely fair and curly-haired boy of about five. Being poor workers, my temporary landlord and landlady were glad to earn a little extra money, and as their lodgings consisted of only two small rooms and a kitchen, and a relative had come to town for the *fiesta,* all of them slept in the room which adjoined mine, the grownups on the floor, on mattresses borrowed from obliging neighbours, and the boy in a small rickety bed.

Dead to the world, I slept like a log until my companions came clattering in to wake me up. Upon consulting my watch, I could hardly believe that three hours had passed since I had closed my eyes, and although I longed to remain where I was, several strong hands grabbed hold of me, and before I was properly awake, I was hustled down several flights of wooden steps, then down the street, and finally into a little shop, where I was fitted out with a large straw hat, a bright vermilion neckerchief, and white rope-soled slippers, decorated with vermilion tape. When the old man who ran the shop saw that a certain rather expensive type of hat was being chosen for me and my companions, with apologies he suggested that we buy cheaper ones. He went on, telling us that most likely we would lose our intended purchases, or that they would be destroyed, and that he ventured to prophesy that before long we would be back in his shop to buy new hats.

As it happened, his guess was right, for, sure enough, next morning we returned for a new supply.

Although during the feast of Saint Fermin no one has ever been robbed by the honest Basques, and even a drunkard's purse and other valuables are perfectly safe, the large straw hats are looked upon as anybody's property, or articles to be treated roughly.

Having disguised me as a Basque, my lively escort marched me to a tavern. There, apparently, while I had slept, my companions had joined a gang which had its own small brass band. And so it came about that before I realized what was happening, I was accepted as the newest member of this company of musicians and dancers. The event having been duly celebrated with wine, we set out in the direction of the bullring, band and banner in front, followed by dancers, and a rearguard consisting of a number of men who carried two demijohns filled with wine, and a variety of food-stuffs, including a huge kind of two-handled casserole which contained a hot stew.

Things had happened so quickly ever since I had been awakened, that it was only when we reached the sunny side of the arena that I began to realize what kind of a gang I had joined. One by one, other similar groups – all with their own little brass bands – marched and danced in to take their places near us, trumpets blared, big drums were thumped, and, behind each group, long banners were held aloft by men. Seeing that ours advertised a certain brew of beer, I asked one of my new buddies who happened to be standing alongside me, what was the meaning of this. To my surprise and consternation, he explained that the members of the gang I had joined were given free entry to the bullring, besides free wine and food, all of which was paid for by the brewery whose beer was being advertised on our banner. If ever I meet "Litri," Ortega or Carmona, the three *matadores* who performed that afternoon, I shall tell them about my gate-crashing in old Pamplona. In the meantime I must say that I thoroughly enjoyed myself, and that if the beer produced by the brewery is as good as the wine and food with which we were supplied, it can leave nothing to be desired.

During the bullfight, an *espontáneo* – one of the over-enthusiastic spectators who sometimes leap into the ring – managed to dodge the policeman and officials who are always on the look-out for such hot-heads. He was a young man of about twenty-five, and wore a white shirt and trousers and rope-soled slippers of the same colour, and round his neck a vermilion kerchief, and round his waist a sash to match. Before the surprised bullfighters had time to stop the intruder, he rushed towards the bull, who happened to be standing in the middle of the arena, ominously turning his head from side to side, wondering where to make his next attack. Without even a jacket or a piece of cloth wherewith to play the bull, the reckless *espontáneo* raced straight at the beast, which lowered its head and charged. Evidently the man hoped to side-step, and to reach the safety barrier before the beast could turn and catch up with him. However, man and bull met full on, with the result that the former was tossed high up into the air, to fall to the ground with a sickening thud. Having recovered from their surprise, some of the bullfighters rushed up, and with their capes drew away the bull, whereafter the victim of this mad escapade was carried out, apparently dead. Some time later, when it was officially announced that the dare-devil was not seriously hurt, a tremendous cheer went up from thousands of spectators. Such is the bravado of some *espontáneos,* but surely the one of this interlude must have been an outstandingly crazy one, almost a suicide.

The bullfight over, youths invaded the ring, and after having let them romp about, pretending to be fighting bulls, and *toreros,* it was our turn to climb over the barrier. Banners were unfurled, bands struck up, and the different gangs re-formed behind them, to dance their way out into the street. As, together with my merry group, I emerged into the open, there, lo and behold, among a crowd of spectators, craning their swan-like necks, and smiling sweetly, I caught sight of two old friends I had seen in Barcelona, in Seville and in Madrid . . . none other than the two precious young Englishmen, "Milo" and "Mila!"

I realized that evening how small the world can be, for whilst strolling about near the main square, waiting for the fireworks to begin, I recognized two other acquaintances in the persons of the balloon-vendors whom I had met during the Flower Festival in faraway Puente Areas. When I went to speak to them, it took them quite a while before they recognized me in my Basque disguise, and when one of my companions offered them his wine-skin, they quickly seized the golden opportunity in both hands.

At the cattle fair – which is held in a vast shaded field near the ancient citadel – I bumped into another old friend. Together with some of my companions I had gone to see the masses of horses, mules, donkeys and cattle which were being sold there, when, to my companion's astonishment, a young gipsy horse-dealer came to embrace me warmly. He was a nephew of the Guajiro whom I had befriended in Seville. These meetings so impressed the members of my gang that they said, "You seem to know everybody in Spain." Among many other items on the official programme was a picturesque procession of the city elders, most of whom wore quaint frock-coats, and, in some cases, picturesque official robes. Mace-bearers in knee-breeches walked along slowly and solemnly, and behind the procession came *cabezudos,* men wearing huge comical heads made of painted cardboard, and these, together with giants on high stilts, delighted the children. Outside one of the churches, men dressed in regional costumes performed several complicated Basque dances, the origin of which is lost in antiquity.

On the way back towards the centre of the town, we stopped to have a look round a market-place where only garlic was sold. The white bulbous roots were plaited together into long thick strings *(ristras)* and masses of these were hung up in stalls, or were piled up high on the ground. It being a local custom for revellers to walk about with a string of garlic hanging down from their necks, my companions bought one or two apiece, and although I did not like the idea of carrying about such a weight, a string was hung round my neck, whereafter we resumed our gay wanderings, going to crowded taverns to eat or drink something, to try our luck in raffles, and at about midnight to go for a while to the Chapel of Saint Fermin, where many devout, and not a few unsteady, tipplers offered short prayers. Whenever I suggested going to bed, my seemingly tireless companions laughed, and as my room was under the roof, they always told me, "Come on, *Abuelo,* there's plenty of time to go to the sparrows." It was during this *fiesta* that one of my greatest hankerings of my Spanish tour was fulfilled . . . I was photographed on a wooden horse! Yes, my great wish became a reality; and this is how it came about. Whilst walking across the crowded main square, there, almost in the middle of it, I spied one of those street photographers with two magnificent steeds, one of them a great big fiery beast, and the other a nice quiet-looking kind of Shetland pony, with a friendly look in his glass eyes. The marvellous sight made me stop and stare like a child looking at a Christmas tree, and when my friends asked me if I was feeling unwell, I just shook my head, and continued to stare, all the while longing to have the courage to make my dreams come true.

When, after a dramatic silence, during which my companions watched me as if on guard against the first symptoms of raving lunacy, I told them about my great ambition, they, also, were bitten by the wooden-horse bug, and so, soon after having stormed the photographer, we were busy choosing costumes which hung from two racks. Some disguised themselves as Mexican *charros,* with formidable wooden revolvers in holsters, others preferred American cowboy rig-outs, and one or two of the lazy ones among us just remained with what they wore. After having been photographed in pairs, the party warmed up, and to the amusement of onlookers we staged a hold-up after which I was grabbed and manhandled into a flowing skirt, to be photographed, pretending to make eyes at a *charro* who acted his part very well on the big horse, on the head of which a huge *sombrero* was placed.

For several practical reasons, I never travel far without taking with me a rope lasso. When coiled up properly and tightly, it takes but little room, and, besides coming in handy for many things, it provides me with excellent exercise when I feel like doing a little rope-spinning or lassoing of different objects. The rope I had brought with me from London was in constant use in Pamplona, where, with it, I entertained a great many people, performing all manner of tricks. Even during the bullfight already described, I was made to lasso several spectators, including two unsuspecting young French tourists who sat in front of us, annoying the members of my gang by shouting and yelling at the wrong time. When the loop fell round the pair, before they and I knew what was happening, the rope was snatched from me by two of my neighbours, and the poor Frenchmen were dragged from their seats, up the stand and out through an exit. I wonder what they had to say about bullfights and barbarous Basques when they returned to their homes in France.

On another occasion, at night, when we were waiting for the firework display to begin, my companions asked me to entertain them and bystanders with a little rope-spinning. Being in a merry mood, I did as requested, but the novelty of my show attracted so many onlookers that a policeman came elbowing his way through the crowd, to inform me that it was against rules and regulations to hold street-shows in busy thoroughfares, and that if I wanted to collect money, I would have to move to a side-street. When my friends told him that I was a visitor from abroad and an author, he looked at my Basque costume, next at my face, and then joined in the laughter of the crowd.

The daily programme being more or less the same throughout the week of the great *fiesta,* after having seen the bulls run through the town in the early morning, I had plenty of time to make excursions to nearby towns and villages. For this sort of thing I found my motor-cycle to be ideal, for apart from the cheapness of running it, I could go a long way in a few hours, and to places a car would have reached with difficulty.

Pamplona, about 1,400 feet above sea-level, is situated in the centre of an agricultural region, but it is also noted for its industries which, though not on a large scale, bring prosperity to the town. In country districts, chestnut, walnut, oak and fruit trees abound, meadows are green and slopes are richly clad with pines and ferns of different varieties, and in some more sheltered parts orange, lemon and palm trees thrive, and vines are cultivated wherever the soil is suitable. Many of the hardy and conservative peasants cling to the traditional two-wheeled ox-carts with elaborately carved yokes covered by a sheepskin. The Basques, who call themselves *Euskaldunak* – a word derived from their language, Euskara – have remained totally unaffected by the various occupations to which they were submitted after long and bitter fighting. Even the Romans who conquered them, failed to leave behind a lasting impression, save that of religion.

Whilst having something to eat in a little inn in a village I visited, I saw a Galician knife-sharpener coming down the street, pushing before him his wheel-barrow-like machine, at the same time playing a tune on his little Pan pipe. Hearing it, the inn-keeper turned to me and said, "This means rain." Puzzled by this laconic remark, I asked the man to explain what made him say that, whereupon he told me that in those parts it was a common belief that whenever a Galician knife-sharpener turns up in the region, he brings rain with him.

Though even peasants in these regions enjoy a much better education than people of the same standing get anywhere in Spain, many of them are surprisingly superstitious, and not a few believe in witch-craft. As pointed out before, Basques are rugged, strong and athletic, and the most typical among them are much fairer-skinned than Spaniards, especially so, those who live in the South. Fair hair and light-coloured eyes are not uncommon among them, but the women, though vivacious and good-looking, lack the gay spirit and grace of their cousins further South.

Whenever I returned to Pamplona after one of my excursions, I found my friends carrying on the spree. Occasionally they had a snooze in some tavern, and after a swim in the river they were ready to start afresh, whereas I, their "Grandfather," believed in going to "the sparrows" to have a lie down, but invariably I was hauled out long before I was ready, and thus, during that hectic week, my daily average of sleep was about three hours. How true the popular Navarrese song my seemingly untiring friends used to sing. Part of it goes as follows:

En las fiestas de San Fermin	At the feast of San Fermin
Es todo una gran locura,	Everything is a great madness
No dejan a uno dormir	They do not let one sleep
Pero el vino todo 10 cura.	But the wine cures it all.

And the chorus.

Ay Gabino! Ay Gabino!
Cómo te vas a poner,
Con la bota, con la bota, llena de vino
Y el chorizo, y el chonzo Pamplonês.

Oh Gabino! Oh Gabino!
What kind of a mess are you going to make of yourself,
With the wine-skin, with the wine-skin, full of wine,
And the sausage, and the sausage, of Pamplona?

Among the interesting things I saw in the town was a small museum in which are kept numerous gifts the famous violinist, Sarasate, received from Royal and other personages. Sarasate, who died in 1908 at the age of sixty four, was a native of Pamplona where he was beloved by everybody. Even after having reached the height of his glory and fame, during the feast of Saint Fermin he often played the violin in the main square, and sometimes in humble taverns. In my story in Chapter XV, about the last Duke of Frias, I have already referred to Sarasate, and as I had a very remote link with the great virtuoso, my visit to the museum meant more to me than it would have done otherwise.

On the last day of the feast, which ends at midnight, about an hour or so before that time, groups of men and boys walk through the streets slowly, carrying in their hands lighted candles. Even if no small brass bands accompany the various groups, a slow and mournful song is sung, and when it comes to the words, "Poor San Fermin dies," the singers stagger and lie down on the ground, soon after to rise and to begin the song over again. And, indeed, by that time most of the musicians and merry-makers must be nearly dead, for the spree has been going on for a solid week, without interruption, day and night.

Though looking distinctly the worse for wear, my companions carried on as usual, and when they told me they had made up their minds to escort me as far as Zaragoza, I became apprehensive. "This is our annual *chufla*" (a Basque slang word meaning "binge"), they said, "and we have lots of friends on the way. After having seen you safely to Zaragoza, we shall return home to work for another year." Coming from my friends at that time, the word "safely" failed to inspire me with confidence, and when I pictured my gang on motor-cycles, calling on the "lots of friends on the way," I held my breath and blinked my eyes.

To make a long and amusing story short, in order to avoid accidents, I had a faked telegram sent to me, urging me to return to Barcelona by train as soon as possible. This did the trick, for it made my good and over-enthusiastic friends decide to return home by train, for by that time even they began to realize that their glorious spree had lasted long enough.

After affectionate farewells, the last I saw of them was when they departed, loaded with presents for their respective families, wine-skins slung over their shoulders, and, hanging from their necks, heavy strings of garlic. Despite hoarseness, they sang the song about Gabino, and when it came to the last verse:

Al terminarse las fiestas	When the feast ends
Se va uno por su camino,	One goes on one's way,
Muy alegre y sin pesetas	Very happy and without money
Con su bota va Gabino.	With his wine-skin goes Gabino.

they waved a final farewell and cheered loudly.

As, during excursions from Pamplona, I had seen most of the regions between that town and Zaragoza, save an uninteresting arid stretch of about sixty miles, I looked forward to another experience on a train. The regions between Zaragoza, Lérida and Barcelona I had traversed during the early stages of my tour, but unfortunately time did not permit me to visit the nearby Pyrenees, of which I had seen something nearly four months earlier.

The last ten days had been so hectic that I looked forward to a much-needed rest on the train, but it was not to be. As usual, I took a third-class ticket, but owing to the exodus from Pamplona after the *fiesta,* the train was packed. Into my compartment were squeezed two elderly stolid Basque farmers, three happy boot-blacks who had done a good trade, and a family of five, which included a toddler and a voracious suckling. Our veritable travelling menagerie left Pamplona at 4 p.m. and as the sun had been blazing down all day, and was still high up in the sky, soon the temperature and atmosphere in our compartment became trying, to put it mildly. The two old farmers' black smocks smelt strongly of cattle, the boot-blacks had a bouquet all their own, and the baby and the toddler contributed with an odour suggestive of a cat-house in a Zoological Garden. When the woman peeled oranges for her children, and the farmers began to smoke thin black cigars, the acrid stench of which mingled with that produced by the boot-blacks' rank-smelling cigarettes, I could not help wondering if, perhaps I, also, contributed a whiff to the olfactory pot-pourri of our crowded compartment. The farmers, whose faces and aquiline noses looked as if they had been carved out of mahogany, sat in silence, looking at fields and farm-houses with expert eyes, and when, at long intervals, they made a short remark concerning something they had seen, they spoke in Basque. The hoot-blacks were jolly fellows who laughed and joked all the time. Of course, they had with them wine-skins, and whenever one of them felt like wetting his parched palate, before doing so he offered everybody his *bota.* The farmers always refused with thanks, saying that during railway journeys they preferred water, of which they had brought a supply in an earthenware jar. Every available place was stacked up with bundles, paper parcels and wicker-baskets filled with food, and whenever somebody felt like eating, and bread, sausage, cheese or fruit were unpacked, everybody was asked to partake in the meal.

We had been travelling about two hours when a young man who wore civilian clothes appeared at the door of our compartment. Having turned up the lapel of his jacket to reveal an official badge, he asked for passes and passports. When I produced mine, he looked at it and me with surprise, evidently taken aback to find a tourist travelling third class in such mixed company. "Where have you come from?" he asked rather officiously. "From Pamplona," I replied. "But", he came back, "the last entry on your *triptico* was made in Santillana, nearly two weeks ago. Where have you been since then?"

"Oh," I said, "all over the country; Santander, Bilbao, San Sebastian and many other places, including a week in Pamplona to see the great *chufia* (spree). You see, I was so busy enjoying myself that I forgot all about the *triptico.*"

This made the two boot-blacks laugh boisterously, and even the two stolid farmers grinned. However, the official took a very different view of the matter, so I told him that I had with me a special recommendation to the military and civil authorities, but before I had time to find it among my papers, one of the hitherto sphinx-like farmers rose from his seat, and, shaking a horny warning finger at the official, began to bellow, now in Spanish, "The manner and tone in which you speak to this *caballero,* a welcome visitor from abroad, is shame to our country, and having to listen to what you say, I take it as a personal insult. Who and what do you think you are? Begone at once, or when we get to Zaragoza I shall deal with you as you deserve!"

To my astonishment, the official handed me back my passport as quickly as he could, and made off down the crowded corridor of the train, whilst the farmer shouted insults and threats after him. Even after having resumed his seat, the man in the black smock went on mumbling to himself, but presently he apologized to me for what had happened, and then resumed his staring out of the window.

I was glad when the sun set and the temperature became cooler, and it came as a great relief to all of us grown-up people when, at last, the children dropped off to sleep. After many stops and country stations, at about 11 p.m. the slow-moving train steamed in to Zaragoza, where some of our coaches were to be hooked on to the Madrid-Barcelona express. We must have been waiting for well over two hours when the news began to circulate that the engine of the express had broken down, and that there would be a delay. Sellers of lemonade, fruit and contraband bread came along the corridors, shouting their wares, and some of them did a roaring trade. It was only after we had been shunted outside the station that porters remembered that they had to load many boxes and crates into the goods van, so after much vociferation and argument, the work was done, carrying the heavy loads, instead of wheeling them along the platform. The boot-blacks having taken their leave like departing friends, there was more room in our compartment, and when I asked the two farmers how far they were going, they told me that they would be getting off the train at the next station. I was interested to watch how little water they drank at a time; and when I asked them why they were so careful with it, they replied that the supply they had with them came from their home, and went on to explain to me that it was not advisable to drink the water of any region to which one was not accustomed, the change being likely to cause a stomach upset.

This brings me to an important point tourists will do well to remember. People who have travelled in foreign parts are apt to tell one that almost everywhere abroad potable water is bad or even dangerous. In the vast majority of cases this is nonsense, for the natives who drink the water are perfectly healthy people who thrive on the liquid wells and fountains provide for them. However, when those same people travel through regions where mineral and other influences change the taste and properties of the water, they take good care to drink as little as possible, unless it be wine or bottled mineral water. In Spanish villages and towns I have met natives who, upon tasting water that was brought to their houses, could tell immediately from which fountain it was drawn. It is a well-known fact that Spanish bullfighters, who have to do a great deal of travelling from one region to another, drink only wine and certain bottled mineral waters of their fancy. This they do because changing from one kind of water to another might easily cause an internal upset, and thus temporarily incapacitate them for their dangerous work. For the same reason, my travelling companions, the two Basque farmers, took with them a supply of water from their home.

Daylight was beginning to appear when the Madrid-Barcelona express crawled into Zaragoza station. Instead of hurrying to make up for time lost, the railway officials took things tantalizingly easy, but at long last our now long convoy began to move, and when the sun rose I found myself in familiar country, through which, four months before, I had ridden on my motor-cycle. Here and there landmarks brought back memories, and when we approached our destination, I had some wonderful views of the grotesque jagged peaks of Monserrat with its weird rock formations.

The train arrived in Barcelona five and a half hours late, but apparently nobody worried, and I, though tired, dishevelled and dirty, was glad to have made the trip. Soon after my motor-cycle had been unloaded, and my equipment strapped on to it, I rode towards the centre of the town, and thence to some hills near the outskirts where my good friends and hosts, Julio and Rosemary, had their house. I could hardly believe it that since having set out from there, on my machine alone, I had covered three thousand five hundred miles, which means that with journeys by car, motor-bus and by train, I had travelled well over five thousand miles.

The servants must have heard me approach, for before I arrived at the gate, they were there to welcome me, and as my hosts happened to be out, after a much-needed bath and a meal, I went up to my room where, in the shape of a glorious *siesta,* to have my first decent sleep in an exhausting though unforgettably delightful fortnight. When my friends returned home and found me in their sitting-room, still half asleep, much reduced in weight, sun-burnt, and my voice so husky that I could hardly speak, they roared with laughter. "Heavens!" they shouted, "you sound as if you had laryngitis, and you look as if you had been in the wars!" "Not in the wars," I half croaked, half whispered in reply, "only to the feast of Saint Fermin, and after it the whole night, and until noon to-day in a packed third-class compartment of a train. If my companions of the big spree were here now, and if you had been on that railway journey with me, you would understand, but, nevertheless, I would not have missed those experiences for anything in the world, so cheers for the good old *fiesta* of Saint Fermin, and cheers for my friends, the Basques!"

CHAPTER 23

BARCELONA – RETURN TO LONDON VIA PARIS AND CALAIS

Towards the end of July I made preparations for my return to London. As it was getting uncomfortably hot in Barcelona, many people who could afford it left for cooler regions, some going to nearby seaside resorts and others to places situated among the foothills of the Pyrenees. Although, as far as I was concerned, it looked as if my adventures had come to an end, several others were in store for me.

One morning, remembering the useless rubber soles that fat rascal of a Basque boot-black had cunningly tacked on my shoes – some four months previously, shortly before I had set out on my tour – I returned to the *café* outside which he carried on his trade, for it was my intention, just for fun, to let him have a piece of my mind. Whilst I sat at a table, waiting for my intended victim to appear, several other boot-blacks came to offer me their services, but the jovial ex-sailor, baker in the Argentine, and ex-jail-bird for having "hopped" his ship, remained invisible. Eventually, when I let another *lustrador* give my shoes a shine, whilst he worked away I asked him if "El Gordo" ("Fatty") had gone away. "Oh, no," came the reply, "he is still knocking about here, but we don't see much of him nowadays." After that, every time I passed near that *café,* I looked out for the fat rascal; but in vain.

Three days before I said *adios* to Barcelona and Spain, I witnessed a most original and amusing bullfight, in which only boys took part. Naturally, the bulls, though fierce, were small, but all the youthful performers wore proper bullfighters' costumes, and all of them acted as if they were famous *matadores,* especially so a nipper of twelve who became the star turn of the afternoon. Save for the absence of horses and *picadores* (lancers), everything was done exactly as in a display given by veterans, though with the slight difference that a grown-up expert – who wore leather chaps and the *vaquero* costume of Andalusia – was there with a cape, ready to help the boys when they got themselves into trouble, which some of them did frequently. For sheer swank and bravado, the greatest and most arrogant *matador* could not have surpassed the good-looking nipper of twelve, and when he killed his bull with the first thrust of his *estoque,* the applause with which he was rewarded was terrific, and when he did his round of honour, masses of presents were thrown at his feet, including a pair of shoes a lady had taken off and flung into the ring in the excitement. Some of the other performers were not as lucky and skilful, and consequently several of them sustained nasty knocks, and there were a few narrow escapes from serious injury, or even worse. However, despite such incidents, the boys enjoyed themselves thoroughly, though, as the occasion demanded, they took themselves and their dangerous work very seriously.

Every time, before a bull was let into the arena, a man who wore white knee-breeches, white shoes, stockings, a kind of cavalier's jacket and a Napoleon hat – all of the same colour – took up his position in the middle of the ring, on a low wooden platform which was painted white. When everything was ready, he raised a bugle to his lips, and blew a challenging call, which was the signal for the trap-door to be raised, and the bull to be released into the arena. With his bugle held to his lips, the man in white remained absolutely motionless, like a marble statue. Then, with a wild rush and fearful snorts, the bull came tearing into the bright sunlight, horning the wooden barrier as he passed. Presently, catching sight of the white figure, he lowered his head, and charged it at full speed, but, at the last moment, when it seemed that all was over for the daring performer, the bull came to a sudden standstill. For a little while he stared suspiciously at the rigid figure before him, and then, evidently not liking the looks of the mysterious object, he scratched the ground with a foreleg and threw sand on his back – which is a sure sign that a bull is looking for trouble. Then, as if puzzled and somewhat afraid, the beast began to move backwards, but all the time keeping its eyes fixed on the man in white, who did not bat an eyelid. Having described a semi-circle round the statuesque figure, the bull changed his mind, and charged it from behind, again to stop when he was only a few inches from it. Such charges were repeated three or four times, until some of the boy bullfighters jumped into the ring to wave their capes. The sight of these made the bull turn his attention to them, and at an opportune moment the man in white made off towards the wooden barrier, to the applause of the public. The pedestal on which he had stood having been removed by attendants, the real bullfight began.

The trick described above is called *suerte de Don Tancredo,* so named after a certain Tancredo Lopez who first introduced it to Spain. Tancredo Lopez was a Valencian who had wished, at one time, to become a star of the bullring. On his tours through Latin America, whilst acting as assistant to a *matador,* he saw this novel trick being practised by a Mexican – nick-named "Orizabeño" – who was later killed whilst performing the act. Lopez did it on his return to Spain, in 1899, whereafter it became popular, but after he had been badly gored several times, the authorities forbade the trick. Later the ban was lifted, but Lopez was ousted and eclipsed by imitators – among them one or two women – who came in with many variations of the original act, which was to personify a marble statue on a low white pedestal. Tancredo Lopez died, ignored and forgotten – except for his Christian name – in the Charity Hospital of Valencia in 1923.

Our Don Tancredo of that afternoon in Barcelona was successful with every bull, until one who had charged him from behind nearly got him. This is how it came about. After the beast had stopped its wild career, to stare at and sniff the motionless figure, and was beginning to lose interest in it, a spectator who was seated in the front row shouted something, which made the bull turn his head. As he was standing very close to the performer, one horn caught him behind a knee, causing him to fall off the pedestal. If ever a marble statue came to life quickly, it was our poor Don Tancredo. Before he had time to rise, the bull was on top of him, but almost at the same instant, as if by magic, two hitherto invisible men appeared with capes to entice the bull away. Leaving his hat and bugle behind, the man in white made for the wooden barrier as fast as his knee-breeches allowed him, but before he reached safety, the bull caught sight of him, and, giving chase, caught up with the desperate fugitive as he vaulted over the boards, and just in time to give him an extra lift in the posterior, sending him spinning high up into the air, and to land on the other side with a thump.

Though badly shaken and bruised, the man recovered in time to take his place in the middle of the arena before the next bull was released through the trap-door, but this time it was a limping white Napoleon who climbed on to the pedestal, and when he blew his bugle, it seemed to me that the call lacked the defiance of those he had played before having met his Waterloo. Despite this, however, I could not help admiring him for his pluck, for surely, whilst standing there, rigid, and probably holding his breath, he must have longed to be far away, with better company near him than that of the bull, who, after the first charge, snorted and sniffed in his direction with ominous suspicion.

There was almost a riot when the show came to an end, people cheered those of the boys who had distinguished themselves, and a crowd of urchins invaded the arena to chair the *matador* of twelve. Two hours later, when I sat outside a *café* in the centre of the town, I heard a great noise coming towards me, and after a while appeared a mass of wildly cheering and shouting boys. Above this avalanche of youngsters, carried on the shoulders of several enthusiasts, came the little hero of the afternoon, still wearing the glittering costume of a *matador*. Though visibly tired, dishevelled and most uncomfortable in his position, he smiled proudly and waved back at those of the people who clapped their hands as he was being carried past them.

On the following day, when I went to a grocer's store with my hostess, there I was introduced to a boy of about sixteen who had also distinguished himself during the juvenile bullfight. His boss, for whom the boy worked as errand boy, told me that the youth never missed an opportunity to be near bulls, or to handle and study them and their ways, when any were about. Although for all the risks the boy had run on the previous day, and for all the knocks received and bruises sustained, he had received only a hundred *pesetas* (roughly one pound), he was delighted, and he looked forward to the day when he would be given another opportunity to show his courage and skill. His boss – who did not like bullfights – told me jokingly, "I don't understand the boy's mentality. He loves bulls, and he enjoys looking after them, and yet, on the other hand, he goes to torment and to kill them."

Having taken leave of a number of friends, when everything was ready for my return journey to London, Julio, my host, came to see me off at the station. Whilst the two of us walked through the main hall, towards the platform from which the train was to leave, suddenly Julio stopped, and, catching hold of one of my arms, exclaimed, at the same time pointing towards a man who hurried along in front of us, carrying a brand-new leather brief-case, "Look, I'll be hanged if this isn't 'El Gordo' the Basque boot-black who played the trick on you with the rubber soles!"

The man must have overheard what was spoken, for he turned round, and upon recognizing us, rushed up to greet us most warmly. After this, for a few moments, I looked him up and down, wondering if my eyes were deceiving me. Instead of dirty and greasy dark-blue overalls, "El Gordo" now wore brand-new light-coloured gabardine trousers, with creases so neatly pressed that one could have sharpened a pencil on them. His shoes and leather belt were of excellent quality, and as it was rather hot, he wore no jacket, but a fine linen shirt with his monogram beautifully embroidered on the breast pocket.

"*Atorrante!*" (Argentine slang for "low-down bounder"), I exclaimed, "what is the meaning of this transformation? Do you remember those rubber soles, and the dirty trick you played on me when you tacked them on my shoes? They came off two days after I set out from here, and I had to throw them away, up among the hills where, for all I know, they are still lying by the wayside. Come, you bounder, tell me what you are doing here."

Grinning up to his ears, the fat one waved a hand, and began by saying that the shoe-shining business was a thing of the past, as far as he was concerned, and that, therefore, I had better forget about those rubber soles. "Now," he went on, raising his head, and acting the part of a very proud and haughty man, "now I am in important business; I deal in foreign currencies, or, to be more explicit and quite frank, I am working for a boss who deals in black market money. Yes, and a splendid job mine is; short hours, and if I hook a good fish or two, most lucrative. And, of course, we have one or two other side-lines."

Laughing sarcastically, Julio interrupted, "What the devil do *you* know about foreign currencies and rates of exchange? Come on, don't be ridiculous!"

"Ridiculous?" the fat one came back, grinning all over, and with a cunning smile in his eyes. "I'll show you what you call ridiculous.

Just listen, and then tell me if you still think I know nothing about foreign currencies and rates of exchange." With this "El Gordo" began to rattle off the various rates of exchange he offered for the buying or selling of French, Belgian and Swiss francs, Italian *liras,* Portuguese *escudos,* and so on. This done, he said, "But, standing here, talking to you, finds me no clients. I must be off to the platform from which the international express is due to leave within half an hour, so *adios* and good luck to you."

And, indeed, as I stood on the platform alongside the train which was to take me to the French border, there was "El Gordo," rushing hither and thither, sometimes boarding the train, or again taking a passenger aside, evidently "hooking a good fish or two," and when the train began to move, and I waved final farewells to my grand host and friend, Julio, a little further along the platform I saw the bulky figure of "El Gordo" who, holding his leather brief-case above his head, waved it to and fro, thus adding a professional touch to his *adios* to me.

The journey back to Port Bou – the Spanish border town – was uneventful and pleasant, but when, upon arriving there, the Customs House officials saw my motor-cycle, as on the occasion of my entry into Spain, I ran into red tape. Though polite and obliging, the officials explained to me that according to laws and regulations I could not take the machine across the border in the train, but that I must *ride* it into French territory, and there load it on the train in Cerbère. My luggage and equipment, they said, could be conveyed to the said town on the train, and they promised that they would see to it that everything arrived safely. There being no alternative, I made ready to race the train across the high mountain pass where I had met with so much adventure four months before. But there was another hitch. According to regulations which demand that motor vehicles carried on trains have no petrol in their tanks, I had emptied the last drop out of mine, prior to embarking in Barcelona; so now, in Port Bou, the first thing I had to do before tackling the mountain pass was to look for sufficient petrol to take me over to Cerbère. As I had given away my last remaining coupons in Barcelona, I had to look for somebody who would let me have some *estraperlo* (black market) "juice," but fortunately I obtained this without difficulty, and so, without delay I set out, uphill, following the steep winding road I had ample reason to remember well. At the Spanish border-post officials had been advised by telephone that I would be arriving soon, and that I would be in a great hurry. Therefore, I found them waiting for me, and soon after I had handed in my passport and papers connected with the motor-cycle, they were returned to me, duly stamped and signed, and I resumed my race with the officials' best wishes. The same thing, more or less, happened at the French post, and then began the descent towards nearby Cerbère. By that time I was so used to ticklish mountain roads, and even tracks, that I felt quite at ease on my machine, and as no violent *mistral* blew, and I was not being towed, as on the former occasion when I made this crossing, all went well, and I arrived at the station in good time to catch the train. However, before boarding it, I ran into another serious difficulty. The Spanish money with which I was left was not sufficient to pay for the transport of the motor-cycle from Cerbère via Paris to London, and as, for reasons incomprehensible to me, nobody would give me French currency for two of the five pounds I had been allowed to take out of England, I found myself in a most unpleasant predicament, until a perfect stranger – who happened to be a Spaniard – came to my rescue, lending me the necessary francs, with the understanding that, if possible, I would reimburse him at my convenience.

During the long night journey from Cerbère to Paris I was left with so little French money that I could not afford to have a meal, but as it was very hot in my compartment – in which travelled two middle-aged women, a man, his wife and their two hopefuls, a boy aged about seventeen and a girl of fifteen – I began to feel so thirsty that, after having counted my francs, I bought myself a bottle of lemonade, for which, incidentally, I was charged an exorbitant price. When my travelling companions unpacked baskets filled with most appetising foods and wine, spread napkins, over their laps, and generally prepared to begin their epicurean onslaught, unlike Spaniards, they did not offer me to partake in their meal. I am mentioning this, not because I would have accepted the offer, even if it had been made, but just to show how conventions and customs between neighbouring countries can vary. Despite the stifling heat, after darkness had fallen, the windows and door were closed hermetically, electric lights were switched off, leaving only one of bluish-purple colour to give a faint light, and everybody, save myself, wriggled into position to sleep. The boy, who wore the shortest of shorts, covered his long spindly shanks with a shawl, and soon after, all I could hear was the rhythmic rattling of wheels as they passed over joints of the rails, and a concert of deep breathing, wheezing, puffing, gurgling and snoring. When the atmosphere in the compartment became unbearable, I went to stand in the corridor, and at long intervals when the train stopped at a station, I paced up and down the platform. Towards morning, when I returned to my seat to rest my legs, I found the sleepers in various weird positions, two leaning against each other, others doubled up, or with their legs on the laps of others. I was glad when we reached Austerlitz station in Paris, where I shared a taxi with an Englishman who appeared to be as short of francs as I was. The two of us were busy putting our light luggage into the vehicle, when a porter came rushing up to give me an unsolicited hand, and when we were ready to depart, and my companion gave him fifty francs for having done nothing, the porter protested, saying that the tip was an insult. He made such a noise, and became so offensive that, to his blank astonishment, I cut loose, slanging him in gutter French. When I finished my verbal barrage by saying that if he did not go away forthwith, there would be serious trouble between the two of us, the man slunk away, mumbling to himself, and every now and again waving the fifty franc note in disgust. Soon after this tiff we were on our way to the Gare du Nord, but although my taxi companion invited me to go with him to meet some friends of his, I preferred to spend the next five hours alone, waiting for the Calais express to leave. I had just enough francs left to be able to give a reasonable tip to a porter in Paris, and to another in Calais, so I did not want to go and sponge on perfect strangers who would be sure to entertain me. Besides my reserve for tips, I had enough money to have a cup of *café au lait* and a *croissant* or two, and as I had eaten nothing since having had a light lunch in Barcelona, my stomach expressed its disapproval by growling and snarling. I was about to go to a nearby *café* when I remembered that my hair needed cutting, but as my funds were not sufficient for this operation and coffee as well, for a few moments I stood, unable to decide which of the two it was to be: *café au lait et des croissants, ou me faire couper les cheveux.* Eventually I took a coin out of my pocket, and, spinning it, said to myself, "Heads it's coffee and *croissants,* tails it's a hair-cut." Heads it was, so across the road I went to a nearby *café,* and after having attended to my inner man, there being no place where one could sit in the station, I wandered about its close vicinity, indulging in window-shopping, looking at books, and watching passers-by.

Whilst standing near the entrance to a subway which leads into the station, I witnessed a short one-act comedy which amused me immensely. A typical *Parisienne* came promenading along with a poodle on a lead. As the dog passed the iron railing of the entrance to the subway, he lifted a leg, and, as ill-chance would have it, at that moment a man came up the steps. For a brief moment he acted as if he were under the impression that it had begun to rain, but upon realizing what had wetted him, he raced up the last few steps, and then ensued a scene, the faithful re-enacting of which would be beyond the capabilities of the best comedian. The whole incident was over in less than a minute, for after having listened to the protests of the injured party for a few moments, the woman called the man an insolent *espèce* of this and that, and marched away with a disdainful shrug of her shoulders.

During the next four hours I had to wait before being allowed to board the train, I got to know the contents of all the book-stalls and shop windows in and near the station, but, at last, my weary walking up and down came to an end.

The trip to Calais was quite pleasant, and after having got rid of my remaining francs to *porteurs* who behaved and made a noise like hungry sea-gulls when a shrimp is washed up on a beach, I boarded the Cross-Channel steamer, on which I had to stand in a long queue until we were in the harbour of Dover. This queuing for having passports inspected, I found to be so trying that it is a wonder to me that tourists bother to come to spend their money in Britain. However, in fairness to the Home Office officials, it must be said that these cherubim, and the "flaming sword which they turn in every way, to keep the way" (to quote from the Book of Genesis) into the British Garden of Eden, were quite polite, and in the case of Americans most pleasant and almost effusive, for evidently these cherubim realize that the golden apples for the British Treasury's tree of life come from America. The Customs House official who dealt with me was a very different type to the one ill-fortune had guided me to on departing from England. Now, on my return, when I was asked if I had anything to declare, and I replied, "not a sausage," I was asked no further questions, my luggage was marked with chalk, and I was allowed to depart.

During the railway journey from Dover to London, I found it difficult to believe that on the previous day I had still been in Spain, and that during the past four months I had covered many hundreds of miles, travelling all over the vast Iberian Peninsula. I saw myself saying *adios* to the Spanish border officials outside their post on that high and ticklish Pyrenean pass, and then hurrying down towards Cerbère in France, where I had to catch the train. With great gusto I remembered something that had happened whilst I zigzagged my way down the steep incline, something I forgot to mention when, in this chapter, I described this experience.

Accustomed to winding mountain roads, every now and again, when I could see stretches of it below me, I looked out for vehicles which might be coming uphill towards me, and thus to guard against a surprise at some sharp bend. Seeing no cars, I merrily rounded curve after curve, and, whilst doing this, the thought ran through my head that, very soon, I would be back in England where traffic keeps to the left-hand side of the road. Instinctively and half absent-mindedly, I went over to the left, and as I approached a hair-pin bend, suddenly, as if from nowhere, appeared a large touring car, coming uphill towards me. For a fraction of a second I was so taken aback that I hesitated and flustered, and then I swerved across the road to the right side, and as I passed the car, its driver – who must have had as big a fright and surprise as I – put his head out of the window, to bellow at me, "BURRO!" And, indeed, I had been an ass, but even at the time it struck me that this exclamation was a grand finale to a marvellous tour, and now I hope that by the time the reader and the carping critic who have accompanied me through all these many pages, come to these last lines, they will not exclaim as that Spanish motorist did, "BURRO!"

And with this, gentle reader, I say to you, "I hope you have enjoyed my story, *mil gracias y buena suerte,* a thousand thanks, and good luck to you."

OUR CURRENT LIST OF TITLES

Abdullah, Morag Mary, *My Khyber Marriage* - Morag Murray departed on a lifetime of adventure when she met and fell in love with Sirdar Ikbal Ali Shah, the son of an Afghan warlord. Leaving the comforts of her middle-class home in Scotland, Morag followed her husband into a Central Asia still largely unchanged since the 19th century.

Abernathy, Miles, *Ride the Wind* – the amazing true story of the little Abernathy Boys, who made a series of astonishing journeys in the United States, starting in 1909 when they were aged five and nine!

Atkinson, John, *Afghan Expedition* – The author travelled to Afghanistan in 1838. He had been designated the Superintending Surgeon of a massive British invasion force resolved to place a sympathetic ruler on the Afghan throne. Soon after Atkinson was released from duty, and thus escaped the catastrophe which awaited his comrades. During the subsequent rebellion the British political agent was beheaded and an estimated 16,000 British soldiers and their dependents were slaughtered in a week by the vengeful Afghans. This book is a must for anybody interested in Afghanistan – then and now.

Beard, John, *Saddles East* – John Beard determined as a child that he wanted to see the Wild West from the back of a horse after a visit to Cody's legendary Wild West show. Yet it was only in 1948 – more than sixty years after seeing the flamboyant American showman – that Beard and his wife Lulu finally set off to follow their dreams.

Beker, Ana, *The Courage to Ride* – Determined to out-do Tschiffely, Beker made a 17,000 mile mounted odyssey across the Americas in the late 1940s that would fix her place in the annals of equestrian travel history.

Bird, Isabella, *Among the Tibetans* – A rousing 1889 adventure, an enchanting travelogue, a forgotten peek at a mountain kingdom swept away by the waves of time.

Bird, Isabella, *On Horseback* in *Hawaii* – The Victorian explorer's first horseback journey, in which she learns to ride astride, in early 1873.

Bird, Isabella, *Journeys in Persia and Kurdistan, Volumes 1 and 2* – The intrepid Englishwoman undertakes another gruelling journey in 1890.

Bird, Isabella, *A Lady's Life in the Rocky Mountains* – The story of Isabella Bird's adventures during the winter of 1873 when she explored the magnificent unspoiled wilderness of Colorado. Truly a classic.

Bird, Isabella, *Unbeaten Tracks in Japan, Volumes One and Two* – A 600-mile solo ride through Japan undertaken by the intrepid British traveller in 1878.

Blackmore, Charles, *In the Footsteps of Lawrence of Arabia* - In February 1985, fifty years after T. E. Lawrence was killed in a motor bicycle accident in Dorset, Captain Charles Blackmore and three others of the Royal Green Jackets Regiment set out to retrace Lawrence's exploits in the Arab Revolt during the First World War. They spent twenty-nine days with meagre supplies and under extreme conditions, riding and walking to the source of the Lawrence legend.

Boniface, Lieutenant Jonathan, *The Cavalry Horse and his Pack* – Quite simply the most important book ever written in the English language by a military man on the subject of equestrian travel.

Bosanquet, Mary, *Saddlebags for Suitcases* – In 1939 Bosanquet set out to ride from Vancouver, Canada, to New York. Along the way she was wooed by love-struck cowboys, chased by a grizzly bear and even suspected of being a Nazi spy, scouting out Canada in preparation for a German invasion. A truly delightful book.

de Bourboulon, Catherine, *Shanghai à Moscou (French)* – the story of how a young Scottish woman and her aristocratic French husband travelled overland from Shanghai to Moscow in the late 19th Century.

Brown, Donald; *Journey from the Arctic* – A truly remarkable account of how Brown, his Danish companion and their two trusty horses attempt the impossible, to cross the silent Arctic plateaus, thread their way through the giant Swedish forests, and finally discover a passage around the treacherous Norwegian marshes.

Bruce, Clarence Dalrymple, *In the Hoofprints of Marco Polo* – The author made a dangerous journey from Srinagar to Peking in 1905, mounted on a trusty 13-hand Kashmiri pony, then wrote this wonderful book.

Burnaby, Frederick; *A Ride to Khiva* – Burnaby fills every page with a memorable cast of characters, including hard-riding Cossacks, nomadic Tartars, vodka-guzzling sleigh-drivers and a legion of peasant ruffians.

Burnaby, Frederick, *On Horseback through Asia Minor* – Armed with a rifle, a small stock of medicines, and a single faithful servant, the equestrian traveler rode through a hotbed of intrigue and high adventure in wild inhospitable country, encountering Kurds, Circassians, Armenians, and Persian pashas.

Carter, General William, *Horses, Saddles and Bridles* – This book covers a wide range of topics including basic training of the horse and care of its equipment. It also provides a fascinating look back into equestrian travel history.

Cayley, George, *Bridle Roads of Spain* – Truly one of the greatest equestrian travel accounts of the 19th Century.

Chase, J. Smeaton, *California Coast Trails* – This classic book describes the author's journey from Mexico to Oregon along the coast of California in the 1890s.

Chase, J. Smeaton, *California Desert Trails* – Famous British naturalist J. Smeaton Chase mounted up and rode into the Mojave Desert to undertake the longest equestrian study of its kind in modern history.

Chitty, Susan, and Hinde, Thomas, *The Great Donkey Walk* - When bio-grapher Susan Chitty and her novelist husband, Thomas Hinde, decided it was time to embark on a family adventure, they did it in style. In Santiago they bought two donkeys whom they named Hannibal and Hamilcar. Their two small daughters, Miranda (7) and Jessica (3) were to ride Hamilcar. Hannibal, meanwhile, carried the baggage. The walk they planned to undertake was nothing short of the breadth of southern Europe.

Christian, Glynn, *Fragile Paradise: The discovery of Fletcher Christian, "Bounty" Mutineer* – the great-great-great-great-grandson of the *Bounty* mutineer brings to life a fascinating and complex character history has portrayed as both hero and villain, and the real story behind a mutiny that continues to divide opinion more than 200 years later. The result is a brilliant and compelling historical detective story, full of intrigue, jealousy, revenge and adventure on the high seas.

Clark, Leonard, *Marching Wind, The* – The panoramic story of a mounted exploration in the remote and savage heart of Asia, a place where adventure, danger, and intrigue were the daily backdrop to wild tribesman and equestrian exploits.

Clark, Leonard, *A Wanderer Till I Die* – In a world with lax passport control, no airlines, and few rules, the young man from San Francisco floats effortlessly from one adventure to the next. When he's not drinking whisky at the Raffles Hotel or listening to the "St. Louis Blues" on the phonograph in the jungle, he's searching for Malaysian treasure, being captured by Toradja headhunters, interrogated by Japanese intelligence officers and lured into shady deals by European gun-runners.

Cobbett, William, *Rural Rides, Volumes 1 and 2* – In the early 1820s Cobbett set out on horseback to make a series of personal tours through the English countryside. These books contain what many believe to be the best accounts of rural England ever written, and remain enduring classics.

Codman, John, *Winter Sketches from the Saddle* – This classic book was first published in 1888. It recommends riding for your health and describes the septuagenarian author's many equestrian journeys through New England during the winter of 1887 on his faithful mare, Fanny.

Cunninghame Graham, Jean, *Gaucho Laird* – A superbly readable biography of the author's famous great-uncle, Robert "Don Roberto" Cunninghame Graham.

Cunninghame Graham, Robert, *Horses of the Conquest* – The author uncovered manuscripts which had lain forgotten for centuries, and wrote this book, as he said, out of gratitude to the horses of Columbus and the Conquistadors who shaped history.

Cunninghame Graham, Robert, *Magreb-el-Acksa* – The thrilling tale of how "Don Roberto" was kidnapped in Morocco!

Cunninghame Graham, Robert, *Rodeo* – An omnibus of the finest work of the man they called "the uncrowned King of Scotland," edited by his friend Aimé Tschiffely.

Cunninghame Graham, Robert, *Tales of Horsemen* – Ten of the most beautifully-written equestrian stories ever set to paper.

Cunninghame Graham, Robert, *Vanished Arcadia* – This haunting story about the Jesuit missions in South America from 1550 to 1767 was the inspiration behind the best-selling film *The Mission*.

Daly, H.W., *Manual of Pack Transportation* – This book is the author's masterpiece. It contains a wealth of information on various pack saddles, ropes and equipment, how to secure every type of load imaginable and instructions on how to organize a pack train.

Dixie, Lady Florence, *Riding Across Patagonia* – When asked in 1879 why she wanted to travel to such an outlandish place as Patagonia, the author replied without hesitation that she was taking to the saddle in order to flee from the strict confines of polite Victorian society. This is the story of how the aristocrat successfully traded the perils of a London parlor for the wind-borne freedom of a wild Patagonian bronco.

Dodwell, Christina, *Beyond Siberia* – The intrepid author goes to Russia's Far East to join the reindeer-herding people in winter.

Dodwell, Christina, *An Explorer's Handbook* – The author tells you everything you want to know about travelling: how to find suitable pack animals, how to feed and shelter yourself. She also has sensible and entertaining advice about dealing with unwanted visitors and the inevitable bureaucrats.

Dodwell, Christina, *Madagascar Travels* – Christina explores the hidden corners of this amazing island and, as usual, makes friends with its people.

Dodwell, Christina, *A Traveller in China* – The author sets off alone across China, starting with a horse and then transferring to an inflatable canoe.

Dodwell, Christina, *A Traveller on Horseback* – Christina Dodwell rides through Eastern Turkey and Iran in the late 1980s. The Sunday Telegraph wrote of the author's "courage and insatiable wanderlust," and in this book she demonstrates her gift for communicating her zest for adventure.

Dodwell, Christina, *Travels in Papua New Guinea* – Christina Dodwell spends two years exploring an island little known to the outside world. She travelled by foot, horse and dugout canoe among the Stone-Age tribes.

Dodwell, Christina, *Travels with Fortune* – the truly amazing account of the courageous author's first journey – a three-year odyssey around Africa by Landrover, bus, lorry, horse, camel, and dugout canoe!

Dodwell, Christina, *Travels with Pegasus* – This time Christina takes to the air! This is the story of her unconventional journey across North Africa in a micro-light!

Duncan, John, *Travels in Western Africa in 1845 and 1846* – The author, a Lifeguardsman from Scotland, tells the hair-raising tale of his two journeys to what is now Benin. Sadly, Duncan has been forgotten until today, and we are proud to get this book back into print.

Ehlers, Otto, *Im Sattel durch die Fürstenhöfe Indiens* – In June 1890 the young German adventurer, Ehlers, lay very ill. His doctor gave him a choice: either go home to Germany or travel to Kashmir. So of course the Long Rider chose the latter. This is a thrilling yet humorous book about the author's adventures.

Farson, Negley, *Caucasian Journey* – A thrilling account of a dangerous equestrian journey made in 1929, this is an amply illustrated adventure classic.

Fox, Ernest, *Travels in Afghanistan* – The thrilling tale of a 1937 journey through the mountains, valleys, and deserts of this forbidden realm, including visits to such fabled places as the medieval city of Heart, the towering Hindu Kush mountains, and the legendary Khyber Pass.

Gall, Sandy, *Afghanistan – Agony of a Nation* - Sandy Gall has made three trips to Afghanistan to report the war there: in 1982, 1984 and again in 1986. This book is an account of his last journey and what he found. He chose to revisit the man he believes is the outstanding commander in Afghanistan: Ahmed Shah Masud, a dashing Tajik who is trying to organise resistance to the Russians on a regional, and eventually national scale.

Gall, Sandy, *Behind Russian Lines* – In the summer of 1982, Sandy Gall set off for Afghanistan on what turned out to be the hardest assignment of his life. During his career as a reporter he had covered plenty of wars and revolutions before, but this was the first time he had been required to walk all the way to an assignment and all the way back again, dodging Russian bombs *en route*.

Gallard, Babette, *Riding the Milky Way* – An essential guide to anyone planning to ride the ancient pilgrimage route to Santiago di Compostella, and a highly readable story for armchair travellers.

Galton, Francis, *The Art of Travel* – Originally published in 1855, this book became an instant classic and was used by a host of now-famous explorers, including Sir Richard Francis Burton of Mecca fame. Readers can learn how to ride horses, handle elephants, avoid cobras, pull teeth, find water in a desert, and construct a sleeping bag out of fur.

Glazier, Willard, *Ocean to Ocean on Horseback* – This book about the author's journey from New York to the Pacific in 1875 contains every kind of mounted adventure imaginable. Amply illustrated with pen and ink drawings of the time, the book remains a timeless equestrian adventure classic.

Goodwin, Joseph, *Through Mexico on Horseback* – The author and his companion, Robert Horiguichi, the sophisticated, multi-lingual son of an imperial Japanese diplomat, set out in 1931 to cross Mexico. They were totally unprepared for the deserts, quicksand and brigands they were to encounter during their adventure.

Grant, David, *Spirit of the Vikings: A Journey in the Kayak Bahá'í Viking From Arkosund, Sweden, to Odessa, Ukraine* – David Grant takes his kayak on an adventure-filled and spiritual journey from Sweden to Odessa on the Black Sea.

Grant, David, *The Wagon Travel Handbook* - David Grant is the legendary Scottish wagon-master who journeyed around the world with his family in a horse-drawn wagon. Grant has filled *The Wagon Travel Handbook* with all the practical information a first time-wagon traveller will need before setting out, including sections on interior and exterior wagon design, choice of draught animals, veterinary requirements and frontier formalities.

Gray, David and Lukas Novotny, *Mounted Archery in the Americas* - This fascinating and amply illustrated book charts the history of mounted archery from its ancient roots on the steppes of Eurasia thousands of years ago to its current resurgence in popularity in the Americas. It also provides the reader with up-to-the-minute practical information gleaned from a unique team of the world's leading experts.

Hanbury-Tenison, Marika, *For Better, For Worse* – The author, an excellent story-teller, writes about her adventures visiting and living among the Indians of Central Brazil.

Hanbury-Tenison, Marika, *A Slice of Spice* – The fresh and vivid account of the author's hazardous journey to the Indonesian Islands with her husband, Robin.

Hanbury-Tenison, Robin, *Chinese Adventure* – The story of a unique journey in which the explorer Robin Hanbury-Tenison and his wife Louella rode on horseback alongside the Great Wall of China in 1986.

Hanbury-Tenison, Robin, *Fragile Eden* – The wonderful story of Robin and Louella Hanbury-Tenison's exploration of New Zealand on horseback in 1988. They rode alone together through what they describe as 'some of the most dramatic and exciting country we have ever seen.'

Hanbury-Tenison, Robin, *Mulu: The Rainforest* – This was the first popular book to bring to the world's attention the significance of the rain forests to our fragile ecosystem. It is a timely reminder of our need to preserve them for the future.

Hanbury-Tenison, Robin, *A Pattern of Peoples* – The author and his wife, Marika, spent three months travelling through Indonesia's outer islands and writes with his usual flair and sensitivity about the tribes he found there.

Hanbury-Tenison, Robin, *A Question of Survival* – This superb book played a hugely significant role in bringing the plight of Brazil's Indians to the world's attention.

Hanbury-Tenison, Robin, *The Rough and the Smooth* – The incredible story of two journeys in South America. Neither had been attempted before, and both were considered impossible!

Hanbury-Tenison, Robin, *Spanish Pilgrimage* – Robin and Louella Hanbury-Tenison went to Santiago de Compostela in a traditional way – riding on white horses over long-forgotten tracks. In the process they discovered more about the people and the country than any conventional traveller would learn. Their adventures are vividly and entertainingly recounted in this delightful and highly readable book.

Hanbury-Tenison, Robin, *White Horses over France* – This enchanting book tells the story of a magical journey and how, in fulfilment of a personal dream, the first Camargue horses set foot on British soil in the late summer of 1984.

Hanbury-Tenison, Robin, *Worlds Apart – an Explorer's Life* – The author's battle to preserve the quality of life under threat from developers and machines infuses this autobiography with a passion and conviction which makes it impossible to put down.

Hanbury-Tenison, Robin, *Worlds Within – Reflections in the Sand* – This book is full of the adventure you would expect from a man of action like Robin Hanbury-Tenison. However, it is also filled with the type of rare knowledge that was revealed to other desert travellers like Lawrence, Doughty and Thesiger.

Haslund, Henning, *Mongolian Adventure* – An epic tale inhabited by a cast of characters no longer present in this lackluster world, shamans who set themselves on fire, rebel leaders who sacked towns, and wild horsemen whose ancestors conquered the world.

Hassanein, A. M., *The Lost Oases* - At the dawning of the 20th century the vast desert of Libya remained one of last unexplored places on Earth. Sir Hassanein Bey, the dashing Egyptian diplomat turned explorer, befriended the Muslim leaders of the elusive Senussi Brotherhood who controlled the deserts further on, and became aware of rumours of a "lost oasis" which lay even deeper in the desert. In 1923 the explorer led a small caravan on a remarkable seven month journey across the centre of Libya. **Heath, Frank**, *Forty Million Hoofbeats* – Heath set out in 1925 to follow his dream of riding to all 48 of the Continental United States. The journey lasted more than two years, during which time Heath and his mare, Gypsy Queen, became inseparable companions.

Hinde, Thomas, *The Great Donkey Walk* – Biographer Susan Chitty and her novelist husband, Thomas Hinde, travelled from Spain's Santiago to Salonica in faraway Greece. Their two small daughters, Miranda (7) and Jessica (3) were rode one donkey, while the other donkey carried the baggage. Reading this delightful book is leisurely and continuing pleasure.

Holt, William, *Ride a White Horse* – After rescuing a cart horse, Trigger, from slaughter and nursing him back to health, the 67-year-old Holt and his horse set out in 1964 on an incredible 9,000 mile, non-stop journey through western Europe.

Hope, Thomas, *Anastasius* – Here is the book that took the world by storm, and then was forgotten. Hope's hero Anastasius was fearless, curious, cunning, ruthless, brave, and above all, sexy. He journeyed deep into the vast and dangerous Ottoman Empire. During the 35 years described in the book (1762-1798) the swashbuckling hero infiltrated the deadly Wahhabis in Arabia, rode to war with the Mamelukes in Egypt and sailed the Mediterranean with the Turks. This remarkable new edition features all three volumes together for the first time.

Hopkins, Frank T., *Hidalgo and Other Stories* – For the first time in history, here are the collected writings of Frank T. Hopkins, the counterfeit cowboy whose endurance racing claims and Old West fantasies have polarized the equestrian world.

James, Jeremy, *Saddletramp* – The classic story of Jeremy James' journey from Turkey to Wales, on an unplanned route with an inaccurate compass, unreadable map and the unfailing aid of villagers who seemed to have as little sense of direction as he had.

James, Jeremy, *Vagabond* – The wonderful tale of the author's journey from Bulgaria to Berlin offers a refreshing, witty and often surprising view of Eastern Europe and the collapse of communism.

Jebb, Louisa, *By Desert Ways to Baghdad and Damascus* – From the pen of a gifted writer and intrepid traveller, this is one of the greatest equestrian travel books of all time.

Kluckhohn, Clyde, *To the Foot of the Rainbow* – This is not just a exciting true tale of equestrian adventure. It is a moving account of a young man's search for physical perfection in a desert world still untouched by the recently-born twentieth century.

Lambie, Thomas, *Boots and Saddles in Africa* – Lambie's story of his equestrian journeys is told with the grit and realism that marks a true classic.

Landor, Henry Savage, *In the Forbidden Land* – Illustrated with hundreds of photographs and drawings, this blood-chilling account of equestrian adventure makes for page-turning excitement.

Langlet, Valdemar, *Till Häst Genom Ryssland (Swedish)* – Denna reses-kildring rymmer många ögonblicksbilder av möten med människor, från morgonbad med Lev Tolstoi till samtal med Tartarer och fotografering av fagra skördeflickor. Rikt illustrerad med foto och teckningar.

Leigh, Margaret, *My Kingdom for a Horse* – In the autumn of 1939 the author rode from Cornwall to Scotland, resulting in one of the most delightful equestrian journeys of the early twentieth century. This book is full of keen observations of a rural England that no longer exists.

Lester, Mary, *A Lady's Ride across Spanish Honduras in 1881* – This is a gem of a book, with a very entertaining account of Mary's vivid, day-to-day life in the saddle.

MacDermot, Brian, *Cult of the Sacred Spear* – here is that rarest of travel books, an exploration not only of a distant land but of a man's own heart. A confederation of pastoral people located in Southern Sudan and western Ethiopia, the Nuer warriors were famous for staging cattle raids against larger tribes and successfully resisted European colonization. Brian MacDermot, London stockbroker, entered into Nuer society as a stranger and emerged as Rial Nyang, an adopted member of the tribe. This book recounts this extra-ordinary emotional journey, regaling the reader with tales of pagan gods, warriors on mysterious missions, and finally the approach of warfare that con-tinues to swirl across this part of Africa today.

Maillart, Ella, *Turkestan Solo* – A vivid account of a 1930s journey through this wonderful, mysterious and dangerous portion of the world, complete with its Kirghiz eagle hunters, lurking Soviet secret police, and the timeless nomads that still inhabited the desolate steppes of Central Asia.

Marcy, Randolph, *The Prairie Traveler* – There were a lot of things you packed into your saddlebags or the wagon before setting off to cross the North American wilderness in the 1850s. A gun and an axe were obvious necessities. Yet many pioneers were just as adamant about placing a copy of Captain Randolph Marcy's classic book close at hand.

Marsden, Kate, *Riding through Siberia: A Mounted Medical Mission in 1891* – This immensely readable book is a mixture of adventure, extreme hardship and compassion as the author travels the Great Siberian Post Road.

Marsh, Hippisley Cunliffe, *A Ride Through Islam* – A British officer rides through Persia and Afghanistan to India in 1873. Full of adventures, and with observant remarks on the local Turkoman equestrian traditions.

MacCann, William, *Viaje a Caballo* – Spanish-language edition of the British author's equestrian journey around Argentina in 1848.

Meline, James, *Two Thousand Miles on Horseback: Kansas to Santa Fé in 1866* – A beautifully written, eye witness account of a United States that is no more.

Muir Watson, Sharon, *The Colour of Courage* – The remarkable true story of the epic horse trip made by the first people to travel Australia's then-unmarked Bicentennial National Trail. There are enough adventures here to satisfy even the most jaded reader.

Naysmith, Gordon, *The Will to Win* – This book recounts the only equestrian journey of its kind undertaken during the 20th century - a mounted trip stretching across 16 countries. Gordon Naysmith, a Scottish pentathlete and former military man, set out in 1970 to ride from the tip of the African continent to the 1972 Olympic Games in distant Germany.

Ondaatje, Christopher, *Leopard in the Afternoon* – The captivating story of a journey through some of Africa's most spectacular haunts. It is also touched with poignancy and regret for a vanishing wilderness – a world threatened with extinction.

Ondaatje, Christopher, *The Man-Eater of Pununai* – a fascinating story of a past rediscovered through a remarkable journey to one of the most exotic countries in the world — Sri Lanka. Full of drama and history, it not only relives the incredible story of a man-eating leopard that terrorized the tiny village of Punanai in the early part of the century, but also allows the author to come to terms with the ghost of his charismatic but tyrannical father.

Ondaatje, Christopher, *Sindh Revisited* – This is the extraordinarily sensitive account of the author's quest to uncover the secrets of the seven years Richard Burton spent in India in the army of the East India Company from 1842 to 1849. "If I wanted to fill the gap in my understanding of Richard Burton, I would have to do something that had never been done before: follow in his footsteps in India…" The journey covered thousands of miles—trekking across deserts where ancient tribes meet modern civilization in the valley of the mighty Indus River.

O'Connor, Derek, *The King's Stranger* – a superb biography of the forgotten Scottish explorer, John Duncan.

O'Reilly, Basha, *Count Pompeii – Stallion of the Steppes* – the story of Basha's journey from Russia with her stallion, Count Pompeii, told for children. This is the first book in the *Little Long Rider* series.

O'Reilly, CuChullaine, (Editor) *The Horse Travel Handbook* – this accumulated knowledge of a million miles in the saddle tells you everything you need to know about travelling with your horse!

O'Reilly, CuChullaine, (Editor) *The Horse Travel Journal* – a unique book to take on your ride and record your experiences. Includes the world's first equestrian travel "pictionary" to help you in foreign countries.

O'Reilly, CuChullaine, *Khyber Knights* – Told with grit and realism by one of the world's foremost equestrian explorers, "Khyber Knights" has been penned the way lives are lived, not how books are written.

O'Reilly, CuChullaine, (Editor) *The Long Riders, Volume One* – The first of five unforgettable volumes of exhilarating travel tales.

Östrup, J, *(Swedish), Växlande Horisont* – The thrilling account of the author's journey to Central Asia from 1891 to 1893.

Patterson, George, *Gods and Guerrillas* – The true and gripping story of how the author went secretly into Tibet to film the Chinese invaders of his adopted country. Will make your heart pound with excitement!

Patterson, George, *Journey with Loshay: A Tibetan Odyssey* – This is an amazing book written by a truly remarkable man! Relying both on his companionship with God and on his own strength, he undertook a life few can have known, and a journey of emergency across the wildest parts of Tibet.

Patterson, George, *Patterson of Tibet* – Patterson was a Scottish medical missionary who went to Tibet shortly after the second World War. There he became Tibetan in all but name, adapting to the culture and learning the language fluently. This intense autobiography reveals how Patterson crossed swords with India's Prime Minister Nehru, helped with the rescue of the Dalai Lama and befriended a host of unique world figures ranging from Yehudi Menhuin to Eric Clapton. This is a vividly-written account of a life of high adventure and spiritual odyssey.

Pocock, Roger, *Following the Frontier* – Pocock was one of the nineteenth century's most influential equestrian travelers. Within the covers of this book is the detailed account of Pocock's horse ride along the infamous Outlaw Trail, a 3,000 mile solo journey that took the adventurer from Canada to Mexico City.

Pocock, Roger, *Horses* – Pocock set out to document the wisdom of the late 19th and early 20th Centuries into a book unique for its time. His concerns for attempting to preserve equestrian knowledge were based on cruel reality. More than 300,000 horses had been destroyed during the recent Boer War. Though Pocock enjoyed a reputation for dangerous living, his observations on horses were praised by the leading thinkers of his day.

Post, Charles Johnson, *Horse Packing* – Originally published in 1914, this book was an instant success, incorporating as it did the very essence of the science of packing horses and mules. It makes fascinating reading for students of the horse or history.

Ray, G. W., *Through Five Republics on Horseback* – In 1889 a British explorer – part-time missionary and full-time adventure junky – set out to find a lost tribe of sun-worshipping natives in the unexplored forests of Paraguay. The journey was so brutal that it defies belief.

Rink, Bjarke, *The Centaur Legacy* – This immensely entertaining and historically important book provides the first ever in-depth study into how man's partnership with his equine companion changed the course of history and accelerated human development.

Ross, Julian, *Travels in an Unknown Country* – A delightful book about modern horseback travel in an enchanting country, which once marked the eastern borders of the Roman Empire – Romania.

Ross, Martin and Somerville, E, *Beggars on Horseback* – The hilarious adventures of two aristocratic Irish cousins on an 1894 riding tour of Wales.

Ruxton, George, *Adventures in Mexico* – The story of a young British army officer who rode from Vera Cruz to Santa Fe, Mexico in 1847. At times the author exhibits a fearlessness which borders on insanity. He ignores dire warnings, rides through deadly deserts, and dares murderers to attack him. It is a delightful and invigorating tale of a time and place now long gone.

von Salzman, Erich, *Im Sattel durch Zentralasien* – The astonishing tale of the author's journey through China, Turkistan and back to his home in Germany – 6000 kilometres in 176 days!

Schwarz, Hans *(German),* *Vier Pferde, Ein Hund und Drei Soldaten* – In the early 1930s the author and his two companions rode through Liechtenstein, Austria, Romania, Albania, Yugoslavia, to Turkey, then rode back again!

Schwarz, Otto *(German),* *Reisen mit dem Pferd* – the Swiss Long Rider with more miles in the saddle than anyone else tells his wonderful story, and a long appendix tells the reader how to follow in his footsteps.

Scott, Robert, *Scott's Last Expedition* – Many people are unaware that Scott recruited Yakut ponies from Siberia for his doomed expedition to the South Pole in 1909. Here is the remarkable story of men and horses who all paid the ultimate sacrifice.

Shackleton, Ernest, *Aurora Australis* - The members of the British Antarctic Expedition of 1907-1908 wrote this delightful and surprisingly funny book. It was printed on the spot "at the sign of the Penguin"!

Skrede, Wilfred, *Across the Roof of the World* – This epic equestrian travel tale of a wartime journey across Russia, China, Turkestan and India is laced with unforgettable excitement.

The South Pole Ponies, *Theodore Mason* – The touching and totally forgotten story of the little horses who gave their all to both Scott and Shackleton in their attempts to reach the South Pole.

Stevens, Thomas, *Through Russia on a Mustang* – Mounted on his faithful horse, Texas, Stevens crossed the Steppes in search of adventure. Cantering across the pages of this classic tale is a cast of nineteenth century Russian misfits, peasants, aristocrats—and even famed Cossack Long Rider Dmitri Peshkov.

Stevenson, Robert L., *Travels with a Donkey* – In 1878, the author set out to explore the remote Cevennes mountains of France. He travelled alone, unless you count his stubborn and manipulative pack-donkey, Modestine. This book is a true classic.

Strong, Anna Louise, *Road to the Grey Pamir* – With Stalin's encouragement, Strong rode into the seldom-seen Pamir mountains of faraway Tadjikistan. The political renegade turned equestrian explorer soon discovered more adventure than she had anticipated.

Sykes, Ella, *Through Persia on a Sidesaddle* – Ella Sykes rode side-saddle 2,000 miles across Persia, a country few European woman had ever visited. Mind you, she traveled in style, accompanied by her Swiss maid and 50 camels loaded with china, crystal, linens and fine wine.

Trinkler, Emile, *Through the Heart of Afghanistan* – In the early 1920s the author made a legendary trip across a country now recalled only in legends.

Tschiffely, Aimé, *Bohemia Junction* – "Forty years of adventurous living condensed into one book."

Tschiffely, Aimé, *Bridle Paths* – a final poetic look at a now-vanished Britain.

Tschiffely, Aimé, *Coricancha*: A fascinating and balanced account of the conquest of the Inca Empire.

Tschiffely, Aimé, *Don Roberto* – A biography of Tschiffely's friend and mentor, Robert Cunninghame Graham.

Tschiffely, Aimé, *Little Princess Turtle Dove* – An enchanting fairy story set in South America and displaying Aimé Tschiffely's love, not only for children and animals, but also for South America.

Tschiffely, Aimé, *Mancha y Gato Cuentan sus Aventuras* – The Spanish-language version of *The Tale of Two Horses* – the story of the author's famous journey as told by the horses.

Tschiffely, Aimé, *Ming and Ping*: An adventure book for older children. The title characters go exploring South America together. They meet many tribes of Indians and learn about their way of life. Exhilarating and effortlessly instructive.

Tschiffely, Aimé, *Round and About Spain:* Tschiffely sets off to explore Spain, but this time his steed is a motorbike, not a horse! With wit, wisdom and a sharp eye for the absurd, he travels to all four corners of this fascinating country and makes many friends along the way. So much has changed since the Second World War that that this book is a unique snapshot of Spain as she was in 1950.

Tschiffely, Aimé, *The Tale of Two Horses* – The story of Tschiffely's famous journey from Buenos Aires to Washington, DC, narrated by his two equine heroes, Mancha and Gato. Their unique point of view is guaranteed to delight children and adults alike.

Tschiffely, Aimé, *This Way Southward* – the most famous equestrian explorer of the twentieth century decides to make a perilous journey across the U-boat infested Atlantic.

Tschiffely, Aimé, *Tschiffely's Ride* – The true story of the most famous equestrian journey of the twentieth century – 10,000 miles with two Criollo geldings from Argentina to Washington, DC. A new edition is coming soon with a Foreword by his literary heir!

Tschiffely, Aimé, *Tschiffely's Ritt* – The German-language translation of *Tschiffely's Ride* – the most famous equestrian journey of its day.

Ure, John, *Cucumber Sandwiches in the Andes* – No-one who wasn't mad as a hatter would try to take a horse across the Andes by one of the highest passes between Chile and the Argentine. That was what John Ure was told on his way to the British Embassy in Santiago – so he set out to find a few certifiable kindred spirits. Fans of equestrian travel and of Latin America will be enchanted by this delightful book.

Warner, Charles Dudley, *On Horseback in Virginia* – A prolific author, and a great friend of Mark Twain, Warner made witty and perceptive contributions to the world of nineteenth century American literature. This book about the author's equestrian adventures is full of fascinating descriptions of nineteenth century America.

Weale, Magdalene, *Through the Highlands of Shropshire* – It was 1933 and Magdalene Weale was faced with a dilemma: how to best explore her beloved English countryside? By horse, of course! This enchanting book invokes a gentle, softer world inhabited by gracious country lairds, wise farmers, and jolly inn keepers.

Weeks, Edwin Lord, *Artist Explorer* – A young American artist and superb writer travels through Persia to India in 1892.

Wentworth Day, J., *Wartime Ride* – In 1939 the author decided the time was right for an extended horseback ride through England! While parts of his country were being ravaged by war, Wentworth Day discovered an inland oasis of mellow harvest fields, moated Tudor farmhouses, peaceful country halls, and fishing villages.

Von Westarp, Eberhard, *Unter Halbmond und Sonne* – (German) – Im Sattel durch die asiatische Türkei und Persien.

Wilkins, Messanie, *Last of the Saddle Tramps* – Told she had little time left to live, the author decided to ride from her native Maine to the Pacific. Accompanied by her faithful horse, Tarzan, Wilkins suffered through any number of obstacles, including blistering deserts and freezing snow storms – and defied the doctors by living for another 20 years!

Wilson, Andrew, *The Abode of Snow* – One of the best accounts of overland equestrian travel ever written about the wild lands that lie between Tibet and Afghanistan.

de Windt, Harry, *A Ride to India* – Part science, all adventure, this book takes the reader for a thrilling canter across the Persian Empire of the 1890s.

Winthrop, Theodore, *Saddle and Canoe* – This book paints a vibrant picture of 1850s life in the Pacific Northwest and covers the author's travels along the Straits of Juan De Fuca, on Vancouver Island, across the Naches Pass, and on to The Dalles, in Oregon Territory. This is truly an historic travel account.

Woolf, Leonard, *Stories of the East* – Three short stories which are of vital importance in understanding the author's mistrust of and dislike for colonialism, which provide disturbing commentaries about the disintegration of the colonial process.

Younghusband, George, *Eighteen Hundred Miles on a Burmese Pony* – One of the funniest and most enchanting books about equestrian travel of the nineteenth century, featuring "Joe" the naughty Burmese pony!

We are constantly adding new titles to our collections, so please check our websites:

www.horsetravelbooks.com – www.classictravelbooks.com
The Equestrian Wisdom & History Series: www.lrgaf.org
www.aimetschiffely.org

Lightning Source UK Ltd.
Milton Keynes UK
UKOW03f0920090217

294001UK00001B/299/P